Takis Constandinides

AN OCEAN LINER BOUND FOR DISTANT LANDS

From a water color by Sears Gallagher

THE EARTH AND ITS PEOPLE · BOOK THREE

NATIONS
BEYOND THE SEAS

BY

WALLACE W. ATWOOD

AND

HELEN GOSS THOMAS

REVISED EDITION

GINN AND COMPANY

BOSTON · NEW YORK · CHICAGO · LONDON

ATLANTA · DALLAS · COLUMBUS · SAN FRANCISCO

The Athenæum Press
GINN AND COMPANY · PRO-
PRIETORS · BOSTON · U.S.A.

FOREWORD TO THE TEACHER

"Nations beyond the Seas" is the third book of a series of geographies on the single-cycle plan. The first book, "Home Life in Far-away Lands," introduces pupils to geography through a series of imaginary journeys to distant lands, in the course of which the simpler relationships between man and the conditions of his natural environment are demonstrated. The second book, "The Americas," begins the systematic study of the earth by countries and regions, covering, as the title implies, North America and South America. "Nations beyond the Seas" completes this study by treating the countries and regions of the Eastern Hemisphere.

In every problem of human geography there are two factors of equal importance: the people and the place. To understand the activities of any group of people, a clear picture of the place in which they live is essential. Hence the basic framework of "The Americas" and "Nations beyond the Seas" is regional, and the maps, pictures, and text combine to visualize for children the natural regions which form the stage setting for the activities of the people in all parts of the world.

The division of the lands into natural regions may be based on any one of several geographic factors, depending on the nature of the study to be pursued and the age and background of the students. The factor used in "The Americas" and "Nations beyond the Seas" is the surface of the land because it is the simplest and the most easily visualized by children. Four simple types of natural regions suffice to classify land surfaces in a broad way: young, rugged mountains; old, worn-down mountains; uplands and plateaus; lowlands and interior plains. Each type has its distinctive characteristics, and each exerts certain well-defined influences on the activities of people.

One of the greatest advantages in this regional classification is that it lends itself to consistent use throughout the world, and makes possible the effective use of correlated study. Throughout "The Americas" and "Nations beyond the Seas" similar regions are carefully correlated, and pupils are called upon constantly to apply knowledge in hand to the solution of new problems.

The value of the regional background cannot be too strongly stressed. It provides the "why" for the "what," and makes geography a series of stimulating problems in cause-and-effect relationships. It offers unlimited opportunity for the discussion of thought-provoking questions such as "Why is Italy the most important of the Mediterranean countries?" or "Why is it unlikely that Australia will ever be able to support as many people as the United States?" A ten-minute discussion of this kind will do more to fix facts permanently in mind than an hour of old-fashioned book study.

The use of the regional method by no means implies neglect of political divisions. Each individual country receives due attention, and each one is illuminated against a vivid regional background.

One of the new and outstanding features of "Nations beyond the Seas" is its treatment of the possessions of the European nations in close association with the home countries. The study of the British Isles is followed immediately by studies of the other parts of the British Empire in the Eastern Hemisphere. Similarly, the colonies of France, of the Netherlands, and of all other European countries which have outlying possessions are treated directly after the home country.

This procedure applies to the countries of Europe the plan which has been used so long and so successfully in connection with the United States and its possessions. It is sound pedagogically and geographically, for the home countries and their possessions are so intimately interrelated that to be studied with full understanding they need to be presented in the closest possible association. For three years previous to the publication of this book, this new plan of organization was tried out in the schools of one of the large Eastern cities. The teachers using it reported unanimously that it conserves time, quickens interest, and gives pupils a keener appreciation of the relationships between the home countries and the possessions than has ever been attained under the old plan of dissociated study.

Like the other books in the series, "Nations beyond the Seas" is divided into convenient units of study, each of which is introduced by a motivated approach which challenges the interest of the pupil and gives him an objective toward which to work. The motivation takes a variety of forms according to the subject matter of the study units. Many of the approaches present problems for solution, and many call for some form of self-activity on the part of the pupil.

Each study unit closes with exercises or tests which enable the pupil to prove his knowledge of the important geographic facts and relationships which he has discovered. Much time and thought have been given to making the tests varied and interesting, and many suggestions are offered for extra work for pupils who work faster than the average of the class.

The maps provide the pupil with a rich field for the discovery of facts of physical, economic, and political geography. Each study unit calls for thoughtful map-reading, and throughout the book map work and text study are intimately interwoven. One of the most valuable features of the maps is the showing of product data against the regional background, whereby the pupil is constantly reminded of the association of certain kinds of economic activity with certain types of regions.

In order to save the time ordinarily wasted by pupils in hunting blindly for places on maps, every map is indexed in atlas style, and wherever in the text the pupil is directed to locate a place on a map, the index is given.

Every picture in the book has been selected for the purpose of playing a definite rôle in the visualization of the lesson units, and every one is an integral part of the plan of study. The pictures are provided with legends which include descriptions, explanations, and questions, and which greatly increase their usefulness.

The vocabulary has been checked by a graded word list prepared by Dr. B. R. Buckingham and Dr. E. W. Dolch. This graded word list contains about 20,000 entries. In making it, fifteen published and unpublished vocabulary studies were combined and then supplemented by original material secured from more than 16,000 children. The returns from this independent investigation were used to fill in the many gaps which were evident even after the fifteen previous studies had been combined. Finally, the graded word list was organized on the basis of meanings rather than on the basis of word forms. Not infrequently one meaning of a given word was found to be suitable for a primary grade, while another meaning of the same word might belong to a much higher grade.

A comparison of the text of "Nations beyond the Seas" with this graded word list gives assurance that its vocabulary is well within the grasp of the pupils for whom the book is intended. Wherever words likely to be new to pupils are introduced, they are explained; and avoidance of reading difficulties leaves the pupils free to give their undivided attention to the subject matter.

The authors of this series believe that the highest function of geographical study is to break down the barriers of provincialism and to foster in American youth a just and sympathetic attitude toward the people of other countries and their problems. The books are offered to the school public in the earnest hope that they may play a worthy part in training American boys and girls for intelligent and broad-minded citizenship.

WALLACE W. ATWOOD
HELEN GOSS THOMAS

CONTENTS

CONTENTS

LIST OF COLORED MAPS

The Castle of Chillon on Lake Geneva

NATIONS BEYOND THE SEAS

THE OLD WORLD

I. THE EASTERN HEMISPHERE AND ITS PEOPLE

1. FOREWORD

The New World and the Old World. During your study of North America and South America you learned that the white men who explored and settled the two continents of the Western Hemisphere came from Europe. When the people of Europe learned of the new-found lands on the western side of the Atlantic Ocean, they began to call the Americas the New World. Later, the lands of the Eastern Hemisphere which had been known so much longer came to be called the Old World. These names have never been given up, and we still call the lands of the Western Hemisphere the New World, and those of the Eastern Hemisphere the Old World. Australia was discovered and settled much later than the Americas, but since it is located in the Eastern Hemisphere we include it among the lands of the Old World.

The older nations. We speak of the people of a country as the *nation*. Long before the discovery of America the people of some of the older nations in Europe had written books and plays, made wonderful monuments and statues, and painted beautiful pictures. When you visit the Mediterranean countries, you will see the remains of temples, palaces, and arches which the Greeks and Romans built more than a thousand years before Columbus was born, — buildings so beautiful that architects copy their designs to this very day. All over western Europe you will see churches and castles which were built in the days when people thought that Europe, Asia, and Africa were all the lands there were in the world. *See Figures 1 and 2.*

You may have seen copies of some of the statues made long ago by the Greek sculptors, or of some of the paintings of the "old masters," as the earliest of the famous European painters were called. Every art student of today studies the work of the early Greek sculptors and the old masters of painting, and every student of literature reads the plays and poetry written by the Greeks and Romans of long ago.

The people of some of the older nations had also made many wonderful discoveries and invented many useful things long before they knew anything about the Americas. For example, the ship's compass, which makes it possible for sailors to know their directions at sea, was invented by the Chinese over seven hundred years ago. In Europe one of the greatest inventions made before the discovery of America was the printing press. Can you explain why this was a very important invention?

New nations from old nations. As people from Europe settled in the New World, the Americas became new homelands for people of the older nations. You already know that most of the white people of South America and southern North America are of Spanish or Portuguese descent, while the people of Canada are mostly of British or French descent.

1

Figure 1. The Arch of Titus and the Colosseum at Rome, in Italy. The arch was built by an emperor of the Romans in the year 81. How long ago was that? Be- yond the arch you can see the ruins of the huge am- phitheater called the Colosseum, which was used by the Romans as a place for holding outdoor entertainments.

Do you know why we speak English in our country? It is because the largest numbers of people in the United States are descended from people who once lived in Great Britain and Ireland, the European countries where the English language is spoken. But many of the other nations of Europe are also repre- sented in our population. Perhaps you your- self are descended from people who were born in one of the countries on the continent of Europe, or you may have neighbors and friends whose families came to the United States from one of those countries years ago.

In our own country and other countries of the Americas there are some people who have come from Asia and Africa, or whose families came from there. They too help to make up the new nations of the Western Hemisphere, but they are much fewer in number than the people of European descent.

Our trade with the Old World. Ever since the earliest days of settlement, the people of the New World have traded with the people of Europe. Today ships carry more goods back and forth between ports of western Europe and ports on the Atlantic coast of the United States than between any other parts of the world. Turn to the map on pages 338–339 and prove that this is true. Notice also how much trade there is between the countries of western Europe and the countries of South America which border the Atlantic Ocean.

Our own country also carries on much trade across the Pacific Ocean with the people of Japan, China, and the Philippine Islands, and our trade with the people of the East Indies, Africa, Australia, and New Zealand amounts to many millions of dollars each year. Turn again to the map (pp. 338–339) and find all the lands named in this paragraph.

The lands of the Eastern Hemisphere. The lands of the Eastern Hemisphere, or the Old World, are the continents of Europe, Asia, Africa, and Australia, with all the neighbor- ing islands. Any map of the world will show you that Europe and Asia form one great stretch of land. When we wish to speak of

Figure 2. One of the old châteaus, or castles, in France. This beautiful château was built as a home for a French nobleman in the year 1390. How many years before Columbus discovered America was that? How much older is the château than the oldest building now standing in the town, city, or state in which you live?

this great land mass as a whole, we call it Eurasia. Europe forms the western part of it, and Asia the central and eastern parts.

As you study about the lands of the Old World, keep these questions in mind:

1. In what parts of the Old World do the people live and work much as we do in our country, and why?

2. In what parts of the Old World do the people live and work very differently from the way we do, and why?

3. In what parts of the Old World do the people live and work somewhat as those in the tropical parts of the Americas do, and why?

Sentences to complete. Give the correct words to complete the following sentences. You may use the map on pages 334–335 if you need to.

1. The continents of the New World are _ _ _ _ _ _ _ _ _ _ and _ _ _ _ _ _ _ _ _ _.

2. The continents of the Old World are _ _ _ _ _ _, _ _ _ _, _ _ _ _ _ _, and _ _ _ _ _ _ _ _ _.

3. Eurasia is made up of the continents of _ _ _ _ _ _ and _ _ _ _.

4. Africa is separated from Europe by the _ _ _ _ _ _ _ _ _ _ _ Sea.

5. The islands southeast of Australia form the country of *New Zealand*

Some things to do. 1. If you were born in some country of the Old World, locate that country on a wall map or on the map on pages 330–331.

2. If you were born in the United States, ask your father or mother what country of the Old World was the homeland of your family before they came to America. You may find that your father's people came from one country, and your mother's from another. On the map locate the Old World countries which you can claim as family homelands.

Special credit work. 1. Find out at least six other languages besides English which are spoken by people in various countries of Europe. Use a wall map or the map on pages 330–331 to show your classmates the country where each language is spoken.

2. Many interesting stories for boys and girls written by people in the Old World have been *translated*, or turned, into English. Try to find such a story and read it. Tell the story briefly to your classmates, and point out the author's country on the map.

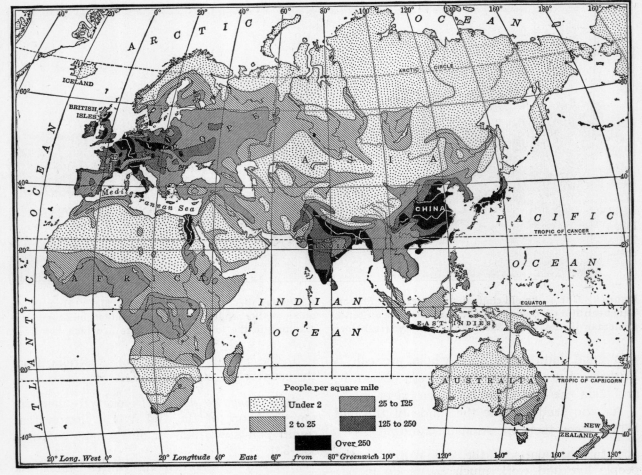

Figure 3. Distribution of people in the Old World.

2. FIRST GLIMPSES OF THE OLD WORLD

In your study of the Americas you discovered that some parts of the New World are very densely, or thickly, settled, and that other parts are very sparsely, or thinly, settled. You will find that the same thing is true in the Old World. Some parts of the Old World are more crowded with people than any part of the New World is, and other parts are almost without people. As you study this section, watch for reasons for these differences in the distribution of population.

Lands crowded with people. On Figure 3 find the three large areas in the Old World which are most crowded with people. In what continent are two of the areas? In what continent is the third?

One of the densely populated areas which you have found on the map is in eastern Asia. There, in China and the islands of Japan, about 550 million people live crowded together. The second densely populated area is in India and Burma. About 400 million people live there. The third area of dense population is the western half of Europe, where over 385 million people live.

Reasons for crowding. Can you think of any reasons why so many people live crowded together in the areas that you have located on the population map? Figure 4 and the map on pages 6–7 will help you to discover why these parts of the Old World are so densely populated.

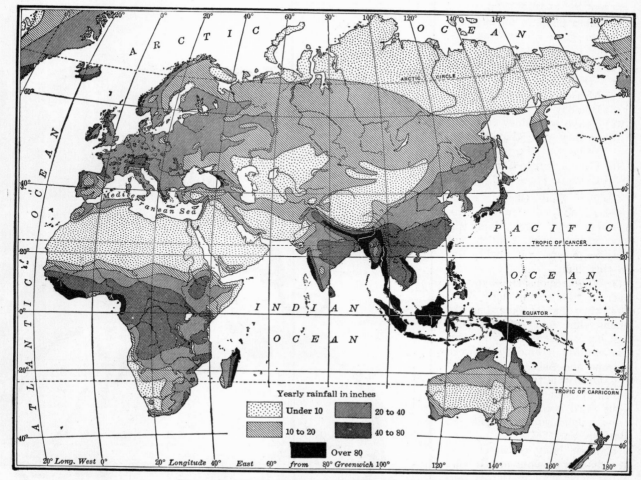

Figure 4. Distribution of rainfall in the Old World.

Turn first to the regional map of the Old World on pages 6–7 and locate the three very thickly populated areas of Eurasia that you found on Figure 3. Are they mostly mountainous lands, or have they large stretches of plains?

Now study Figure 4. Remember that in order to be well suited to most kinds of farming a region should have at least 20 inches of rain each year. What does Figure 4 show about the rainfall in the three most densely populated parts of Eurasia?

You will remember that most of the people of the New World live in well-watered lowlands in the north and south temperate zones, where the temperature changes from season to season and the surface and climate are well suited to farming. Use the map on pages 6–7 and Figures 3 and 4 to prove that

1. Except for the Deccan Plateau of India, the most thickly populated parts of the Old World are largely in the north temperate zone.

2. The three large areas of densest population in Eurasia are not in the coldest or highest parts of the Old World.

3. Within each of these three areas of Eurasia there are large stretches of lowland plains.

4. Most parts of the crowded areas of Eurasia have between 20 and 80 inches of rain each year.

Turn over to page 8.

MAP STUDIES

1. Plan a flight in an airplane in seven great "hops" as follows:

   (1) London (C2) to Moscow (F2)
   (2) Moscow to Bombay (H4)
   (3) Bombay to Tokyo (N3)
   (4) Tokyo to Sydney (O8)
   (5) Sydney to Cape Town (E8)
   (6) Cape Town to Cairo (F3)
   (7) Cairo to Paris (D2)

2. Over what thickly populated region shall you be flying on your first hop? Name a large city between London and Moscow where you might stop on this flight.

3. What regions shall you fly over on your second hop? Why have they fewer people than the plains that you saw on your first hop? Where shall you cross the natural boundary between Europe and Asia?

4. Over what two very crowded parts of Asia shall you fly on your third hop? At what large cities might you stop between Bombay and Tokyo?

5. What body of water shall you fly over on your fourth hop? What zone shall you cross during your flight over the Pacific Ocean?

6. What body of water shall you fly over on your fifth hop? In what zone shall you be during your flight from Sydney to Cape Town? At what other city in Australia might you stop on that flight?

7. What regions shall you fly over on your sixth hop, from Cape Town to Cairo? What zone shall you cross on that flight? What desert shall you see as you cross the tropic of Cancer? What river valley shall you be following as you approach Cairo? What other large city could you visit near Cairo?

8. What sea and what mountains shall you fly over on your last hop, from Cairo to Paris?

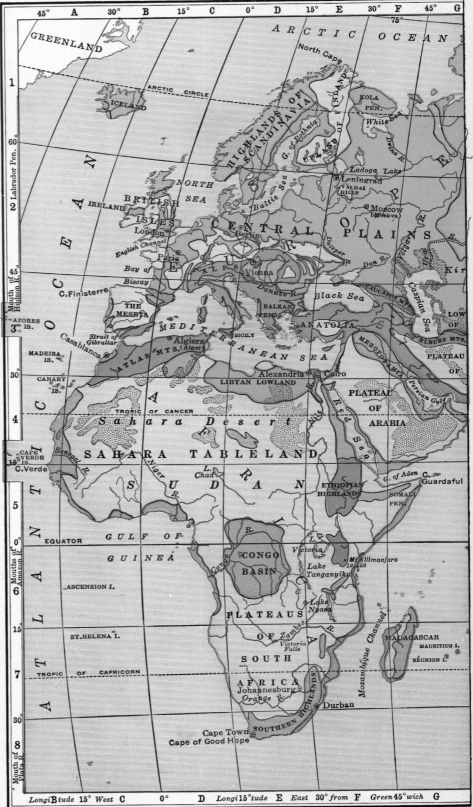

[979]

6

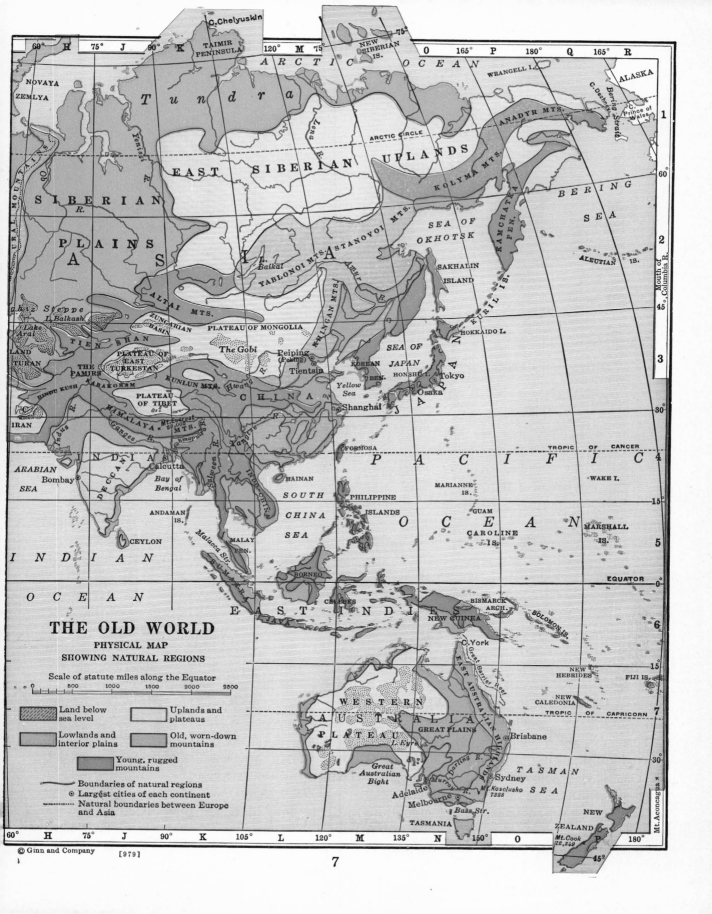

THE OLD WORLD

PHYSICAL MAP
SHOWING NATURAL REGIONS

Scale of statute miles along the Equator

0   500   1000   1500   2000   2500

Land below sea level

Lowlands and interior plains

Young, rugged mountains

Uplands and plateaus

Old, worn-down mountains

— Boundaries of natural regions
⊙ Largest cities of each continent
------- Natural boundaries between Europe and Asia

© Ginn and Company

[979]

7

Photograph by Pictorial Clubs, Inc.

Figure 5. A view in the Plateau of Arabia, where so little rain falls that it is hard for people to make a living. A scanty growth of grass and widely scattered pools of water make it possible for small groups of wandering Arabs to live in this dry region by keeping flocks of sheep and goats, and a few camels and horses.

Lands with very few people. Turn to Figure 3 again and find the three largest sections of the Old World where very few people live. You will discover that one of them is in Asia, another in northern Africa, and the third in Australia.

In your study of the Americas you learned that the most thinly populated parts of the New World are chiefly the parts which are the highest, driest, or coldest. Compare the maps on pages 4, 5, and 6–7 and see if you can find similar reasons for the most thinly populated parts of the Old World.

First study the population map again. What one of the thinly populated sections is partly north of the arctic circle? What reason can you give for the few people there?

Turn next to the regional map on pages 6–7. What kind of surface do you find in the great sections of very sparse population? Taken as a whole, are those sections made up chiefly of lowland plains, or more largely of mountains and plateaus?

Now turn to the rainfall map on page 5. How does it help to explain the locations of the very thinly settled sections?

What you have discovered. You have discovered that, except for part of India, the three largest sections of dense population in the Old World are mostly in the north temperate zone; that within them are large stretches of lowland plains; and that they have over 20 inches of rain each year.

Think over what you have learned about the work of the people in regions of the same kind in the Americas, and then make a list of the kinds of work that you think the people of the thickly populated parts of Eurasia do. Keep your list and check it as you learn more about these Old World lands.

You have also discovered that the great sections of the Old World which have very few people are largely high lands or dry lands, and that part of the very thinly settled section of Asia is a very cold land. The regions that have less than 10 inches of rain each year are true deserts. Why is it hard for people to make a living in very dry lands?

De Cou from Ewing Galloway, N. Y.

Figure 6. A picture taken in the crowded harbor of one of the great seaports of China. The eastern part of China is so densely populated that many people live in small boats in the river mouths and harbors along the coast. Some of them make their living by carrying goods from place to place in their house boats.

What have you learned about the life and work of people in the high, rugged mountains and in the deserts of the New World? Make a list of the kinds of work that you think the people do in regions of the same kind in the Old World. Keep this list with your first one, and check it as you learn more about these regions.

Figures 5 and 6 show some interesting contrasts between Arabia, which is one of the very thinly populated parts of Asia, and China, which is one of the most crowded parts. Study both pictures carefully.

Flying over the Old World. Suppose you had an airplane of your own and could fly wherever you pleased. In the column at the left of the map on pages 6–7 you will find suggestions for a trip by airplane in the Old World. As you work out the map studies, try to imagine that you are really flying over the Old World lands.

Making choices. Prove that you are getting acquainted with the Old World by choosing the right ending for each sentence below.

1. Most of Eurasia is in the
north temperate zone.   south temperate zone.
torrid zone.

2. The greater part of Africa is in the
north temperate zone.   south temperate zone.
torrid zone.

3. The continent of the Old World which is wholly in the Southern Hemisphere is
Asia.   Australia.   Africa.

4. The most densely populated sections of the Old World are largely regions of
high mountains.   plateaus.   lowland plains.

5. The yearly rainfall in the three large areas of dense population in Eurasia is
enough for farming.   too little for farming.
too much for farming.

Water less than 500 ft. deep

Land below sea level

Floating ice

Tundra

Grasslands and cultivated areas

Temperate forests

Semideserts, deserts, and barren mountain slopes

Oases

EUROPE

Scale of miles

0   100   200   300   400   500

II. OUR NEAREST NEIGHBORS IN THE OLD WORLD

Foreword. The part of the Old World that the people of our country visit most often is Europe. One reason is that Europe is nearer to us than any other part of the Old World. Another is that most of the people of the United States are descended from European people. How many countries of Europe can you name without looking at a map?

Turn to the map of the world on pages 330–331 and name the European countries that border the Atlantic Ocean. These are our nearest neighbors in Europe. Do you know how we keep in touch with them?

Transatlantic travel. The fastest ships cross the Atlantic Ocean from New York City to British or French ports in four and a half days. A considerably larger number of boats make the crossing in from six to nine days. There are also airplane routes across the Atlantic. Planes flying the northern route, from Newfoundland to Ireland, make the trip in less than twenty-four hours. *See Figures 7 and 10.*

Hundreds of thousands of people travel by boat each year between the countries on the opposite sides of the north Atlantic Ocean. Millions of tons of freight are carried by ships between those countries, and millions of letters pass back and forth. Ideas and news also travel back and forth easily, and they help the people of North America and Europe to know each other better.

Sending messages. Telegraph cables that rest on the sea bottom are used to send messages quickly from one side of the ocean to the other. Radio stations in the United States and others in western Europe keep in constant touch with one another, and by using

the radio it is possible for people in North America and people in Europe to telephone to one another.

Some comparisons. In the lists on pages 330–331 find the area of Europe and the area of the United States. Comparing their size will show you that Europe is somewhat larger than the United States. But the United States is a single country, while Europe is divided into about thirty different countries.

Courtesy of United States Lines

Figure 7. Great ocean liners, or passenger ships, such as the one shown here, make fast trips between New York and ports of western Europe. A ship of this size carries about 1200 passengers.

What is true, then, of the size of the European countries compared with our country?

Turn to pages 330–331 again and trace the parallel of 40° north latitude across the map of the world. Notice that this parallel divides the United States about in halves. What part of Europe does it cross? Now trace the parallel of 60° north latitude and the arctic circle across the map. Do these lines cross the United States? What part of Europe do they cross? What can you say now about the locations of Europe and the United States with reference to the equator? with reference to the north pole?

Turn over to page 14.

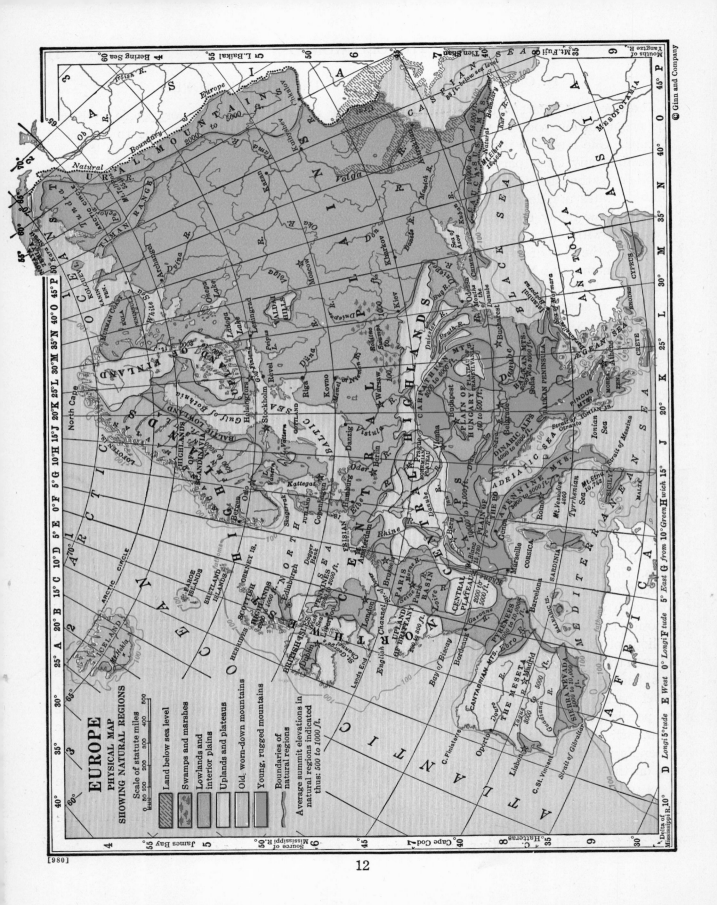

EUROPE

PHYSICAL MAP

SHOWING NATURAL REGIONS

Scale of statute miles

Land below sea level

Swamps and marshes

Lowlands and interior plains

Uplands and plateaus

Old, worn-down mountains

Young, rugged mountains

Boundaries of natural regions

Average summit elevations in natural regions indicated thus: 500 to 1000 ft.

© Ginn and Company

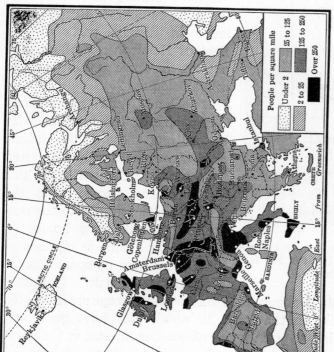

Figure 9. Distribution of people in Europe.

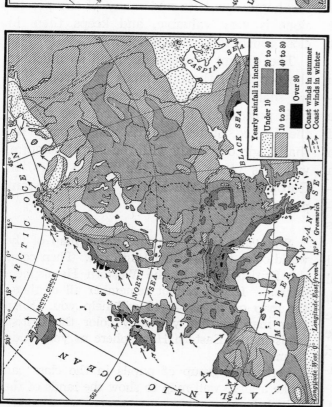

Figure 8. Distribution of rainfall in Europe.

MAP STUDIES

1. In what part of Europe do you find young, rugged mountains? 2. Name the two mountain regions which have the highest summits. 3. How does Mont Blanc (*G6*) in the Alps compare in height with Mount Elbrus (*O7*) in the Caucasus? 4. What mountains in the Americas are of the same kind as those in southern Europe? 5. In what ways do you think the people of the young, rugged mountains in Europe probably make their living?

6. Find the Central Plains, the Paris Basin, the Plain of the Po, and the Plain of Hungary. 7. Compare this map with Figure 8 and give two reasons why these plains are well suited to farming.

8. Find the Northwest Highlands and the Central Highlands. 9. What large region of old, worn-down mountains forms part of the Northwest Highlands? 10. In the Central Highlands of Europe the landscape is much like that in parts of the Appalachian Highlands of North America. Can you explain why?

11. Notice how irregular the western coast line of the Scandinavian Peninsula is. This coast is broken by long, narrow fiords which will remind you of southeastern Alaska and southern Chile.

12. What sea separates the Scandinavian Peninsula from the British Isles? 13. What sea extends far into the Central Plains of Europe? 14. What large sea borders Europe on the south? 15. What do you find on Figure 8 to show that northwestern Europe lies in the path of the rain-giving westerly winds?

16. Use Figure 9 to compare the density of population in central and southern Europe with the density in northern Europe. What reasons can you give for the difference? 17. Compare the density of population in the western half of Europe with that in the eastern half, and give reasons for the difference.

Figure 10. One of the great Atlantic-type air liners that fly at high speed across the ocean carrying passengers and mail. It is 109 feet in length and has four high-powered engines.

Since Europe lies so much farther north than the United States, you might expect its climate to be much colder. This, however, is not true, except in the northern sections of Europe which are far inland. Do you know why? If you cannot tell the reason now, be on the lookout for it as you learn more about the European countries.

The natural regions of Europe. When you were studying the lands of the Western Hemisphere, you found that the way people live and work depends largely on the kind of region in which they make their home. In order to understand how the people live in different parts of Europe, you need to get acquainted with the natural regions of the continent. To do this, work out the map studies on page 13.

Lands held by European nations. You will remember that the United States has several possessions in different parts of the world, and that we found parts of the British Empire in North America, South America, and the West Indies. We also found French and Dutch possessions in the Western Hemisphere. Do you remember where they are?

We shall find that the British, French,

Belgians, Dutch, and a few of the other nations of Europe hold lands in distant parts of the Eastern Hemisphere. Many, but not all, of these possessions are called colonies.

Homelands and possessions. The people of the homelands in Europe and those of the distant possessions are keenly interested in each other. One reason for this is that many people from the home countries go out to the possessions to make new homes, or to work for a time as representatives of business companies or as government officials. Naturally enough, their relatives in Europe are interested in the lands to which they have gone, and they, in turn, seldom lose interest in the home country. Another reason is that trade between the home countries and many of the possessions is very valuable, and keeps them in close touch with one another.

The distant possessions mean so much to the people of the homelands in Europe that we shall study the European countries and their possessions together, just as we studied the United States and its possessions. We shall begin our study with the British Empire, which is made up of the British Isles, in Europe, and all the British lands in distant parts of the world.

Something to do. On an outline map of the world color the British Isles in red. Then color the British lands in the Western Hemisphere in pink. If you cannot remember all of them, the map on pages 42–43 will help you. Keep your map so that you may color the British lands in the Eastern Hemisphere as you study them.

Perhaps a group of pupils in the class can make a large wall map to show the lands of the British Empire.

THE BRITISH EMPIRE

I. A GREAT FAMILY OF NATIONS

Foreword. In the early days of exploration, before anyone knew how many continents there were on the earth, the British sailors were among the most daring men who went to sea. They visited many distant parts of the world, and when they returned to their homes in the British Isles they told of the far-away lands and the strange people they had seen.

Later the British sent out colonists to settle in some of these distant lands, and formed business companies to carry on trade with others. Through settlement and trade they gradually gained possession of many different parts of the earth, until today they control more land than any other nation. Their vast empire includes lands in every continent, and its area of more than thirteen million square miles is nearly one fourth of the entire land area of the earth.

Contrasts within the empire. The various parts of the British Empire differ greatly from one another. In some parts the winters are long and cold, and in others the weather is always warm. Other parts are desert regions, and still others are lands where the rainfall is so heavy that there is danger from floods.

Map work. Before you read further about the British Empire, turn to page 43 and work out the map studies there.

The people of the empire. In the lands belonging to the British Empire there are more than five hundred million people, or about one fourth of all the people on the earth. Of this great number, less than one fifth are white people and more than four fifths are people of the darker-skinned races. Some of the groups of people within the empire are among the most advanced nations of the world, while others are among the most backward nations.

The people who live in the British Isles are the English-speaking people of Europe, and most of the white people in all parts of the British Empire use the English language. In many of the colonies there are native people who use their own language, but more and more of them are learning to speak English because they need it in order to trade with the white people.

World-wide interests of the British people. All the large firms carrying on business in distant parts of the British Empire have offices in one or another of the great cities of the British Isles, and many of the business firms of the home country have branch offices in the dominions and colonies. Thus the British people have business interests in all parts of the world.

On any day of the year, at any one of the large seaports of the British Isles, you might see ships arriving from other parts of the empire or sailing off to those distant lands. If you should visit the wharves frequently, you would discover that people and goods are always traveling back and forth between the home country and the colonial lands.

In almost every British family there is someone who has gone to live in one of the distant parts of the empire, or someone who has joined the navy or is an officer or a seaman on some passenger ship or freighter which crosses and recrosses the oceans.

The divisions of the empire. When you were studying North America, you learned that Canada is a dominion of the British Empire. How many other dominions did you discover in studying the map on pages 42–43?

The dominions are almost like independent countries, for the people govern themselves. Each of the colonies has a governor sent out from the home country, but the people themselves also have a share in the government.

Besides the dominions and colonies, there are parts of the empire called protectorates and dependencies. They are lands where the British protect the native people and help them with their government.

The self-governing parts of the British Empire form what is called the British Commonwealth of Nations. The word *commonwealth* comes from the old English words *common weal*, which mean "common good," or "for the good of all." The members of the commonwealth are Great Britain and Northern Ireland and the British dominions.

It is in the lands of the commonwealth that most of the white people of the British Empire live. Although these groups of people are widely scattered over the world, they help one another through friendship and trade. Helping one another works for the good of all, and thus they form a real commonwealth of nations.

Where are these ships going? A shipowner in the British Isles is sending out five ships to distant parts of the empire. The place where each ship is going is described below. Write the names of the places in a list, in the order in which they are described. When you have finished, check your list by the map on pages 42–43 to make sure it is correct.

1. To a British dominion in North America.
2. To the largest of the British lands in Asia.
3. To a British dominion in Africa.
4. To a British dominion which occupies a whole continent.
5. To the dominion farthest southeast from the British Isles.

II. THE BRITISH ISLES

Foreword. The British Isles are made up of the two large islands known as Great Britain and Ireland, and the many small islands close by. The map on pages 22–23 shows that Great Britain has three political divisions, and Ireland two. What are their names?

England, Scotland, Wales, and Northern Ireland are under one government and form the United Kingdom of Great Britain and Northern Ireland. Eire, which occupies the greater part of the island of Ireland, is a self-governing member of the British Commonwealth of Nations.

The British Isles make up less than 1 per cent of all the lands of the empire, and yet they have nearly 10 per cent of all the people, and they are one of the most densely populated parts of Europe. Do you know why it is that so many people can make a living in these islands? Watch for reasons as you study this chapter.

1. THE HOMELAND OF THE BRITISH

When you were studying the United States, you learned that the people of New England began very early to use the sea for fishing and trading, and that later on trading helped them to develop manufacturing. The story of the British people is somewhat like that of the New Englanders. For hundreds of years they have been using the sea for fishing and trading, and today they carry on more dollars' worth of foreign commerce, or trade with other countries, than any other nation in the world. Our own country ranks second in foreign commerce.

During the last one hundred and fifty years the British people have also become a great manufacturing nation, and manufactured goods are by far the most valuable products that they sell to the people of other countries.

As you study this section, find reasons why the British have become leaders among the commercial, or trading, nations of the world, and also among the industrial, or manufacturing, nations.

gaelic gulf-stream

Photograph by Elizabeth T. Wilson, R. I. Nesmith and Associates

Figure 11. A view among the beautiful Lakes of Killarney in southwestern Ireland. In the center of the picture are the ruins of an old castle. Many of the upland regions of the British Isles are as hilly and mountainous as this. Do you think they make especially good farm lands? Give a reason for your answer.

Map study. Begin your study of the British Isles by using the map on pages 22–23 to answer the following questions:

1. Is the coast line of the British Isles smooth and regular or crooked and irregular? 2. What does this suggest about the number of good harbors for ships? 3. What bodies of water surround the British Isles? 4. What narrow bodies of water separate Great Britain from France?

5. What range of old, worn-down mountains do you find in England? 6. In what part of England are these mountains? 7. How should you describe the rest of England? 8. Is Wales chiefly an upland or a lowland country?

9. In what part of Scotland do you expect to find the most people? Why? 10. Look at Figure 9 on page 13 and see if your answer to the first part of question 9 was correct. 11. How does the central part of Ireland differ from the northern and southern parts? 12. In what country is the central plain of Ireland?

The higher lands of the British Isles. You have discovered from the map that much of the land in the British Isles is hilly or mountainous. The mountains are old and worn down, and the uplands are lands with rounded hills and gently sloping valleys. In northern England and in Scotland and Ireland there are lake districts much like our own beautiful lake districts in New England and in the Adirondack Mountains. *See Figure 11.*

The continental glacier and its work. Do you remember about the great ice sheets, or continental glaciers, which long ago covered the northern part of North America? At about the same time that these ice sheets formed in North America a great ice sheet formed in the Scandinavian Peninsula of Europe and spread over the northern part of that continent. It brought about changes in Europe similar to those caused by the ice sheets in North America. Figure 12 shows how much of Europe was covered by the continental ice sheet.

As the great mass of glacier ice moved slowly over the highlands of Scotland and the Pennine Chain of England, it wore down the higher parts and rounded the mountain peaks. When the ice finally melted away, it left loose rock material known as *glacial drift* spread over the land which it had covered. Fortunately, the glacial drift left in the British Isles is not so coarse and bowldery as that in New England, and therefore it is not so great a handicap to farming.

Figure 12. A map showing how much of Europe was covered by the continental ice sheet of long ago. Notice that as the ice spread southward from the Scandinavian Peninsula it covered all parts of the British Isles except the southernmost part of England.

The lowlands of the British Isles. In studying the map you discovered that there are three important lowland regions in the British Isles. The largest one is in England, and within it are the best farm lands of that country, and also many of the largest industrial, or manufacturing, centers. In the farming sections you will see grainfields and pastures bordered by beautiful hawthorn hedges instead of by wooden fences or stone walls. *See Figure 13*.

The lowland of Scotland forms a narrow belt between the Scottish Highlands on the north and the uplands of southern Scotland on the south. It is a beautiful region of green fields which are used for pastures and mixed farming, and scattered through it are many little villages and a few large cities. It is in this lowland region that most of the people of Scotland live. Explain why.

The lowland of Ireland extends from coast to coast across the central part of the island. Much of the land in this region is so low that it is swampy, but it makes good pasture land. In all parts of Ireland the summers are cool, the winters mild, and the rainfall abundant. For this reason the grass stays green throughout most of the year. Ireland is often called the "Emerald Isle." Can you explain why?

Mineral wealth. Turn to the map on pages 22–23 and find the places where coal is mined in England, Scotland, and Wales. Notice that there are coal mines in the lowlands as well as in the uplands. The fact that there is much coal in Great Britain will help you to understand why manufacturing is so important there. Study the map again and name a metal ore that is mined in several different parts of England. What kind of manufacturing, then, do you expect to find in some of the English industrial centers?

The "drowned" coast line. You discovered in studying the map that the coast line of the British Isles is very irregular. That is because long, long ago the land sank and the sea water came into the lower ends of the river valleys. For this reason we say that the river mouths have been "drowned." We call a drowned river mouth an *estuary*.

The estuaries provide the British Isles with many large, deep harbors for ships. That is one reason why the British have always been seafaring people; that is, people who make much use of the sea. *See Figure 14*.

The shallow bordering seas. Turn to the map on page 12 and find the brown line in the water around the British Isles. Notice that it is marked *100 fathoms*. Along that line the water is 100 fathoms, or 600 feet, deep.

During your study of North America you learned that the 100-fathom line marks the outer edge of the continental shelf, or the part of the land which lies under water much shallower than the deep oceans. Turn to the map on page 12 again, and you will see that the British Isles are surrounded by shallow seas.

© F. Frith & Co., Ltd., Reigate

Figure 13. Plowing in the southern part of the plain of England. Contrast the surface of the land here with that shown in Figure 11. Where in Scotland and Ireland may you expect to find land as level as this?

Courtesy of Grace R. Stevens

Figure 14. Two villages on the southwestern coast of England. One village is on the top of a sea cliff, and the other is at the foot. How do you think some of the people of the lower village make their living?

Famous fishing grounds. Do you remember the famous fishing grounds called "banks" which are found on the continental shelf bordering northeastern North America? The North Sea and the other shallow seas bordering northwestern Europe are also rich fishing grounds, because they too are feeding places for millions of fish. That is why fishing has always been an important kind of work along the shores of the British Isles. *See Figure 15.*

A climate problem. You have already discovered that the British Isles are in the same latitude as Labrador, and you know that Labrador is so cold that very few people live there. The map on page 340 will help you to understand why northwestern Europe is warmer than the eastern part of North America in the same latitude. What ocean current moves northeastward across the Atlantic Ocean toward northwestern Europe? Is it a cold current or a warm current?

How oceans affect climate. Wherever you travel you will find that ocean waters have much to do with the climates of the bordering lands. In the first place, they make coast lands cooler in summer and warmer in winter than interior lands in the same latitude.

The next point for you to remember is that there are warm currents and cold currents in different parts of the oceans. The warm currents make the air just above them warm, while the cold currents make the overlying air cold. When air warmed by an ocean current is blown over a land surface, the temperature of the air over that land becomes warmer. What happens when air cooled by an ocean current is blown over a land surface?

The oceans also have much to do with the rainfall of the bordering lands. Winds that blow from the oceans bring rain-bearing clouds to the lands, and therefore all coast lands where winds blow steadily or frequently from the sea have abundant rainfall throughout the year.

Temperatures in the British Isles. The reason the British Isles are so much warmer than Labrador is that they lie in the path of the westerly winds of the Northern Hemisphere. These winds, blowing across the north Atlantic Ocean, carry air warmed by the Gulf Stream and the Gulf Stream Drift to the British Isles and other parts of northwestern Europe. Thus this part of Europe has a much warmer climate than the part of

London Times

Figure 15. Fishing boats putting out to sea from Yarmouth, a fishing port on the east coast of England. Boats of this kind are used for herring-fishing.

North America on the opposite side of the Atlantic Ocean in the same latitude.

The British Isles are seldom very cold in winter or very hot in summer. That is because the islands are not large, and therefore all parts of them are affected by the temperatures of the surrounding waters.

Since in the winter the waters surrounding the islands do not cool off so fast as the land, the air that blows inland from the sea keeps the winter weather from being very cold. For this reason the temperature seldom falls to the freezing point (32° Fahrenheit) in the lowlands of these islands.

During the summer the air over the land becomes warm, for the summer days are long in the latitude of the British Isles. But the surrounding waters do not warm up so fast as the land, and the cool breezes which blow inland from the sea keep the summer temperatures from being uncomfortable.

Rainfall in the British Isles. The westerly winds bring large quantities of moisture to the British Isles, giving them a rainy climate. The western sides of the islands and the mountainous parts have from 70 to 80 inches of rain a year, and the lowlands have from 25 to 40 inches in most sections. This, as you know, is plenty of rain for agriculture. The driest section is in the lowland northeast of London. Can you explain why?

Some things to explain. Explain what is meant by each of the following words and phrases:

continental glacier　　　　seafaring people
estuary *mouth of a river*　foreign commerce
fathom *6 feet*　　　　　commercial nation
continental shelf　　　　industrial city

Giving reasons. Complete each sentence below by giving reasons for the fact which it states:

1. Many parts of the British Isles are not well suited to farming because *they are hilly Mountains*

2. There are no sharp peaks in the mountains of Great Britain because *the mount are old and worn down*

3. The British Isles have many good harbors because *there are many drowned river mouths*

4. The British Isles have a mild, rainy climate because *they are in the path of the westerly winds*

5. They are much warmer than Labrador because *they are warmed by winds that blow over the Gulf Stream*

Something to prove. If you can answer the following questions correctly, you will prove that you already know some of the reasons why the British people are one of the greatest commercial and industrial nations of the world.

1. Why is it easy for people who live on islands to carry on trade with people in other parts of the world?

2. How does a "drowned" coast line help people to make use of the sea?

3. How does an abundance of coal help a nation to carry on manufacturing?

4. For what important kind of manufacturing is iron ore the principal raw material?

5. Why is a densely populated country better prepared to carry on manufacturing than a sparsely populated country?

6. How does foreign commerce help a country to increase its manufacturing?

Special credit work. Find out how much rain falls each year where you live, and tell how it compares with the rainfall in the British Isles.

Figure 16. Buckingham Palace, the home of the British king. The British recognize the king as the head of the government, but the real power lies in the hands of the prime minister and other officers of the people.

Figure 17. The Houses of Parliament, seen from across the Thames. The British Parliament is somewhat like our Congress, and is made up of members from England, Scotland, Wales, and Northern Ireland.

2. THE CAPITAL OF THE BRITISH EMPIRE

Every visitor to Great Britain wishes to see London, just as every visitor to our country wishes to see New York City. New York, you will remember, is the largest city of the New World. London is the largest city of the Old World. Within the city limits live about four and a half million people, and crowded closely around it live nearly four million more.

Find London on the map on pages 22–23 (*G5*). In what part of England is it located? On what river? Can you suggest any reasons why a great city should have grown up at that place?

A great center of government. London is the capital of the United Kingdom of Great Britain and Northern Ireland. Figure 16 shows the palace where the king lives, and Figure 17 shows the great building where the British Parliament meets to carry on the government of the kingdom.

London is the capital of the British Empire also. In this great city are offices where matters concerning the self-governing dominions are cared for, and others where men in charge of certain affairs of the colonies and dependencies do their work.

A busy, crowded city. The traffic in London reminds us of New York and the other large cities of our country. The sidewalks are crowded with people, and the streets are filled with taxicabs, busses, and private automobiles. Beneath the ground there is a network of subways for electric trains. Thousands of people use the subways to travel back and forth between their homes and their places of work.

The shops and stores in London are much like those in our own large cities. The business buildings are large, and many are ten or twelve stories high, but there are no huge skyscrapers such as we have in the United States. *See Figure 18.*

Old London. Figure 19 shows that London spreads out on both sides of the river Thames. In the midst of the great city of today is Old London, on the north bank of the river near London Bridge. (See 11 on Figure 19.) Here the first settlement was made, more than two thousand years ago. The map on pages 22–23 will help you to understand why a town grew up at this place. Notice that the river Thames flows from west to east across southern England.

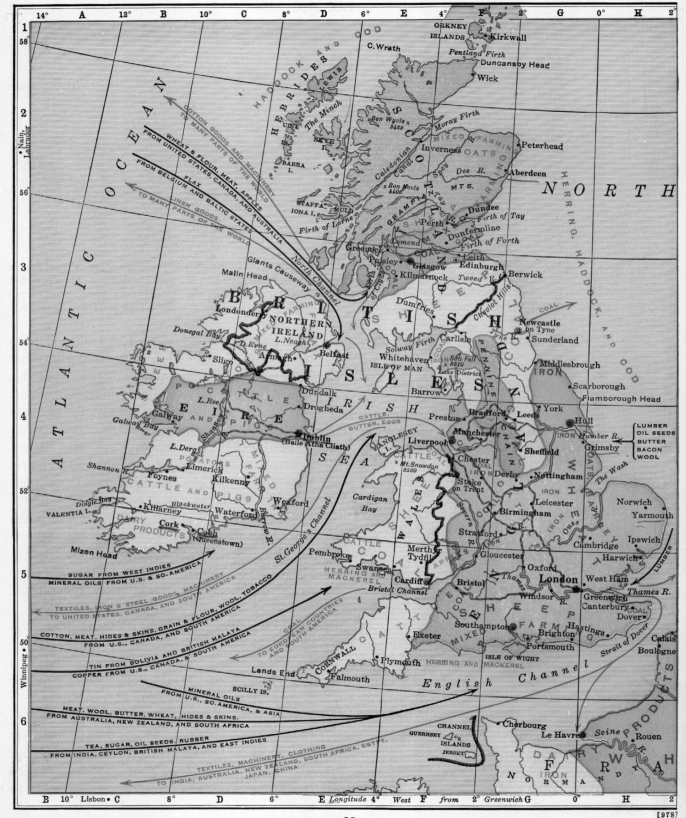

[978]

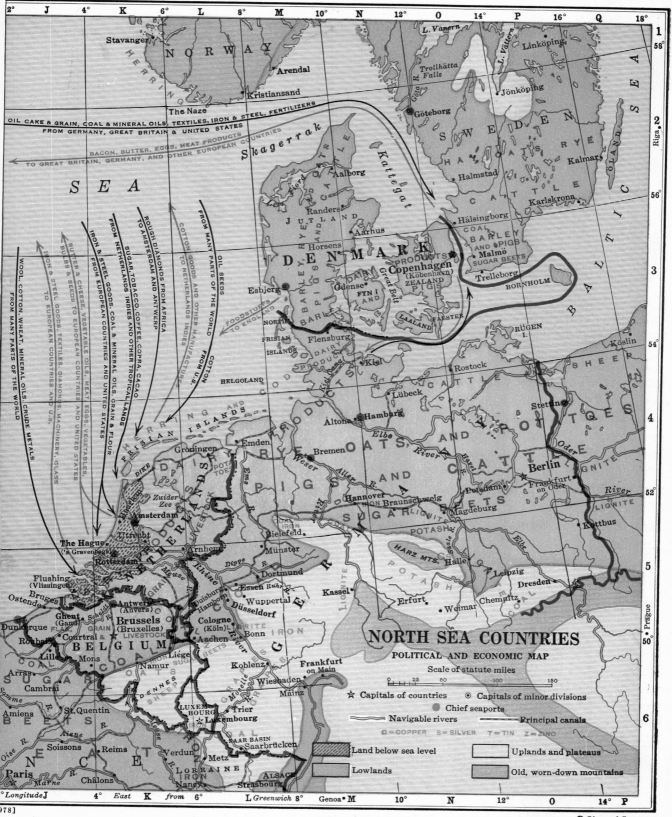

© Ginn and Company

Philip D. Gendreau, N. Y.

Figure 18. The square in London which the British call Piccadilly Circus. Five busy streets come together here, all of them lined with shops and stores, hotels, restaurants, and moving-picture theaters.

For a long distance upstream from its mouth the Thames is wide and deep, and is bordered by low, swampy land. The place farthest east where the river was narrow enough and the ground dry enough for a bridge to be built in the early days was near where London Bridge stands today. The first bridge was probably narrow and made of wood, but it was very important; for it was here that roads from the southern parts of England met to cross the Thames, and then spread out to north and west.

Because the bridge was the meeting point for the roads of southern England, a settlement grew up at its northern end; and as time went on, this "bridge town" became the most important trading center of Great Britain. As you read further, watch for reasons why it has grown to be one of the world's greatest cities.

Today Old London is the heart of the business section of the great city. Like Lower Manhattan in New York, it is crowded with workers during the day; but at night, after the banks and offices have closed, most of the buildings are empty and the streets are quiet.

Some famous buildings. In Old London, surrounded by business buildings, is St. Paul's Cathedral. This great church has a beautiful dome which towers above the surrounding roofs. The best shops, theaters, and hotels, and the famous museums and art galleries are in the part of the city west of Old London. Here too are the Houses of Parliament and Westminster Abbey, a beautiful old church in which there are statues and busts of people whom the British admire and respect.

Parks and gardens. As London has grown and spread over the lowlands on both sides of the Thames, the people have saved many open spaces for public parks and gardens. Thus there are many pleasant places where the people of this great, crowded city may enjoy themselves out of doors. Find some of the parks on Figure 19.

A famous observatory. We shall surely wish to visit the famous observatory in the part of London known as Greenwich. The observatory is a domed building with a big telescope for studying the stars. It is well known the world over because it marks the place of the prime meridian of longitude, or the meridian of 0°. Find Greenwich on the map on pages 22–23 (*H 5*) and on Figure 19.

You will remember that the meridians are the imaginary north-south lines which pass around the earth through the poles. They are numbered by degrees east and west from Greenwich. Since there are 360 degrees in a circle, the meridian of 180° is just halfway around the earth in either direction, west or east, from Greenwich. Use a globe to prove that this is true. Is our own country in longitude east from Greenwich, or in longitude west from Greenwich?

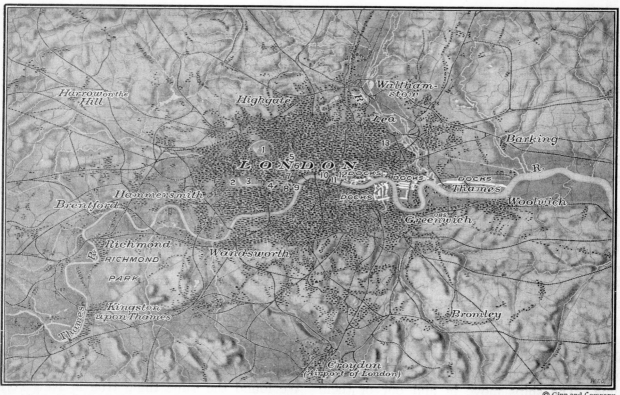

Figure 19. A relief map of London and its surroundings. The numbers show the location of the following places of interest: 1, Regent's Park; 2, Kensington Gardens; 3, Hyde Park; 4, Buckingham Palace; 5, British Museum; 6, National Gallery; 7, Trafalgar Square; 8, Westminster Abbey; 9, Houses of Parliament; 10, St. Paul's Cathedral; 11, London Bridge; 12, Tower of London; 13, Victoria Park. Find the airport of London.

Down the Thames. We shall find it interesting to make the trip to Greenwich on a passenger boat which runs down the Thames. Just beyond the limits of Old London we shall pass the Tower of London, a great stone building erected as a fortress hundreds of years ago. Part of it is now a museum where many relics of historical interest are kept. Then we shall come to the Tower Bridge, shown in Figure 20. Study Figure 20 and its legend.

Ocean shipping. The busiest part of London's water front extends along the Thames for several miles below the Tower Bridge. There we shall see many large ocean freighters and passenger ships which have come from distant parts of the British Empire and from other countries of the world. They have brought to London large cargoes of raw materials, such as wool, hides, and rubber, and great quantities of foodstuffs, such as meat, butter, eggs, tea, and fruits. Many of the huge storage warehouses which line the water front are filled with imported products for the British people, and many others with British goods to be shipped away.

Turn to the map on pages 22–23 and study the imports of London. From what distant parts of the British Empire do large quantities of foodstuffs and raw materials come to London?

Now study the exports of London. What kind of goods are they — foodstuffs, raw materials, or manufactures? To what parts of the British Empire do large quantities of the exports go?

The tides at London. Each day in the year there are two periods when the ocean waters rise to a high level, and two periods when they sink to a low level. Because of the tides the waters rise and fall twice a day in all the harbors and river estuaries along the ocean coasts. At London the Thames is about 25 feet lower at low tide than at high tide, and at low tide the water is too shallow for the larger ocean ships.

Docks for the large ships. Because of the changes in tide, large ocean ships cannot safely tie up at wharves along the banks of the Thames. If they did, they would sink into the mud on the river bottom at low tide. For this reason many large docks of a special kind have been built along the river downstream from the Tower Bridge.

The docks are giant basins of deep water shut off from the river by big gates. Each one is large enough to hold many ships at a time. The ships move in and out of them at high tide. Then the gates are closed, and they keep the water from flowing out of the docks when the tide falls. In this way the ships are perfectly safe while they are being unloaded and loaded again.

London's growth as a seaport. You have learned why London very early became the most important trading center of Great Britain. Can you think of any reasons why it became a busy seaport also?

You can see from the map that the Thames is navigable from London to the sea, and that its mouth is not far distant from the continent of Europe. The British began very early to trade with their neighbors on the Continent. It was natural, then, that ships should bring their cargoes up the Thames to the town that was already the leading trading center and from which goods could be sent in all directions over the roads.

It was also natural that when railroads were built the leading seaport and trading center of Great Britain should become the greatest railroad center. The railroads helped to increase trade, and so London has continued to grow as a seaport. Today it is not only the leading port of the British Isles but one of the greatest ports of the whole world. Besides all the goods which it receives from distant lands for use by the British people, it imports large quantities of goods for *re-export* to other countries.

A great manufacturing center. As you would expect, London, with its many railroads and its great shipping business, is a great manufacturing center. Give as many reasons as you can to explain why. Remember that manufacturers must have raw materials, power, and workers for their factories, and good means of marketing their products.

Among all the different industries of London the making of clothing and the preparation of foodstuffs are the most important. We found the same thing true in New York City. What reason can you give for it?

A great airway center. The map on page 128 shows that London is the airway center of Great Britain. Notice that it is connected by airlines with all parts of Europe and with distant parts of the world.

A world city. The longer we stay in London, the more we realize that it is not only a great British city but a great world city. Its ships trade in all the great seaports of the earth, and its people carry on business in nearly every country. Its banks are among the wealthiest in the world, taking a leading part in the work connected with the exchange of money between all the commercial nations. Because of this work we call London a great *financial center*.

London is also a great *cultural center*, where people from many lands gather to study art and music, to use the books in its wonderful libraries, and to study the collections in its famous museums.

Figure 20. An airplane view of part of London, looking up the Thames. In the upper left corner of the picture is the dome of St. Paul's Cathedral. In the center is the Tower Bridge, and just beyond it, at the right, is the old

Surrey Flying Services' Photograph from Orient and Occident

Tower of London. The lower central portion of the Tower Bridge can be lifted to allow boats to pass through. The large ocean ships, however, dock downstream from the bridge, where the water is deeper.

Something to prove. By answering the following questions prove that you understand why London has always attracted people and trade.

1. Why did London become the most important trading center of Great Britain a long time ago?

2. Why did London make an early start as a seaport?

3. Why has London become the greatest railroad center of Great Britain?

4. How did the building of railroads help to increase the foreign commerce of London?

5. Why has London become a great manufacturing center?

6. Why do so many people from all parts of the world visit London?

Something to explain. Explain what has been done to make it possible for large ocean ships to load and unload at London. Use Figure 19 in making your explanation.

3. OTHER SEAPORTS OF THE BRITISH ISLES

Because the long, irregular coast line of the British Isles provides so many good harbors, British trade is carried on through many different seaports. But although there are many ports, Liverpool is the only one which can be compared with London in importance. London and Liverpool together carry on more than half of all the trade of the British Isles.

Find Liverpool on the map on pages 22–23 (*F4*). On what sea is it located? What ports of Ireland are located on that sea? What is the leading port of Scotland? In what part of Scotland is it located? What is the leading port of Wales?

As you study about these and other seaports of the British Isles, try to discover how their trade is connected with the work and needs of the people of Great Britain and Ireland.

Aerofilms Ltd.

Figure 21. A small part of the water front at Liverpool, as it looks from an airplane. The basins where ships are loading and unloading cargoes are the deep-water docks. All the wharves between the docks are lined with storage warehouses, and on some of them there are railroad tracks. Can you tell why this is so?

English Seaports

Liverpool. If you are on a ship coming into Liverpool from the south, you will see the low hills of Ireland and Wales for some hours before you reach the end of your journey. Trace your route on the map on pages 22–23, and try to imagine that your ship is now moving slowly into the harbor of Liverpool.

There are many other ships coming and going in the harbor. Judging from the map, from what countries do you think some of them have come? What have they brought to Liverpool? What do you think those that are leaving are carrying away?

The harbor and the docks. Liverpool is on the estuary of the Mersey River. Because of the rise and fall of the tides in the harbor, the people of Liverpool have had to build docks that can be closed by gates like those at the port of London. The docks extend along the river for about seven miles, providing space for many ships to load and unload at one time. Like the docks at London, they are bordered by huge warehouses for the storage of all kinds of goods. *See Figure 21.*

The large freighters that come to Liverpool load and unload in the docks, but the great ocean liners land their passengers at a floating wharf which rises and falls with the tide. A bridge, also built to change its position with the changing level of the water, connects the wharf with the land.

A great trading center. Liverpool is the port through which most of the British trade with the United States, Canada, and South America is carried on. Its exports of British products are greater than those of London, but its imports are less. How does the location

Aerofilms Ltd.

Figure 22. An airplane view of a part of Manchester, showing the ship canal. Notice the factories and the railroad tracks along the canal. The long rows of buildings at the left are the homes of mill workers. This great industrial city is about thirty-five miles inland, but the ship canal has made it a busy port.

of Liverpool help to explain its large trade with the Americas?

At Liverpool, as at London, the leading imports are foodstuffs and raw materials, and the leading exports are manufactured goods. Among the imports, cotton ranks first. About half of it comes from our Southern States, but large quantities also come from Egypt, and smaller quantities from India, Peru, Brazil, and other countries. Which of the countries named is part of the British Empire?

Some of the cotton is used in mills near Liverpool, but most of it goes farther inland to a great cotton-manufacturing district which centers around Manchester. Find Manchester on the map on pages 22–23 (*F4*) and notice that it is connected with the estuary of the Mersey by a canal. This is the Manchester Ship Canal, and a good many of the boats loaded with cotton and other imports pass by the docks at Liverpool and carry their cargoes directly to Manchester. *See Figure 22.*

The next most valuable imports of Liverpool are meat, hides and skins, grain and flour, and wool. They come chiefly from the United States, Canada, and Argentina. Which of these countries is a British dominion?

You have discovered that Liverpool is the great gateway through which raw cotton enters England. It is also the principal gateway through which cotton goods manufactured in English mills are shipped to distant parts of the world.

Other work in Liverpool. Like all great ports, Liverpool is a manufacturing center because of its advantages for receiving raw materials and shipping away manufactured

Aerofilms Ltd.

Figure 23. A glimpse of the port of Southampton from the air. The large passenger liner at the right is in a dry dock for repairs. Find some other ocean liners in the picture.

goods. It is also a very important *terminus*, or ending place, for railroads from all parts of Great Britain. The railroads that meet here bring large quantities of manufactured goods from all parts of the island to be shipped to distant lands, and carry back large quantities of raw materials and foodstuffs to the inland industrial centers.

Two ports on the North Sea. On the map (pp. 22–23) find Hull (*G4*) and Newcastle on Tyne (*G3*). These are England's leading ports on the North Sea. Because of their location, much of their trade is with the countries bordering that sea and the Baltic Sea.

Hull, on the estuary of the Humber River, is one of England's great gateways for imports of food and raw materials. Among its imports are butter and bacon from Denmark, lumber from countries on the Baltic Sea, and wool from many distant lands. The wool goes to a great woolen-manufacturing district which you will learn about later.

Newcastle, on the estuary of the river Tyne, is chiefly a coal-exporting port. What do you find on the map (pp. 22–23) to explain this fact? While you are looking at the map, find the place where iron ore is mined near Middlesbrough (*G3*). That city has great blast furnaces and steel mills. Steel from Middlesbrough and abundant coal have helped to make Newcastle a great center for the manufacture of machinery and steel ships. The lower Tyne, like the lower part of the Delaware River in our country, is one of the great shipbuilding centers of the world.

Southampton. Southampton, on the southern coast of England, is the port used by some of the largest passenger ships that cross the Atlantic. It was chosen as a port for these great liners because the harbor is deep and well protected from storm waves. *See Figure 23.*

Southampton also carries on much foreign commerce. Foodstuffs and raw materials from distant lands come to this port to be sent inland by rail, and manufactured goods from inland cities are shipped away. Southampton itself is becoming a manufacturing center of importance. Can you explain why?

A list to make. The five most important English ports are described below. Write their names in a list in the order in which they are described. Put stars against the two ports which together carry on half of all the trade of the British Isles.

1. The port which carries on the most trade with distant parts of the British Empire in the Eastern Hemisphere.

2. The port which carries on the most trade with the Americas.

3. The port on the southern coast, used by some of the largest transatlantic liners.

4. Two ports which carry on much trade with countries bordering the North Sea and the Baltic Sea.

Courtesy of Grace R. Stevens

Figure 24. The railroad bridge over the Firth of Forth in Scotland. The bridge is built of steel and is one of the longest in the whole world.

Ports of Scotland

The firths. The Scotch people call the drowned river mouths of their country *firths*. The deep firths of the highland region in the north are much like the fiords of Norway, but those of the central lowland are shallower and more like the estuaries of England. On the map on pages 22–23 find the Firth of Clyde (*E3*) and the Firth of Forth (*F2*). Notice that they lead into the very heart of the central lowland of Scotland. *See Figure 24.*

Glasgow and the river Clyde. If you take a boat trip up the Clyde to Glasgow, you will see huge ship-building yards on both sides of the river. The shipyards begin at Glasgow and extend downstream for many miles, and they make the Clyde the greatest shipbuilding river in the world.

The river Clyde was formerly so shallow that ocean ships could not enter it, but it has been deepened by dredging so that large ships can go upstream to Glasgow. The deepening of the river brought so much shipping to Glasgow that this city is now the leading seaport of Scotland. Its population of more than a million makes it the second largest city of the British Isles.

Glasgow is a great manufacturing city, partly because it is a busy seaport, and partly because coal is found close by. Among its great variety of manufactures, ships' engines are of special importance. Explain why.

From Glasgow to Edinburgh. A trip from Glasgow to Edinburgh takes us through the central lowland of Scotland. As we travel through this region we shall see that the people carry on mixed farming. Fields are planted to grain, vegetables, and fodder crops, and cattle and sheep are grazing in the pastures. Why is this lowland the principal farming region of Scotland?

Edinburgh and its port. Edinburgh is a beautiful old city lying at the foot of several hills. On one of the hills is an old castle which was built long ago to protect the city. Before Scotland was united with England in government Edinburgh was the home of the Scottish kings and queens, and Holyrood Palace, where they lived, is still used at times by the British king and queen. Edinburgh has long

Philip D. Gendreau, N.Y.

Figure 25. A view of Edinburgh. On the hill at the right is Edinburgh Castle, which is very old. The first settlement of Edinburgh grew up around this hill, for the castle served as a fortress where the people could defend themselves from attack by enemies.

Figure 26. A ship loading coal at Cardiff. From the map on pages 22-23 name the parts of the world to which large quantities of Welsh coal are exported.

been a center of learning, and for this reason the printing and publishing of books, magazines, and atlases is very important there. *See Figure 25.*

The port of Edinburgh is the smaller adjoining city of Leith on the Firth of Forth. Most of the exports of Scotland pass through the port of Glasgow, but Leith is important for its imports, especially of foodstuffs.

Dundee. Farther north, on the Firth of Tay, is the port of Dundee. Here we can visit mills which use large quantities of jute from India. Jute is a plant fiber, and it is used to make twine, rope, and coarse kinds of cloth known as burlap and gunny cloth. Great numbers of sacks, or bags, made of gunny cloth are also manufactured at Dundee, and are exported to distant lands for use in shipping various kinds of farm products.

Cardiff and Belfast

The chief seaport of Wales. On the map on pages 22-23 find Cardiff, the chief seaport of Wales (*F5*). This city is near one of the largest coal fields in Great Britain and is a great coal-exporting center. *See Figure 26.*

Welsh coal is so well suited to smelting that the manufacture of metals and metal products is the most important industry of this part of Great Britain. Cardiff and other cities of the region have large blast furnaces for smelting iron ore, steel mills, and factories for the manufacture of iron and steel products. Most of the iron ore is imported, chiefly from Spain. Tin, copper, and other metal ores are also imported from distant lands to be smelted with Welsh coal and used for the manufacture of many different metal products. The tin is used largely in the manufacture of tin plate, of which tin cans are made.

The seaport of Northern Ireland. Turn to the map again and find Belfast, the capital and chief seaport of Northern Ireland (*E3*). What is the leading import of this city?

Belfast has an excellent harbor lined with shipyards which will remind you of Glasgow. Where do you think the shipbuilders get their supplies of coal, iron, and steel?

The imports of flax suggest that Belfast is also a textile-manufacturing city. Have you ever seen any of the beautiful Irish linens? Belfast is the center for their manufacture. The farmers in the surrounding country raise flax, but they can supply only a small part of all the fiber that is needed by the linen mills. From what countries are large quantities of flax imported? What connection is there between manufacturing and export trade at Belfast?

Reminders of seaports. Name one or more British seaports which come to your mind when you think of the following imports and exports:

1. Imports of raw cotton and exports of cotton goods.
2. Imports of flax and exports of linen goods.
3. Exports of manufactured goods from Scotland.
4. Exports of coal from British mines.
5. Imports of metal ores.
6. Imports of wool.

4. SOME GREAT MANUFACTURING DISTRICTS

The British people began manufacturing very early, and today they are one of the greatest manufacturing nations in the world. As you study further, you will discover that manufacturing in Great Britain owes its growth to somewhat the same conditions which have led to the growth of manufacturing in the northeastern part of the United States. Can you suggest what some of these conditions are?

The industrial districts and the coal fields. Figure 27 shows where the principal industrial, or manufacturing, districts of the British Isles are located. Compare this map with the map on pages 22–23, and you will see that nearly every industrial district in Great Britain is on or near a coal field. The only important exception to this rule is the industrial area around London. The abundance of coal for power has been one of the principal reasons for the growth of British manufacturing.

The Textile Industries

A very old industry. One of the oldest industries in Great Britain is woolen-manufacturing. It began hundreds of years ago in the part of England known as Yorkshire, on the eastern side of the Pennine Chain. In those early days all the wool came from sheep pastured in the Pennines, and the spinning and weaving were done by hand. Textile machinery has now taken the place of the spinning wheels and hand looms of long ago, and all the work is done in mills. Today Yorkshire is one of the greatest woolen-manufacturing districts in the world, chiefly because it made such an early start, but also because it has abundant supplies of coal for power. Find this woolen-manufacturing district on Figure 27.

The pasture lands of Great Britain still provide much wool, but not nearly enough for all the mills, and vast quantities are im-

Figure 27. Industrial districts of the British Isles.

ported from distant lands. Much of it comes from the British dominions of Australia, New Zealand, and the Union of South Africa, and large quantities are imported from Argentina, Uruguay, and the Falkland Islands. About half of all the imports of wool come to the port of London. What two seaports nearer the Yorkshire industrial district also import wool? *Paisley*

Leeds and Bradford. On the map on pages 22–23 find Leeds and Bradford (*G4*), the leading cities of the woolen-manufacturing district. In these cities and in the neighboring towns and villages the making of woolen goods is far more important than any other kind of work. The woolen cloth made in the British mills is some of the best in the world, and it finds markets all over Great Britain and in many distant lands. Much of the cloth that is exported goes by train across the Pennines to the great port of Liverpool. *See Figure 28.*

© Sport & General Press Agency, Ltd., London

Figure 28. Scouring newly woven pieces of woolen cloth in a mill near Leeds. Scouring, or cleansing, is one of the processes of finishing the cloth.

Cotton-manufacturing in Lancashire. You already know that the city of Manchester, on the western side of the Pennines, is the center of a district where huge quantities of cotton goods are manufactured. This part of England is known as Lancashire, and it is the greatest cotton-manufacturing district of the whole world. Hundreds of thousands of people in Manchester and the neighboring towns make their living by working in spinning mills, weaving mills, and mills for dyeing and finishing cotton cloth. Find this great cotton-manufacturing district on Figure 27.

Cotton-manufacturing in England began much later than woolen-manufacturing, for there was no home supply of raw cotton, and it was only about one hundred and fifty years ago that large quantities of cotton began to be grown in our Southern States, on which the British depend for their greatest supplies. Today cotton-manufacturing is one of the most important of all the British industries, and it provides the most valuable of all British exports.

There are two principal reasons why cotton-manufacturing developed west of the Pennines. One was that Lancashire is on the windward side of England, and therefore it has a moister climate than Yorkshire. If cotton fibers are dry, they are apt to snap in the spinning, and therefore a moist climate is a great advantage in cotton-manufacturing. The other reason was that Lancashire is so conveniently located for receiving raw cotton from the United States. Here, as in the Yorkshire woolen district, abundant coal has helped greatly in the growth of manufacturing.

Vast quantities of cotton goods are shipped from Lancashire to the British colonies, to tropical lands in distant parts of the earth, and to China, where there are millions of people who wear cotton clothing. Through what port do most of these goods leave England?

Textile districts in Scotland and Ireland. Scotland has a cotton-manufacturing district centering around Glasgow, and a woolen-manufacturing district in the valley of the river Tweed, but they are far less important than the great textile districts of Lancashire and Yorkshire in England.

The greatest linen-manufacturing district in the British Isles is in Northern Ireland, centering in and around the city of Belfast. What connection did you discover between this industry and the foreign trade of Belfast?

Rayon-manufacturing. The newest textile industry in Great Britain is the manufacture of rayon goods. There are rayon mills in Yorkshire and several other parts of England, and for the making of rayon fiber large quantities of wood pulp are imported.

Industries depending on Iron and Steel

Iron ore in Great Britain. On the map on pages 22–23 find the places where iron ore is mined in Great Britain. The abundance of iron ore and coal has led to the development of many industries which make use of iron and steel. The mines of Great Britain provide about two thirds of the iron ore used in the blast furnaces. The rest of the ore is imported, chiefly from Spain, northern Africa, and Sweden.

London Times

Figure 29. A steel plant in England as it looks at night. After dark the bright glow from the steel furnaces reddens the sky for miles around.

You already know that there are blast furnaces and steel mills at Middlesbrough and in southern Wales. There are others at various places where iron ore and coal can be brought together easily. *See Figure 29.*

Birmingham and the "Black Country." On the map on pages 22–23 find Birmingham (*G4*). This is the largest city of the great industrial district known as the "Black Country." The Black Country has many coal mines, and it is crowded with towns which manufacture all kinds of products of iron and steel. *See Figure 30.*

The special work of the Black Country began long ago when first iron ore and then coal were discovered in the district. Most of the iron ore has now been used up, and the district no longer makes much iron and steel. Huge quantities of these metals come from other parts of Great Britain to the Black Country, where they are used to make all kinds of iron and steel products, from needles and nails to automobiles and locomotives. *See Figure 31.*

Birmingham has become the largest city and the greatest manufacturing center of the Black Country chiefly because it is a meeting point for roads, railroads, and canals from all directions. Because it is the great railroad center of the Black Country, it is the principal distributing point for the manufactures of that district.

Sheffield. A short distance south of the woolen-manufacturing district on the eastern side of the Pennines is another industrial district where huge quantities of iron and steel products are made. This district centers around Sheffield. You may have heard of Sheffield knives, for this city long ago became famous for its manufactures of cutlery, or cutting tools.

Find Sheffield on the map on pages 22–23 (*G4*). The discovery of iron ore and coal gave this city its start long ago as a center for the manufacture of iron and steel. Today all kinds of small tools and hardware are made in Sheffield and the neighboring towns, and Sheffield scissors, knives, razors, and other cutlery are sold in many distant parts of the world.

From Ewing Galloway, N. Y.

Figure 30. British miners at a coal mine near Birmingham. Coal-mining provides work for many thousands of men in Great Britain. Why are the coal-mining districts also manufacturing districts?

© Sport & General Press Agency, Ltd., London

Figure 31. In an automobile factory near Birmingham. The framework and engines of these cars have been completed, and are ready for the bodies.

© Sport & General Press Agency, Ltd., London

Figure 32. An ocean freighter being built in one of the shipyards on the river Tyne. What advantages has Great Britain for building ships of steel?

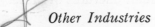

Other Industries

The English potteries. Between the Birmingham iron-and-steel district and the Lancashire cotton district are the "pottery towns." The largest of them is Stoke on Trent. These towns manufacture all kinds of pottery, from the finest china to the coarsest earthenware. Find the pottery district on Figure 27.

The principal raw material used in the making of pottery is clay, and the pottery towns grew up long ago where large deposits of clay suitable for this work were found. Today much of the best clay has been used up, and supplies are brought from other parts of England. But the pottery towns still lead in this industry, partly because they made such an early start, and partly because they are on a rich coal field.

Shipbuilding. You already know of three places in the British Isles where shipbuilding is a great industry. Where are they? There are still other centers of this industry at various places along the coast, for the British people need thousands of ships to carry on their trade with other parts of the world. They have more merchant ships than any other nation, and they build ships for many nations besides themselves. *See Figure 32.*

The variety of manufactures. You know now what the most important British manufactures are, but there are many, many others. In fact, it would be hard for you to think of anything that is not manufactured somewhere in the British Isles. The number of different industries is enormous, and far more people are engaged in manufacturing than in any other kind of work.

Something to prove. Prove your knowledge of the great industrial districts of the British Isles by giving the correct names to complete the following sentences. As you do so, point to the district on the map and explain its advantages for the kind of manufacturing for which it is famous.

1. The great cotton-manufacturing district centers around _____ in _____.

2. The great woolen-manufacturing district centers around _____ and _____, in ____ _____.

3. The two leading districts in the manufacture of iron and steel products center around _____ and around _____.

4. The greatest center for the smelting of metal ores is in southern _____.

5. The great linen-manufacturing district centers around _____ in Northern _____.

6. The greatest shipbuilding district is along the river _____ in _____.

5. FARMING AND FISHING

Thus far we have visited the British seaports and industrial districts where trade and manufacturing are the most important kinds of work. In the country districts we shall find farmers raising crops and live stock, and on the shallow seas surrounding the islands we shall find many fishermen busy with their work. What reasons can you suggest for the importance of farming and fishing in the British Isles?

Glimpses of the farming districts. In the lowlands of the British Isles, away from the cities, you will find many small farms and many large country estates. On the estates there are fine old houses surrounded by parklike grounds, and even the farmers' cottages are unusually attractive with their thatched roofs, their neatly trimmed hedges, and their flower gardens. *See Figure 33.*

Scattered through the farming districts are many little villages with narrow streets and thatched cottages overgrown with roses. Some of the villages have a factory or two, but they are chiefly market centers for the surrounding farm lands.

The need for food. As you travel through the farming regions, you will see very little land lying idle. The British Isles are so densely populated that as much land as possible must be used for raising crops and live stock to provide the people with food. But the islands are so small and so many parts of them are hilly or mountainous that the amount of good farming land is limited, and so the farmers can produce only part of the food that is needed. For this reason large quantities of foodstuffs are imported from other parts of the world.

© F. Frith & Co., Ltd., Reigate

Figure 33. A farmyard in the southern part of England. From what you see in the picture, what products do you think this farmer probably sells to the market men in the nearest town or city?

Specialized farming. In order to make the best possible use of the farm lands, most of the farmers specialize in certain products, just as the farmers in New England do. Near each of the larger cities there are dairy farms and poultry farms. Some of the farmers specialize in raising pigs, for the English people are very fond of bacon. Others specialize in raising vegetables and fruits for the city markets.

On the map on pages 22–23 find the Scilly Islands (*D6*) and the Channel Islands (*F6*). The climate of these islands is very mild, and the farmers raise early vegetables to send to the markets in the British cities.

Wheat lands. The drier part of the plain of England, northeast of London, is the only part of the British Isles where the climate is well suited to wheat. This is a winter-wheat section, where the farmers plant the seed in the autumn and harvest the grain in the early summer. *See Figure 34.*

The wheat farmers also raise crops to fatten cattle for market. They buy the cattle from Ireland and Scotland, and from

By Ewing Galloway, N. Y.

Figure 34. Harvesting winter wheat on an English farm. The wheat is being cut with a reaper, and the two men at the left are stacking the bundles in shocks to dry in the sun. At what season of the year was this picture taken? Give a reason for your answer.

other parts of England. In what belt in our country do the farmers fatten large numbers of cattle for market?

How the hilly lands are used. Many of the hilly lands of the British Isles are used as pastures, partly for cattle, but more largely for sheep. In this way they help to provide the British people with wool and meat. *See Figure 35.*

Some parts of the hilly lands belong to wealthy people who keep them for private hunting grounds, and others are play-grounds for all who wish to visit them. The beautiful lake district of England and the part of Scotland where Loch Lomond is located are visited each year by thousands of British people and by many tourists from other lands.

British fisheries. If you were to take a trip around the coasts of the British Isles, you would soon discover that the people depend on the shallow seas surrounding the islands and also on

the waters farther north between Scotland and Iceland for part of their food supply. The fishermen bring in cod, herring, haddock, sole, mackerel, and other kinds of fish.

On the map on pages 22–23 find Aberdeen in Scotland (*F 2*), and Hull, Grimsby, and Yarmouth in England (*G–H 4*). These are the four greatest fishing ports of the British Isles. On what sea are they located? You can easily guess from their location that the North Sea is the greatest of the fishing grounds near the British Isles.

At the fishing ports you will see many sights to remind you of the fishing ports along the coast of North America from New England to Newfoundland. You may be there when the steam trawlers and the smaller sailing boats are starting off for the fishing banks, or when they return loaded with fish. Near the wharves where the fishing boats land their catch you will see racks for

Figure 35. Sheep grazing in the Highlands of Scotland. The rougher parts of the British Isles make excellent sheep pastures, and Great Britain is one of the leading sheep-raising countries of Europe.

drying codfish, and buildings where herring are smoked and cured. You will also see the special trains that hurry the fresh fish to the cities farther inland. *See Figure 36.*

Thousands of boys in the coastal towns grow up loving the sea, and many of them become fishermen while they are still very young. Some who begin work as fishermen later become sailors on the British merchant ships which cross and recross the seas.

Some things to explain. Explain why

1. The shallow seas around the British Isles are rich fishing grounds.

2. The irregular coast line of the British Isles helps the fishermen.

3. The British Isles provide large markets for fish.

Some farming questions. In answering these questions, you will need to recall some of the things that you learned about farming in the United States.

1. Suppose two American farmers, one from the corn belt and the other from New England, should visit the farming districts of the British Isles. Which one would see more things to remind him of home? Why?

2. More acres of land in the British Isles are planted to oats and hay than to any other crops. How is the climate suited to the raising of oats and hay?

3. Find the wheat lands of the British Isles on the map on pages 22–23. What "climate reason" can you give to explain why they are located there rather than farther north or west?

4. Why are there no great cattle ranches in the British Isles?

5. Why are there many dairy farms, poultry farms, and market gardens near the large cities in the British Isles?

6. Why is it impossible for the farmers of the British Isles to supply enough food for all the people?

Figure 36. A view of one of the fish wharves at Aberdeen, Scotland. At the left are some of the fishing boats, and at the right are quantities of codfish, cleaned and ready to be salted and dried. Of what New England fishing port does this remind you?

6. EIRE

The self-governing part of Ireland is named for the island itself. Ireland is its English name, but Eire is its name in the language that all the Irish spoke long ago. Today many of the Irish speak English only, but self-governing Ireland is called by its true Irish name.

Ireland is quite different from Great Britain, for it is chiefly an agricultural country. Do you know why farming, rather than manufacturing, is the principal work there?

Farm lands and pasture lands. As you travel throughout Eire, you will notice that more of the land is used for pasture than for crops. That is because much of the lowland region is swampy and the uplands are hilly. Many of the swampy and hilly lands are not well suited to the raising of crops, but they are covered with rich green grass which makes excellent pasturage for cattle.

A visit to an Irish farm. If we visit one of the better farms, we shall learn that the farmer uses about one fourth of his land for

© E. M. Newman from Publishers Photo Service, Inc.

Figure 37. Irish farmers at a milk station. The farmers sell the cream, which is separated from the milk at the station, and take the skimmed milk home to feed to their pigs and chickens.

Manufacturing. Because of the lack of coal, Eire is not an important manufacturing country. There are a good many small factories for making such things as clothing, shoes, and furniture, but the leading industries are those which make use of the farm products. Among them the making of butter and cheese, the milling of grain, the curing of bacon, and the refining of sugar are especially important.

To help to make up for the lack of coal, a large power plant has been built on the river Shannon near Limerick, and the hydroelectricity is sent over wires to Dublin and other cities.

Seaports and trade. On the map on pages 22–23 find Dublin (Baile Atha Cliath), the capital and largest city of Eire (*D 4*). It is the chief port for trade with Great Britain. *See Figure 39.*

After what you have learned about the work of the farmers in Eire, you will not be surprised to find that live cattle, butter, eggs, and bacon are among the leading exports of the country. Large quantities of

crops, and the rest for pasture. In the farmyard we shall find pigs and chickens, and in the pastures we shall see dairy cows and beef cattle. We may see several fine horses too, for the Irish are very fond of horses, and they raise many for hunting and racing.

Near the house we shall find a vegetable garden, and when we visit the cultivated fields we shall learn that the farmer's chief crops are potatoes which he raises for food, and oats, hay, and other crops which he raises to feed his live stock. He may also raise some sugar beets to sell. He makes his money chiefly by selling live cattle and pigs, poultry, eggs, and cream. *See Figure 37.*

Peat bogs. As we travel throughout Eire we shall not find any great coal-mining districts as we did in Great Britain, for Eire has but few coal seams thick enough to be worth mining. But we shall not go far before we see people working in the peat bogs. Peat is a fuel which is formed in swamps and bogs by the decaying of leaves, wood, and roots. The people dig it from the bogs, cut it in blocks, and dry it. It is of no use for making steam power, but it provides the people in the country districts with fuel for use in their homes. *See Figure 38.*

Philip D. Gendreau, N. Y.

Figure 38. A glimpse of a peat bog in Eire. Each of these women will carry home an armful of peat for the fire over which she does her cooking.

<small>Philip D. Gendreau, N.Y.</small>

Figure 39. One of the busy streets in the city of Dublin, the capital of Eire. Notice the "two-story" electric cars in the picture.

these farm products are shipped from Dublin across the Irish Sea to Liverpool.

In exchange for their exports of foodstuffs, the Irish import large quantities of British manufactured goods. Dublin is the chief center for the distribution of these products. How does its location explain its importance as a gateway for trade with England?

Cork, on the southern coast of Eire, is another port from which large quantities of foodstuffs are shipped to Great Britain. Find Cork and Cobh on the map on pages 22–23 (C5). Cobh is on an island in the harbor of Cork, and it is a port of call for some of the great passenger liners which run between America and England.

At Foynes, on the Shannon estuary, there is a base where seaplanes flying the north Atlantic airway between Newfoundland and Ireland land and take off.

Some things to explain. 1. Explain why (1) England provides good markets for the surplus farm products of Eire, and (2) Eire provides good markets for English manufactured products.

2. Explain why the leading exports of Eire are live-stock products.

7. THE GROWTH OF BRITISH MANUFACTURING AND COMMERCE

The most valuable exports from Great Britain are (1) cotton goods, (2) machinery, (3) iron and steel goods, (4) coal, and (5) woolen goods. The most valuable imports are (1) meats, (2) wool, (3) cotton, (4) butter, (5) wheat and flour, and (6) mineral oils.

By studying these lists you should be able to answer the following questions:

1. What kind of work in Great Britain provides a large surplus of products for export?

2. What great needs of the British people are supplied in part through foreign commerce?

Advantages for manufacturing. In visiting the industrial districts of Great Britain you discovered that British manufacturing owes its growth largely to the following advantages:

1. An abundance of coal for power.

2. Large supplies of iron ore.

3. A dense population, providing millions of factory workers and a large home market for manufactured goods.

4. Many good seaports, making it easy to import raw materials and export manufactured goods.

5. Large markets for manufactured goods in distant parts of the British Empire.

In addition to these advantages, we should remember that the British made an early start in manufacturing, gaining the lead over nations which began later.

In Great Britain, as in the United States, the building of railroads and the more recent use of automobiles and motor trucks for transportation have also helped greatly in the growth of manufacturing.

Fuel and power handicaps. In spite of all their advantages for manufacturing, the British people have certain handicaps to overcome. They have almost no petroleum, and so they must get nearly all their fuel oil, gasoline, and lubricating oil from distant lands.

BRITISH EMPIRE

	AREA IN SQUARE MILES
Great Britain	88,745
Northern Ireland	5,237
Eire	26,601
Possessions in Europe	124
Union of South Africa	472,550
Other possessions in Africa	3,350,835
India	1,575,187
Burma	261,610
Other possessions in Asia	177,332
Australia	2,974,581
New Zealand	103,723
Pacific Islands	199,585
Canada	3,694,863
Newfoundland and Labrador	152,734
Other possessions in America	115,940
Total	13,199,647

	POPULATION
Great Britain	44,795,357
Northern Ireland	1,279,745
Eire	2,989,700
Possessions in Europe	277,000
Union of South Africa	9,589,898
Other possessions in Africa	50,130,000
India	388,998,000
Burma	14,667,146
Other possessions in Asia	13,513,000
Australia	6,997,326
New Zealand	1,573,810
Pacific Islands	1,768,000
Canada	11,506,655
Newfoundland and Labrador	304,718
Other possessions in America	2,544,000
Total	550,934,355

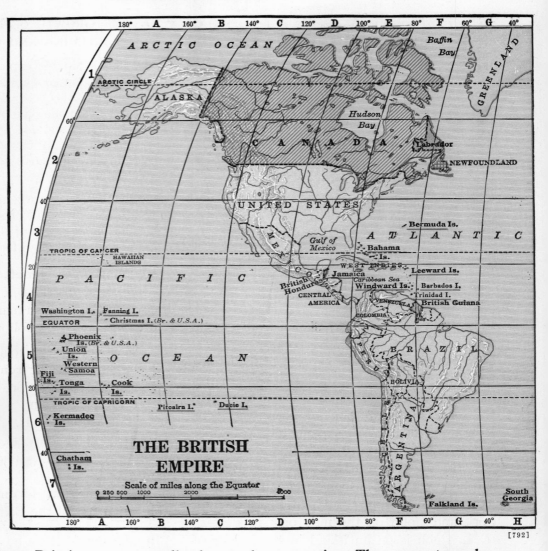

THE BRITISH EMPIRE

Scale of miles along the Equator

[792]

The rivers of Great Britain are too small to provide much water power for making electricity. The people make good use of what water power they have, but they must depend on steam power to make most of their electric power. This is a great handicap, for water power is the cheapest source of electricity.

The need for raw materials and markets. The British people need more iron ore than their mines can produce, and they have few metal ores other than iron in their country. Therefore they must purchase additional supplies of iron ore and many kinds of metals from other countries. They cannot produce enough wool for their woolen mills, and because of the cool climate they cannot grow any of the cotton needed for their cotton-manufacturing industry. In order to keep their mills and factories running, they must import large quantities of these and many other raw materials from distant lands.

Even though Great Britain is densely populated, the people do not need all the goods produced in the manufacturing plants. The manufacturers must find large markets in other lands if they are to sell all they produce.

Turn over to page 44.

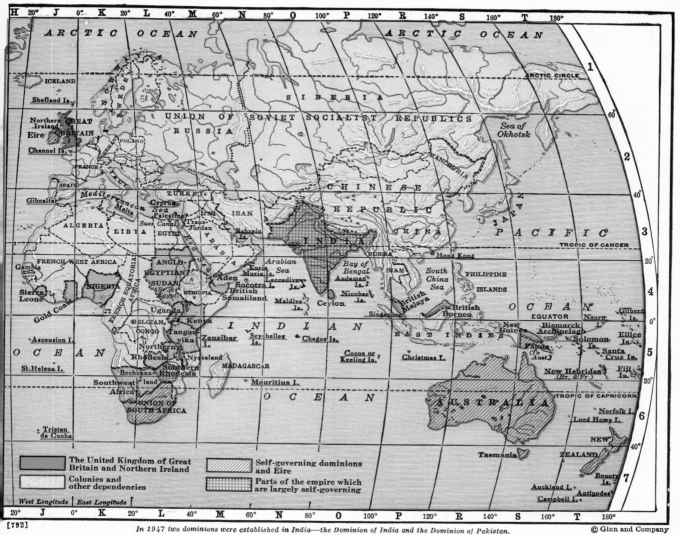

In 1947 two dominions were established in India—the Dominion of India and the Dominion of Pakistan.

© Ginn and Company

MAP STUDIES

1. About how far north of the equator are the British Isles? Give your answer in degrees of latitude. 2. What part of North America is in the same latitude as the British Isles? 3. What British lands are in temperate North America? 4. Which one of them extends north of the arctic circle? 5. What British possessions in the Western Hemisphere are tropical lands?

6. What continent in the Eastern Hemisphere is a British dominion? 7. In what part of that dominion is the climate best suited to white people? Why? 8. What other British dominion is southeast of Australia? 9. In what zone is that dominion?

10. What large part of Asia belongs to the British Empire? 11. What part of India is within the tropics? 12. What tropical island off the southern coast of India belongs to the British?

13. What British dominion is located in the southern part of Africa? 14. In what zone is most of that dominion? 15. What does that fact suggest with reference to the healthfulness of the climate for white people?

16. Name the British possessions which extend northward in an unbroken line from the Union of South Africa to Egypt. 17. What can you say about the climate of those possessions? 18. In what oceans do you find islands belonging to the British people?

Figure 40. Loading locomotives for export at Newcastle, England. The ship, the loading machinery, and the locomotives were all built at Newcastle.

© Sport & General Press Agency, Ltd., London

The problem of food supply. The British Isles are so small, the population is so dense, and so many of the people are engaged in manufacturing that the farmers and fishermen cannot supply enough food for all the people. Therefore the British must buy part of their foodstuffs from countries which have extra supplies to sell.

The growth of commerce. From all these facts you can see that as population has increased in Great Britain, and manufacturing has become the most important kind of work, the British people have been faced with three great problems:

1. How to obtain enough raw materials for their factories.

2. How to increase their food supplies.

3. How to find markets for their surplus manufactures; that is, the manufactures which they do not need themselves.

They have solved these problems by building up a great fleet of merchant ships and developing a large foreign trade. In this work they have been helped greatly by their island location and their irregular coast line with its many good harbors. *See Figure 40.*

Long ago the British began to send trading ships to distant lands, and it was partly through trade that they gained the lands of their great empire. As they became colonizers, or settlers of new lands, they developed farming and other kinds of work in their colonies which would help to supply the home factories with raw materials and the home markets with food. As more and more people went to live in the colonies, they provided *colonial markets* for manufactured goods from the home country; and today the British people have an enormous trade with their colonial possessions.

At the same time the British have been building up trade with foreign countries, buying raw materials and foodstuffs from them, and selling them manufactured goods. Thus commerce and manufacturing have grown side by side, each one helping the other.

A very important reason for the remarkable growth of British commerce and manufacturing is the people themselves. They have always been a strong, energetic nation; and because of this, they have been able to make the best use of the resources of their little island country and to find ways of overcoming its handicaps.

Map work. Use the map on pages 22–23 to answer the following questions:

1. What foodstuffs and raw materials do the British import from their dominions in the Old World? from their lands in the Americas? from the East Indies?

2. What metals do the British import in large quantities from the Americas? What fuels do they import from the United States?

3. What distant parts of the British Empire provide valuable markets for manufactures?

Special credit work. Many kinds of cloth from British mills are sold in drygoods stores in our country. Visit such a store and ask if you may have samples of British goods to show to your classmates.

Sentences to complete. Complete the sentences below by giving the correct names to fill the blank spaces:

1. The British Isles are made up of the two large islands of _____ _____ and _____ and many small islands.

2. The three parts of Great Britain are _____, _____, and _____.

3. Ireland is divided politically into _____ _____ and the self-governing country of ____.

A list to make. Write down the names of the cities described below. When you have finished, you will have a list of the eight largest cities in Great Britain.

1. The capital of the British Empire. *London*

2. The leading seaport of Scotland. *Glasgow*

3. The great industrial city of the Black Country. *Shefield*

4. The great cotton-importing port of Great Britain. *Liverbool*

5. The largest city of the Lancashire cotton-manufacturing district. *Manchester*

6. An English city famous for the manufacture of cutlery. *Shefield*

7. The largest city of the Yorkshire woolen-manufacturing district.

8. The old Scottish city near the Firth of Forth.

Matching cities and manufactures. Each city in the first column below is noted for one of the kinds of manufactures given in the second column. Match the cities and their manufactures correctly.

Belfast	cotton goods
Birmingham	iron and steel goods
Cardiff	linen goods
Glasgow	pottery
Leeds	ships
Manchester	tin plate
Stoke on Trent	woolen goods

Something to prove. Prove by answering the following questions that you understand why the British are a great manufacturing nation:

1. What advantages have the British for getting raw materials from all parts of the world!

2. What mineral resource have they which provides power for their mills and factories?

3. Why have they no trouble in getting workers for their mills and factories?

4. What advantages have they for marketing manufactured goods?

A trade test. 1. Some of the important imports and exports of the British Isles are given below. Make a list of those which are imports, and another of those which are exports.

coal	machinery	cotton goods
flax	raw wool	iron and steel
meats	linen goods	wheat and flour
butter	raw cotton	woolen goods
iron ore	mineral oils	hides and skins

2. Explain why the British people need to import large quantities of the products in your first list.

3. What kind of work provides all but one of the products in your second list?

Giving reasons. Complete each sentence below by giving reasons for the fact which it states:

1. The British are more nearly able to supply their needs for fish than for any other important kind of food because _____.

2. The British people produce more food-stuffs per acre of farm land than the people of the United States do, yet they have to import large quantities of foodstuffs because _____ _____.

3. The building of merchant ships is a very important kind of work in the British Isles because _____.

4. It is fortunate that Great Britain has many good harbors because _____.

5. London is the largest city of the British Isles because _____.

6. Liverpool is the leading seaport for trade with the Americas because _____.

7. Trade with the United States is very important to the manufacturers of Lancashire because _____.

8. The people of Eire are able to help to provide the people of England with foodstuffs because _____.

9. Eire is not a great manufacturing country because _____.

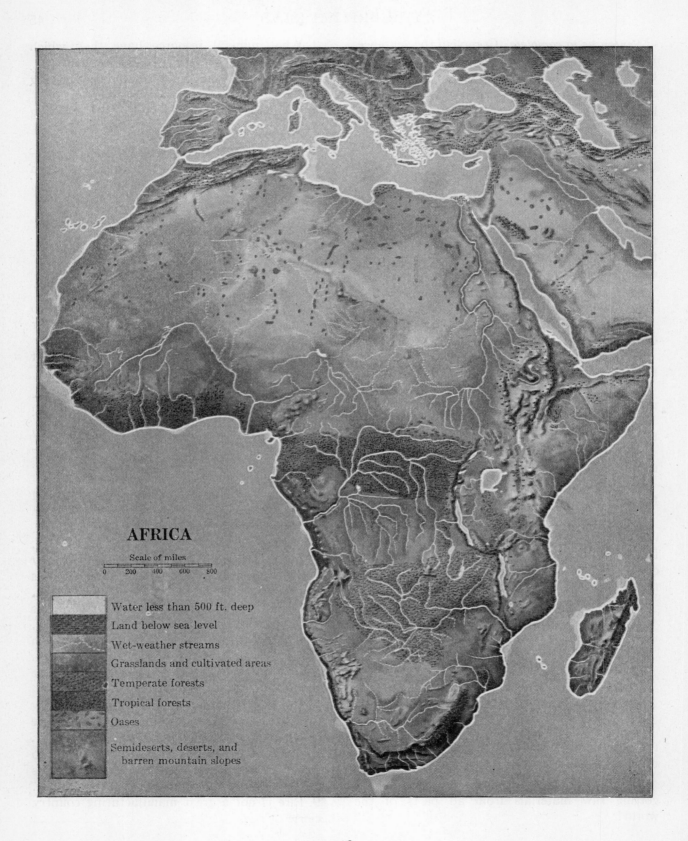

AFRICA

Scale of miles

0   200   400   600   800

Water less than 500 ft. deep

Land below sea level

Wet-weather streams

Grasslands and cultivated areas

Temperate forests

Tropical forests

Oases

Semideserts, deserts, and
    barren mountain slopes

III. BRITISH LANDS IN AFRICA

Foreword. Across the Mediterranean Sea from Europe lies Africa. In this great continent there are but three independent countries: Egypt, Ethiopia, and Liberia. All the rest of the African lands belong to one or another of the European nations.

About one third of the continent of Africa is under the control of the British people. Find the British lands in Africa on the map on pages 42–43 and name the one that is a self-governing dominion. The rest are colonies, protectorates, and dependencies.

As you study about the lands in Africa which are controlled by the British and other European nations, find answers to the following questions:

1. Of what value are possessions in Africa to the European nations?

2. In what ways are the European people helping the native people of Africa?

1. Africa and its People

Do you know why so much of Africa is controlled by European nations? This section will help you to discover some of the reasons.

The native peoples. Africa is the homeland of the Negro race; and even though many people born in Europe or descended from Europeans now live in certain parts of the continent, there are far more colored people than white people there.

Before the coming of the white men most of the natives of Africa obtained their food by hunting, fishing, and gathering wild nuts, fruits, and berries. Some of them had little gardens where they raised a few vegetables, but their farming was of the simplest kind.

Some of the native people of Africa now work on farms and plantations and in mines owned by white people, and some help to care for live stock. Many, however, still live almost as simply as their forefathers did.

People from Asia. Many of the people now living in the northern part of Africa are descendants of white people who came from southwestern Asia long ago. Other Asiatic people, who have come to Africa more recently, are natives of India. They have been brought to some of the British possessions to work on plantations and to help in the building of railroads. Since their homeland is warm, they are able to work in a hot climate.

People from Europe. Most of the white people who have settled in Africa during the last hundred years have come from Europe, principally from the Netherlands, France, Germany, and Great Britain.

Among the Europeans who have become interested in Africa, the British and the French have done more than any other nations to develop farming, mining, and stockraising in that continent. Little by little, through their work in Africa, they have come to control many of the most valuable lands of the continent.

Why Europeans control most of Africa. One reason so much of Africa is under the control of Europeans is that most of the groups of native people are very backward, and they have never learned to make the best use of the lands in which they live. Therefore, when white men from Europe came to Africa and began to develop the farm lands and grazing lands and to open mines and build railroads, it was natural that they should become the rulers of the native peoples.

Getting acquainted with Africa. The British lands in Africa include so much of the continent that you will find it helpful to get better acquainted with Africa as a whole before you study them. The maps on pages 48 and 49 will help you to do this. Before you read further, work out the map studies on page 49.

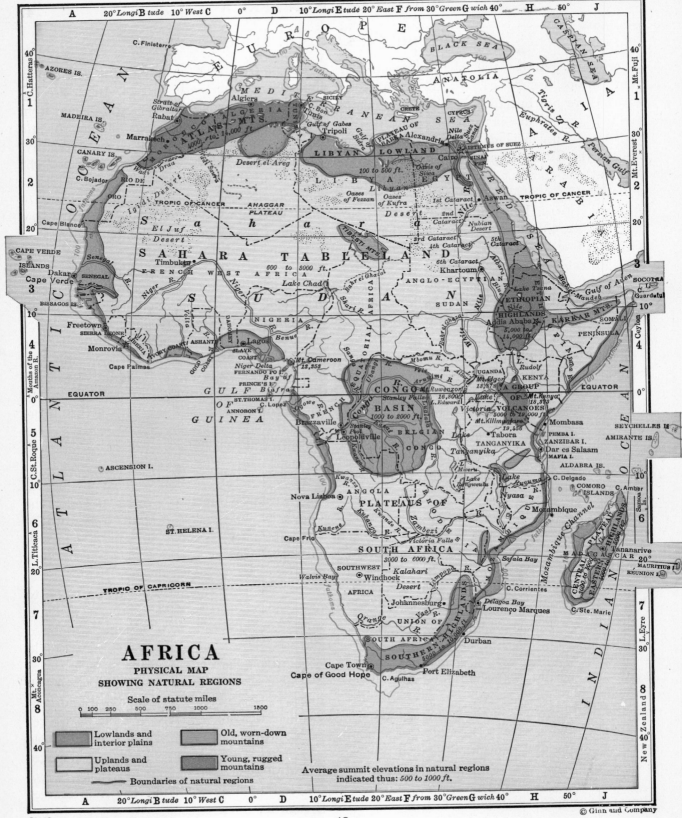

AFRICA

PHYSICAL MAP

SHOWING NATURAL REGIONS

Scale of statute miles

| Lowlands and interior plains | Old, worn-down mountains |
| Uplands and plateaus | Young, rugged mountains |

Boundaries of natural regions

Average summit elevations in natural regions indicated thus: 500 to 1000 ft.

© Ginn and Company

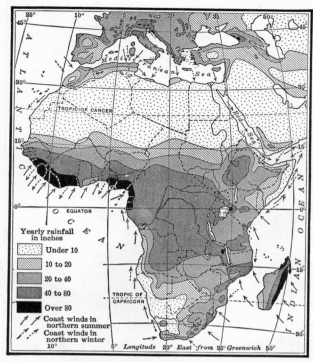

Figure 41. Distribution of rainfall in Africa.

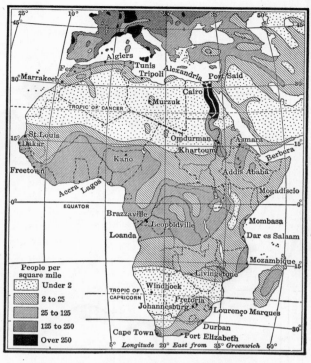

Figure 42. Distribution of people in Africa.

MAP STUDIES

1. On the map opposite this page trace the tropics of Cancer and Capricorn across Africa. 2. Is most of Africa between the tropics, or outside the tropics? 3. What does that tell you about the climate? 4. What parts of Africa do you think are most healthful for white people? Why?

5. Through what large river basin of Africa does the equator pass? 6. From Figure 41 describe the rainfall in the Congo Basin. 7. What kind of forests do you expect to see in that hot, rainy region? Check your answer by the map on page 46.

8. Where in Africa do you find young, rugged mountains (see map opposite)? old, worn-down mountains? 9. Find Mount Kilimanjaro, the highest mountain in Africa (G5). How high is it? Is there any mountain peak in the United States as high as that? 10. Describe the surface of the land in the greater part of Africa.

11. What does Figure 41 show about the rainfall in the great plateau region of northern Africa? 12. What great desert is located there?

13. Find the Sahara Desert on the map on page 46. 14. How do you account for the oases there? 15. What river valley forms a long, narrow oasis through the eastern part of the Sahara Desert? 16. How does the population of the northern part of that valley compare with the population in the rest of the desert? in the rest of Africa?

17. On the map opposite find the region of northern Africa known as the Sudan. 18. Does it have more rainfall than the Sahara, or less? 19. The Sudan is a *savanna*, or tropical grassland. Turn to the map on page 46 and notice that the tropical forest of the Congo Basin is bordered on the north, east, and south by savannas. 20. In your studies of the Americas where did you find a tropical forest bordered on the north and south by savannas? In the basin of what river is that forest?

21. On Figures 41 and 42 find the part of Africa south of the tropic of Capricorn. 22. What connection can you see between the distribution of rainfall and the distribution of population in that part of the continent?

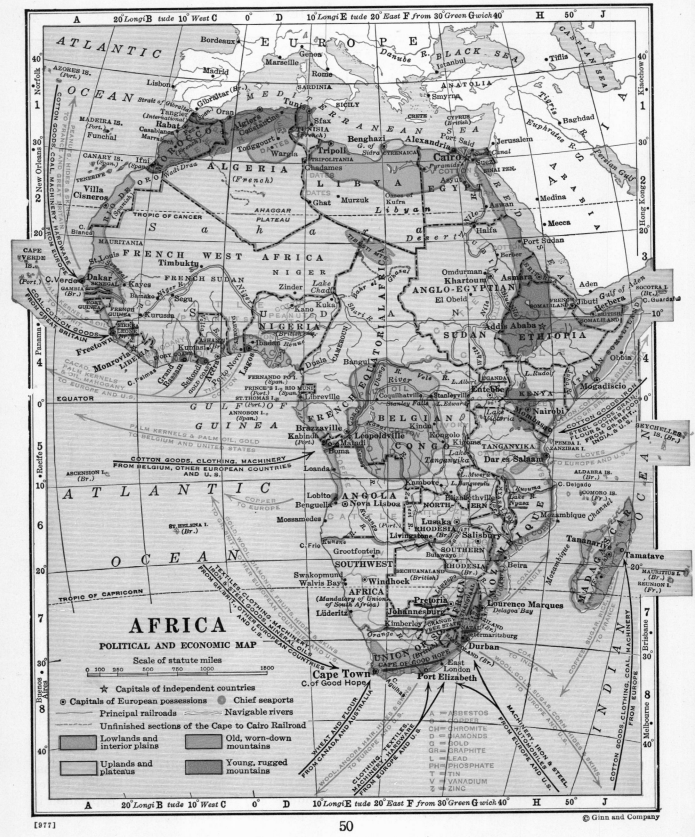

AFRICA

POLITICAL AND ECONOMIC MAP

Scale of statute miles

★ Capitals of independent countries
◉ Capitals of European possessions — Chief seaports
Principal railroads — Navigable rivers
Unfinished sections of the Cape to Cairo Railroad

Lowlands and interior plains
Old, worn-down mountains
Uplands and plateaus
Young, rugged mountains

A = ASBESTOS
C = COPPER
CH = CHROMITE
D = DIAMONDS
G = GOLD
GR = GRAPHITE
L = LEAD
PH = PHOSPHATE
T = TIN
V = VANADIUM
Z = ZINC

[977]

50

© Ginn and Company

Dr. Malan

Finding reasons in climate. Give a "climate reason" for each of the following facts:

1. Many of the native peoples of Africa do not like to work hard.

2. The Congo Basin and the other tropical lowlands of Africa are unhealthful for white people.

3. The largest numbers of white people in Africa live north of the tropic of Cancer and south of the tropic of Capricorn.

Something to do. 1. Turn to the map on pages 334–335 and tell what European people first explored the coast of Africa. How does the location of their home country help to explain their explorations along the African coast?

2. Trace the route of Vasco da Gama, the Portuguese sea captain who first found the route around Africa to India in 1497–1498.

3. Study the routes of exploration in southern and central Africa by Livingstone and Stanley. David Livingstone was a Scotchman. Henry M. Stanley was born in Wales, but he lived most of his life in the United States. How many years after Vasco da Gama made his voyage did Livingstone begin his explorations in Africa? Can you think of any reasons why the coasts of Africa were well known long before the interior was explored?

2. THE UNION OF SOUTH AFRICA

In 1910 four British colonies — Cape of Good Hope, Natal, Transvaal, and Orange River Colony (now called Orange Free State) — united to form the self-governing dominion known as the Union of South Africa. This dominion is about four fifths as large as Alaska and is the most important British possession in Africa. The first European settlers there were Dutch people, and today there are more Boers, or South Africans of Dutch descent, than British people in the Union.

Find the Union of South Africa on the map on page 50 and study its exports and imports. Judging from the exports, what kinds of work

Pix

Figure 43. Part of Cape Town, showing Table Mountain in the background. The white cloud that often rests on the mountain is called its "tablecloth." Find Cape Town on the map on page 50 (*E8*). What reason does the map suggest for the name of this city?

do you think are most important in this dominion? Judging from the imports, do you think South Africa is a great manufacturing country? Check your answers to these questions as you study this section.

Map work. On the map of the British Empire which you are making, color the Union of South Africa pink.

An ocean voyage. Almost any week in the year we could leave England on a ship bound for Cape Town, in South Africa. We might make the ocean journey without a stop, or we might go on a ship which stops at Ascension Island and St. Helena Island. Find these islands on the map on page 50 (*B5* and *C6*). They are British islands, and they serve as stations in the south Atlantic Ocean where ships may stop for repairs or to take on supplies of food and coal. They are also radio stations where messages may be received and forwarded through the air.

Cape Town. At the end of a voyage of about seventeen days our ship will reach Cape Town, and we shall find ourselves in one of the best and most attractive harbors of South Africa. *See Figure 43.*

By Burton Holmes from Ewing Galloway

Figure 44. A ship taking on wool and coal at Durban. Notice the bales of wool in the freight car. Durban is a more important port than Cape Town because it is better located to serve all of the more thickly settled part of South Africa. *See Figure 42.*

Cape Town is the port of South Africa nearest to England, and it is a port of call, or stopping place, for ships sailing back and forth between Australia and the British Isles. Since nearly half the trade of South Africa is with the home country, Cape Town is an important seaport. It is also the second city in size in South Africa.

Other gateway cities. Other seaports where we might land in South Africa are Port Elizabeth, East London, and Durban. They are on the southeast coast, and are connected by railroads with Cape Town and with the inland cities. They serve as gateways through which products of many of the mines, ranches, and farms farther inland pass on their way to distant lands. Durban, the largest of the three, is the leading seaport of South Africa. It is also an important coaling station for ships, and coal is one of its chief exports. Locate Durban on the map on page 50 (*G8*) and find the place where the coal comes from. Then study Figure 44.

Natural regions of South Africa. Turn to the map on page 48 and study the coast of South Africa. Notice that on the east there is a narrow coastal lowland. Notice also that if we travel inland from any one of the seaports of South Africa, we must climb the slopes of an old mountain region. The mountains are much higher than the Appalachian Mountains of our own country, for they rise from 5000 to 10,000 feet above the sea. From their summits the land slopes downward to the interior plateau.

The people of South Africa call the interior plateau the *veld*. When we reach the veld, we shall find ourselves in a gently rolling region from 3000 to 4000 feet above the sea. The highest part is in the east and is called the high veld.

How temperatures differ in the natural regions. The map shows that South Africa is close to the tropic of Capricorn, in the warmest part of the south temperate zone. You will get a good idea of its latitude if you will remember that Durban is about as far south of the tropic of Capricorn as New Orleans is north of the tropic of Cancer. With this in mind, you will not be surprised to learn that the weather is never very cold, even in the winter. What are the winter months in the south temperate zone?

Temperatures differ, however, in the different regions. The eastern coastal lowland is hot in summer and warm in winter, and there is never any frost there. The veld, which is much higher, is warm in summer, but not nearly so hot as the coastal lowland; in winter it is so cool that frosts often occur.

Differences in rainfall. South Africa lies in the belt of the southeast trade winds. When these winds reach the coast of Africa, they are heavily laden with moisture which they have gathered up in blowing over the Indian Ocean. As they rise to cross the mountains, they become cooler and give up much moisture. For this reason there is abundant rainfall on the eastern lowland and on the eastern slopes of the mountains.

By the time the winds have crossed the mountains and begun to move down the western slopes they have lost much of their moisture. Therefore the rainfall on the western slopes and in the high veld is lighter, and it grows less and less as the winds move farther and farther northwest.

Courtesy of South African Railways and Harbours

Figure 45. A sheep ranch in the South African grassland known as the veld. In the veld the rainfall grows less and less from east to west like the rainfall in the interior plains of the United States.

Differences in vegetation. The word *vegetation* means plant and tree growth. When we speak of the *natural vegetation* of a region, we mean the plants and trees that grow without the help of man. When we speak of the *cultivated vegetation*, we mean the plants and trees planted and cared for by the people. As we travel from east to west across South Africa, we shall find that the vegetation changes from region to region because of differences in elevation and rainfall.

The subtropical belt. On the warm, moist eastern lowland the vegetation is subtropical, or almost tropical. Palm trees and wild banana plants grow there, and the people raise sugar cane and other subtropical crops.

The eastern mountain slopes. We shall find that the subtropical vegetation extends inland to an elevation of about 1000 feet. Then, as we begin to climb the mountain slopes, we shall see grasses and bushes of the temperate zone, and on the higher and cooler slopes, above 4000 feet, we shall find temperate forests.

The grassland. When we reach the high veld on the northwestern side of the mountains where the rainfall is lighter, we shall be in a temperate grassland which will remind us of the prairies of our country. There are few trees here except those along the streams and those which have been planted for shade. As you would expect, large numbers of cattle and sheep graze on the natural grasses. *See Figure 45.*

Scrubland and desert. Farther west we pass into a still drier part of the veld, which is called *scrubland*. Here the vegetation is made up of poor grasses and shrubs. Goats graze in this region, but the pasturage is too poor for cattle and sheep. Before we reach the western coast, we find that both plants and animals have disappeared. We are now in a desert where there is too little rain for vegetation of any kind, and bare, rocky hills and sand dunes surround us.

The southwestern corner of Africa. The region around Cape Town, in the southwestern corner of Africa, has quite a different climate from the rest of the Union. In the summer it is hot and dry like the coast farther north. At that time of year the grass is withered by the hot sun and the landscape is brown and dusty. But this part of the con-

© Publishers Photo Service, Inc.

Figure 46. Lunch time in a diamond compound at Kimberley. The miners are given food and living quarters in the compounds, but they cannot go outside the inclosures while they are working in the mines.

tinent is just far enough south so that during the winter season in the Southern Hemisphere, when all the wind belts move northward, it is in the belt of the westerly winds of that hemisphere. These winds, blowing from the Atlantic Ocean, bring rain. The people are thankful for the winter rains because when they come fresh grass springs up, wild flowers blossom in abundance, and the landscape changes from brown to green.

Proving your acquaintance with South Africa. You are now well enough acquainted with South Africa to complete each of the following sentences correctly:

1. South Africa is in the warmest part of the _____ _____ zone.

2. In South Africa winter begins in the month of ____ and summer begins in the month of _____.

3. The eastern coast of South Africa is a moist, subtropical region because _____.

4. The high veld is a temperate grassland because _____.

5. The western part of South Africa is a desert because _____.

6. The southwestern tip of the country has winter rains because _____.

 *Mineral Wealth*

A great mining country. On the map on page 50 find the places in South Africa where diamonds and gold are mined. The wealth of gold and diamonds taken from the mines in this British dominion has made it one of the great mining countries of the world.

A wonderful discovery. In 1867 a glittering white pebble was found among the playthings of the children of a farmer in the South African veld. A neighbor recognized the stone as a diamond, and it was sold for 500 pounds in English money, or about $2400.

Not long after, someone discovered a place in the veld where the stream gravels contained diamonds. When the discovery became known, thousands of men from all over the world rushed to South Africa and began hunting for the precious stones.

An even greater discovery was made when the miners found the "parent rock" from which the diamonds had been washed by the streams. Today, near the spot where the first diamond mines were located, is the city of Kimberley. Ever since mining began there, South Africa has produced most of the clear, perfect diamonds obtained in the world.

The diamond mines. The diamonds are obtained from rock material mined deep beneath the ground by native workmen. The rock is brought to the surface and spread out on the ground, where it is allowed to lie for a year or more until it decays and crumbles. Then, by washing it, the precious stones are obtained. Most of the rough diamonds are shipped to Europe, where they are cut and polished, and from Europe the polished diamonds are sent to various parts of the world.

The native workmen at the diamond mines are kept in fenced inclosures called *compounds* which are guarded almost like prisons. They are usually engaged for a period of three months, and when they leave they are

Pix

Figure 47. Two pictures taken deep underground in a Rand gold mine. At the left you see two miners drilling a hole into which they will put dynamite to blast the gold-bearing rock. At the right you see the first of a string of small cars, run by electricity, bringing ore from a tunnel in the mine.

carefully searched to make sure they are not carrying away any diamonds. *See Figure 46.*

There are diamond mines at several other places in the veld besides Kimberley, and the largest single mine is near the city of Pretoria. Find Pretoria and Kimberley on the map on page 50 (*F 7*).

The gold mines. In 1885 another discovery was made in South Africa, which has meant more to the people than the diamonds. This was the discovery of gold in the high veld near the present city of Johannesburg. That district has become the greatest gold-mining center in the world, producing nearly half the world's output of gold each year. Valuable as the diamonds are, the gold of South Africa is worth many times as much.

The gold comes from deep mines located along a ridge called the "Witwatersrand," but the people usually call the gold-mining district simply "the Rand." *See Figures 47 and 48.*

Mining and the growth of cities. Since the discovery of diamonds and gold in the high veld, more and more European people have gone to live in that region, and many towns and cities have grown up. Kimberley, as you know, has grown up in the midst of the diamond fields. Pretoria, which is the seat of government of the dominion, has increased its population since the opening of the great diamond mine close by. Johannesburg made its start the year after gold was discovered in the Rand. Today it is the largest city and the chief railroad center of the Union.

Coal and iron. You already know that coal is mined in the highland region some distance north of Durban, and that some of it is exported. Coal is also mined in the Rand,

alloy = not pure metal

Authenticated News Photo

Figure 48. The buildings of one of the great gold-mining plants in the Rand. Here the ores are crushed and treated in other ways to obtain the metal. You can see the mine shaft at the right.

and is a great help in providing power to run the machinery in the gold mines.

There are large quantities of iron ore in the northeastern part of the country, but until quite recently the Union has had no iron-and-steel industry, and so not much of the iron ore has been mined. A steel plant has now been built in Pretoria, and if the manufacture of iron and steel increases, iron-mining will increase also.

What mining means to the people. Mining is the most important kind of work in South Africa, and it has helped more than anything else to make the people of the Union prosperous. The gold mines and the diamond mines have made many of the white people wealthy, and they provide work for thousands of natives. Copper, tin, manganese, and platinum are also mined in the Union, but their value is small compared with that of the gold or the diamonds. Mining also plays a large part in the trade of South Africa. Gold is by far the most valuable export, and millions of dollars' worth of diamonds are shipped to Europe each year.

Farm Lands and Pasture Lands

Crops and live stock. Next to mining, the raising of crops and live stock is the most important kind of work in South Africa. From what you have learned about the climate of the country, do you think more land is used for farming or for grazing? Judging from the exports shown on the map on page 50, what crops do you think the South Africans raise in greater quantities than they need for themselves?

The South African corn belt. Corn is the chief food of the millions of native people in South Africa, and it is the principal grain crop of the Union. Most of it is raised in the northern, or warmer, part of the high veld, where the summer temperatures and rainfall are much the same as in the western part of our own corn belt. Much more corn is produced than the people themselves need, and the Union is one of the leading corn-exporting countries of the world.

Nearly every corn-belt farmer of South Africa keeps cattle, which he pastures on the

From Ewing Galloway, N. Y.

Figure 49. Threshing wheat on a farm in the Union of South Africa. What do you find among the imports (map, p. 50) which shows that the South Africans do not raise all the wheat they need?

Photograph by Ewing Galloway, N. Y.

Figure 50. A South African farmer at work in his pineapple field. In what tropical possession of the United States are pineapples an important crop?

wild grasses of the veld and fattens for market on corn. Many of the farmers near the large cities have dairy herds, and some of them cut part of their corn while it is green and use it as ensilage, as dairy farmers in our own country do.

Other grain crops. The European people of South Africa prefer wheat flour for their bread, just as we do. The wheat fields of the Union are nearly all in the southwestern region, and the wheat is grown during the season of the winter rains and harvested in the early summer. *See Figure 49.*

In the drier farm lands the farmers raise Kafir corn, just as farmers in the drier parts of our interior plains do. The natives use Kafir corn for food, and much is also used to feed cattle.

Sugar cane and fruit. On the warm, well-watered lowland bordering the eastern coast, especially near Durban, there are sugar plantations and groves of orange, grapefruit, and lemon trees. You will remember that sugar

cane needs a warm, moist climate, and that citrus fruits can be grown successfully only where there is little or no danger of frost. Farther north in the lowland, where the temperatures are still warmer, the people raise bananas, pineapples, and other tropical fruits. *See Figure 50.*

On the high veld, where the temperatures are cooler, there are orchards of apples, pears, and other temperate-zone fruits. In southwestern Africa, near Cape Town, the people raise peaches, citrus fruits, and large quantities of grapes. Some of the grapes are raised to be eaten fresh, some to be dried to make raisins and currants, and some to be used in the making of wine. *See Figure 51.*

Fruit is becoming more and more important among the products of South Africa. The people eat large quantities themselves, and each year they are exporting more and more fresh fruit, canned and dried fruits, and fruit jam to Great Britain.

The fresh fruit is exported in ships which have cold-storage compartments for it, and it leaves South Africa in the late summer and early autumn of the Southern Hemisphere. Since the seasons are just opposite in the

From Ewing Galloway, N. Y.

Figure 51. Picking peaches in an orchard near Cape Town. Why is this part of South Africa well suited to fruit crops which are likely to be damaged by frost?

Photograph by Publishers Photo Service, Inc.

Figure 52. Packing grapes for export in a vineyard near Cape Town. The grapes are packed with great care so that they will not be damaged on the long ocean voyage to the British Isles.

Northern Hemisphere, it reaches Great Britain when spring is beginning in that country and before there is any fresh fruit from the home orchards. For this reason fresh fruit from South Africa brings high prices in the British markets. *See Figure 52.*

Handicaps to farming. Although the people of South Africa raise more fruit, corn, and sugar cane than they need, these crops play a much less important part in the export trade than do the products of the mines and the grazing lands. South Africa is not a great farming country because so much of it has less than 20 inches of rain.

The plateau region provides millions of acres of land level enough for farming, but only in the eastern part is there rain enough for the growth of crops. A few areas in the drier lands are irrigated, and a few others are cultivated by dry-farming methods. Plans for irrigating more land have been made, and if they are carried out, more of the plateau will be used for raising crops.

Considering the handicaps to farming in a large part of South Africa, you will not be surprised to learn that at present stock-raising is more important than the raising of crops.

Cattle-raising. Altogether, there are about ten million cattle in the Union. As you would expect, the largest numbers graze on the better pastures of the high veld. The early Dutch settlers raised large numbers of cattle for draft, or work, animals, and some of the Boer farmers still use oxen for plowing and other farm work. Today most of the cattle are raised for beef and dairy products; and as you already know, they are fed partly on corn and other forage crops. *See Figure 53.*

Sheep and goats. The number of sheep in South Africa is three or four times the number of cattle. Sheep are found in all but the wettest and driest parts of the Union. You will remember that sheep can graze on pastures that are too dry for cattle. They can also graze on the better pasture lands after the cattle have been there, for they can nibble grass that is too short for cattle to get hold of.

Most of the sheep in South Africa are raised for their wool, and huge quantities of wool are exported each year. There are only five great wool-exporting countries in the world, and South Africa is one of them. The others are Australia, Argentina, New Zealand, and Uruguay.

Goats are also raised in large numbers in South Africa, and many of them graze in pastures that are too poor for sheep. The South African veld has more Angora goats and produces more mohair than any other region in the world. Mohair is the long, fleecy hair of Angora goats. *See Figure 54.*

Special credit work. Imagine that you have gone to South Africa and that for a year you have been in the kind of work that interests you most there. Write a letter to a friend at home, asking him to go into business with you. Tell him just where you are, what kind of work you are doing, and why you think he would like South Africa.

By Burton Holmes from Ewing Galloway

Figure 53. How some of the South African farmers plow their fields. Teams of as many as eight or ten oxen are often used for this work.

Manufacturing and Trade

Advantages for manufacturing. As yet South Africa is not a manufacturing country of any importance, but in recent years the number of industries has been increasing. There is plenty of coal, and the population is growing larger each year, providing greater markets for manufactured goods. Johannesburg and Durban are the chief industrial centers. What raw materials produced in the Union might be used to build up manufacturing industries?

Exports and imports. From the map on page 50 name the principal exports of South Africa. To what two classes of goods do they belong? To what class of goods do most of the leading imports belong?

Raw materials from the mines and pasture lands are by far the most important exports, followed by certain foodstuffs from the farms. The imports, as you have discovered, are chiefly manufactured goods.

About two fifths of the exports of South Africa go to Great Britain, and about half of all the imports come from there. What reasons can you give for this large trade between the dominion and the home country?

There is a smaller amount of trade of the same kind between South Africa and some of the industrial countries on the continent of Europe. Our own country buys some of South Africa's raw materials, and we help to supply the people of the Union with many kinds of manufactured goods, especially automobiles. We also supply them with much of their gasoline and other mineral oils.

Southwest Africa

A former German colony. On the map on page 50 find Southwest Africa (*E7*). This part of Africa was once a German colony, but after the close of the First World War, in 1918, its government was placed in the hands of the people of the Union of South Africa. In that war the Germans were defeated by the American, British, and French Allies, and Germany lost all its colonies.

Figure 42 on page 49 will show you that Southwest Africa is thinly populated, and Figure 41 will show you why. Explain the reason. Most of the people are natives, but there are a few Europeans who are interested in mining or in stock-raising. Copper and vanadium are mined in the northeast, and diamonds are found along the coast in the south.

Courtesy of South African Railways and Harbours

Figure 54. Angora goats in South Africa. The first goats of this kind in the Union were brought from the Plateau of Anatolia in southwestern Asia.

cape town
Port Elizabeth
Durban

THE CAPE TO
CAIRO ROUTE
———— Railroad service
- - - - - Steamer "
======= Automobile "
Scale of miles
0   250 500   1000   1500

Figure 55. The transcontinental route of travel from Cape Town to Cairo. The shaded areas on the map are the British lands in Africa.

A combination test. This test is a combination of making choices and giving reasons. In each sentence you are to choose the correct word or phrase from those in parentheses and then complete the sentence by giving the reason for the fact which it states.

1. South Africa is not a great (mining) (grazing) (farming) country because _____.

2. The high veld is a (desert) (grassland) (temperate forest) because _____.

3. The most important work in the high veld is (mining) (farming) (lumbering) because ____ _____.

4. The eastern coastal lowland has (too little) (plenty of) (too much) rain for farming because _____.

5. The southwestern corner of Africa is suited to the growth of (winter wheat) (corn) (sugar cane) because _____.

6. South Africa is a great (cotton-growing) (wool-producing) (manufacturing) country because _____.

7. Much of the trade of South Africa is with (the United States) (India) (Great Britain) because _____.

3. BRITISH LANDS IN TROPICAL AFRICA

The map on pages 42–43 shows that there is an unbroken line of British lands in Africa extending from the Union of South Africa northward to the independent country of Egypt. Name these British lands in order from south to north. In what zone are they? Which one of them borders the Red Sea? What tropical lands bordering the west coast of Africa belong to the British? What British possession is located east of Ethiopia?

Can you suggest reasons why these tropical lands in Africa are of value to the British people? Keep this question in mind as you read about these lands.

Map work. As you study the tropical possessions of the British in Africa, color them pink on the map of the British Empire which you are making.

The Cape to Cairo Route

A transcontinental route of travel. On the map on page 50 find Cairo, the capital of Egypt (*G1*). From Cape Town we can travel overland to Cairo by what is known as the Cape to Cairo route. It is a long, slow journey, partly by railway, partly by river steamer and lake boat, and partly by road, and it will take us six or seven weeks. Trace the Cape to Cairo route on Figure 55 and show where travel is by railroad, by river steamer on the Congo and the Nile, by lake boat, and by automobile. Notice how much of this transcontinental route passes through British lands. What lands does it pass through which do not belong to the British?

The Cape to Cairo Railway. The British people began to plan the Cape to Cairo Railway many years ago. Figure 55 shows that the southern section of the railway has been completed from Cape Town to Bukama, on the Congo River in Belgian Congo, and the northern section from Khartoum to Halfa in Anglo-Egyptian Sudan and from Aswan to Cairo in Egypt. River boats now carry passengers between Aswan and Halfa, but in time this missing link in the railway will probably be built.

Between the northern and southern sections of the Cape to Cairo Railway much railroad-building remains to be done. Perhaps the missing railroad links will never be constructed, for the "Air Age" may make them unnecessary. Some years ago the British established an airway between London and Cape Town by way of Cairo. Planes carrying passengers and mail fly over this route, making the trip in a small fraction of the time required for the overland journey.

By Burton Holmes from Ewing Galloway

Figure 56. Victoria Falls. These falls are a mile wide and 360 feet high — more than twice as high as Niagara Falls. Just below the falls the railroad from Cape Town to Bukama crosses the gorge of the Zambezi on a steel bridge 400 feet above the river.

Southern Rhodesia and Northern Rhodesia

The opening-up of Rhodesia. As the British people became interested in developing the resources of South Africa, some of them moved farther north across the Limpopo River and then across the Zambezi River. Find these rivers on the map on page 50.

Among the men who were most interested in this northward movement was Cecil Rhodes. He became a great leader in South Africa, and he did more than anyone else to open up the region north of the Limpopo for British settlement. In time this part of Africa was named Rhodesia in his honor. Rhodesia is now divided into two colonies: Southern Rhodesia and Northern Rhodesia.

From South Africa to Rhodesia. If we travel northward by train from South Africa to Rhodesia, we shall pass through the eastern part of the British protectorate of Bechuanaland. This great stretch of plateau country includes most of the Kalahari Desert; and as you might expect, it is thinly populated. Most of the people are natives, who raise cattle, sheep, and goats. The few Europeans live in the east, near the railroad.

Southern Rhodesia. All Southern Rhodesia lies in the plateau region of southern Africa, in the belt of the southeast trade winds. The greater part of the plateau is over 4000 feet above sea level, but it slopes down to the Limpopo River on the southeast and to the Zambezi River on the northwest.

Although Southern Rhodesia is wholly within the tropics, the greater part of the country has a subtropical climate and is healthful for white people. That is because so much of the plateau is over 4000 feet in elevation.

The rainfall varies from 35 inches in the east to 15 inches in the west, which is enough for the abundant growth of grass in all parts of the country, and some forest growth in the east. Explain why the rainfall grows less from east to west. Southern Rhodesia does not extend far enough west to have any desert lands.

Some wonderful falls. On the map on page 48 find the Victoria Falls in the Zambezi River (*F6*). These falls were discovered by David Livingstone. They are more wonderful than our own Niagara Falls, and thousands of tourists visit them each year. *See Figure 56.*

By Burton Holmes from Ewing Galloway

Figure 57. Long-horned cattle of the kind raised chiefly by the native people of Rhodesia and South Africa. They are not high-grade beef animals, but they supply the natives with meat and milk, and provide considerable quantities of hides for export.

The people of Rhodesia are planning to use part of the water power at the Victoria Falls to make electricity, just as the people of our country and Canada use part of the water power at Niagara. In what ways will this use of the falls help the people of Rhodesia?

A cattle-and-corn country. Like the high veld in South Africa, Southern Rhodesia is a cattle-and-corn country. It is not, however, a good sheep country, for sheep need a cooler climate to be healthy and to produce thick wool. Cattle-raising is the most important work of the Europeans and also of the natives, and meat is exported. Corn is the most important crop because it is the chief food of the natives and because it is used to fatten cattle and pigs. Tobacco and oranges are the chief crops grown for export. *See Figure 57.*

Some products of the earth. Turn to the map on page 50 and name the chief mineral products of Southern Rhodesia. This country is a very important producer of chromite ores and asbestos. Chromite ores contain a mineral called chromium, which is used with iron to make certain very hard kinds of steel. Asbestos, you will remember, is a mineral made up of fine, silky fibers which will not burn and which can be woven into cloth. You may have seen asbestos mats or asbestos packing around steam pipes. What other uses of asbestos can you name?

Of even greater importance than the chromite and the asbestos is the gold which is mined in Southern Rhodesia, and which is by far the most valuable export of the colony.

Trade with distant lands. Since Southern Rhodesia has no seacoast, its trade with distant lands is carried on through the ports of neighboring countries with which it is connected by railroads. Some of its trade passes through Durban and Cape Town, but much more passes through the port of Beira in the Portuguese colony of Mozambique.

Turn to the map on page 50 and compare the length of the railroad routes from Salisbury, the capital of Southern Rhodesia, to Beira, to Durban, and to Cape Town. Then explain why the Rhodesians export and import more goods through the Portuguese port than through the British ports.

A country which could support more people. Southern Rhodesia is not a densely populated country, and less than one twentieth of the people are Europeans. The Europeans are by no means all British, for many are descendants of Dutch settlers, and others of German and of French settlers. Many more white people could make a living in Southern Rhodesia, for the country is larger than our state of Montana, and there are still large stretches of good land that are not in use. The greatest need is for more roads and railroads to open up more of the land for settlement.

Northern Rhodesia. Northern Rhodesia is a country much like Southern Rhodesia, except that it is somewhat warmer because it is nearer the equator. The southern part is well suited to cattle-raising, and there are large copper mines in several places. As a whole, however, this colony is not so well developed as Southern Rhodesia because it has fewer Europeans and therefore fewer ranches, farms, and mines. Turn to the map on page 50 and tell what metal ores besides copper are mined in Northern Rhodesia.

Something to discuss. Discuss the British development of South Africa, Southern Rhodesia, and Northern Rhodesia with your classmates, and try to decide why the greatest progress has been made in South Africa and the least in Northern Rhodesia.

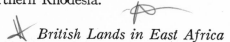

British Lands in East Africa

Lands of the Lake Plateau. On the map on page 50 find Uganda, Kenya, Tanganyika, and Nyasaland. These are the British lands of East Africa. Except for the narrow coastal lowland of eastern Kenya and Tanganyika they are in the plateau of East Africa.

This region of Africa is sometimes called the Plateau of the Great Lakes, or the Lake Plateau. The map on page 50 will show you why. First find Lake Victoria (*G 5*). Then find the chain of long, narrow lakes beginning with Lake Albert, northwest of Lake Victoria, and extending in a curve to Lake Nyasa (*G 6*). You can see these lakes still more clearly on the relief map on page 46.

The long, narrow lakes lie in a deep trough called the "rift valley of Africa," and they are among the most beautiful lakes in the world. As you already know, Lake Tanganyika serves as part of the Cape to Cairo route of travel. Lake Victoria is not one of the rift-valley lakes, but it serves in the same way.

The coastal lowland. The coastal lowland of Kenya and Tanganyika is hot and rainy

By Cowling from Ewing Galloway, N. Y.

Figure 58. Natives of East Africa hanging sisal fiber on lines to dry. What country of the Americas produces large quantities of sisal hemp for export?

and covered with tropical forests. Its hot, moist climate is unhealthful for white people, and few of them live there. Many of the natives gather coconuts from the coconut palms that grow on the lowland and dry the "meat" to make copra for export, just as the natives of the Philippine Islands do. Others work on plantations where sisal hemp is grown for export. *See Figure 58.*

The plateau lands. Since the plateau lands of East Africa are much higher than the coastal lowland, their climate is much better for white people. They receive less rain than the coastal lowland, and are chiefly grasslands. In the midst of the plateau there is a group of old volcanic mountains which tower above the surrounding lands. Among them is Mount Kilimanjaro, the highest mountain in Africa. Although it is near the equator, its peak is always covered with snow. Why?

Work in the plateau. Many of the natives of the plateau raise cattle, and both the natives and the Europeans raise corn. On many of the native farms and also on plantations owned by white people coffee is grown for export. The leading export crop, however, is cotton, which is raised chiefly by the natives,

From Ewing Galloway

Figure 59. How cloves are prepared for export in Zanzibar. The natives are spreading the cloves evenly on mats to dry in the sun.

especially in Uganda. Cotton-growing is being encouraged by the British and is becoming more important each year. Most of the crop is shipped to England. What reason can you give for this?

East African ports and their trade. On the map on page 50 find the island of Zanzibar (*G5*). This little tropical island is a British protectorate, and on it is a seaport of the same name. Zanzibar is a great trading center, and one of the chief ports of East Africa. In the harbor you will see ships from many distant lands, and on the streets you will meet merchants from many different countries.

Zanzibar and the neighboring island of Pemba produce most of the world's cloves. Cloves are the dried unopened flower buds of a certain kind of tropical tree. *See Figure 59.*

Other important ports of East Africa are Mombasa, in Kenya, and Dar es Salaam, in Tanganyika. At those ports and at Zanzibar you will see ships unloading manufactured goods and taking on products of the East African farms and plantations. Most of the trade is with Great Britain and India. What East African product do you think the British want the most? Why?

British Lands in the Northeast

Map studies. Before you read further, use the map on page 50 to work out the following map studies.

1. On the map find Anglo-Egyptian Sudan and British Somaliland. 2. What bodies of water border these British lands? 3. What large river flows northward through Anglo-Egyptian Sudan? 4. Judging from this map, what do you think are the most important kinds of work in Anglo-Egyptian Sudan? 5. What do the people raise that might be sold in Lancashire, England?

6. What canal connects the northern end of the Red Sea with the eastern end of the Mediterranean? 7. Turn to the map on pages 338–339 and decide whether this canal is important to the British people in carrying on trade with Australia, New Zealand, and the parts of the empire in Asia and eastern Africa.

The Suez Canal. The Suez Canal, which you have located on the map, is about 100 miles long, and it has no locks because it was cut through very low land. It was opened in 1869, and is of great commercial importance because it provides a water route from western Europe to eastern Africa, Asia, and Australia several thousand miles shorter than the route around the southern tip of Africa. The canal is in Egypt, but it is owned by a private company in which the British are the largest shareholders. Furthermore, the canal is guarded by British troops. Why is it of advantage to Great Britain to have a large share in the control of this important waterway?

The British allow the ships of all nations to pass through the Suez Canal, just as our country allows the ships of all nations to use the Panama Canal. The ships pay certain charges to the canal company for going through. *See Figure 60.*

British Somaliland. This part of Africa is a very dry land with few people, but there is an advantage to the British people in holding it. It lies opposite Aden, one of the

Figure 60. A glimpse of Port Said, at the northern entrance to the Suez Canal. Why do large numbers of British ships pass through this canal each year?

British possessions in southwestern Asia, and its position helps the British to control the southern entrance to the Red Sea.

Anglo-Egyptian Sudan. As you may guess from its name, the southern portion of this country lies in the part of Africa known as the Sudan, where there is enough rain for the growth of grass. The northern portion is part of the Sahara Desert.

Figure 42 on page 49 shows that most of the people of this British land live in a belt bordering both sides of the Nile River. Turn to the map on page 50 and find Khartoum (*G3*). Notice that it is located at the junction of the two main branches of the Nile. The Blue Nile comes from the well-watered Ethiopian Highlands, and the White Nile rises in a rainy part of Africa near the equator. Both branches provide abundant water for irrigation along their banks. You will learn more about the use of the Nile for irrigation when you visit Egypt.

The people of Anglo-Egyptian Sudan raise much cotton on their irrigated lands, and cotton is the chief export. The fiber is separated from the seeds in gins imported from England, and is sent by train to Port Sudan, on the Red Sea, for shipment to Liverpool.

The people raise also large quantities of a grain called millet, and various other food crops. In the southern grasslands many of the natives raise cattle, sheep, and goats and prepare the hides and skins for export to Europe. Wild elephants roam the southern grasslands and are hunted by the natives, who eat the meat and sell the ivory tusks to traders for export.

With its irrigated lands for farming and its large areas of grasslands for the raising of stock, Anglo-Egyptian Sudan can produce much greater quantities of raw materials and foodstuffs than it does today, and many people believe that as more Europeans go to make their homes there it will become one of the most important countries of Africa.

By Ewing Galloway, N·Y·

Figure 61. Passengers going aboard a small river steamer at Omdurman in Anglo-Egyptian Sudan. How can you tell from the map on page 50 that this boat must have come from the south?

From Ewing Galloway, N. Y.

Figure 62. Boats loaded with cacao for export from the Gold Coast. The harbors are so shallow that ocean ships anchor off shore, and cargoes are carried to and from them in small boats of this kind.

Khartoum is the capital of the country and has the largest European population of any of the towns and cities. Omdurman, just across the Nile from Khartoum, is the old native capital and has the largest native population. *See Figure 61.*

The West Coast Possessions

Locating the British lands in West Africa. On the map on page 50 find Gambia (*B3*), Sierra Leone (*B4*), Gold Coast and Ashanti (*C4*), and Nigeria (*D4*). Which of these British possessions in West Africa is the largest?

The tropical coast. The west coast of Africa, from Gambia to the mouth of the Congo River, is one of the hottest and rainiest parts of the continent. From Figure 41 on page 49 tell how much rain falls along the coast of the Gulf of Guinea. Because of the heat and moisture the climate is very unhealthful for white people, and the few white people who live on the coastal lowlands are mostly traders.

The natives carry on farming in a simple way to supply themselves with food. Many of them work for Europeans on cacao planta-

tions, or raise cacao themselves for export. You will remember that we visited cacao plantations in Brazil and learned how the "beans" are taken from the seed pods and prepared for export. The Gold Coast produces more cacao than any other part of the world.

The natives also gather the fruit of the oil palms which grow wild in the tropical forests of this hot, rainy coast. The pulp and the kernels, or seeds, of this fruit provide palm oil, which is used in Europe and the United States for making soap and for other purposes. Large quantities of the kernels and the oil are exported from West Africa.

The savannas. Farther inland, where the land is higher and the rainfall less, the forests give way to the savannas of the Sudan. The northern half of Ashanti and the greater part of Nigeria are in the Sudan. The natives of these tropical grasslands carry on farming and raise many cattle. Their principal export crop is peanuts, which are sent to Great Britain and other European countries for use in making vegetable oil.

In Nigeria the natives have long raised cotton and woven coarse cotton cloth for clothing. The British government has helped them to raise more and better cotton, and the better grades are exported to England. Another important product of Nigeria is tin. The mines are under the control of the government, and the ore is exported to Wales.

West African trade. More than half of the trade of the British possessions in West Africa is with the home country. In exchange for cacao, palm kernels, cotton, peanuts, tin, and other products which they get from these possessions the British send cotton goods for clothing for the natives, machinery, tools, and other manufactures. *See Figure 62.*

Special credit work. Find out who built the Suez Canal and why it was easier to build than the Panama Canal.

A check. Turn to Figure 55 on page 60 and see if you can name correctly all the British possessions in Africa. If you have any trouble doing so, you need to study the map on pages 42–43 again.

An identification test. After your study of the British lands in Africa you should be able to tell what each phrase below describes.

1. The cape at the southern tip of Africa.
2. The city which is the greatest gold-mining center in the world.
3. The highest mountain in Africa.
4. The canal in Egypt controlled largely by the British.
5. The city which is the center of the oldest diamond-mining district of Africa.
6. The falls in Africa which are greater than Niagara.
7. The river in which these falls are located.
8. The capital of Anglo-Egyptian Sudan.
9. The transcontinental route of travel from northern Africa to southern Africa.
10. Two lakes which serve as part of this transcontinental route.
11. The great desert in northern Africa.
12. The people of Dutch descent in South Africa.
13. The river which forms part of the northern section of the Cape to Cairo route.
14. The tropical grassland south of the Sahara Desert.
15. The river which forms part of the central section of the Cape to Cairo route.
16. The interior plateau of South Africa.

Finding reminders. Tell where a person from each of the following places in the Americas would find a place in the British lands in Africa to remind him of home.

1. The corn belt of the United States.
2. A sheep ranch in Argentina.
3. A gold-mining center in Colorado.
4. The cotton belt of the United States.
5. A coffee plantation in Brazil.
6. A tin-mining camp in Bolivia.
7. A cacao plantation in Ecuador.
8. A sisal-hemp plantation in Yucatan.

Giving reasons. Complete each sentence below by giving reasons for the fact which it states.

1. Of all the British possessions in Africa the Union of South Africa is the one which has attracted the most white people because _.

2. In time Anglo-Egyptian Sudan will probably be of much greater value to the British than it is today because _ _ _ _ _ _ _ _ _ _ _ _ _ _ _ _.

3. The British are encouraging cotton-growing in Uganda, Anglo-Egyptian Sudan, and Nigeria because _ _ _ _ _ _ _ _ _ _ _ _ _ _ _ _ _ _.

4. The British are interested in mining the tin of Nigeria because _ _ _ _ _ _ _ _ _ _ _ _.

5. The greater part of the wool exported from South Africa goes to England because _.

6. Fresh fruit from South Africa finds ready markets in Great Britain because _.

7. Although the British possessions in East Africa are within the tropics, they are fairly well suited to settlement by white people because _.

8. Although British Somaliland is thinly populated, it is of value to the British people because _.

9. The British possessions in Africa provide good markets for British manufactures because _.

Getting cargoes. Name one or more ports of the British lands in Africa where a British ship might go to get each of the following products. You may use the map on page 50 for this work if you find it necessary.

tin	coffee
coal	mohair
wool	sisal hemp
cloves	palm kernels
cotton	hides and skins
cacao	gold and diamonds

Special credit work. 1. Find a book which tells about Cecil Rhodes and his work in South Africa, and make a report to your class.

2. Find out what the Rhodes scholarships are and what a boy must do to win one.

ASIA

Scale of miles

0   200   400   600   800   1000 1200 1400

Water less than 500 ft. deep
Land below sea level
Floating ice
Tundra
Wet-weather streams
Grasslands and cultivated areas
Temperate forests
Tropical forests
Oases
Semideserts, deserts, and
barren mountain slopes

IV. BRITISH LANDS IN ASIA

Foreword. About half of all the people in the world live in Asia, and of all the people in that great continent over one third live in India and other lands which are parts of the British Empire. The natives of these British lands are not people of the black race, like the Negroes of Africa. Most of them are brown-skinned people, but the various groups differ from one another in race, religion, and customs.

The British have done much to help the native people of these Asiatic lands. They have made living conditions more healthful for them, and they have taught them better ways of farming and doing other kinds of work. They have also built roads and railroads, improved the harbors, and developed foreign trade, giving the natives a better chance to market their surplus products in distant lands.

As you read this chapter, try to find out why the British became interested in the lands of Asia, and why these lands are valuable parts of the British Empire.

Getting acquainted with Asia. Before you visit the British lands in Asia, you will find it helpful to get somewhat better acquainted with the continent as a whole. First study the colored relief map opposite this page. Find (1) the parts of Asia which have too little rain for farming; (2) the parts where there are extensive grasslands and cultivated areas; (3) the part with the greatest stretches of temperate forests; (4) the cold, frozen part known as the *tundra*.

Now work out the map studies on page 71.

Map work. After you have finished the map studies, color the British lands in Asia pink on the map of the British Empire which you are making. Use the map on pages 42–43 as a help.

1. A VOYAGE TO INDIA

We are going to board a steamship at London and travel by way of the Suez Canal to India. This is the route most commonly followed by ships going from western Europe to seaports of Asia, Australia, and New Zealand. Trace it on the map on pages 42–43. Point to the places along this important trade route where we may expect to see British flags flying.

Courtesy of Canadian Pacific Steamships

Figure 63. The Rock of Gibraltar, as it looks from ships passing eastward through the strait. The port of Gibraltar, on the lower land back of the Rock, is an important fueling station for ships.

Gibraltar. We enter the Mediterranean Sea through the Strait of Gibraltar, which is about 8 miles wide at its narrowest point. What two continents are separated by this narrow strait? What European country lies on the northern side of the strait?

On the north, which is to our left as we pass eastward through the strait, is the Rock of Gibraltar, shown in Figure 63. There we see British flags, which tell us that the Rock of Gibraltar belongs to Great Britain, instead of to Spain, as we might easily suppose. This huge rock has been made into a fortress which gives the British control of the western gateway to the Mediterranean.

Turn over to page 72.

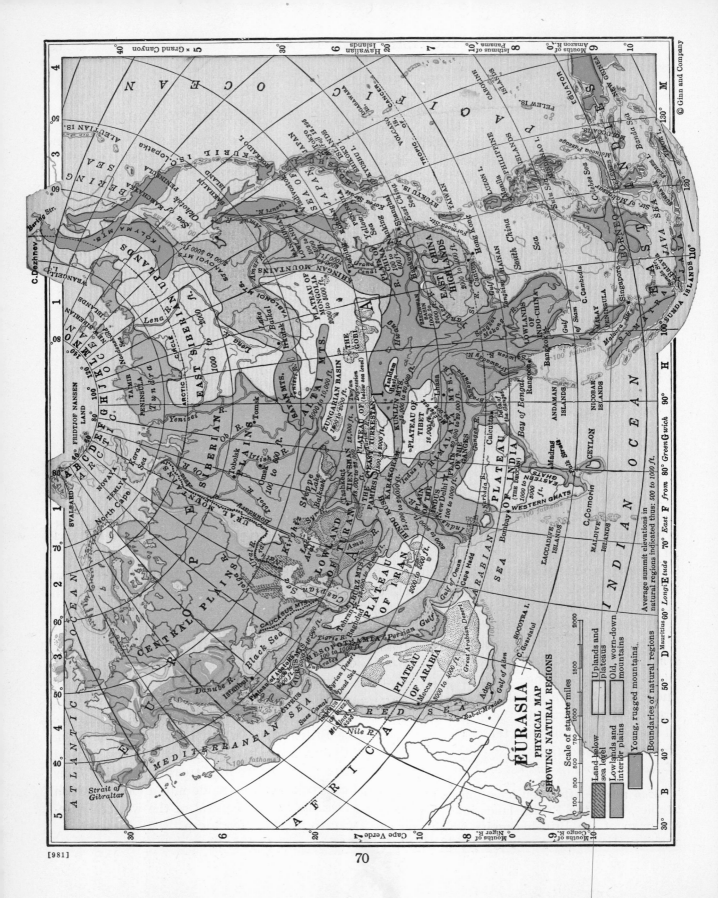

EURASIA
PHYSICAL MAP
SHOWING NATURAL REGIONS

© Ginn and Company

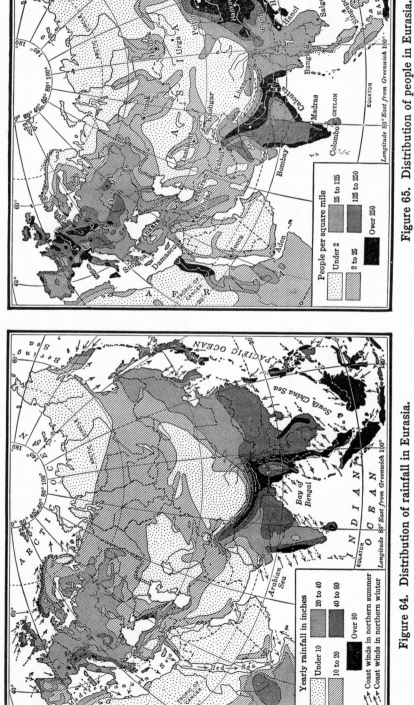

Figure 65. Distribution of people in Eurasia.

Figure 64. Distribution of rainfall in Eurasia.

MAP STUDIES

1. What mountain ranges, river, and inland sea form the natural boundary between Europe and Asia? 2. What plains lie east of the Ural Mountains? 3. In what direction do the rivers of those plains flow? 4. What lowland lies east of the Caspian Sea? 5. How do these Asiatic plains compare in density of population with the Central Plains of Europe? 6. What reason for this difference does Figure 64 suggest?

7. Find the plateaus of Arabia, Iran, and India on the physical map and on the rainfall map. 8. Which of these plateaus do you expect to find densely populated? Why? Check your answer by Figure 65. 9. On the physical map find the Indus and Ganges rivers in India and name the mountains in which they rise. These are the highest mountains in the world. What kind of mountains are they? 10. Name the highest peak in the Himalayas and give its elevation.

11. Describe the surface of the part of Asia which stretches northeastward from the Himalaya Mountains to Bering Sea. 12. Give two reasons why this part of Asia is thinly populated. 13. What part of eastern Asia is as densely populated as India? 14. What reason can you give for the many people there? 15. Is Asia mostly a continent of lowland plains or of mountains and plateaus? 16. Do most of the people live in the cooler part of the continent or the warmer part?

deciduous
coniferous

loess = иши

© From Ewing Galloway, N. Y.

Figure 66. One of the buildings of the Hebrew University in Jerusalem. This university, established in the new homeland of the Jews, will make Jerusalem a great center of learning.

Malta. Sailing eastward, we come to the narrowest part of the Mediterranean Sea, between the island of Sicily and the coast of northern Africa. Here we pass the island of Malta, which is the most important port of call for ships passing back and forth through the Mediterranean. If we stop at Malta, we shall see British flags flying from the public buildings, showing that this little island is another British possession. It is a great British naval and air base and a fueling and repair station for ships.

Cyprus. To the north of our route, near the eastern end of the Mediterranean Sea, is the island of Cyprus, which has been governed by the British since 1878. The people are mostly farmers, and before the island came under British control their crops were often badly damaged by droughts. The British have helped the people by building irrigation works.

The British in the Near East

A stop at Haifa. Our next stop is at Haifa, a seaport on the coast of Palestine, at the eastern end of the Mediterranean Sea. Here a number of British officials leave the ship. They have been sent out from London to help in the government of Palestine. Palestine is in southwestern Asia, which is the part of the world known as the "Near East." Find Palestine on the map on page 75 (*B–C 4*).

Palestine. Palestine is the old homeland of the Jews, where Jesus lived and carried on his great work as a religious teacher. For that reason it is called the "Holy Land." For hundreds of years before the First World War Palestine belonged to Turkey. At the end of that war its government was placed in the hands of the British, and a plan was worked out to make Palestine a new homeland for the Jews.

During the years that followed, many Jews went to live in Palestine, principally from the countries of eastern and central Europe. Many of them bought farm lands in Palestine, while others went into business in the cities and towns.

In May, 1948, the British withdrew from Palestine, and the Jews proclaimed their independence. The exact boundaries of their state still remain to be determined, however. The population of Palestine is made up more largely of Arabs than of Jews, for the country was inhabited chiefly by Arabs when it belonged to Turkey. The Arabs have disliked the plan for making Palestine a national homeland for the Jews, and there has been much trouble between the two groups.

Turn to Figure 64 on page 71 and study the rainfall of the lands bordering the eastern end of the Mediterranean Sea. Notice that there is a narrow belt along the coast where the yearly rainfall is over 20 inches. This belt is a coastal plain. Farther inland the land grows hilly and mountainous, and the rainfall grows less.

Photo by Lionel Green

Figure 67. Part of Jerusalem. Most of the Arabs in Palestine are Mohammedans, and the domed building in the foreground of the picture is a Mohammedan mosque, or place of worship. The buildings in Jerusalem are made of stone or sun-dried mud bricks instead of wood. What reason can you suggest for this?

Most of the people of Palestine are farmers. Their chief crops are wheat, barley, and oranges, olives, and other fruits. You will remember that wheat and barley need less moisture than most grains. Olive trees also can be grown where the rainfall is rather light. The rougher and drier parts of Palestine are better suited to grazing than to farming, and so the raising of sheep and goats has always been important.

The old city of Jerusalem was the Jewish capital in the days of Jesus, and it is still the capital of Palestine. Thousands of tourists visit Jerusalem and other parts of the Holy Land each year. *See Figures 66 and 67.*

The rift valley. Along the eastern margin of Palestine are the Sea of Galilee, the Jordan River, and the Dead Sea. These bodies of water lie in a deep, narrow trough somewhat like the rift valley of East Africa. The trough is so deep that the surface of the Dead Sea is 1292 feet below the level of the Mediterranean.

The Dead Sea has no outlet, and so its waters are salt like those of Great Salt Lake.

There are falls in the Jordan River which are being put to work to supply Palestine with hydroelectricity. One power plant has been built, and two more are planned. The electricity is used in the cities, and to run some of the railroads.

Trans-Jordan. Trans-Jordan is an Arab country with a king of its own. It had been under British authority since the First World War, but became independent early in 1946. Trans-Jordan is east of the rift valley and is part of the desert plateau of Arabia. Most of the people are Bedouin Arabs, and they live a wandering life with their camels, sheep, and goats. Locate Trans-Jordan on the map on page 75 (C 4–5).

Through the Suez Canal. Leaving Haifa, our ship heads directly toward the northern entrance to the Suez Canal. We stop at Port

Photo by Lionel Green

Figure 68. Part of the water front at Aden. Aden is a center where coffee, hides, and skins from neighboring regions of Arabia and Africa are collected for export, and from which cotton goods from Great Britain are distributed to those lands. How can you tell from the picture that this coast receives very little rain?

Said, where we see British flags flying, and then steam southward through the canal. There is little to see on this trip except the bare, sandy desert through which the canal has been cut. We stop again at the British port of Suez, at the southern end of the canal, and then pass out into the Red Sea.

Aden. At the southern end of the Red Sea we pass through the narrow strait called Bab-el-Mandeb and head toward the port of Aden. There we stop for some hours to take on coal and to unload some cotton goods.

On the map on page 75 find Aden and its port of the same name (*D–E8*). This area at the southwest corner of the peninsula of Arabia belongs to the British and is a valuable possession because it gives them control of the southern entrance to the Red Sea. The port of Aden serves as a fueling station for ships and as a trading center for the people of southern Arabia and the people of Somaliland on the neighboring coast of Africa. *See Figure 68.*

Across the Arabian Sea. From Aden we sail across the Arabian Sea to Bombay, on the western coast of India. The trip from

London has taken about three weeks. If we had traveled around the southern tip of Africa instead of through the Suez Canal, it would have taken us several weeks longer. If we had been in a hurry to reach Bombay, we could have flown from London to India in four days.

Something to discuss. Discuss with your class the value of Gibraltar, Malta, Port Said, Suez, and Aden to Great Britain. Try to decide why it is worth while to the British to hold them.

In connection with this discussion you will find it helpful to answer the following questions:

1. Why do the British, more than most nations, need fueling and repair stations for ships along the great water highways of the world?

2. Why is the route between western Europe and Asia by way of the Suez Canal especially important to the British people?

3. How might British trade and shipping suffer if the Strait of Gibraltar, the Suez Canal, and the strait called Bab-el-Mandeb were controlled by nations which were unfriendly to Great Britain?

4. How does Great Britain help other countries of the world by keeping the Suez route open for the ships of all nations?

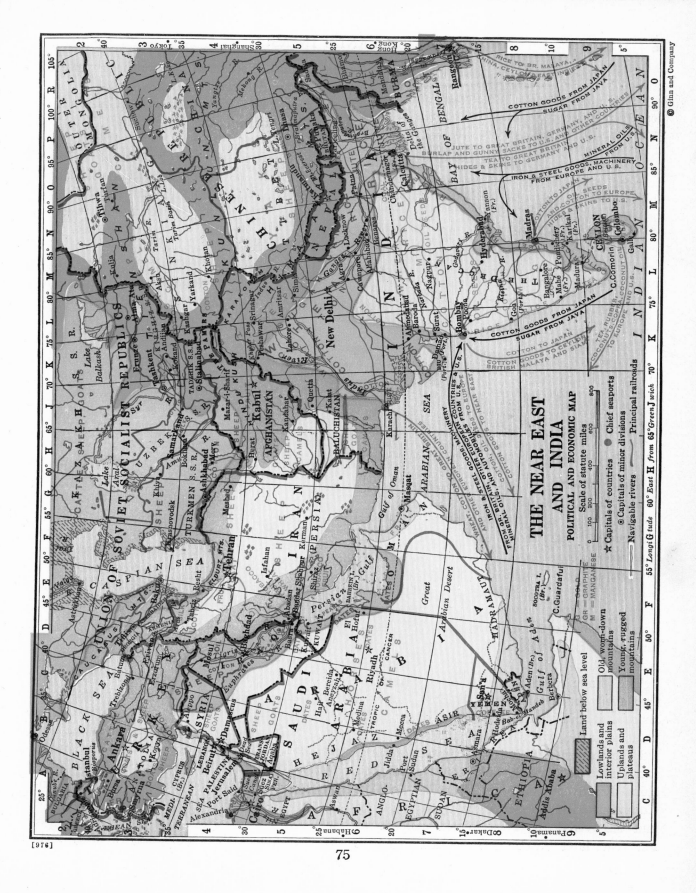

THE NEAR EAST
AND INDIA

POLITICAL AND ECONOMIC MAP

Scale of statute miles

☆ Capitals of countries
● Chief seaports
⊙ Capitals of minor divisions
— Navigable rivers
— Principal railroads

Land below sea level
Lowlands and interior plains
Uplands and plateaus
Old, worn-down mountains
Young, rugged mountains

© Ginn and Company

[976]

2. INDIA, BURMA, AND CEYLON

As you already know, India is one of the most densely populated countries in the world. It is more than half as large as the United States, and is by far the largest and most important of the British lands in Asia. Within it live about three hundred and ninety million people, or over two thirds of all the people of the British Empire.

As you study about India, find answers to the following questions:

1. How can so many people make a living in this part of Asia?

2. How did the British come to control this densely populated country?

3. Why was India of value to the British people?

4. What have the British done to help the people of India?

A Country won through Trade

Early trade with India. For hundreds of years before the discovery of America the people of India and other countries of eastern Asia had been supplying the wealthy people of Europe with silks, spices, and precious stones. Camel caravans brought these products overland to the eastern end of the Mediterranean Sea, where they were met by trading ships from the European countries.

The trade with India was so profitable that every trading nation of Europe wanted a share in it, but the transportation of goods by camel caravan was slow and uncertain. This led the seafaring nations of Europe to search for a route by which they could send their ships directly to the ports of India. In 1492 Columbus tried to reach India by sailing west, and discovered the New World instead. A few years later Vasco da Gama, a Portuguese sea captain, discovered the southern route to India around Africa.

James Sawders

Figure 69. Part of one of the gateways to an old Hindu temple in the southern part of India. The temple was built about two hundred years ago.

A commercial race. After Da Gama's discovery, Portugal, the Netherlands, France, and Great Britain became competitors in a commercial race for control of the trade with India. Each one built trading stations along the coast of India, and there was great rivalry between them. Great Britain won this race, and that is why India became a part of the British Empire.

Trade and government. As the British increased their trade with India, they found it necessary to send soldiers to protect their merchants against some of the natives, and this led them to take a more and more active part in the government of the country. At times, too, they had to settle troubles between various groups of the native people, and this gave them still more power. So, by gradual stages, India came under British control.

The people of India. The people of India are a great mixture of races, and among them are many different groups who speak different languages and have different religions. The largest religious group is that of the Hindus, who make up about two thirds of the total population. The next largest is that of the Moslems, who are Mohammedans by religion. In the cities and towns there are beautiful temples and mosques, and religion plays a large part in the life and customs of the people. *See Figure 69.*

Nowhere in the world are there greater contrasts in wealth and education than among the people of India. Some of the native princes are very rich, and there are many wealthy merchants. But the masses of the people are pitifully poor, and only about twelve in every hundred can read and write. The British have opened many schools in the cities and larger towns, but schools in the country districts are few and far between. On the other hand, many educated Indians are among the most highly cultured people in the world, and India has produced great scholars, writers, and scientists.

The political divisions of India. Until the year 1947 India was divided into two groups of territories: the provinces of British India, which made up about three fifths of the country, and the Indian, or Princely, States.

The central government of British India was headed by a British governor general, but for some time each province had enjoyed about as much freedom in managing its own affairs as each of our states has under our Federal government.

There were 562 Indian states of varying size. All of them were under the protection of the British government, but each one was ruled by its own native prince.

For a long time certain Indian leaders had been demanding full independence for their country. Great Britain said that as soon as British India could set up a strong central government of its own, it would be given the standing of a dominion. The Hindus and the Moslems, however, could not agree on a united central government, and there was so much trouble between them that finally, in 1947, British India was divided into two dominions.

The parts of British India in which the people are mostly Hindus became the Dominion of India. The parts in which the people are mostly Moslems became the Dominion of Pakistan. Each of the Princely States was left free to decide whether to join one of the dominions or to become independent. Great Britain agreed that after June, 1948, India and Pakistan should decide whether or not to remain members of the British Commonwealth of Nations.

The Land and the Climate

Map work. Before you read further, use the map on page 75 to work out the following map studies.

1. Trace the tropic of Cancer across India. 2. The part of India south of that line is called *peninsular India.* Explain why. 3. What plateau makes up most of peninsular India? 4. What seems to be the most important kind of work there? 5. What kind of land do you find north of the Deccan? 6. This region is called the plain of northern India. Judging from its latitude, what can you safely say about its climate? 7. What kind of work is most important in this region?

8. The map shows that the plain of northern India is made up of the basins of three great rivers and their tributaries. What rivers are they? 9. Which one flows into the Arabian Sea? 10. Which two flow into the Bay of Bengal? 11. In what mountains do all three rivers rise? 12. What have you already learned about those mountains? 13. Now turn to Figure 64 on page 71 and tell whether or not most of India has enough rain for farming.

The natural regions of India. You have learned from the map that India is a warm country with abundant rainfall, and that it may be divided into three great natural regions: (1) the high, rugged mountains on the north, (2) the great northern plain, and (3) the plateau region called the Deccan.

The northern plain is remarkably level, and the soils are fine and very fertile, for they have been laid down by the great rivers that rise in the Himalayas and flow through India to the sea. The Deccan is from 1000 to 3000 feet above the sea; and while it is by no means level, it is not too rough for farming. In the northwestern portion of this region there are rich lava soils like those in the Columbia Plateau of our country.

With all these facts in mind, what can you say about the suitability of the greater part of India for farming?

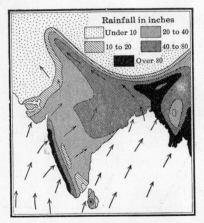

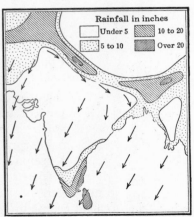

Figure 70. Distribution of rainfall in India during the period of the summer monsoons.

Figure 71. Distribution of rainfall in India during the period of the winter monsoons.

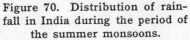

The arrows on both maps show the direction of the winds.

The monsoon winds and rains. You may have heard people say that India is a monsoon land. The word *monsoon* means "seasonal," and India is called a monsoon land because its winds change with the seasons.

During the northern summer the interior of the great continent of Asia becomes very warm. The warm air over the land tends to rise, and the cooler air from over the oceans moves inland close to the earth. Because of this movement of air, India has winds from the southwest in the northern summer. These winds begin to blow in June and usually last until sometime in October. They are called the *summer monsoons*. As they blow from the southwest toward India, they gather up much moisture in crossing the Indian Ocean. When they strike the land, they are forced to rise. In rising they are cooled, and the rain falls. Thus the summer monsoons are wet monsoons and bring much rain to India during the hot months of the year. *See Figure 70.*

The monsoon rains are especially heavy on the western coast of peninsular India, where the winds first strike the land. They are also very heavy in Burma, where the winds strike the land after crossing the Bay of Bengal.

In the northern winter the interior of Asia becomes very cold. The cold air is heavy, and it settles to the ground and then moves outward from the center of the continent. This outward movement of air gives India winter winds from the northeast. These winds usually begin in December, and they are called the *winter monsoons*. Figure 71 shows that much less rain falls in India during the period of the winter monsoons than during the period of the summer monsoons. These northeast winds, blowing toward India from over the land instead of the sea, are dry monsoons, for they bring very little moisture with them. Therefore the mild winter is the dry season in India.

Rainfall and farming. The seasonal distribution of rainfall in India plays an important part in the life and work of the people. During the rainy season the farmers raise crops such as rice, sugar cane, and cotton, which need much heat and moisture. During the dry season they raise wheat, millet, and other crops which can get along with less moisture. In this way most of the farmers of India get at least two crops a year from their land. That is one reason why so many people can live in India.

In some years the monsoon rains are late in coming, and much less rain falls than usual. At such times the crops are poor, and millions of the people suffer from hunger. Famines, as such periods of food shortage are called, have occurred many times in India in the past, and in some of the worst famine years hundreds of thousands of people have died of hunger. Conditions are better now, for the British have built railroads in India, and food supplies can be sent quickly to the famine areas from other parts of the country.

A monsoon test. Prove that you understand about the monsoon conditions in India by completing each sentence below:

1. India is called a monsoon land because

--.

2. The winds that blow over India in the northern summer come from the __(direction)__ and are called the _____ _____ or the ___ _____. They bring much ____ to India because _____.

3. The winds that blow over India in the northern winter come from the __(direction)__ and are called the _____ _____ or the ___ _____. They bring little ____ to India because _____.

From Bombay to Calcutta

Bombay. Our ship has brought us across the Arabian Sea to Bombay, the second largest city of India and the leading seaport of the western coast. In its harbor, which is one of the best in the world, we shall see ships from many distant lands. Find Bombay on the map on page 75 (*K7*) and study Figure 72.

Judging from the map, what do you think our ship may have brought from London to Bombay? What do you think it is likely to carry back from Bombay to England? What

Figure 72. A view of Bombay. This seaport of western India is a city of over a million people, among whom are many wealthy Indian merchants and many British business men and officials.

Figure 73. A dry-goods shop in Bombay. Goods of many different kinds are sold in little shops like this, but there are also many larger stores.

do you find among the exports which suggests that Bombay is a manufacturing city?

In Bombay we shall see many things to remind us of the work that the British are doing in India. Along the water front there are large docks and warehouses like those in any great European port, and in the business section there are modern banks and office buildings. In the manufacturing district we shall see many different kinds of mills and factories equipped with up-to-date machinery from England. Among them are more than eighty cotton mills, for Bombay is the leading cotton-manufacturing city of India.

We shall also see a large railroad station in Bombay, for the British have built railroads to connect this seaport with other parts of India. Its location on the western coast and its railroads make Bombay the gateway city for the west-central part of India and the chief port through which imports from Great Britain enter the country.

Although we shall see much that is new and modern in Bombay, we shall also see many things to remind us that India is a very old country

Imperial Institute, London

Figure 74. Threshing rice in India. The bullocks are trampling the grain to separate the seeds from the stalks. Rice is the chief food of millions of the people of India. The crop is sown in June and harvested in January. Can you explain why?

Courtesy of Canadian Pacific Steamships

Figure 75. Drawing water for irrigation from a well in India. Can you explain how the bucket is lowered into the well and then lifted, full of water?

where the people are slow to change their ways of living and working. On the sidewalks Englishmen in European clothes pause to chat with Indian merchants in native dress and bright-colored turbans. In the streets modern automobiles pass slow-moving oxcarts and two-wheeled carts pulled by natives. If we visit the little native shops, we shall find them nothing more than stalls opening on the sidewalks. *See Figure 73.*

The tropical west coast. Leaving Bombay, we steam southward for about 800 miles along the west coast of India, where the monsoon rains are very heavy. The western margin of the Deccan is called the Western Ghats, and it rises so near the sea that there is only a very narrow lowland along the coast. This coast is densely populated by natives who make their living by raising rice and tropical crops which need much heat and moisture. Few white people care to live here because of the hot, moist climate.

The eastern coastal lowland. When we round the southern end of the peninsula and turn northward, we find that the eastern

margin of the plateau (the Eastern Ghats) is some distance inland and that there is a lowland from fifty to a hundred miles wide along the coast. Here too the population is very dense, and most of the people make their living by farming. Among the crops which they raise are rice, cotton, sugar cane, and tropical fruits. Although the total rainfall for the year in this region is heavy, most of it comes between June and December, and the crops that are grown during the dry season have to be irrigated. *See Figures 74 and 75.*

Madras. On the map on page 75 find the city of Madras (*M 8*). Madras is the third largest city of India, and the ocean gateway for the southeastern part of the country. It has no natural harbor, but the British have made an excellent one by building great breakwaters such as we saw at some of the ports along the west coast of South America. They have also built railroads to connect Madras with other parts of India. Like Bombay, Madras has cotton mills and exports raw cotton and cotton goods. It also has tanneries which make use of hides and skins from the plateau.

From Madras to Calcutta. From Madras we sail northeastward toward the great delta which the Ganges and the Brahmaputra rivers have built out into the Bay of Bengal. On this low delta plain is the great city of Calcutta. Find Calcutta on the map on page 75 (*N 6*).

The approach to the great delta is dangerous for large ships, for there are hidden sand bars beneath the water. For this reason we take on a special pilot when we are still 120 miles from Calcutta. He guides the ship safely into the mouth of the Hooghly River, which is one of the larger outlets, or distributaries, of the Ganges. Calcutta is 80 miles inland on the Hooghly. The river has been deepened by dredging, so that ocean ships may go upstream to docks in the city.

Another gateway city. At Calcutta the British have provided all kinds of modern machinery for loading and unloading ships, for this city is an even greater seaport than Bombay. Turn to the map again and name its leading exports. What raw materials do you find among them? What manufactured goods?

Calcutta is the largest city of India, and the ocean gateway for the most fertile and most densely populated part of the northern plain. Many of its buildings, streets, and shops are modern, for it was planned and built by the British. Most of its people, however, are natives, and the city has its bazaars, or open markets, where the native people buy and sell goods, and its temples and mosques.

Jute-manufacturing. Besides being a great seaport, Calcutta is a busy manufacturing city. Along the river front you will see many jute mills, for Calcutta is the world's leading center for jute-manufacturing. In the mills

Figure 76. Bales of raw jute in a mill at Calcutta. The jute mills in this city provide work for many thousands of people. What city in Scotland is an important jute-manufacturing center?

the fibers of jute stems are spun into yarn and woven into the coarse cloth which we call burlap. *See Figure 76.*

Each year shippers of cotton, coffee, sugar, and many other farm products in many different countries need large quantities of burlap and millions of gunny sacks, or burlap bags. For this reason almost every country in the world buys jute or jute products from India. What countries of the Americas do you think are good customers for burlap and gunny sacks?

Map discoveries. Turn to the map on page 75 and find answers to the following questions:

1. In what way is the location of Calcutta like the location of New Orleans?

2. What seaport of the West Indies is in the same latitude as Calcutta? (See western margin of map.)

3. Why has Calcutta become the great jute-manufacturing center of India?

4. Why has Bombay, rather than Calcutta, become the great cotton-manufacturing center?

Something to explain. Large quantities of burlap manufactured in mills in Calcutta are shipped to New Orleans. What reason can you give for this fact?

James Sawders

Figure 77. An Indian farmer plowing with a wooden plow drawn by a pair of "humped" bullocks, as they are called from the humps on their backs. Humped cattle are common in all parts of India.

Farm Lands and Inland Cities

A great agricultural country. Let us imagine that we have an airplane in which to fly over India. No matter what season we choose for the trip, we shall see countless people at work in the fields, for three fourths of the natives are farmers, and the climate is so warm that farm work goes on the year round.

Except in the mountains at the north the surface of India is well suited to farming, and most of the country is well watered. Thus the latitude, the surface, and the rainfall combine to make India one of the great agricultural countries of the world. In addition to these natural advantages the dense population provides cheap labor, or workers, and therefore India can produce large quantities of crops such as cotton and tea, which require much handwork.

As you would expect in such a thickly settled country, food crops are of the greatest importance, and enormous quantities are needed to supply the home markets. But the people also raise cotton, jute, and certain other crops in sufficient quantities to have a large surplus for export.

Farming scenes. We shall see many differences between the farm lands of India and those of our own country. Most of the farms are small, and few of the people use farm machinery. We shall see them plowing with bullocks, or oxen, or with "water buffaloes," such as we saw in the Philippines, and harvesting their crops by hand. *See Figure 77.*

Farm animals. Although there are millions of cattle in India, we shall not find any great ranches, and we shall see few dairy farms. The cow is a sacred animal to the Hindus, and so they do not eat beef. Because of this, little attention is paid to raising cattle for meat. Milk is used, but almost no effort is made to raise good dairy cows. Cattle in India are valuable chiefly as work animals, and for their hides when they die. Nearly every farmer has a pair of bullocks, which

Imperial Institute, London

Figure 78. Harvesting jute on the Ganges delta in India. After the stalks have been cut, they are soaked in water and the fibers are scraped from them. Then the fibers are dried and packed in bales for shipment to mills in Calcutta or to distant lands.

he uses to draw his plow and to pull the high-wheeled cart in which he carries his produce to market.

The people of India raise many sheep, especially in the Deccan, but neither the wool nor the meat is of very good quality. Goats are found everywhere in the country, for they require little care and can live on the poorest of shrubs and grass. Both sheep and goats are raised chiefly for their skins. As you might expect, hides and skins are important exports from India.

Rice and jute lands. If we fly northeastward from Calcutta, we shall find that the chief crops on the low, flat lands of the great delta are rice and jute. The delta plain is covered with a network of streams, and farm products are carried to market in boats.

Figure 79. Indian girls picking tea leaves on a plantation near Darjeeling. Since the picking is done so often, the tea plantations provide work for many people throughout the year.

Every year, during the rainy season, the rivers rise and overflow their banks, flooding the low delta lands. To avoid danger from floods the people build their houses on mounds of earth in the midst of their fields. In this way they are safe from ordinary floods; but in years when the rains are very heavy and the waters rise unusually high, they have to leave their houses in boats to escape being drowned.

Although the great floods do much damage, the ordinary ones are helpful, for they leave a layer of fine, rich soil spread over the land, and they provide an abundance of moisture for crops. Both rice and jute are crops which need much water while they are growing, and this great delta plain is wonderfully well suited to them. *See Figure 78.*

Tea plantations. If we fly northward to Darjeeling and then eastward along the valley of the Brahmaputra, we shall look down on whole hillsides covered with tea planta-

tions. Tea plants grow best on well-drained hillsides where the yearly rainfall is over 80 inches. In warm countries new leaves keep coming out the whole year long, and in India they are picked at least once, and often twice, a month. *See Figure 79.*

After the leaves have been picked, they are carefully dried and prepared for use. India exports much tea to Great Britain, for the British are great tea-drinkers.

Farming in the Deccan. If we return to Calcutta and then fly southwestward, we shall soon find ourselves crossing the Deccan. This plateau is a region where millions of people make a living on small farms. Turn to the map on page 75 and make a list of the crops that you expect to see growing there.

The principal food crop of the Deccan is millet, though rice is grown in the moister sections. The principal money crops are oil seeds and cotton. The oilseeds include cottonseed, flaxseed, mustard seeds, peanuts, and several other kinds of seeds that are rich in oil. Large quantities of them are exported to Great Britain and other European countries,

Orient and Occident

Figure 80. An Indian farmer hauling his cotton to market in his two-wheeled bullock cart. What two seaports of India use large quantities of cotton from the Deccan in their mills?

where the oil is pressed out of them and used for many different purposes. In the production of cotton India ranks next to the United States, and the greater part of the crop is grown in the Deccan. *See Figure 80.*

An old native city. The largest city of the Deccan is Hyderabad. It is the capital of one of the native states, and the home of its Indian ruler. It is very old, and quite different from the great seaports of India, for it is an inland city and has not yet become a manufacturing center. The most interesting sights in the city are the bazaars, where the people from the country round about sell their farm products and buy cotton goods and other things that they need.

The dry plain of the Indus. If we fly northwestward from Hyderabad to the plain bordering the Indus River, we shall find ourselves in a part of India which has so little rain that the farmers must irrigate all their crops. The British have built huge irrigation works in this region, with thousands of miles of canals and ditches to carry water from the river to the farm lands. On these irrigated lands the farmers raise large crops of wheat, barley, corn, millet, rice, and cotton. *See Figure 81.*

Karachi. The ocean gateway for the plain of the Indus is the seaport of Karachi. Find this city on the map on page 75 (*J6*). What does it export?

For a long time Karachi was only a small settlement, but it has grown fast since the development of irrigation and the building of railroads in the plain of the Indus. Today it is one of the four leading seaports of India, and the capital of the Dominion of Pakistan.

Baluchistan. West of the plain of the Indus is the mountain and plateau region known as Baluchistan. It is a very dry region, and the few people who live there are mostly nomads who wander about with their flocks and herds. Like all nomadic people, they suffer from hunger in years when the little rain on which they depend fails and many of their animals die. In former years these nomads were sometimes driven by hunger to attack and rob the people in the neighboring lowland of India, and it was to stop these attacks that the British took possession of Baluchistan.

The northern plain of India. It will be interesting to fly up the valley of the Indus and then turn southeastward and return to Calcutta by way of the Ganges Valley. On this trip we shall pass over the northern plain of India, which is one of the richest parts of the country. Within it are many of the finest old Indian cities and some of the best farm lands of the country.

In the upper part of the Indus and Ganges valleys we shall find that the principal winter, or dry-season, crops are wheat, barley, and millet, and that they are irrigated by a great system of canals and wells which the British have built. Among the important summer, or wet-season, crops are cotton and sugar cane. Farther east, in the lower plain of the Ganges, where the rainfall is heavier, the cotton fields disappear and the wheat fields give way to rice fields.

James Sawders

Figure 81. A glimpse of the water front in a town on the Indus River. The sacks that you see in the picture are filled with wheat, and they have been brought down the river in flat-bottomed boats. Large quantities of wheat move down the Indus Valley by train and boat for export from the port of Karachi.

The capital of India. In the midst of the northern plain, at a point which long ago became a meeting place for roads, is the old city of Delhi. Today Delhi is the most important inland railroad center of India. Adjoining it is New Delhi, the capital of the Dominion of India. It has modern government buildings, broad streets, and parks and gardens.

On the map (p. 75) find New Delhi (*L 5*) and the town of Simla (*L 4*). In what region of India is Simla? This town is 7000 feet above sea level, and every summer the government officials move up there from New Delhi. Can you explain why a mountain town is used as India's summer capital?

Old cities of the Ganges Valley. As we fly down the Ganges Valley, we shall surely stop at Agra to see the beautiful building called the Taj Mahal. It is made of white marble, and many people think it the most beautiful building in the whole world. *See Figure 82.*

We shall also wish to stop at Benares on the Ganges River. The Ganges is the sacred river of the Hindus, and Benares is the center of their religion. Many thousands of Hindus come to this old city every year to worship in its hundreds of temples and to bathe in the sacred waters of the river.

At Delhi and other places in the northern plain we shall see cotton mills, flour mills, sugar mills, and other modern manufacturing plants which make use of raw materials from the farm lands. But we shall probably be much more interested in the little workshops where native craftsmen make many beautiful things by hand. We shall see some of them carving ivory, others making pottery, and still others hammering copper into beautifully shaped cups, vases, and other forms.

At Agra, Benares, and some of the other old cities we shall see native people weaving beautiful striped silks and gold brocades on hand looms. In fact, all through India we

James Sawders

Figure 82. The Taj Mahal, at Agra. This beautiful marble building was erected about three hundred years ago by an Indian ruler in memory of his wife.

shall find that among the millions of people who cannot read or write there are many who are wonderfully skillful in making beautiful things with their hands. *See Figure 83.*

The Himalaya Mountains

The highest mountains in the world. When you were studying the map of Asia, you learned that the Himalayas are the highest mountains in the world. They rise like a great wall on the northern side of India, and among their summits are snow fields and glaciers which never melt away. *See Figure 84.*

The rainfall on the southern side of the Himalayas is so heavy that the lower slopes are covered with thick forests. The lowest forests are made up of bamboos and many other tropical trees. Higher up, where the air is cooler, there are forests of pines and other evergreen trees, and still higher come the grassy slopes which are too cold for trees.

Work in the mountains. In the mountains north of the Plain of the Indus there are many fertile valleys where the people raise a variety of food crops and keep cattle and sheep. These mountain people are very skillful in the weaving of wool, and they make

beautiful rugs and shawls which are sold in many parts of the world. You have probably heard of the cashmere shawls which are made in the mountain valley of India known as the Vale of Kashmir.

Nepal and Bhutan. On the map on page 75 find Nepal and Bhutan on the southern slopes of the Himalaya Mountains. These are independent kingdoms, but they are in the "British sphere of influence." This means that the British would protect them if any country should try to interfere in their affairs. The people get their living chiefly by farming and raising cattle, and what little trade they have is mostly with India.

Manufacturing and Trade

Handwork. For thousands of years the people of India have been famous for their skillful handwork. Weaving, pottery-making, metal-working, and carving are old, old industries in India, and they are found side by side with the modern manufacturing industries which the British have introduced.

Advantages for manufacturing. The British have been quick to see the advantages which India has for manufacturing. The farms

Herbert Photos, Inc.

Figure 83. An Indian craftsman. He is stamping a design in colors on a piece of cotton cloth which he has woven on a hand loom. Have you ever seen bright-colored printed cotton goods from India?

Acme

Figure 84. The highest mountains in the world. In this picture you are looking at the snow-capped Himalayas from a distance of about eighty miles. Mount Everest, the highest peak, is third from the right. It looks a little lower than its neighbor on the right, but that is because Mount Everest is farther away.

provide large quantities of raw materials, and the dense population insures abundant labor, or workers, for the mills and factories, and large home markets for manufactured goods. The map on page 75 will show you that India also has coal and iron ore.

The leading industries. Because of these advantages for manufacturing, the British have built mills and factories and equipped them with machinery made in England. The leading industries are cotton-manufacturing and jute-manufacturing because cotton and jute are the most important raw materials produced in India. As you know, there are markets all over the world for jute goods. For cotton goods there is a large home market, because India is so warm that the millions of people wear mostly cotton clothing. Another important industry is the manufacture of leather goods. Can you explain why?

Abundant coal and iron ore have led to the growth of iron-and-steel manufacturing in India, but as yet this industry supplies only a small part of the needs of the huge population for products of iron and steel.

The trade of India. From the map on page 75 make a list of the exports of India, dividing them into two classes: (1) products of farming and (2) products of manufacturing. Which kind of work provides more of the exports? Why are there more raw materials than foodstuffs among the exports?

Of all the exports of India, raw cotton is the most important. About half the yearly crop is exported, and normally Japan is the best customer. Great Britain takes about three tenths of all the exports, buying most of the tea and wheat that are shipped away, and large quantities of the raw jute and oil seeds. Our own country is India's best customer for burlap, and a good one for hides and skins.

Now turn to the map on page 75 again and study the imports of India. What do you find there to show that as yet India does

raft= extra

Courtesy of Hamburg-American Line

Figure 85. An elephant piling teakwood in a lumber yard at Rangoon. Have you ever seen chairs, tables, or other pieces of furniture made of carved teakwood?

not manufacture enough cotton cloth to supply the home market? What country exports large quantities of cotton goods to India?

The imports show that India also provides an excellent market for machinery, iron and steel goods, automobiles, and mineral oils. Great Britain and the United States lead in supplying these needs.

Altogether Great Britain supplies about four tenths of all the imports of India. This great country, with its many millions of people, is one of Great Britain's best markets for manufactured goods. It is this fact, more than anything else, that makes India of great value to the British people.

Burma[1]

Rangoon and the Irrawaddy Valley. We shall go by boat from Calcutta to Rangoon. This city is the capital, the largest city, and the seaport of Burma. Find it on the

[1]In 1948 Burma became a republic (the Union of Burma), entirely outside the British Empire.

map on page 75 (*P7*) and notice its location near the mouth of the Irrawaddy River.

The delta of the Irrawaddy River is hot and rainy, and the people raise so much rice there that they have a surplus for export. Farther up the Irrawaddy Valley the rainfall is somewhat less than on the delta, and the people raise millet, cotton, and other crops in addition to rice.

Petroleum and teak. The most valuable mineral product of Burma is petroleum from oil fields in the Irrawaddy Valley. The crude petroleum goes by pipe line to refineries in and near Rangoon, and large quantities of mineral oils are exported.

Another important export from Burma is a beautiful hardwood called teak. The trees are cut in the dry season and dragged to the rivers, where they are bound together on bamboo rafts. When the rains come and the rivers rise, the rafts of logs are floated downstream to the sawmills. Teakwood is so heavy that the natives use elephants to get the logs out of the forests and to move the lumber in the lumber yards. *See Figure 85.*

Photo by Lionel Green

Figure 86. A field of young rice in Ceylon. Rice is a plant which needs much water, and so the fields are flooded during the early part of its growth. The men in the picture are stirring the muddy soil with bamboo poles to keep down the growth of weeds.

Ceylon[1]

A tropical island. Southeast of India is the pear-shaped island of Ceylon, which is about half the size of England. The center of the island is hilly and mountainous, but there is a lowland around the coast. The lowland is hot and moist because Ceylon is near the equator and has a monsoon climate. The lowland is well suited to rice-growing, and rice is the chief food of the natives. See Figure 86.

Plantation products. In India you found most of the natives working on small farms. In Ceylon many of the natives work on large plantations owned by British and other European planters. On the coastal lowland there are coconut plantations. On the lower mountain slopes in the southwestern part of the island there are rubber plantations, and on the higher slopes in the same section there are large tea plantations. See Figure 87.

In the year 1876 the British government sent several thousand seedlings of Brazilian rubber trees to Ceylon and established the first plantation there. That was the beginning of rubber-growing in southeastern Asia. From Ceylon the plantations spread to British Malaya and the East Indies, and this part of Asia now produces over nine tenths of the world's rubber. From Ceylon rubber is the second most valuable export. Tea ranks first.

Colombo and its trade. Find Ceylon on the map on page 75 and locate its seaport of Colombo (M9). The location of Colombo on the southwest coast of the island makes it an important port of call for ships on their way back and forth between the countries of Europe and the countries of eastern Asia.

[1]Ceylon became a self-governing dominion in 1948.

© Plate Ltd., Ceylon

Figure 87. A tea factory on a plantation in Ceylon. In the factories the tea leaves are carefully cured and prepared for export. The two-wheeled carts carry the tea to the seaport of Colombo.

At Colombo you will see ships being loaded with tea, rubber, copra, coconuts, and coconut oil. These plantation products go chiefly to Great Britain, other European countries, and the United States. Another export product is graphite, a mineral which is mined in Ceylon. One of the uses of graphite is in making the "lead" for pencils.

Many of the ships that come to Colombo bring rice from Burma and neighboring lands. Rice is the leading import, for the people of Ceylon do not raise enough to supply their needs. The next most valuable imports are mineral oils, chiefly from Burma, and cotton goods, which come largely from India.

Can you name these products? Name each agricultural product described below.

1. A plant fiber grown in India, used in factories in Bombay and Madras, and also exported in large quantities.

2. A plant fiber grown on the Ganges delta and used in many factories in Calcutta.

3. The leading crop grown for food by the people of India, Burma, and Ceylon.

4. A plantation product exported from both India and Ceylon, much of it going to England.

5. The important raw material for manufacturing exported from Ceylon.

3. BRITISH POSSESSIONS IN THE FAR EAST

When we speak of the "Far East," we mean China, Japan, and the neighboring countries of eastern Asia. Another name for the Far East is the Orient, which means simply "the East," and we often call the people of that part of the world Orientals.

The lands of the Far East are shown on the map on page 298. Turn to that map and find British Malaya (*B6*), the British lands in Borneo (*C6*), and the island of Hong Kong (*C4*). These are the British possessions in the Far East. As you study about each one, try to decide why it is of value to the British people.

British Malaya. British Malaya is in the southern part of the Malay Peninsula, which stretches southward from Burma. The interior of the country is mountainous, but along both coasts there are lowland plains. These plains are hot and rainy. They are used for raising rice, the principal food of the people, and for plantations of rubber, coconuts, pineapples, and other tropical products.

Rubber plantations. British Malaya produces about one half of all the world's rubber, and this important raw material is the most valuable export of the country. Most of the large plantations are owned by British and other European rubber companies, and altogether they cover hundreds of thousands of acres. More than two thirds of the plantation laborers are natives of India, and the rest are mostly Chinese and Malays.

On the plantations the rubber trees are set out in rows and carefully tended. Every other day, early in the morning, the laborers "tap" the trees by removing a thin shaving of the bark with a sharp knife. This starts the flow of the creamy-colored latex, which drips into small cups fastened to the trees. *See Figure 88.*

Later in the morning the laborers collect the latex in pails and carry it to the factories on the plantations. In the factories the latex is treated in such a way that it thickens. When it is thick enough, it is "milled," or pressed into long, narrow sheets, and the sheets are hung up to dry. When they are dry enough, they are packed in boxes or bales and sent to Singapore for export. About half the rubber goes to the United States, and the rest mostly to Europe. From some of the plantations liquid latex is sent to Singapore, and tank steamers carry it to the United States.

Tin-mining. British Malaya is also the leading country in the production of tin, providing about one third of the world's supply. The tin ore is found near the surface of the ground, mixed with clay, sand, and gravel. At some of the mines the workmen use huge hose to loosen the ore-bearing earth and to wash it into troughs where the ore is separated from the worthless rock material. At others great dredges which are run by electric power are used instead of hose.

From the mines the tin ores are sent to smelting plants at Singapore and on the island of Penang, and nearly all the tin from the smelters is exported. Much of it goes to the United States, and much to the southern part of Wales. Can you explain why?

Courtesy of Canadian Pacific Steamships

Figure 88. A tapped rubber tree on a plantation in British Malaya. The latex flows into a little metal trough and then drips into the cup below.

James Sawders

Figure 89. A glimpse of the water front at Singapore. The boats with the arched coverings of straw matting are called sampans. Hundreds of them are used at Singapore to transfer goods from one ship to another and to carry goods back and forth between ships anchored in the harbor and warehouses on the shore.

Singapore. On the map on page 298 find the city of Singapore (*B6*) at the southern entrance to the Strait of Malacca. Singapore is called the "Gateway to the Orient," and it is one of the greatest seaports and trading centers of the world. Can you suggest any reasons for its growth?

Turn to the map on pages 338–339, and you will see that all ships using the shortest route between ports of Europe or India and ports on the eastern coast of Asia must swing around the southern end of the Malay Peninsula. You will also see that the southern entrance to the Strait of Malacca is the meeting place for ships on this great trade route.

Singapore is located on a little island of the same name. In 1819, when the British gained possession of the island, it had only a few hundred people. Today the seaport alone has more than half a million people.

It is the location of Singapore which accounts for its wonderful growth. Into its harbor come ships from all over the world, and many of them exchange cargoes there. Others bring goods to be distributed from Singapore to neighboring parts of Asia and the East Indies, and carry away rubber, tin, and other products of Malaya and the neighboring lands. *See Figure 89.*

After the First World War the British made Singapore a strong naval and air base, and it became one of the stopping places on the airway that links England with India and Australia. For these reasons and because of its great trade, Singapore is one of the most valuable outposts of the British Empire.

Figure 90. A street in Hong Kong. Notice the Chinese rickshaw at the left, the Chinese coolies carrying burdens hung from yokes on their shoulders, and the Chinese signs outside the shops.

British lands in Borneo. The large island of Borneo is one of the East Indies. The greater part of it belongs to the Netherlands, but Great Britain controls three sections in the northwest which together are half again as large as England. Most of the population is made up of natives and of people from other Far Eastern lands, and they get their living by raising various tropical products.

The British have established rubber plantations in their part of the island, and rubber is one of the leading exports. In the sections known as Sarawak and Brunei there are rich oil fields, and from the refineries in these fields mineral oils are exported. Most of the trade of the British part of Borneo is carried on through the great seaports of Singapore and Hong Kong.

Hong Kong. The small island of Hong Kong, off the south coast of China, was ceded, or transferred, to Great Britain by the Chinese in 1841. The island is separated from the mainland by a narrow strait, and a small part of the mainland has been leased to the British. The harbor is between the island and the mainland, and there are docks for ships on both sides.

Hong Kong, like Singapore, is a great seaport and trading center where ships from all parts of the world stop and exchange cargoes. It is also one of the chief gateways through which the exports of China are shipped to distant lands. The population of the city is chiefly Chinese, but the British control the government. Many wealthy Chinese merchants have their headquarters in Hong Kong, where they are under British protection. *See Figure 90.*

British islands in the South Pacific Ocean. Among the large number of small tropical islands in the South Pacific Ocean there are many which have come in one way or another to belong to the British. Find these British islands on the map on pages 42–43. Some of them are low islands of coral rock, and others are the tops of volcanic mountains which rise high above the sea. The higher islands have heavy rainfall because the winds that strike them rise, become chilled, and give up their moisture. The mountain slopes of these islands are densely forested, and the coastal lowlands are fringed with coconut palms.

The native people of these islands find life very easy. They need but little clothing, and small huts thatched with palm leaves provide them with shelter from the sun and rain. Coconut trees, banana plants, and breadfruit trees furnish much of their food, and the rest comes largely from the sea, for the natives are skillful fishermen.

It is because these islands can be used as fueling and repair stations for British ships, as radio and cable stations, and, in time of war, as naval and air bases that the British care to hold them.

Testing yourself. Each of the cities listed below this exercise belongs to one of the following phrases. Write the names in their correct order.

1. The largest city of India and the world's greatest jute-manufacturing center.
2. The center of the Hindu religion.
3. The capital of the Dominion of India.
4. India's leading cotton-manufacturing city.
5. The capital and largest city of Palestine.
6. The seaport of Ceylon.
7. The great seaport of British Malaya, called the "Gateway to the Orient."
8. A British port in southwestern Arabia.
9. The gateway for the Indus Valley and the capital of the Dominion of Pakistan.
10. The seaport of Burma.
11. The seaport of southeastern India.
12. The city in India where the Taj Mahal is located.

Aden	Calcutta	Madras
Agra	Colombo	New Delhi
Benares	Jerusalem	Rangoon
Bombay	Karachi	Singapore

Can you name these places? You have learned that the British hold several important places which give them control of the great shipping route from western Europe to eastern Asia. Name the place which guards

1. The western gateway to the Mediterranean.
2. The narrowest part of the Mediterranean.
3. The northern entrance to the Suez Canal.
4. The southern entrance to the Red Sea.
5. The southern entrance to Malacca Strait.

Making choices. Choose the correct ending for each of the following sentences:

1. The chief food crop of India is

millet.   sugar cane.   rice.   wheat.

2. The most important raw material for manufacturing produced in India is

rubber.   hides and skins.   wool.   cotton.

3. The most important raw material for manufacturing produced in British Malaya and Ceylon is

jute.   cotton.   rubber.   wool.

4. British Malaya produces about one third of the world's supply of

manganese.   copper.   iron.   tin.

5. The most valuable export of Ceylon is

tea.   coconuts.   sugar.   rice.

6. Valuable supplies of petroleum are obtained from oil fields in

British Malaya.   Burma.   Ceylon.

7. The exports of India are chiefly products of

mining.   farming.   lumbering.   fishing.

8. The imports of India are largely

manufactures.   foodstuffs.   raw materials.

9. The leading exports from India to Great Britain are

cotton and rice.   tea and raw jute.   sugar and coconuts.

10. The United States is India's best customer for

raw jute and tea.   cotton and wheat.   burlap.

Sentences to complete. Complete each sentence below correctly:

1. The highest mountains in the world are the ---------.
2. The winds which bring rain to India are the ------ --------.
3. The plateau of India is called the ------.
4. The eastern and western margins of the plateau are called the ------.
5. The sacred river of the Hindus is the ------.
6. The beautiful building at Agra is the ------ ------.
7. The island off the south coast of China which belongs to the British is ---- ----.
8. The island southeast of India which is a self-governing dominion is ------.

Some things to explain. Explain what the British have done in India to (1) help the farmers; (2) provide better means of transportation; (3) educate the people; (4) prevent famines.

Special credit work. Try to find a book which describes the Taj Mahal and tells about its history. Report to your class on this subject.

AUSTRALIA
AND
NEIGHBORING ISLANDS

Scale of miles

0   200   400   600   800

Water less than 500 ft. deep

Floating ice

Wet-weather streams

Grasslands and cultivated areas

Temperate forests

Tropical forests

Semideserts, deserts, and
barren mountain slopes

Great Barrier Reef

V. THE COMMONWEALTH OF AUSTRALIA

Foreword. After our visits to the British lands in Asia, where we saw so many dark-skinned people and heard so many strange languages, Australia will seem almost like home. Nearly all the Australians are people of British descent, and so they speak the English language. They have adopted a "White Australia policy," which means that they have laws which make it almost impossible for people of the darker-skinned races to settle in their country. They want only white people, and they prefer British settlers to all others.

Turn to pages 330–331 and compare Australia and the United States in size and population. Notice that while Australia is almost as large as our country, it has only about one twentieth as many people. In fact, the number of people in the entire continent is considerably smaller than the number living in New York City.

Below are some questions for which you will want to find answers as you study about Australia. Read them through, and then make a list of any other questions about the island continent that you would like to have answered.

1. How does Australia happen to be part of the British Empire?

2. What is there about Australia that has led many people from the British Isles to settle there?

3. What natural resources has Australia, and how are the people developing them?

4. What problems must the Australians solve in developing their country?

5. Why is the population of Australia so much smaller than the population of the United States?

Map work. Begin your study of Australia by working out the map studies in Group I on page 97.

1. DISCOVERY AND SETTLEMENT OF AUSTRALIA

Turn to the map on pages 334–335 and tell what European explorers visited Australia about the time when the first settlements were being made on the eastern coast of our country. What parts of the coast of Australia did they see? Which coast of Australia was visited much later by an Englishman? Do you know why the Dutch made no settlements in Australia, and why the British, who came much later, now hold the entire continent?

Dutch explorations. As it happened, the Dutch discoverers of Australia saw some of the least attractive parts of the continent, for the northern coast is a moist, tropical land, and the parts of the western and southern coasts which they saw are very dry. When they learned that there were no silks, spices, or precious stones to be had in Australia, they went away disappointed, and they lost interest in this new-found land. More than a hundred years passed before any of the people of Europe attempted to learn more about this southern continent.

The first settlements. Captain James Cook, a famous British explorer, visited the southeastern part of the coast of Australia in 1770 during a journey around the world. That part of the coast has a mild climate with abundant rainfall, and is attractive to white people. Captain Cook took possession of the entire eastern coast in the name of the British king; and when he returned to England, he made such a favorable report concerning it that the British decided to send settlers to Australia.

The first settlement was made in 1788, on the shore of the large natural harbor where Sydney is now located. Within a few years other settlements were made on the eastern and southeastern coasts of Australia. Find Sydney on the map on page 96 (*F5*) and then turn over to page 98 and study Figure 93.

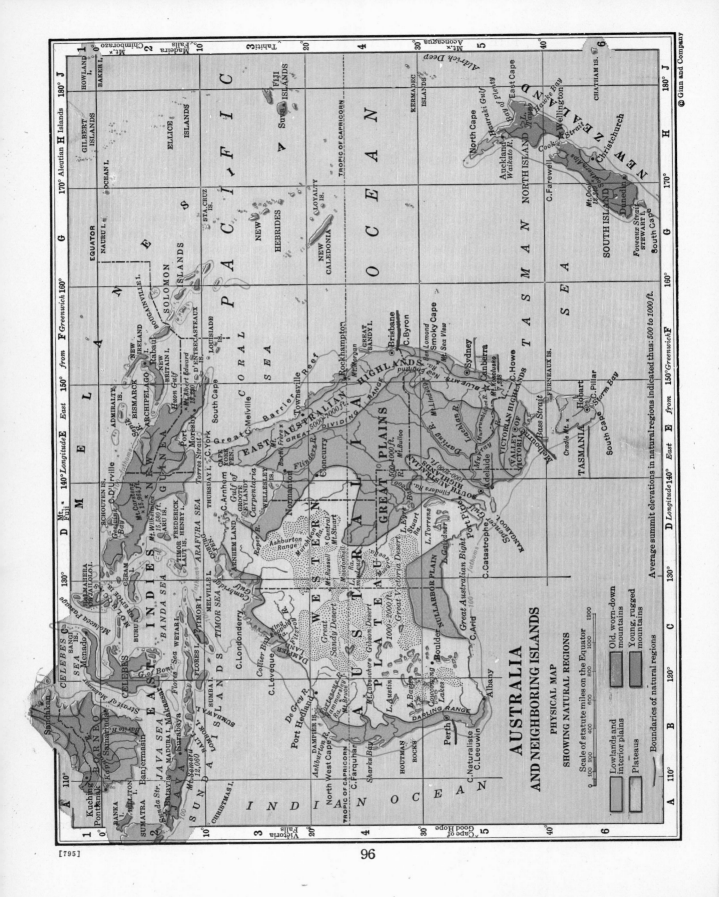

AUSTRALIA
AND NEIGHBORING ISLANDS
PHYSICAL MAP
SHOWING NATURAL REGIONS

Scale of statute miles on the Equator

Average summit elevations in natural regions indicated thus: 500 to 1000 ft.

Lowlands and interior plains

Plateaus

Old, worn-down mountains

Young, rugged mountains

Boundaries of natural regions

© Ginn and Company

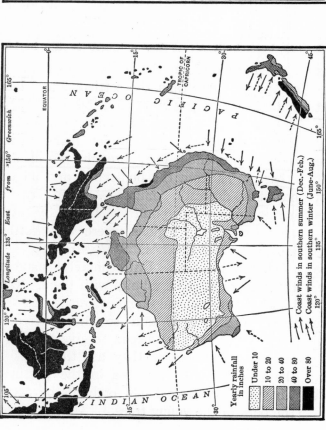

Figure 91. Distribution of rainfall in Australia.

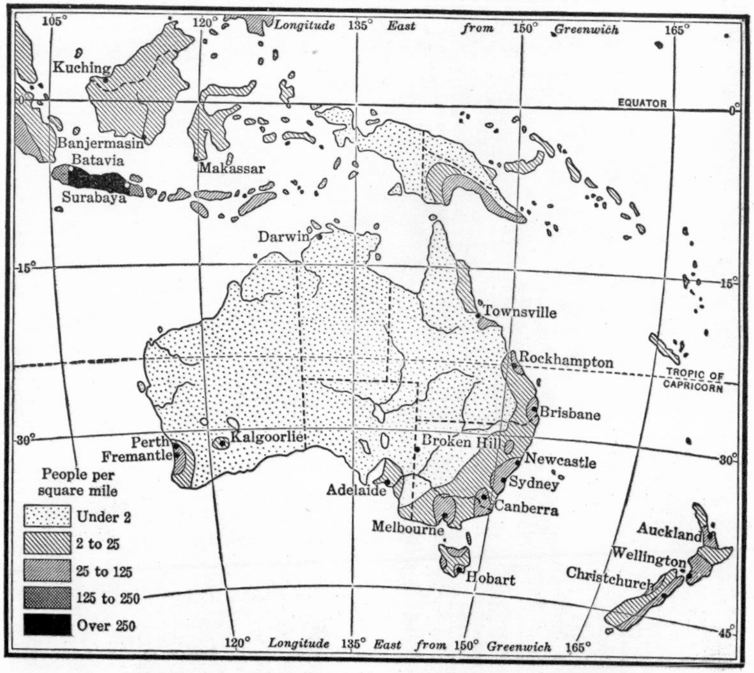

Figure 92. Distribution of people in Australia.

MAP STUDIES

Group I

1. What part of Australia is in the tropics? 2. What part is in the south temperate zone? 3. Where in Australia do you find the highest mountains? 4. What kind of mountains are they? 5. What mountains in the United States are of the same kind? 6. Find Mount Kosciusko, the highest peak in Australia (E5). How high is it?

7. What does Figure 91 show about the rainfall along the eastern coast of Australia? 8. What region lies west of the eastern highlands? 9. How does the rainfall of that region compare with the rainfall along the eastern coast? 10. What reason can you suggest for the difference? 11. What do you think is probably the most difficult problem which the farmers of the Great Plains of Australia have to solve?

12. Find the Murray and Darling rivers (E5). 13. These two rivers and their tributaries form the only great river system of Australia. What use do you think the people probably make of them? 14. What region lies west of the Great Plains? 15. What can you tell about that region by comparing the physical map with the rainfall map?

Group II

1. What does Figure 92 show about the number of people in the greater part of Australia? 2. What parts of the continent are most densely populated? 3. Do most of the people live north of the tropic of Capricorn or south of it? What reason can you give for this fact?

Group III

1. What parts of Australia have over 40 inches of rain a year? 2. What parts of the coast have less than 20 inches? 3. About how much of Australia should you say has too little rain for agriculture without irrigation?

Photograph from Wide World Photos, Inc.

Figure 93. An airplane view of the harbor of Sydney showing some of the piers and docks for ships. The harbor is large and very deep, and is well protected from stormy winds and waves, for it is nearly surrounded by hilly land. Notice the large bridge that has been built across the entrance to the harbor.

The native people. The British settlers found themselves in an almost empty continent. The few natives were black-skinned people who lived chiefly by hunting and by digging up the roots of plants which they could eat. There are still some of these "blackfellows," as the British call them, left in Australia, but they live in the interior of the continent and are never seen by visitors to the coastal cities. *See Figure 94.*

The native plants and animals. The British also found themselves in a land of strange plants and animals. There, for the first time, they saw tree ferns and forests of tall eucalyptus trees such as are shown in Figure 95. There too they discovered the animals that are known as "marsupials," which carry their young in pocketlike pouches on the under side of the body. The kangaroo is the marsupial which we know best.

Changes made by the settlers. In the eastern part of Australia the settlers found land suitable for raising crops and live stock; and as time went on, more and more people came from Great Britain to make new homes in the island continent. They brought wheat and other grains from the homeland, and all the common domestic animals — sheep, cattle, horses, pigs, and poultry. Little by little they turned the regions where they settled into farms and ranches. *See Figure 96.*

The rabbit pest. Unfortunately, some of the settlers brought rabbits with them. Rabbits have no natural enemies among the animals of Australia, and so they increased very fast. Soon they began to give the farmers great trouble, for they ate the crops in the fields and the grasses in the pastures. They even destroyed new orchards by eating the bark of the young trees.

Keystone View Company

Figure 94. Australian " blackfellows " hunting kangaroos with their spears. The man at the right in the picture has a young kangaroo slung over his shoulder.

Keystone View Company

Figure 95. A forest of tree ferns and eucalyptus in Australia. Nowhere else in the world do ferns grow so large and tall as they do in the island continent.

The people of Australia have tried all kinds of ways to get rid of the rabbits, but they are still a great pest. Many of the farmers and stockmen have built wire fences all around their fields and pastures to keep the rabbits out, and many employ "rabbiters" to shoot, poison, and trap these destructive little animals.

The discovery of gold. In 1851 gold was discovered in eastern Australia. This led to a series of "gold rushes," and during the next ten years more than half a million men hurried to Australia, hoping to make their fortunes in the gold fields. Although millions of dollars' worth of gold were obtained within a few years, many of the gold-seekers had no success. In time they gave up the search, and many, instead of going home, remained in Australia to become farmers or to raise live

stock. Thus the discovery of gold helped greatly to increase the population of Australia.

The growth of the early settlements. The early settlements in Australia were along the coast, and the first towns grew up where there were good harbors. The most important of these towns were Sydney, Melbourne, Adelaide, Brisbane, and Perth. Today these are the largest cities of Australia, and each one is the capital of an Australian state. Find each one of them on the map on page 105 and name the state of which it is the capital. Find also the Northern Territory, the island of Tasmania, and Papua, in the island of New Guinea. Tasmania is a state of Australia, and Papua is a territory. Before the First World War the part of New Guinea north of the territory of Papua, with the neighboring islands of the Bismarck Archipelago, belonged to Germany.

Figure 96. A flock of sheep on a ranch in the state of South Australia. The ancestors of the best Australian sheep were brought from England in 1797. How long ago was that? The Australian ranches are very large, and on some of them there are more than 100,000 sheep. For what three different purposes are sheep raised?

Courtesy of Intelligence and Tourist Bureau, Adelaide, South Australia

After that war the Australians were given charge of the government of these lands.

The formation of the commonwealth. The states of Australia were for many years separate British colonies. But as time went on, the people felt that a central government would be of great benefit to all, and in 1901 the Commonwealth of Australia was formed, including the entire continent and the island of Tasmania. As you know, the commonwealth is a self-governing British dominion.

The capital city. When the commonwealth was formed, Sydney and Melbourne, the two largest cities, both wished to be the capital of the country. To settle the question, a beautiful location in the mountains between Sydney and Melbourne was chosen for the capital and named Canberra. There was no settlement there, and so a whole new city was laid out. Canberra is a very beautiful city with broad streets and many fine buildings. Among the government buildings is the Parliament House, which you see in Figure 97.

Giving explanations. Give an explanation for each of the following statements:

1. The Dutch were the discoverers of Australia, but the British were the first to settle there.

2. The first settlements in Australia were along the eastern and southeastern coasts.

3. The British settlers made better use of the land than the natives had ever made.

4. The population of Australia increased very fast in the ten years following 1851.

Something to do. Turn to page 336 and make a list of the five largest cities of Australia with their populations. Add the populations, and then make a statement telling about what proportion of the people of Australia live in the five largest cities.

in 125

2. CLIMATE AND DISTRIBUTION OF PEOPLE

There is no land in the world where the climate has more to do with the distribution of people than it has in Australia. Do you know why? Begin your study of this problem by working out the map studies in Group II on page 97.

After your study of the map the following statements will not surprise you:

1. More than nine tenths of all the people of Australia live south of the tropic of Capricorn.

2. Four fifths of all the people live within 100 miles of the sea on the eastern, southeastern, and southwestern coasts.

Keep these facts in mind as you read this section, and be on the watch for reasons to explain them.

The tropical north and the temperate south. You have learned from the maps that the northern part of Australia is in the tropics, while the southern part is in the south temperate zone. Because of this the lowlands at the north are hot lands, while those at the south are much cooler and have frosts during four or five months of the year.

Seasonal temperatures. During January, which is the warmest month in the Southern Hemisphere, the average temperature of most of Australia is over 80°, and in places it is over 90°. Along the southern border it drops to 70°, and in the island of Tasmania to 62°.

In July, the coldest month, the temperature is about 70° along the northern margin of the continent, about 50° along the southern margin, and about 40° in Tasmania. In the south, where frosts occur, the winter temperatures drop at times to 32° or less.

The summer and winter temperatures in southern Australia show that the temperate part of the continent has no great extremes of heat or cold. The winters are much milder

Commonwealth Government Photo

Figure 97. The Parliament House in Canberra. Here representatives from the Australian states meet to carry on the government of the country just as our Congress meets in the Capitol at Washington.

there than in the Northern states of our country, and snow seldom falls except in the highest parts of the mountains. The summers are warm, but the weather is seldom uncomfortably hot.

Explain now why most of the people of Australia live in the southern part of the continent. Remember the race to which nearly all the people belong.

Differences in rainfall. Turn to page 97 and work out the map studies in Group III. These will show you that Australia is a land with great differences in rainfall.

Why the interior of Australia has little rain. The map shows that about two thirds of Australia has less than 20 inches of rain. Winds from the ocean bring rain to certain parts of the coast; but since they give up most of their moisture there, the interior of the continent is dry.

The arid Western Plateau. Most of the great desert of Australia is in the Western Plateau. Vast stretches of this region are sandy deserts, and most of the remainder has no vegetation except the poorest of desert shrubs. People cannot live in the desert sections unless they get everything they need from outside, and so there are hundreds of square miles of the plateau without a single inhabitant. In places there are mountains rising above the surface of the plateau. They cause the winds to give up enough moisture so that on their windward sides (the sides toward the wind) there is enough vegetation for a few people to make a living by raising sheep.

Toward the north in the plateau, where there is more rain, there are savannas suitable for raising cattle, but few settlers have chosen to live there. Explain why.

Some arid coast lands. The very dry part of Australia extends to the central part of the western coast, and to the shore of the Great Australian Bight (or Bay) on the south. Therefore these coast lands are almost as thinly populated as the dry interior.

The monsoon rains. The extreme northern part of Australia is a monsoon land, and the heavy rains there are brought by monsoon winds. You will remember that the monsoon winds which bring rain to India blow from the southwest during the northern summer, when the interior of Asia is very warm. The monsoons that bring rain to northern Australia blow from the northwest during the southern summer, when the interior of Australia is very warm. They bring much rain to the northern coast because they come from the ocean.

Turn to Figure 91 on page 97 and find the arrows that stand for the wet monsoons of northern Australia. Find also the arrows that show the direction of the winds in northern Australia during the southern winter. Notice that these are winds from the southeast. Since they blow outward from Australia, they are dry monsoons, and so, during the winter, northern Australia has little rain.

After your visit to India, with its millions of people, you might well expect the monsoon region of Australia to be densely populated. But, as Figure 92 (p. 97) shows, it is one of the very thinly populated parts of the continent. That is because nearly all the people of Australia belong to the white race, and white people find it very hard to do out-of-door work such as farming in the heat of the monsoon climate. So long as the Australians refuse to allow people of the darker-skinned races to settle in their country, the monsoon region will remain thinly populated.

Rain from the southeast trades. The abundant rain on the eastern coast of Australia is brought chiefly by the southeast trade winds, which come from the Pacific Ocean. As they reach the land and are forced to rise they give up much moisture on the seaward side of the eastern highlands. They blow steadily throughout the year, and so the eastern coast has rain at all seasons, and is well suited to farming. For this reason it is one of the most densely settled parts of the continent.

Rain from the westerlies. The southwestern corner of Australia and the southern coast between Adelaide and Melbourne are regions of winter rain and summer drought. Like the southwestern corner of Africa, they extend far enough south to have the westerly winds in the southern winter, when all the wind belts migrate northward. The westerlies, coming from the Indian Ocean, bring rain.

The first rains usually come in May and the last in October, but July is the rainiest month. In the summer the winds that blow over these two regions come from the land and bring little moisture. Thus the six months beginning with November and ending with April are very dry.

Tasmania is far enough south to have winds from the west throughout the year, and so it has rain at all seasons.

Like the temperate section of the eastern coast, the coastal regions which have rain from the westerlies are densely populated, for the climate is healthful for white people and the moisture is sufficient for farming.

Commonwealth Government Photo

Figure 98. An Australian farmer harvesting wheat. "Wheat work" in Australia is done with machinery just as it is in our own wheat lands. Australian wheat is winter wheat, planted in the autumn and harvested in the late spring or early summer. What are the autumn months in Australia? the spring months?

Something to prove. Prove that you understand the climate of Australia and its effect on the distribution of population by completing each sentence below correctly:

1. Temperatures grow cooler from north to south in Australia because _____.

2. The extreme northern part of Australia has heavy rain in the southern summer because ___ _____.

3. The monsoon region of Australia is thinly populated because _____.

4. The eastern coast of Australia has rain at all seasons because _____.

5. Tasmania has rain at all seasons because _____.

6. Southwestern Australia and the southern coast between Adelaide and Melbourne have winter rains and summer drought because ____ _____.

7. The eastern, southeastern, and southwestern coasts of Australia are the most densely populated parts of the continent because _____ _____.

8. The interior of the continent is very dry because _____.

9. Very few people live in the interior because _____.

3. WORK IN THE WELL-POPULATED REGIONS

Before you read this section, turn to the map on page 105 and find the parts of Australia where you might expect to see the people doing the following kinds of work:

raising wheat	raising sugar cane
growing fruit	mining metal ores
mining coal	raising live stock

Judging from the map, what regions of Australia do you think provide the most products for export to distant lands?

 Southwestern Australia

The southwestern corner of the continent. The winter rains from the westerly winds save the southwestern corner of Australia from being a desert, and make it possible for many people to live there. The well-watered region includes the narrow coastal lowland and the bordering part of the plateau.

How work varies with rainfall. The rainfall in southwestern Australia is heaviest along the coast and grows less and less farther inland. Thus there are distinct rainfall belts crossing

Courtesy of Tourist and Publicity Bureau, Perth, Western Australia

Figure 99. A view of one of the gold mines at Kalgoorlie, in Western Australia. Kalgoorlie is a town of about 5000 people, and its prosperity depends wholly on gold-mining. Why is there no farming or sheep-raising in this part of Australia?

this region, which have much to do with the work of the people.

In the coastal belt, where the rainfall is over 30 inches, there are valuable forests of hardwood trees. On the cleared lands the people carry on mixed farming and dairying. On the hillsides they have planted orchards and vineyards, and fruit is exported.

Farther inland, where the rainfall is from 15 to 25 inches, there is a winter-wheat belt; and still farther inland, where the land is too dry for wheat, there is a sheep-raising belt. Then comes the desert, which is too dry even for grazing. See Figure 98.

Perth and its seaport. The largest city and principal business center of southwestern Australia is Perth, which is twelve miles from the coast. This city is the western terminus of the only transcontinental railroad in Australia. Find the railroad on the map on page 105.

The seaport of Perth is Fremantle. Because of its location on the west coast of Australia, Fremantle is the first port of call for steamers from England. Find this sea-

port on the map on page 105 (B5) and name its leading exports.

Gold-mining centers. The map shows that gold is one of the leading exports from Perth. Turn to the map on page 105 and find the places where the gold comes from. The gold-mining centers are the only towns of any importance in the great Western Plateau. See Figure 99.

At Kalgoorlie and the other gold-mining towns the greatest problem is to obtain food and water for the people. The region is much too dry for farming, and there are no streams to provide water for drinking or irrigation. When the mines were first opened, camels were used to bring supplies from the coast and to carry back the gold, but railroads have now been built. Water for the people of Kalgoorlie is pumped through pipes from a reservoir near Perth, nearly 400 miles away.

The Eastern Coastal Lowlands

The eastern coast of Australia. On the map on page 96 find the two lowland belts on the eastern coast of Australia. Which one is a tropical lowland? Which is a temperate lowland? Along the remainder of the coast the mountains come so close to the sea that the coastal lowlands are too narrow to be shown on the map. What have you learned about the rainfall on this coast? What kinds of work do you think are important here?

A mixed-farming region. The temperate coastal lowland of New South Wales is one of the best mixed-farming regions of Australia. As we travel through it, we shall see fields of corn, hay, alfalfa, and vegetables, and many herds of dairy cows. The region is especially well suited to dairying because the

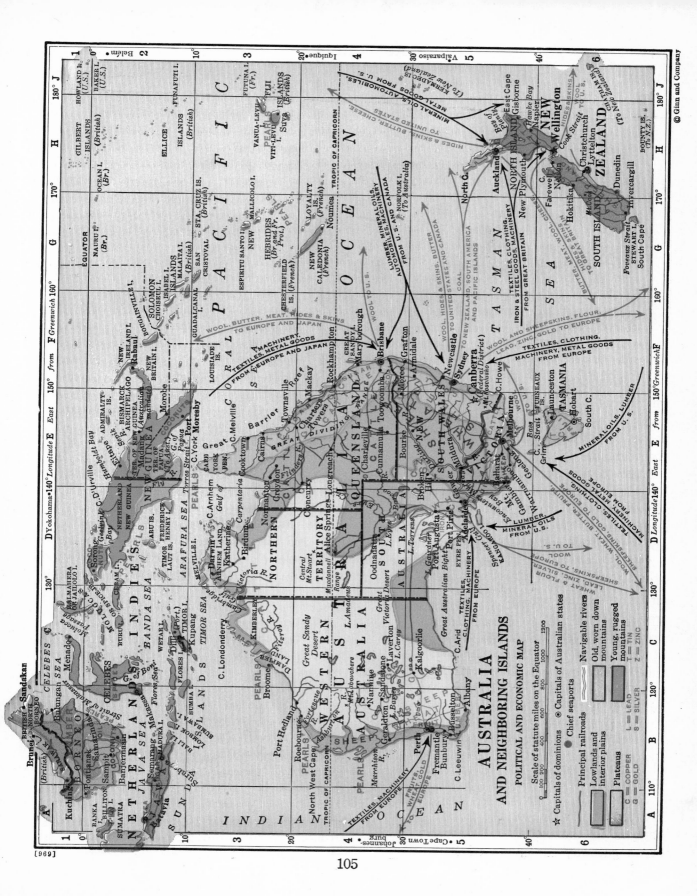

AUSTRALIA
AND NEIGHBORING ISLANDS
POLITICAL AND ECONOMIC MAP

© Ginn and Company

Courtesy of Commissioner for Australia, N.Y.

Figure 100. A dairy farm near the coast in New South Wales. Notice the farmer's house and farm buildings. Why does he not have a silo, as most dairy farmers in our country do?

mild climate allows the cows to graze out of doors at all seasons, and the abundant rain keeps the pasturage fresh and green throughout the year. *See Figure 100.*

In this region we shall also see many orchards of apples, peaches, plums, and pears, and other temperate-zone fruits, and many groves of orange trees. What do the orange trees tell about the danger of frost in the lowland?

The largest city of Australia. On the coast of the temperate lowland is Sydney, the largest city and leading seaport of Australia. Sydney has over a million people, and is one of the great cities of the world. Only two cities in the British Empire — London and Calcutta — are larger. Find Sydney on the map on page 105 (*F5*) and notice that it is the center of the railroad system of New South Wales. What reasons can you suggest for its growth?

Sydney has become a great port because it has one of the finest harbors in the world and is an ocean gateway for much of the richest and most densely populated part of Australia. To its wharves come ships from all over the world, bringing goods to be distributed by rail to all parts of New South Wales and to other states of Australia. When the ships sail away, they carry Australian products which have come to Sydney for export. Name the leading exports by using the map on page 105.

On the hilly shores overlooking the harbor of Sydney you will see many fine houses and many attractive bungalows surrounded by beautiful gardens, and in the business section you will find office buildings, banks, and stores much like those in our own cities. Along the water front, near the wharves and docks, you will find large warehouses, and huge grain elevators where millions of bushels of wheat are stored, waiting to be shipped away. Here too you will see shipyards, flour mills, and many other kinds of manufacturing plants.

Coal and manufacturing. On the map on page 105 find the coal field near Sydney and Newcastle (*F5*). The coal mined there is good for making coke as well as steam power, and it

Commonwealth Government Photo

Figure 101. Part of the iron-and-steel plant at Newcastle. The blast furnaces here produce large quantities of pig iron, which is used in the manufacture of steel for many different purposes.

Courtesy of Commissioner for Australia, N.Y.

Figure 102. A farmer in Queensland gathering pineapples. Where in South Africa did you see pineapple plantations? What likeness is there between that part of South Africa and this part of Australia?

Commonwealth Government Photo

Figure 103. A fruit-grower in Victoria starting for market with a load of pears from his orchard. What season of the year was it in the Northern Hemisphere when this Australian picture was taken?

has helped to make both cities important manufacturing centers. At Newcastle and other places in the district there are iron-and-steel plants which get their iron ore from mines in the state of South Australia. Iron and steel from these plants are used in railroad repair shops, machine shops, automobile-body factories, shipyards, and other manufacturing plants which turn out iron and steel products. *See Figure 101.*

A tropical farming region. On the tropical coastal lowland of Queensland there are sugar plantations which supply the sugar needed by the people of Australia, and also a surplus for export. The people of this region also raise corn, rice, and many tropical fruits such as pineapples and bananas. *See Figure 102.*

This hot, moist lowland is suitable for all kinds of tropical crops, for which there is a good market in temperate Australia. Land is cheaper here than farther south, yet the region is much less densely populated than the coastal lowland of New South Wales. Can you explain why?

The capital of Queensland. On the map on page 105 find Brisbane, the capital and largest city of Queensland (*F 4*). Notice that it is near the southern boundary of Queensland and is the chief seaport and railroad center of that state. Why do you think the largest city of Queensland has grown up here rather than farther north on the coast? Judging from the exports of Brisbane, what do you think is the most important kind of work in southern Queensland?

Along the water front at Brisbane you could visit meat-packing plants, and in a neighboring town you could visit woolen mills. These manufacturing plants should make you feel still more sure that your answer to the question in the last paragraph was correct. Explain why.

The Valley of Victoria. On the map on page 96 find the Valley of Victoria, in which the great city of Melbourne is located (*E 5*). This valley has a mild, pleasant climate with sufficient rain for farming and is one of the more densely populated regions of Australia. The eastern part is chiefly a dairying section,

Commonwealth Government Photo

Figure 104. A busy street in Melbourne. The large building at the right is a railroad station, and the tracks come into it from the left, under the street. Beyond is the river that flows into the bay, and in the distance at the right is a manufacturing district.

and railroad locomotives and cars. Can you explain why these industries have grown up in Melbourne?

A travel test. 1. If you were to travel from Perth to Kalgoorlie on the train, you would cross the rainfall belts of southwestern Australia which so largely determine the work of the people. Arrange the phrases below in the order in which you would see the things they describe.

> wheat farms
> sheep ranches
> useless desert lands
> gold-mining centers
> dairy farms and fruit orchards

2. Give reasons why the people of each belt carry on the kind of work which you have observed there.

while the western part is used more largely for raising beef cattle and sheep. Large quantities of wheat and fruit also are raised in the western section. *See Figure 103.*

Judging from the work of the people in the Valley of Victoria, what do you expect the leading exports of Melbourne to be? Check your answer by the map on page 105.

The capital of Victoria. Melbourne is the second largest city of Australia, and has about a million people. The map shows that it is located at the inner end of a large bay which extends far into the Valley of Victoria, and that it is the center of the railroad system of the state. Thus it is the ocean gateway not only for the valley but also for the southern part of the Great Plains, beyond the Victorian Highlands. *See Figure 104.*

Melbourne, like Sydney, is a manufacturing center. Among its manufactures are mining machinery, farming tools and machinery,

Some things to explain. Give an explanation for the fact that

1. More immigrants, or new settlers, in Australia choose to live in the coastal lowland of New South Wales and the Valley of Victoria than in the coastal lowland of Queensland.

2. The Valley of Victoria and the coastal lowland of New South Wales can support large numbers of people.

3. The state of Queensland supplies the sugar used by the Australians.

4. Brisbane, Sydney, and Melbourne are railroad centers.

5. Sydney is better located than Brisbane or Melbourne to serve as an ocean gateway for all parts of the more densely settled section of eastern Australia.

6. Sydney has become a leading manufacturing center in Australia.

7. The agricultural products of southwestern Australia are like those of the southwestern part of the Union of South Africa.

James Sawders

Figure 105. Australian lumbermen cutting down a giant tree. Notice the size of the trunk compared with the men.

Philip D. Gendreau, N.Y.

Figure 106. Hauling logs from the forest to a sawmill in Victoria. It takes several pairs of horses or oxen to pull a load of a few large logs over the rough roads in the forested highlands.

The Highlands of Eastern Australia

A mountain barrier. Like the Appalachian Highlands of our country, the East Australian Highlands and the Victorian Highlands form a barrier between the coast lands and the plains farther inland. It was some time before the early settlers found routes across the mountains to the interior of the continent, and much longer before railroads were built. Today railroads run from the seaports through the mountains to towns in the Great Plains.

Rainfall and forests. Since the seaward slopes of the mountains have much rain, they are covered with forests, and lumbering is carried on in many places. Many of the lumbering camps are far from the railroads, and the heavy logs have to be taken to the sawmills by ox-teams. Pines and other softwood trees grow in a few places in the highlands, but most of the forests are of hardwoods. For this reason Australia has to import softwood lumber from countries in the north temperate zone. *See Figures 105 and 106.*

Farming and stock-raising in the highlands. Between the ranges of the eastern highlands there are valleys and plateaus which provide fairly large stretches of level land and are used for farming. The principal crops that the farmers raise are the same as those we saw on the temperate coastal lowland,— grain, alfalfa, fruits, and vegetables. Dairying is very important, and the farmers send much butter to the coastal cities.

Many herds of beef cattle graze in the moister, eastern section of the mountains, providing large quantities of meat and hides for export. The drier parts are better for sheep than for cattle, and the thickest "sheep population" in Australia is on the western slopes of highlands in New South Wales and the northern slopes in Victoria.

Mineral wealth. It was the discovery of gold in the eastern highlands that led to the rapid increase in the population of Australia from 1851 to 1861. In places the ores have now given out, and today the greater part of the gold of the dominion comes from Western Australia. Nevertheless, gold is still a product of considerable importance in the eastern highlands. From the map on page 105 tell what other metal ores are mined there.

Courtesy of Commissioner for Australia, N.Y.

Figure 107. A portion of the famous silver-lead mines at Broken Hill in Australia. Find this mining center on the map on page 105 (*E5*). What other metals are found in the ores mined there?

The only mineral product of Australia that rivals gold in value is coal. Most of it comes from the field in New South Wales. This field contains more coal than any other field in the Southern Hemisphere. What do you find on the map on page 105 that shows that the Australians mine more coal than they need for their own use?

The South Australian Highlands. On the map on page 96 find the South Australian Highlands. Here, too, rich deposits of metal ores have been found. In the eastern part of the region is Broken Hill, where some of the richest silver-lead mines in the world are located. These mines have attracted so many people that Broken Hill has a population of more than 25,000. *See Figure 107.*

Farther south, near Spencer Gulf, there are copper mines, and at Iron Knob, on the opposite side of the gulf near Port Augusta, there is a whole hill of high-grade iron ore. The ore mined at Iron Knob is shipped to the coal field in New South Wales for smelting.

In the valleys among the South Australian Highlands the people raise sheep and carry on mixed farming. In the southern part of the region the people raise much wheat and fruit.

The capital of South Australia. The capital and largest city of South Australia is Adelaide. It is a very attractive city, located a few miles inland on a small river which empties into a large bay. An outer harbor, beyond the river mouth, makes Adelaide a seaport. Find this city on the map on page 105 (*D5*). How is its export trade connected with work in the South Australian Highlands?

Tasmania. The island state of Tasmania is part of the eastern highlands of Australia, separated from the mainland by Bass Strait. Therefore the surface is hilly and mountainous. In the western part of the island, which is the more rugged part, there are several important mining centers. Some of the mines produce tin, others produce copper and gold, and still others produce silver, lead, and zinc.

Courtesy of Commissioner for Australia, N.Y.

Figure 108. Apple orchards in a valley among the mountains of Tasmania. At what season of the year in the Northern Hemisphere do apples shipped from Tasmania reach the markets in England?

Photograph from Ewing Galloway, N. Y.

Figure 109. The zinc plant near Hobart, in Tasmania. This plant provides work for over 1000 men. It is located on the shore of the harbor of Hobart, and ships bring the zinc ores directly to its wharves from Adelaide. Find Hobart on the map on page 105 (*E 6*) and estimate the distance from there to Adelaide.

The "orchard state." You already know that Tasmania has plentiful rainfall from the westerly winds. As you would expect, most of the people live in the valleys, where the land is level enough for farming. Most of the farmers carry on mixed farming, and many raise apples as a special money crop.

So many apples are raised in Tasmania that it is often called the "orchard state" of Australia. Every autumn thousands of barrels of apples are shipped to England, where they bring a good price because they arrive at the season when the home supply of apples is low. All the fruit-growers of Australia enjoy this same advantage in sending fresh fruit to England. *See Figure 108.*

During the last few years the Australians have been using some of their fruit to make jams for export to England. This has proved to be a profitable business, for the British serve jams regularly at breakfast.

Hobart. Hobart, on the southeastern coast of Tasmania, is the capital, the largest city, and the chief seaport of the state. In one of the suburbs of Hobart is the zinc plant shown in Figure 109. This is one of the largest plants in the world for refining zinc by means of electricity. Most of the zinc refined here comes from Broken Hill, and the electricity comes from a great hydroelectric plant in the north-central part of Tasmania. Can you explain what advantages Tasmania has for the making of electricity through the use of water power?

Making choices. From the sentences given below select those that you think give the most important reasons why many people have settled in the mountains of eastern Australia.

1. The mountains have a rough surface.
2. They have plentiful rainfall.
3. They are a natural barrier.
4. The mountains have much mineral wealth.
5. They have large stretches of forests.
6. Their scenery is beautiful.
7. The mountains have many rivers.
8. They are near the seacoast.
9. They are well supplied with railroads.

Commonwealth Government Photo

Figure 110. Bales of wool ready to leave a sheep station by ox-cart for the nearest railroad point. The finest quality of wool comes from sheep known as Merinos, large numbers of which are raised in Australia.

Photograph from Ewing Galloway, N. Y.

Figure 111. Water coming from an artesian well 3500 feet deep, in the Great Plains of Australia.

4. THE GREAT PLAINS OF AUSTRALIA

Turn to the map on page 96 and study the location of the Great Plains of Australia. Notice that they lie between the eastern highlands and the interior desert. What does Figure 91 tell you about the rainfall in this region?

Like our own Great Plains, the Great Plains of Australia are grasslands with few trees except along the streams. What kinds of work do you expect to find the people doing?

Cattle pastures. The thinly settled savannas in the northern part of the Great Plains are used chiefly as pastures for beef cattle. Most of the cattle of Australia, however, are found in the well-watered eastern highlands and in the temperate coastal lowlands.

Sheep pastures. The northern part of the Great Plains is too warm for sheep, but farther south on the plains and on the bordering slopes of the eastern highlands more sheep are pastured than in any other area of equal size anywhere in the world.

Nearly all the sheep ranches, or sheep stations, as they are called in Australia, are found where the yearly rainfall is between 10 inches and 30 inches. Many of the larger stations cover as much as 150 square miles, and altogether there are in Australia more than 100,000,000 sheep. *See Figure 110.*

Problems of the sheep ranchers. There are no farmers or stockmen in the world who watch the weather more anxiously than the sheep ranchers of Australia. During a very dry year the grass withers, water is scarce, and the sheep die by thousands. Such conditions often mean ruin for many of the ranchmen. A year with good rainfall brings an abundance of grass and sufficient water, and these, in turn, mean prosperity for the ranchmen.

In the drier pasture lands the problem of getting enough water for the sheep is always serious. Fortunately, the ranchmen in most parts of the Great Plains can get water from beneath the ground by drilling deep wells. Some of the wells are *artesian wells*, which means that the water flows out of them without having to be pumped. Even the wells, however, sometimes fail to provide water in a very dry season. *See Figure 111.*

In the Great Plains the millions of rabbits give the ranchmen much trouble, for seven rabbits will eat as much grass as one sheep. The pastures have to be fenced with wire fine enough to keep the rabbits out, and the ranch-men employ men called "boundary riders" to keep the fences in good condition.

The importance of sheep-raising. Sheep-raising was one of the first kinds of work undertaken by the British settlers in Australia, and it is the leading industry of the commonwealth today. The sheep are raised for both wool and meat, but the wool is much the more important product. Australia is the leading wool-producing country of the world, and wool is by far its most valuable export.

Wheat lands. Among the farm products of Australia wheat is the most valuable export crop. The most important wheat lands are in the southern and southeastern parts of the Great Plains and on the lower slopes of the bordering mountains. The rainfall in these lands varies from 10 to 40 inches, and in the drier parts the farmers use dry-farming methods. When there is a little more rain than usual, the wheat farmers get larger crops; when there is less rain than usual, their crops are small. Thus their prosperity depends largely on the rainfall.

The Australian farmers do their plowing, planting, and harvesting with the best of modern machinery. They plant their seed in April and usually begin to harvest the grain late in December. Do they raise spring wheat or winter wheat?

About half the Australian wheat crop is used at home. The rest is exported, chiefly to Europe. Australia is one of the five leading wheat-exporting countries of the world. The others are Canada, Argentina, the United States, and the Soviet Union. *See Figure 112.*

Irrigated lands. On the map on page 96 find the plains along the lower course of the Murray River and its tributaries. These plains have less than 20 inches of rainfall. The better-watered portions are part of the "wheat belt" of southeastern Australia, but for most crops the rainfall is too light. For

Courtesy of Commissioner for Australia, N. Y.

Figure 112. Loading wheat at a railroad station in the Great Plains of Australia. From the map on page 105 name the two seaports which lead in the export of wheat from eastern Australia.

this reason large areas are irrigated. The water comes from artesian wells and from reservoirs made by damming the streams, and the irrigated lands are used chiefly for fruit-growing and dairying. New irrigation works are being built to make still greater use of the waters of the Murray-Darling system for farming.

Some things to explain. Explain why

1. Temperatures grow cooler from north to south in the Great Plains.

2. Rainfall grows less from east to west in the Great Plains.

3. The most important kind of work in the Great Plains is stock-raising.

4. More cattle than sheep are raised in the northern part of the Great Plains.

5. In the region as a whole, far more sheep than cattle are raised in the Great Plains.

6. Most of the sheep are found in the eastern and southeastern parts of the plains and on the bordering mountain slopes.

7. The wheat lands of the Great Plains are in the southern and southeastern parts of the region.

8. The prosperity of the sheep-raisers and the wheat farmers varies from year to year with the rainfall.

5. Manufacturing, Transportation, and Trade

Give what you think are the correct answers to the following questions, and check them as you read this section.

1. What advantages has Australia for the development of manufacturing?
2. What is the greatest handicap to transportation in Australia?
3. What kinds of work in Australia supply the leading exports?

The growth of manufacturing. Although Australia has coal and produces iron ore and other valuable raw materials, manufacturing has grown rather slowly. The iron-and-steel industry is increasing each year, but as yet it by no means supplies all the needs of the people for iron and steel products. For the most part the leading industries are those which prepare raw materials for home use and export, such as meat-packing, flour-milling, butter-making, and the refining of metal ores, and those which supply products which all the people of the country need, such as the making of clothing and shoes.

The greatest handicap to manufacturing is the small population of the country, for a small population means a small home market for all manufactured products except those which everyone uses. That explains, for example, why the Australians do not manufacture many kinds of heavy machinery. With its abundant coal and its iron ore and other raw materials Australia is well equipped to become a manufacturing country. But the growth of manufacturing will depend largely on the growth of the home markets, and therefore on the growth in population.

The railroads of Australia. You have discovered from the map that each of the more important states of Australia has a railroad system which centers in the capital city on the coast, and that a few railroads in the east extend across the highlands into the Great Plains. The interior of the continent has almost no railroads, and there is only one transcontinental line.

The transcontinental railroad connects the state railroads of South Australia with those of Western Australia, making it possible to travel all the way from Perth to cities on the eastern coast by train. This railroad, as you know, runs across the southern part of the desert of Australia, and there is a stretch of 1000 miles where it does not cross a single permanent stream. In this stretch the problem of getting water for the locomotives and passengers is very difficult.

Many years ago the Australians started to build a north-south transcontinental railroad through the heart of the continent between Port Augusta in South Australia and Darwin, the capital of Northern Territory. It was never finished because there seemed little chance that it would be much used. Recently its north and south sections have been linked by a highway.

A handicap to railroad transportation. Travel and transportation by train in Australia are slower than in Europe or the United States because the railroads of the different states do not use the same gauge. That means that the rails of the different lines are not the same distance apart. Some of the railroads have a narrow gauge of 3 feet, 6 inches; others a "standard gauge" of 4 feet, $8\frac{1}{2}$ inches, as we do in the United States; and still others a broad gauge of 5 feet, 3 inches.

These differences are unfortunate, for locomotives and cars built for one gauge cannot run on rails of another gauge. At the places where the gauge changes, passengers have to change cars, and freight must be transferred from the cars of one line to those of another.

Transportation by air. Australia is so large and so far away from Great Britain that the airways are very important in cutting down the time needed for travel and mail service.

Triangle Photo Service

Figure 113. A huge grain elevator at Sydney. Here millions of bushels of wheat from Australian farms are stored, waiting to be shipped to distant countries.

Australian Government Photograph

Figure 114. A ship from London being loaded with bales of wool at Brisbane. To what cities in England is the wool likely to be sent after it reaches London?

All the larger cities are connected by airlines, and from Darwin, in Northern Territory, there is air service to England. From Sydney an airway runs to the United States by way of New Zealand and Hawaii. *See map, p. 341.*

The trade of Australia. From the map on page 105 make a list of the leading exports of Australia. Which ones come from the ranches and farms? from the mines? Which are food-stuffs? Which are raw materials?

Wool, wheat, butter, meat, fruits, hides and skins, and other products of the ranches and farms are the most valuable exports, and gold, lead, zinc, and other products of the mines are next. These raw materials and foodstuffs go largely to Great Britain and other countries of western Europe. Japan is the next best customer for Australian products in normal times, and our own country takes some of the metals, wool, and skins.

Now study the imports of Australia. To what class of goods do most of them belong? What does our country send to Australia? What country of Asia supplies some of the Australian imports?

It is clear from the imports that the things that the Australians need most from distant lands are manufactured goods. They need also gasoline and other mineral oils, for as yet no petroleum has been discovered in this continent. Why do they need lumber?

Trade with the home country. You will probably not be surprised to learn that Great Britain takes about half of all the exports of Australia and supplies about two fifths of the imports. The home country finds in the commonwealth a very valuable source of raw materials for its factories and of foodstuffs for its people, and a good market for some of its manufactures. *See Figures 113 and 114.*

LANDS TO THE NORTH GOVERNED BY AUSTRALIA

New Guinea and the neighboring islands. On the map on page 105 find the part of New Guinea which is governed by the Australians. The Bismarck Archipelago and several other islands east of New Guinea are also under Australian control. Most of the people of these tropical lands are dark-skinned natives who live largely on bananas, coconuts, and other tropical fruits, and on vegetables which they raise in small gardens. There are also a few Europeans, who are interested in developing coconut plantations and rubber plantations.

Matching cities and states. Each place named in the left column below is the capital and largest city of one of the Australian states named in the right column. Match the cities with the states correctly.

Sydney	Western Australia
Melbourne	Queensland
Adelaide	Tasmania
Brisbane	New South Wales
Perth	Victoria
Hobart	South Australia

A selection test. Select the word or phrase which makes each statement below correct:

1. The two most important kinds of work in Australia are

> mining and manufacturing.
> fishing and lumbering.
> stock-raising and farming.

2. The animals raised in largest numbers in Australia are

sheep.   pigs.   cattle.

3. The leading grain crop of Australia is

corn.   wheat.   oats.

4. For fuel the Australians have abundant

coal.   petroleum.   peat.

5. The leading exports of Australia are products of the

mines.   ranches and farms.   forests.

6. The most valuable export of all is

wheat.   butter.   wool.

7. The imports of Australia are chiefly

manufactured goods. foodstuffs. raw materials.

Some things to explain. Explain why

1. The British buy large quantities of wool and wheat from Australia.

2. Fresh fruit and fruit jams from Australia find a good market in Great Britain.

3. Most of the Australian imports from Great Britain are manufactured goods.

4. Large quantities of the imports of mineral oils are from the United States.

5. The Australians trade more largely with the British than with any other nation.

Sentences to complete. 1. Stock-raising is more important than farming in Australia because much of the well-watered land is _____, and much of the level land is too ___ for crops.

2. The prosperity of the people of the Great Plains of Australia varies from year to year with the _____ because _____.

3. Vast stretches of the interior of Australia will always be useless lands because _____.

4. The tropical northern part of Australia is likely to remain _____ populated unless ____ _____.

5. Airplane transportation is very important in Australia because _____. _____.

Can you explain these differences? 1. Read the following comparisons carefully:

a. Australia is almost as large as the United States.

b. The United States has about

> (1) twenty times as many people as the Commonwealth of Australia;
> (2) fifteen times as much land used for raising crops;
> (3) nine times as many miles of railroads;
> (4) five times as many dollars' worth of foreign trade.

2. Explain why Australia has much more land unsuited to farming than the United States has. Do you think that Australia will ever be able to support as many people as the United States does? Give reasons for your answer.

3. Explain why the railroad mileage of Australia is so much less than that of the United States. Do you think the interior of Australia will ever be covered with a network of railroads, as the interior of the United States is? Give reasons for your answer.

4. The fact that Australia, with about one twentieth as many people as our country, has about one fifth as much foreign trade shows that the Australians depend more largely on foreign trade than we do. What does that suggest about their ability to supply their own needs compared with our ability to supply our needs? What reasons can you give for this difference?

Figure 115. Ships in the harbor of Wellington. Here you will see boats from other parts of the islands of New Zealand, as well as ships from distant lands. Although Auckland carries on more foreign trade than Wellington, this city is the more important center for trade between different parts of New Zealand. In what way is its location better for this domestic, or home, trade than is the location of Auckland?

Courtesy of Wellington Harbour Board

VI. THE DOMINION OF NEW ZEALAND

Foreword. At Sydney we can board a ship which will take us almost directly eastward to Auckland, the largest city of the British dominion of New Zealand. The distance from Sydney to Auckland is 1270 miles, or more than one third of the distance from New York to London. Trace our route on the map on page 105. In the harbor at Auckland we shall see ships from Great Britain, and probably some from the United States and Canada, for most of the New Zealanders are of British descent and trade chiefly with the English-speaking people of the world.

To the people of the British Isles the islands of New Zealand are the "antipodes," which means that these islands are on the opposite side of the earth from the British Isles. Use your globe to prove that these two groups of islands are the antipodes to each other.

Turn to page 4 and compare New Zealand and the British Isles in size and population. What can you say about the density of population in these two groups of islands?

As you read this chapter keep the following questions in mind:

1. Why have people from the British Isles chosen to settle in New Zealand, on the opposite side of the earth?

2. Why are the islands of New Zealand so much less densely populated than the British Isles?

3. How do the British people in New Zealand and the British people in the homeland help to supply each other's needs?

OROC

Figure 116. A little town on a lake in the mountains of South Island, New Zealand. The mountains of South Island are called the Southern Alps. Can you explain why they were given this name?

1. A FAVORABLE LAND FOR SETTLEMENT

The map on pages 334–335 shows that Captain Cook visited New Zealand as well as Australia. It was not until 1840, however, that the British made their first settlement in New Zealand. Do you know why the settlers were pleased with their new home, and what people they found living there?

Wellington — the first settlement. For their first settlement the British chose a place with an excellent harbor on Cook Strait, which separates the North Island of New Zealand from the South Island. This settlement was named Wellington, and today it is the second largest city of New Zealand as well as the capital of the dominion. It is also an important seaport. Find Wellington on the map on page 105 (*H 6*) and study Figure 115.

Other cities. Auckland, farther north on North Island, carries on more foreign trade than Wellington, chiefly because it is the nearest port of call for ships from Sydney and from ports on the western coast of Canada and the United States. About two thirds of all the trade of New Zealand is carried on through Wellington and Auckland.

The largest city on South Island is Christchurch, on the east coast. Much of the trade of South Island is carried on through Lyttelton, the port of Christchurch. Find these two cities on the map on page 105 (*H 6*), and notice the railroads which connect them with other parts of the island.

The native people. Although we shall see mostly people of British descent as we travel through New Zealand, we shall also see many Maoris, as the natives are called. They are tall and strong, with light-brown skin and wavy black hair, and they are far more intelligent than the blackfellows of Australia. They make up about one twentieth of the population of New Zealand, and they carry on farming and stock-raising much as the white people do.

A mountainous country. You will see from the map that both islands of New Zealand are made up largely of young, rugged mountains. There are, however, lowland plains bordering the coast in several places, and among the mountains there are many small but fertile plains. *See Figure 116.*

The mountains of South Island are so rugged and so beautiful that they have been named the Southern Alps. They are not so high as the Swiss Alps, but their summits are snow-capped, and from the snow fields great glaciers extend far down the slopes. Swift-flowing streams with many waterfalls also add to the beauty of the mountains.

The highest peak is called Mount Cook in honor of Captain Cook, and the largest glacier is named Tasman Glacier for the Dutch explorer who first sighted the islands. This glacier is over a mile wide and about eighteen miles long, and is one of the largest mountain glaciers in the world.

The mountains in North Island are lower than the Southern Alps, and among them are a number of volcanic peaks. Some of the volcanoes are dead, while others are still alive. Around the margins of the volcanic mountains are geysers and hot springs like those in Yellowstone National Park. *See Figure 117.*

A favorable climate. Do you remember why the British Isles have a mild climate with no great extremes of heat or cold? New Zealand has a mild climate for the same reason. On the lowlands and the lower slopes of the mountains the winters are never very cold, and uncomfortably hot weather in summer is unusual. If you cannot give the explanation for the mild climate, review what you learned on page 20.

Like Tasmania, New Zealand is far enough south to receive the moist westerly winds at all seasons, and so there is rain throughout the year. On which side of the islands should you expect the rainfall to be heavier? Why? Check your answer by Figure 91 (p. 97).

Figure 91 shows that the heaviest rainfall of all is on the western side of South Island, where the winds are forced to rise to cross the highest mountains of the country. This part of New Zealand has over 80 inches of rain a year. The eastern side of the island is not so well watered, but it is by no means dry. The rainfall in the driest belt is from 20 to 30 inches. This amount of moisture is plenty for the growth of grass and enough for many temperate-zone crops.

Forests and grasslands. Because so much of New Zealand has heavy rainfall, it has large stretches of forests, and the parts of the islands that are cool as well as moist have pine trees and other softwoods which provide valuable lumber for building purposes.

Herbert Photos, Inc.

Figure 117. A geyser in North Island, New Zealand. This geyser spouts hot water and steam high into the air almost continuously, day and night.

The eastern side of South Island and the parts of North Island which have the least rain are chiefly grasslands. The native grass is coarse and wiry and makes poor pasturage; so the people have burned over the grasslands, plowed them, and planted good grass seed imported from England. Thus they have turned poor grasslands into rich pastures where large numbers of cattle and sheep can graze.

Finding likenesses. Sum up the likenesses between New Zealand and Great Britain by completing the following sentences:

1. New Zealand and Great Britain are both small [.......] countries, separated from the nearest continents by _____.

2. They are both in the _____ zone.

3. They both have a mild _____ because _____

4. They both have abundant _____ because _____.

5. They are both healthful lands for white people because _____.

Finding differences. Now make as long a list as you can of ways in which New Zealand is different from Great Britain. Keep this list and add to it as you read more about the Dominion of New Zealand.

Photograph from Ewing Galloway, N.Y.

Figure 118. Shearing sheep in New Zealand. The men are using shears run by electricity to clip the thick wool from the sheep. The shearing season is from October to January. Can you explain why?

2. THE NEW ZEALANDERS AND THEIR WORK

From what you have learned about New Zealand, what kind of work do you think is most important there? Study the exports shown on the map on page 105 and see whether or not you wish to change your answer.

The raising of live stock. So much of New Zealand is hilly and mountainous that it is better suited to grazing than to farming, and the raising of live stock is by far the most important kind of work. The climate is so mild that the grass grows at all seasons and the sheep and cattle can graze out of doors the year round.

The ranchmen raise far more sheep than cattle, partly because sheep can graze on rougher land, and partly because sheep's wool grows thick and fine in the climate of New Zealand. The sheep are raised for both wool and meat; and mutton and lamb, as well as wool, are important exports. *See Figure 118.*

The sheep thrive best where the rainfall is less than 50 inches, and so the sheep stations, or ranches, are mostly on the eastern side of the islands. Figure 119 is a picture of one of them.

The ranches where beef cattle are raised are mostly on the well-watered lowlands and lower hillsides, and there are far more in North Island than in South Island. What export products do the cattle ranches provide?

Dairying. In recent years the people of New Zealand have been giving more and more attention to dairy farming, and they now produce large quantities of butter and cheese for export. Many of the dairy farmers raise special fodder crops to make the cows give more and better milk. *See Figure 120.*

What "refrigerator ships" mean to New Zealand. In the days before there were "refrigerator ships" with compartments in which perishable products could be kept cold or frozen, it was impossible for the people of New Zealand, Australia, and other countries of the Southern Hemisphere to ship fresh meat, butter, or cheese across the warm tropical seas to the countries in the Northern Hemisphere. They could ship such products as wool and hides, but meat, butter, and cheese would spoil on the long, hot voyage.

After refrigerator ships were built and put into service, the people of these southern lands could export a much greater variety of products. To the people of New Zealand, depending so largely on the raising of live stock, this change was especially helpful.

Farm crops. As you would expect, the people of New Zealand raise wheat and other grains, temperate-zone fruits, and vegetables to provide themselves with food. They do not, however, raise any crops of great importance for export. What handicap to farming in New Zealand explains this fact?

New Zealand Government Publicity Photograph

Figure 119. A sheep station near Hawke Bay in North Island, New Zealand. Notice the surface of the land here. Why is it better suited to grazing than to the raising of crops? New Zealand is one of the five great wool-exporting countries of the world. Can you name the other four? You learned about them on page 58.

Forest work. The people of New Zealand are more fortunate than the people of Australia in having forests of softwood trees to provide all the lumber that they need for building and other purposes. Lumbering is carried on in both islands, chiefly to supply the home market.

One of the most valuable trees is the kauri pine, which grows in North Island. It is a tall, straight tree which provides excellent lumber, and it is cut in large quantities. The hardened resin of kauri pines which long ago fell to the ground and rotted away is dug from the earth in North Island and is exported to the countries of western Europe and to the United States. It is called kauri gum, and is used chiefly in the making of varnishes.

Manufacturing. As yet New Zealand is not a great manufacturing country, and its principal industries are those by which the foodstuffs and raw materials from the farms and ranches are prepared for home use or for export. Among the more important manufacturing plants are meat-packing plants, butter factories, cheese factories, flour mills, tanneries, sawmills, woolen mills, clothing factories, and shoe factories.

As time goes on, the people will probably do more manufacturing, for there is coal in New Zealand, and the swift-flowing rivers provide plentiful water power for the making of electricity. But New Zealand, like Australia, needs a larger population in order to become a great manufacturing country.

New Zealand Government Publicity Photograph

Figure 120. New Zealand farmers returning from a dairy factory where they have sold their milk. In New Zealand a "dairy factory" may mean a butter factory or a cheese factory. Large quantities of butter and cheese from New Zealand are sold in Great Britain.

Trade with distant lands. You have only to study the map on page 105 to see that the leading exports of New Zealand are products of the ranches and the dairy farms. For many years wool was by far the most valuable export. More recently butter and frozen meats have outranked wool. Cheese and hides and skins also are valuable exports. *See Figure 121.*

Study the imports, and you will see that they are chiefly manufactured goods. What does our country sell to New Zealand? How do those imports show that New Zealand is a prosperous country?

You will probably not be surprised to learn that Great Britain takes about four fifths of the exports of New Zealand and supplies about half the imports. The dominion produces a large surplus of certain foodstuffs and raw materials that are greatly needed in Great Britain, and offers an excellent market for the manufactured goods which are produced in such great quantities there.

A check. Read the questions on page 117 again. You should be able to think out the answers to them now.

Giving reasons. Give reasons for each of the following facts:

1. Stock-raising is the most important kind of work in New Zealand.

2. Years ago the principal exports of New Zealand were wool and hides and skins. Today butter, cheese, and frozen meats are also very valuable exports.

3. The leading imports of New Zealand are manufactured goods.

4. The trade of New Zealand is chiefly with Great Britain.

5. Although Australia and New Zealand are neighboring countries, their trade with each other is much smaller than their trade with Great Britain.

Map work. Complete your map of the British Empire by coloring New Zealand, Australia, and the outlying lands governed by Australia. Then compare your map with the map on pages 42–43 and see if it is correct in every way.

Special credit work. Try to find a book which tells about the discovery of New Zealand by the Dutch explorer Tasman, and about the visit of Captain Cook. Tell your class of the experiences which these men had with the Maoris.

Courtesy of Wellington Harbour Board

Figure 121. A "refrigerator ship" from London being loaded with crates of cheese at Wellington. The cheese will travel a distance of about 12,500 miles on its trip from Wellington to London.

A REVIEW OF THE BRITISH EMPIRE

A summary. During your study of the British Empire you have learned that the outlying parts of the empire are valuable to the British people chiefly as (1) sources of raw materials and foodstuffs; (2) markets for manufactured goods; (3) places where people from the overcrowded homeland may go to make new homes and still live under the British flag. Give examples to prove that this is true.

You have discovered that most of the outlying parts of the empire carry on more trade with Great Britain than with any other country. That is partly because the home country and the possessions are able to supply many of each other's needs. Give examples to prove that this is true.

Another reason why there is so much trade between the home country and the possessions is that the British allow many of the products imported from the possessions to enter Great Britain "duty free." That means that shippers of such products do not have to pay *duties*, or money charges, for the privilege of selling their goods in Great Britain, as they are obliged to do in many other countries of the world. Certain other products imported from the possessions are charged duty, but the charge is less than is made on the same kinds of goods if they are imported from foreign countries. Thus the British offer the people of the possessions special advantages for marketing surplus products in the home country.

You have learned that Great Britain exercises so little control over the government of the dominions that they are almost like independent countries. What reason can you give for the fact that the people of the dominions are capable of governing themselves? Why are the people of many of the other possessions not so well able to govern themselves?

In some parts of the empire the people are anxious to have much more freedom in governing themselves than the British have as yet given them. The British believe that the people of these lands should be able to read and write and should learn more about doing work and business in modern ways before they are allowed to govern themselves. Do you think the people would be better off if they had self-government at present? Give reasons for your answer.

A check. Check your knowledge of the distant parts of the British Empire by naming each part described below:

1. The British dominion in North America.
2. A British colony in the northern part of North America.
3. The British colony in Central America.
4. The British colony in South America.
5. The British dominion in Africa.
6. The largest of the British possessions bordering the Gulf of Guinea.
7. The British possession bordering Egypt.
8. Four British possessions in the plateaus of East Africa.
9. Two British colonies in Africa named for Cecil Rhodes.
10. Two possessions which give the British control of the southern entrance to the Red Sea.
11. The lands in southwest Asia which were formerly under British protection.
12. The large country in Asia which was divided into two dominions.
13. The British part of the Malay Peninsula.
14. A continent which is a British dominion.
15. The dominion made up of islands which are the antipodes to the British Isles.
16. British possessions in the East Indies.

Naming cities. Write down the names of the cities described below. When you have finished, you will have a list of the ten largest cities of the British Empire.

1. The capital of the British Empire.
2. The largest city of India.
3. The largest city of Australia.
4. The leading seaport of western India.
5. The leading seaport of Scotland.
6. The largest city of the Black Country in England.
7. The capital of the Australian state of Victoria.
8. The largest city of Canada.
9. The great seaport on the western coast of England.
10. The largest city of the Lancashire cotton-manufacturing district in England.

Some things to prove. Give facts to prove that each statement below is true.

1. Certain parts of the British Empire are warm the year round, have abundant rainfall, and are very densely populated.

2. Other parts of the empire are very dry and very sparsely populated.

3. Certain parts of the empire are among the great farming lands of the world.

4. Certain parts are among the great grazing lands of the world.

5. Several parts of the empire are rich in mineral resources.

6. Several parts of the empire are not yet over-populated and are well suited to settlement by white people.

7. Certain parts of the empire will probably never attract large numbers of white people.

An English merchant's problem. Suppose you are a wholesale merchant in England, interested in shipping manufactured goods made in Great Britain to other parts of the British Empire. You have a supply of each kind of goods listed below, and wish to sell them in other parts of the empire. Tell where you would be most likely to find good markets for them, and why.

butter churns	gold-mining machinery
automobiles	threshing machines
woolen goods	jute-manufacturing machinery
electric fans	diamond-mining machinery
cotton gins	electrical wool clippers
airplanes	well-drilling machinery
cotton goods	coal-mining machinery
locomotives	flour-milling machinery
umbrellas	cotton-manufacturing machinery

A British buyer's problem. Imagine that you are a wholesale buyer in Great Britain and must secure from other parts of the British Empire supplies of the products listed below. To what parts of the empire should you send for them?

tea	wheat	diamonds
tin	asbestos	oil-seeds
gold	jute fiber	fresh fruit
copra	raw cotton	raw wool
palm oil	teakwood	graphite
fruit jams	fresh mutton	hides and skins
fresh beef	crude rubber	butter and cheese

Six empire problems. The British people face many problems in connection with their vast empire. Some of these problems are suggested below. Discuss them with your classmates.

1. In the dominions manufacturing is increasing steadily. This means that in time the demands for many of the goods manufactured in the home country will probably decrease. What effect will such a condition have on the people of Great Britain?

2. Suppose that raw materials are used in increasing quantities in the outlying parts of the British Empire where they are produced. How is that likely to affect the surplus of raw materials for export to Great Britain? If in the future the British are not able to get such large quantities of raw materials from their possessions as they have in the past, to what foreign countries can they turn to purchase additional supplies?

3. As population increases in the outlying parts of the British Empire, the demands for food will increase there, and in time the surplus quantities of foodstuffs for export may be smaller. When that time comes, from what foreign countries will the British probably buy more foodstuffs than they do at present? Give reasons for your answer.

4. For many years manufacturing increased very fast in Great Britain. Many people believe that there will be little increase, and possibly even a decrease, in British manufacturing in the future. If this should prove to be true, would Great Britain be able to support a greater population than it does today? If population should increase and manufacturing decrease, what would some of the people have to do?

5. Already Great Britain is over-populated, and at times when business is poor large numbers of people are out of work. To what parts of the empire could those who want steady work in a healthful climate go?

6. Of all the distant parts of the empire, Australia is the one which is most eager to attract new settlers from the British Isles. Explain why. What opportunities for making a good living has Australia to offer to people from the homeland? What other dominions offer similar opportunities?

Acme

Figure 122. The airway " station " at Le Bourget, the airport of Paris. In the central part of the long building are ticket offices and waiting rooms. Travelers arriving at Le Bourget by plane find automobiles waiting to carry them to Paris, a trip which takes three quarters of an hour. Find Le Bourget on Figure 128.

FRANCE AND ITS POSSESSIONS

1. THE REPUBLIC OF FRANCE

Foreword. Across the English Channel from Great Britain lies the Republic of France. The French people are the nearest neighbors of the British, and ships and airplanes are continually traveling back and forth between the two countries.

From Dover on the English coast to Calais on the French coast the distance is less than 25 miles. Every day boats cross and recross the Channel between these two ports, carrying throngs of passengers and tons and tons of mail. The trip takes only an hour and a quarter, but the water is often rough, and therefore many people dislike the crossing. Trains from London and Paris connect with the boats, and one can make the trip between the two capital cities in about seven hours. Trace the route by train and boat from London (*E5*) to Paris (*F6*) on the map on pages 144–145.

If you wish to avoid the rough crossing of the Channel, and save as much time as possible, you can take an airplane from Croydon, just outside London, and land at Le Bourget, just outside Paris, in less than two hours. *See Figure 122.*

Turn to the map on pages 144–145 again and find Calais (*F5*) and Marseille (*G7*). Fast trains make the trip between these two French ports, by way of Paris and Dijon (*G6*), in about fifteen hours. Prove by the map that the shortest route from the North Sea to the Mediterranean is this one across France, and that it is almost wholly a lowland route. Because of these facts, this route is one of the most important highways of travel and transportation in Europe.

The map shows that France is a six-sided country, and that three sides border the water. The Channel coast and the Atlantic

James Sawders

Figure 123. Part of the water front at Marseille. The ships are in one of the docks which have been made by building breakwaters along the coast. Marseille was founded by Greek colonists about 2500 years ago, and it has always been a great center of shipping and commerce. Can you suggest reasons for this fact?

coast make it easy for the French people to carry on trade with the Americas, and the Mediterranean coast makes it easy for their ships to reach Africa, Asia, and Australia.

With these facts in mind you will not be surprised to learn that the French are one of the great commercial nations of the world and that their colonial empire, as their possessions are often called, is next largest to that of the British. Turn to the map on pages 148–149 and name the continent in which most of the French possessions are located. Can you give a reason why the French control so much of that continent?

As you read about France and its possessions, keep these questions in mind:

1. What likenesses and differences are there between the work of the people in France and the work of the people in Great Britain?

2. Are the French possessions more valuable than the British possessions or are they less valuable?

1. French Seaports and their Trade

On the map on pages 140–141 find the four leading seaports of France. Which is the northernmost port? On what body of water is it located? At the mouth of what river is Le Havre? Bordeaux? Near the mouth of what river is Marseille?

By studying the trade of these ports we can discover some of the likenesses and differences between France and Great Britain. Prove by the exports and imports that

1. The French, like the British, carry on much manufacturing.

2. France is not so well supplied with coal as Great Britain.

3. France, like Great Britain, has no great home supply of petroleum.

4. The French, like the British, import foodstuffs and raw materials from North America and South America.

5. The French, like the British, find in their colonies a valuable source of foodstuffs and raw materials, and a valuable market for manufactured goods.

Marseille — the Mediterranean gateway. Marseille is the second largest city of France and the greatest of the French seaports. Study its location more carefully and you will see that it is at the southern end of the Rhône-Saône Valley, some distance east of the Rhône delta. On the map (pp. 140–141) find the canal by which barges may reach Marseille from the Rhône River. Marseille has a good natural harbor, but not a very large one, and its foreign trade is so great that docks, protected by breakwaters, have been built for three miles along the open coast beyond the natural harbor. *See Figure 123.*

Photograph by James Sawders

Figure 124. A glimpse of Le Havre. This is one of the docks where freighters load and unload their cargoes. Le Havre is an important port for passenger liners as well as for cargo ships.

In order to understand the growth of Marseille you need to look at the map on pages 144–145. Trace the Rhône-Saône Valley northward, and you will see that it forms a lowland corridor leading almost to the Paris Basin, the great plain in the midst of which Paris is located. Do you see how natural it is that railroads should follow this lowland corridor to the Mediterranean, and why a great seaport was bound to grow up as an ocean gateway at its southern end?

Because of its location Marseille is the port through which most of the French trade with northern Africa and Asia is carried on. Ships come to its busy wharves from the United States and from the countries of South America also. Among its imports are oilseeds of various kinds from all over the world, and one of its greatest manufacturing industries is the refining of vegetable oils and the making of soaps.

Le Havre and Dunkerque. Le Havre owes its growth to its location at the mouth of the Seine. This river and its valley form a natural highway of travel and transportation through the heart of the Paris Basin, and therefore Le Havre is the chief ocean gateway for this region. Dunkerque has grown up as the port for a great industrial district in the northern part of the plain. What reason does the map on pages 140–141 suggest for the growth of manufacturing in that part of France?

As you would expect from their location, Le Havre and Dunkerque handle much of the French trade with Great Britain and the Americas. At their wharves ships from the Americas unload large quantities of raw materials such as cotton and wool, and take on cargoes of manufactured goods from French mills and factories. *See Figure 124.*

Bordeaux — gateway for the Aquitaine Basin. The plain in southern France which is drained by the Garonne River and its tributaries is called the Aquitaine Basin, and Bordeaux is its ocean gateway. The city is located at the mouth of the Garonne and is the great wine-exporting port of France. What do you find on the map to explain the importance of its exports of wine?

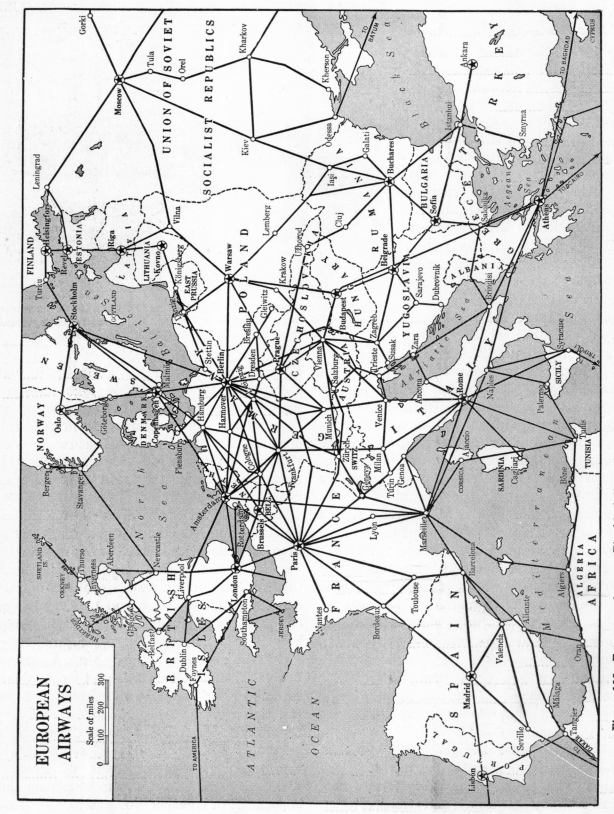

Figure 125. European airways. The black lines show the routes over which passenger airplanes are operated regularly.

Bordeaux is a busy manufacturing city also. Among its leading industries are flour-milling, sugar-refining, coffee-roasting, and the making of chocolate. How are these industries connected with its trade with distant lands?

Ports of lesser importance. As you read about each of these ports locate it on the map on pages 140–141. Although the larger ocean ships cannot go up the Seine beyond Le Havre, smaller freighters go upstream to Rouen (*G4*). Many of them bring cotton from the United States, and Rouen has become one of the great cotton-manufacturing cities of France.

Cherbourg (*F4*) will remind you of Southampton, for it is the port used by many of the great ocean liners which bring passengers to France from the United States and other countries on the western side of the Atlantic.

Farther south is the port of Nantes (*F5*), at the head of the estuary of the river Loire. Nantes shares with Bordeaux some of the French trade with tropical lands.

The railroads of France. Travelers entering France through any one of the seaports find good railroad service to almost any part of the country, and express-train service to Paris. The map on pages 144–145 shows that Paris is the great center of the railroads of France. All the main lines meet there, forming the spokes of a "railroad wheel" of which Paris is the hub.

The inland waterways. Turn to the map on pages 140–141 again and notice that many of the rivers of France are navigable. Notice also that there are many canals connecting the navigable rivers. The rivers and canals form a great system of waterways which are used for transporting freight in barges. We shall find that the people of France and other

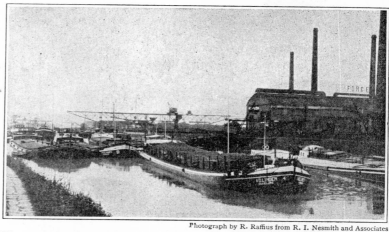

Photograph by R. Raffius from R. I. Nesmith and Associates

Figure 126. Barges on a canal in Strasbourg, a city near the river Rhine in the eastern part of France. They have brought coal from Germany to the manufacturing plant that you see in the picture.

countries which share the Central Plains of Europe use rivers and canals for transporting freight much more than we do in the United States. Such transportation is slow, but it is cheaper than transportation by railroad. For this reason the barges carry chiefly bulky goods, such as coal, lumber, and iron ore, which have a low value in proportion to the space which they take up. *See Figure 126.*

Highways and airways. The French have also covered their country with a great network of motor highways, and they were one of the leading nations in developing regular airplane service for passengers and mail.

Figure 125 shows that Paris and Marseille are the two great airway centers of France. Notice the airlines from different parts of Europe that meet at Marseille. This city is one of the chief centers of the airlines that connect Europe with Africa and southeastern Asia. How does its location help to explain this fact?

Tracing canals. Use the map on pages 140–141 to show how goods may be carried by barge from (1) the Garonne River to the Rhône; (2) the Rhône to the Rhine; (3) the Rhine to the Seine; (4) the Seine to the Loire; (5) the Seine to the Rhône.

Photograph by Ewing Galloway, N.Y.

Figure 127. An airplane view of part of Paris. In the distance you can see part of the little island (the Ile de la Cité) where the first settlement was made. The large open space with the tall column in the center is the Place de la Concorde, and beyond it are the Garden of the Tuileries and the buildings of the Louvre.

Naming ports. Prove your acquaintance with the French seaports by naming correctly each one described below.

1. The greatest seaport of France.

2. The port which is the chief ocean gateway for the Paris Basin.

3. The port where many travelers from England enter France.

4. The port which is the ocean gateway for the Aquitaine Basin.

5. The port which serves an important industrial district of northern France.

6. A port for transatlantic passenger ships.

Something to prove. Prove by the maps on pages 140–141 and 226–227 that the leading imports of France are chiefly raw materials and foodstuffs and that the leading exports are mostly manufactured goods.

2. Paris and the Paris Basin

Paris, like London, attracts people from all over the world. Many come for business or study, and many for pleasure, for Paris is a city of work and of play. It is a city of great beauty also, for the French are very artistic, and they have spent much time, thought, and money in making their capital beautiful.

In Figure 127 you are looking up the river Seine toward the little island where the first settlement of Paris was made, over 1400 years ago. As the settlement grew into a town and then into a city, it spread first to the south bank of the river and then to the north bank. Figure 128 shows that today Paris spreads out for several miles in all directions from the Ile de la Cité (Isle of the City), where the first settlement was located. Study Figure 128 carefully.

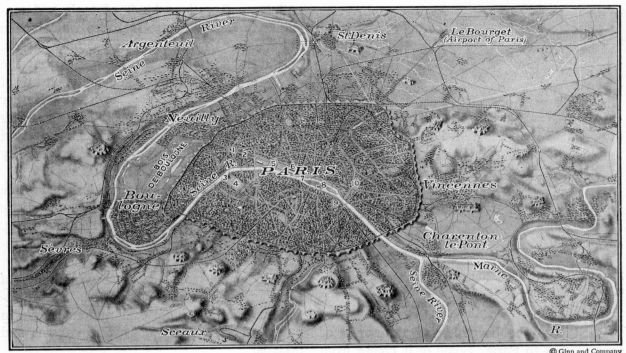

Figure 128. A map of Paris and its surroundings. The numbers show the locations of the following places: 1, Arc de Triomphe; 2, Avenue des Champs-Élysées; 3, Eiffel Tower; 4, Champ-de-Mars; 5, Place de la Concorde; 6, Garden of the Tuileries; 7, the Louvre; 8, Cathedral of Notre Dame (on the Ile de la Cité); 9, Botanical Gardens; 10, Place de la Bastille. Find the beautiful park known as the Bois de Boulogne.

Besides being the capital of France, Paris is one of the largest cities of Europe. Before the war, only London, Berlin, and Moscow, among the European cities, had more people. Like London, it is a great business, industrial, and financial center, and a great center of learning and culture. Can you think of any reasons why Paris has become one of the world's greatest cities?

The heart of the Paris Basin. Find Paris on the map on pages 140–141 (*H4*). Notice that it is in the very heart of the Paris Basin, at the place that can be reached most easily by way of the Seine and its tributaries. The Paris Basin is one of the richest agricultural regions of France, and long ago, when there were no railroads and but few roads, Paris became its principal trading center. Can you explain why?

As time went on, Paris became a meeting place for roads from all parts of the basin, and then for railroads. Thus from the very first the location of Paris has made it a natural center of travel and transportation, and this, in turn, has made it a great center of business and trade.

A great river port. You will remember that in our own country cities like St. Louis, which were once great river ports, lost most of their trade by water when they became great railroad centers. Paris is different, for even after it became a railroad center it continued to grow as a river port.

East and west of the central part of the city the Seine is lined with long stone wharves, where hundreds of barges unload bulky goods for use in the city. Some of the barges come upstream from Le Havre and Rouen, and others come from distant parts of France by way of the canals that lead to the Seine and its tributaries.

Figure 129. The Opera House in Paris, facing the busy square known as the Place de l'Opéra. The ground floor in the hotel at the left is a famous café.

Each year the barges bring thousands of tons of coal to Paris. Some of it comes from the large coal field in the northern part of France, and some of it is imported coal from Great Britain. On the map on pages 140–141 trace the route of the coal barges from the northern coal field to Paris.

A great manufacturing city. Just as London is one of the greatest manufacturing cities of Great Britain, so Paris is one of the greatest manufacturing cities of France. What advantages has it for getting raw materials and distributing manufactured goods?

One of the greatest helps to manufacturing in Paris is the fact that coal can be brought in cheaply by water. The factories are along the banks of the river upstream and downstream from the center of the city, and they extend into the suburbs. Coal comes almost to their doors by barge, and the many railroads which center in Paris distribute their products to all parts of France, to neighboring countries, and to the French seaports for export.

Among the factories on the outskirts of the city are those which make automobiles, cutlery, and various kinds of tools and machinery. Here also are factories which make automobile tires and other rubber goods, chemicals, and glass. Near the center of the city are factories for the manufacture of luxuries such as jewelry, expensive leather goods, and fine furniture. The Parisians have always been famous for their skill and artistic taste in making things of fine quality and great beauty.

Parisian goods in Parisian shops. The best way to learn how skillful and artistic the Parisian workers are is to visit the shops. In the windows you will see wonderful displays of clothing, laces, embroideries, jewelry, leather goods, toys, and other products of Parisian factories and workshops. So beautiful are these products that manufacturers in many other countries copy the patterns and designs.

The greatest industry. By far the most important industry in Paris is the making of women's clothing and hats. French dressmakers and milliners are so artistic that they set the fashions for the women of Europe and America. Buyers from the great stores in the United States and the various European countries visit Paris several times a year to learn the new styles and to purchase the latest gowns and hats to offer to their customers at home.

A busy, beautiful city. Like all great cities, Paris is full of life and activity. The sidewalks swarm with people, and the streets are crowded with automobiles. Electric trains speed through subways underground, and streams of people and automobiles cross and recross the bridges over the Seine. During the day thousands of people are busy in stores, banks, offices, factories, and workshops, and at night thousands seek pleasure and entertainment in the theaters and the gay cafés. *See Figure 129.*

What impresses the visitor most is the

beauty of this great city, — its broad boulevards lined with trees, its public squares with their fountains and monuments, its parks and gardens, and its palaces and churches.

Sight-seeing in Paris. On the right, or north, bank of the Seine are the better hotels and theaters of Paris, the principal business and shopping districts, and the more fashionable homes. There too are some of the museums and art galleries for which Paris is famous. Among them is the Louvre, which contains many of the world's finest paintings and works of sculpture. (See 7 on Figure 128).

From the Louvre you can walk westward through the beautiful Garden of the Tuileries to the large open square called the Place de la Concorde, where there are eight statues, each representing a French city. From there a broad boulevard lined with trees (the Avenue des Champs Élysées) leads to a great open circle in the midst of which stands the Arc de Triomphe (Arch of Triumph). Beneath this arch is the tomb of the "Unknown Soldier" who lost his life in the World War of 1914–1918. Trace the route of this walk on Figure 128 and study Figure 130.

You will surely wish to visit the Ile de la Cité to see the beautiful Cathedral of Notre Dame, which is more than six hundred and fifty years old. On the island you will also see the group of buildings known as the Palace of Justice, where the highest law courts of France are held.

Crossing from the island to the left, or south, bank of the Seine, you will find yourself in a crowded section of Paris known as the Latin Quarter. In this section live thousands of students from all parts of France and many students from other countries, for

© Compagnie Aérienne Française

Figure 130. An airplane view of the Place de l'Étoile, in the middle of which stands the Arc de Triomphe. The French word *étoile* means "star." Do you think this *place* is well named?

the University of Paris, the College of France, the School of Fine Arts, and various other schools and colleges are located here. This section also has several fine museums.

If you walk westward from the Latin Quarter, you will see many of the French government buildings. Among them is the group of buildings where the Senate and the Chamber of Deputies meet. France is a republic, with a president, who is elected for a term of seven years. The Senate and Chamber of Deputies are made up of representatives from all parts of the country, like our Congress and the British Parliament.

You could spend weeks and weeks in Paris without seeing all there is of interest and beauty there. But even a short visit will show you that the French, like the British, have a capital which is a great world city.

Making a summary. Make a summary of the reasons for the growth of Paris, explaining why (1) it long ago became a market center and a river port; (2) it later became a railroad and manufacturing center; and (3) it now attracts people from all parts of the world.

By Burton Holmes from Ewing Galloway

Figure 131. French peasants gathering spinach in a market garden not far from Paris. The Paris Basin is dotted with cities and towns, and with little villages of farming families who go out to their work in the surrounding fields each day.

Farming in the Paris Basin. Travel in any direction you choose from Paris, and you will see people at work in the fields, for the Paris Basin is a great farming region. The westerly winds from the Atlantic Ocean bring ample rain at all seasons and keep the winter weather from being very cold. Thus, in addition to crops sown in the spring, the farmers can raise autumn-sown crops of grain.

Clustered around Paris are many market gardens, and a little farther away are dairy farms. Can you explain why? Elsewhere in the basin most of the farmers carry on mixed farming, though the special money crops differ in different sections. *See Figure 131.*

On many of the farms winter wheat is the principal money crop, for the Paris Basin is one of the chief wheat-growing regions of Europe. More wheat is grown in France than in any other European country except European Russia; but even so the French have to import additional sup-plies of wheat in order to meet their needs. *See Figure 132.*

In the northern part of the plain, sugar beets are the leading money crop, and there are many factories where the sugar is prepared for use. Farther south there are several districts where the farmers raise large quantities of grapes for making wine. In all parts of the region the farmers raise oats and other grains besides wheat, and keep cows, sheep, pigs, and poultry.

Two industrial districts. On the borders of the Paris Basin are two very important industrial districts. One is the iron-mining region of Lorraine in the east, and the other is the coal-mining region in the north. Find these industrial districts on the map on pages 140–141 (*J-K4*) and (*H3*).

Iron and steel in Lorraine. The iron mines of Lorraine are among the richest in the world, and they make France one of the three leading iron-mining countries. The others are the United States and the Soviet Union. Because so much iron ore is mined in Lorraine, this is the

Photograph by Margaret Willis from R. I. Nesmith and Associates

Figure 132. Stacking wheat in the Paris Basin. This is the way the wheat is stored until it is threshed. Why is the Paris Basin a great farming region? Why is winter wheat a leading crop there?

Photograph by Ewing Galloway, N.Y.

Figure 133. An iron-and-steel plant near Nancy, in Lorraine. Huge quantities of iron ore are smelted in Lorraine, and the pig iron is used to make all kinds of iron and steel. Part of the coking coal which is used in the blast furnaces of Lorraine is imported from a rich coal field in the western part of Germany.

leading iron-and-steel manufacturing district of France. The largest city of the district is Nancy. There, and in various other cities and towns in Lorraine, you will see huge blast furnaces and steel mills that will remind you of our Pittsburgh district. *See Figure 133.*

The northern coal field and its industries. By far the most valuable coal field of France is the one in the north, and a great industrial district has grown up there. In Lille and many other cities and towns of the district you will see woolen mills, cotton mills, rayon mills, and linen mills, for this region is the leading textile-manufacturing district of France. Part of the flax for the linen mills comes from the neighboring farm lands, and large quantities of wool and cotton are imported through the port of Dunkerque.

Because the coal of this northern field is good for coking, the district has also become an important center for the smelting of iron ore, the making of steel, and the manufacture of iron and steel products. Most of the iron ore used in this section comes from Lorraine.

France has so much iron ore that there is a surplus for export. In normal times the exports of iron ore go chiefly to Germany; for while the Germans have abundant coal in their country, they have less iron ore than they need. France, on the other hand, with abundant iron ore, has less coal than it needs, and therefore the French people are obliged to import additional supplies of coal, chiefly from Great Britain and Germany.

Giving reasons. Complete each sentence below by giving reasons.

1. The Paris Basin is a great agricultural region because _____.

2. Lorraine is a great center for the manufacture of iron and steel because _____ _____.

3. There is a very important industrial district on the northern border of the Paris Basin because _____.

4. Dunkerque imports large quantities of raw cotton and wool because _____.

5. The French import coal from Great Britain and Germany because _____.

Figure 134. A farmyard in Brittany. The farmhouse and other buildings are of stone covered with plaster, and the roofs are thatched with straw. The peasants of Brittany have little farming machinery, and they do most of their work with the help of oxen. Why is Brittany a poorer farming region than the Paris Basin?

Photograph by Ewing Galloway, N. Y.

3. THE UPLAND OF BRITTANY AND THE AQUITAINE BASIN

On the map on pages 140–141 find the Upland of Brittany to the west of the Paris Basin. Notice that in the north this region extends beyond Brittany into the section of France called Normandy. Find also the Aquitaine Basin, which is drained by the Garonne River and its tributaries. Which do you think is the more important farming region, and why?

A hilly region. In many ways the Upland of Brittany is like the Coastal Hilly Belt of New England. Many of the hills are rocky, and much of the soil is too thin to be good for crops. Grass, however, grows abundantly because of the moist climate. Thus Brittany, like New England, is better suited to the raising of live stock than to the raising of crops, and it has become an important dairying region. Other reminders of New England are the apple orchards on many of the hillsides in Normandy. *See Figure 134.*

The climate of the upland is much milder than that of New England because of the westerly winds from the Atlantic Ocean. The grass in the pastures remains green most of the year, and in certain sheltered spots along the coast spring comes so early that the farmers specialize in raising early vegetables for the Paris market.

Mineral wealth. On the map find the two places in this upland region where iron ore is mined. Unfortunately there is no coal in the region, and so the smelting plants which have been built at Caen and Nantes use imported coal from Great Britain and Germany. The smelting plants use only a small part of the ore that is mined. Part of the surplus is exported, often in the ships which bring the coal, and the rest goes to the northern coal field of France.

A summer playground. The rocky, irregular coast of Brittany, with its many bays and inlets, is dotted with resorts where large numbers of French and British people spend their summer vacations. How do the summer visitors help to provide work for the people?

Breton fishermen. Each bay and river mouth along the coast of Brittany has its little port, and each port has its fleet of fishing boats. The Bretons have been famous fishermen for hundreds of years. Some of them go to Newfoundland and Iceland for cod, and others go to the North Sea for herring. Many work in smaller boats along the coast of Brittany, fishing for sardines. On shore many of the Breton women find work in the factories where the sardines are canned in oil for export. *See Figure 135.*

Farming in the Aquitaine Basin. The Aquitaine Basin is entirely different from the Upland of Brittany; for the land is level or gently rolling, and most of the soils are deep and fertile. Like the Paris Basin, it is a great

Authenticated News Photo

Figure 136. Picking grapes in a French vineyard. From the vineyards the grapes go to "wineries" where the juice is pressed out and made into wine. From what seaport are the wines of the Aquitaine Basin exported?

farming region; but since its climate is warmer, the farmers raise corn as well as wheat. You may think of this basin as the "corn belt" of France, for nearly all the corn of the country is grown there.

Nearly a third of all the vineyards of France are in this warm, sunny plain of the south, and huge quantities of grapes are grown for making wine. French wines take their names from the districts where they are made, and because of their excellent quality some of them find markets in many other countries. *See Figure 136.*

Turning waste lands into woodlands. On the map on pages 140–141 find the strip of coast land known as the Landes (*F 6–7*). For many years this section was a waste of sand dunes which were not only useless but harmful; for the winds from the ocean caused them to move slowly inland, and little by little they were spoiling the bordering farm lands. To stop the eastward march of the dunes the people planted pine trees, and today these one-time waste lands of the Landes provide large quantities of lumber and turpentine. *See Figure 137.*

Photo by Mario Scacheri, Triangle Photo Service

Figure 135. A little fishing port in Brittany, showing the kind of boats used in catching sardines along the coast. Many of the fishing boats have red sails.

Photograph by Ewing Galloway, N. Y.

Figure 137. A "turpentine forest" in southern France. Notice the cups which catch the resin as it drips from the gashes in the pine trees. Where in the United States could you see sights like this?

This turning of waste lands into woodlands means much to the French people, for so much of their country has been cleared of trees to make room for farms that they are not well supplied with forests. This lack of large forests is something you will notice all through the densely settled regions of western Europe, for most of the level land and much of the hilly land have been cleared for farming. Wood, therefore, is scarce and expensive. For this reason the people are caring for the forests which are left in such a way that they may produce yearly "crops" of timber. This, you will remember, is what our government is doing in the national forests of our country.

Some things to explain. 1. Give three reasons why so many of the people along the coast of Brittany get their living by fishing. Remember what led to the growth of fishing along the New England coast.

2. Many of the officers and sailors on French ships are Bretons. Explain why.

3. Explain why the Aquitaine Basin is the corn-growing region of France.

4. Explain why Bordeaux exports large quantities of wine.

4. THE CENTRAL PLATEAU AND THE RHÔNE-SAÔNE VALLEY

On the map on pages 140–141 find the Central Plateau of France and the Rhône-Saône Valley. What do you find in the plateau which suggests that there may be industrial centers there? What have you already learned about the Rhône-Saône "corridor"?

The Central Plateau. Much of this large region is not well suited to farming because the land is hilly and mountainous and much of the soil is poor. In places, however, there are rich lava soils on which the people raise grain and other crops.

As a whole the Central Plateau is better suited to grazing than to farming, and many of the people make their living by keeping live stock. Dairying is important in the northeastern part of the region because there are good markets for dairy products in the cities of the Rhône-Saône Valley. Many of the people of the plateau raise beef cattle, and others raise sheep and goats. Have you ever eaten Roquefort cheese from France? It is made from a mixture of sheep's milk and goat's milk, and takes its name from the town in the southern part of the plateau where it is made.

Coal and manufacturing. The map shows that there are several places in the plateau where coal is mined. These are very small coal fields compared with the one in northern France, but near each one an industrial center has grown up. The chief work in these centers is the making of all kinds of products of iron and steel, from bolts and nails to locomotives and heavy machinery. The iron and steel used in the factories come mostly from Lorraine. St. Étienne is the largest of the iron-and-steel manufacturing cities.

Farther west in the plateau are Clermont-Ferrand, which specializes in the manufacture of automobile tires, and Limoges, famous for the beautiful china which is made there.

A great silk-manufacturing district. On the map on pages 140–141 find Lyon (*J 6*). Notice that it is located where the Rhône River, coming from the Alps, joins the Saône. Lyon is the third largest city of France and the center of the greatest silk-manufacturing district of Europe.

Silk, as you probably know, is the silvery fiber spun by the silkworm in making its cocoon. The raising of silkworms depends on the growing of mulberry trees, for the worms live by eating mulberry leaves. Mulberry trees, in turn, need a fairly warm climate, and the Mediterranean borders of Europe are well suited to their growth.

Figure 138. A silk mill in the Rhône Valley near Lyon. The prosperity of many of the villages and small towns in the Rhône Valley depends on the silk mills, which give employment to many people.

Long ago silk production became an important kind of work in the Rhône Valley of France and in the bordering part of the plateau, and the towns of that region became silk-manufacturing centers. Years ago the industry outgrew the home supplies of raw material, and large quantities of raw silk are now imported from Italy, China, and Japan.

Some of the towns specialize in spinning silk thread, and others in weaving silk cloth. St. Étienne is a center for the making of ribbons. Lyon specializes in dyeing and finishing silk goods, and is the business center of the entire silk industry. *See Figure 138.*

Vineyards and olive groves. If you travel southward through the Rhône-Saône Valley, you will see many vineyards and many groves of olive trees. The Mediterranean borderlands of Europe have winter rains and summer drought, and therefore they are not well suited to the raising of crops which need rain in summer. But grapevines and olive trees grow well in the Mediterranean climate, for they have long roots, which draw up water from far beneath the ground when the surface is dry and dusty. For this reason grapes and olives are two of the most important Mediterranean products.

Because of the abundance of grapes and olives in the Mediterranean region of France, the making of wine and olive oil is of great importance. No doubt you have eaten salad dressing made of olive oil, and perhaps you know that olive oil is also used for making soap. Marseille is the great center for the making of olive oil in France, and it was this industry that gave the city its start in the manufacture of soaps. Today, as you know, its vegetable-oil refineries and soap works use oilseeds of various kinds from many different parts of the world.

Sentences to complete. 1. The Rhône-Saône Valley is a great highway of travel and transportation because _____.

2. Several cities in the eastern part of the Central Plateau manufacture products of iron and steel because _____.

3. Marseille imports raw silk and exports silk goods because _____.

4. Large quantities of grapes and olives are grown in the Mediterranean region of France because _____.

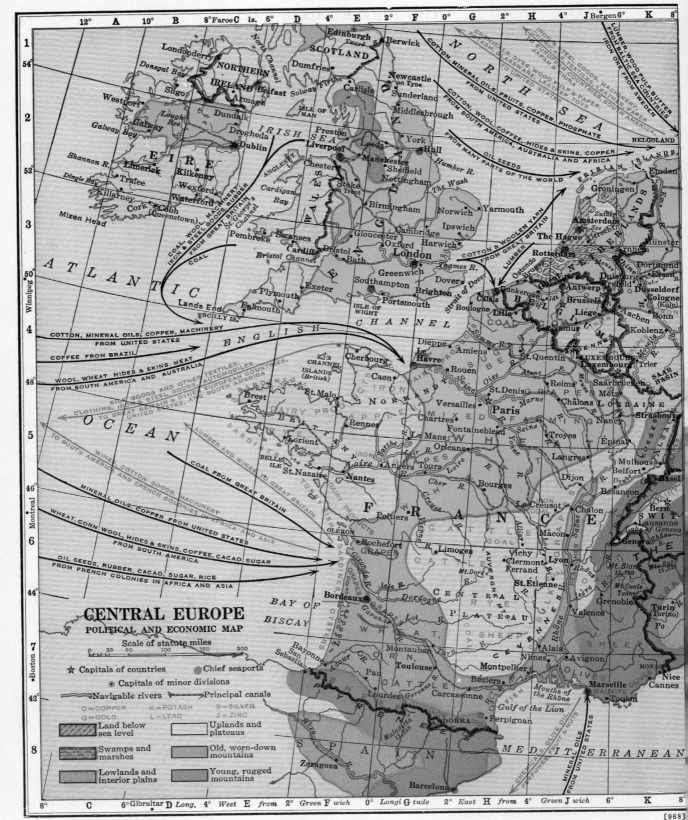

CENTRAL EUROPE
POLITICAL AND ECONOMIC MAP

Scale of statute miles

0 25 50 100 150 200

★ Capitals of countries ● Chief seaports

◎ Capitals of minor divisions

Navigable rivers ➤ Principal canals

C=COPPER K=POTASH S=SILVER
G=GOLD L=LEAD Z=ZINC

Land below sea level

Swamps and marshes

Lowlands and interior plains

Uplands and plateaus

Old, worn-down mountains

Young, rugged mountains

H. Armstrong Roberts

Figure 139. Farmhouses in a valley in the Pyrenees. Notice that the cultivated lands are the small areas of level ground and the gentler slopes. Why is much of the land in the Pyrenees unfit for farming?

5. AMONG THE MOUNTAINS OF FRANCE

From the map on pages 140–141 name two regions of young, rugged mountains of which France has a share. Name also a small region of old, worn-down mountains in eastern France. In what way do you think these mountain regions are of the greatest value to the French people?

Cotton-manufacturing in the Vosges. In the valleys among the Vosges Mountains there are many towns where cotton goods are manufactured. The cotton industry began there long ago when the spinning and weaving were done in the homes of the people. Today the work is done in factories, many of which use hydroelectric power from the mountain streams, and because of its early start, the region is one of the important textile-manufacturing districts of France.

The Rhine Valley. The map shows that east of the Vosges France has a small share of the valley of the Rhine. You will learn more about this valley when you visit Germany. In the French section there are valuable deposits of potash salts, which, you will remember, are used in making fertilizers. These deposits make France second only to Germany in the production and export of potash.

The French Alps. Most of the people in the French Alps live on little farms in the valleys. They keep cattle and goats and raise small crops on their tiny patches of level land. In summer many of them are busy supplying the needs of tourists who come to climb the mountains and enjoy the scenery.

The only large city of the region is Grenoble, on a tributary to the Rhône. Long ago Grenoble became a center for the manufacture of gloves from goatskins, and it is still the great glove-manufacturing city of France. In recent years, however, its industries have increased greatly in number and kind because hydroelectric plants have been built along the swift-flowing mountain streams, providing abundant power for manufacturing.

The Riviera. On the map trace the mountainous coast of the Mediterranean from Marseille to Genoa, in Italy. This coast is called the Riviera, and it is a great winter playground for people from the cooler countries of Europe and America. The mountain wall of the Alps shuts out the cold winds from the north, and the winter weather is so warm that the visitors can enjoy all the out-of-door sports and pleasures that belong to summer in their homelands. *See Figure 140.*

The mountains rise steeply from the blue Mediterranean, and on their slopes are vineyards, olive groves, and acres and acres of roses, hyacinths, sweet peas, and many other lovely flowers. These flowers are grown for use in an industry for which the French are famous, — the making of perfumes from the oil in the blossoms.

Corsica. On the map on pages 144–145 find Corsica (*G7*). This island belongs to France, but the people are of Italian descent. As the island is mountainous, most of the people live along the coasts. They have vineyards and groves of olives and other fruit trees, and they keep sheep and goats.

The Pyrenees. The map shows that the Pyrenees rise like a great wall, separating France from Spain. They form such a barrier that for many years the only railroads connecting the two countries ran around the ends of the mountains. Even now only two railroad lines actually cross the mountains.

In the valleys among the Pyrenees there are a few small villages where the people carry on a little farming, but the principal use of the mountains is for pasturing cattle and sheep from the bordering lowland in the summer. To the French this region is valuable chiefly for its many swift streams which provide hydroelectricity. *See Figure 139.*

Making up for the shortage of coal. By this time you know the answer to the question asked at the beginning of this section. The mountains of France are of great value to the people because their water power helps to make up for the shortage of coal in the country. Already France is using more hydroelectric power than any other European country except Italy, and it will probably use still more in the future.

One of the many uses of hydroelectricity in France is in obtaining aluminum from its ore, bauxite. The bauxite mines are in the southern part of the country, east of the Rhône Valley, and they make France the world's leading producer of this important ore.

© Publishers Photo Service, Inc.

Figure 140. Monte Carlo, a famous winter resort on the French Riviera. Monte Carlo is the largest town in the little principality of Monaco. Find Monaco on the map on pages 140–141 (*K7*).

A Small Neighbor of France

Andorra. Hidden away in the heights of the Pyrenees, between France and Spain, is tiny Andorra. It is an independent country, but it enjoys the protection of the French nation. Its people number less than 5500, and their little villages are in valleys which can be reached only through mountain passes which are buried in snow for half the year. They make a poor living with their flocks and herds; but they care more for freedom than for comfort, and they do not seem to mind being almost forgotten by most of the world.

A playground test. 1. Tell where you would go in France in the winter time to enjoy summer sports.

2. Tell where you would go in the summer time to enjoy mountain climbing.

3. Tell where you would go in the summer to enjoy the pleasures of the seashore.

4. Explain why the Pyrenees have few summer visitors compared with the Alps.

EUROPE
POLITICAL MAP
SHOWING PRINCIPAL RAILROADS

Scale of statute miles

0 50 100 200 300 400 500

★ Capitals of countries
⊙ Capitals of minor divisions
● Chief seaports

Navigable rivers
Principal canals
Principal railroads

Land below sea level
Swamps and marshes
Lowlands and interior plains
Uplands and plateaus
Old, worn-down mountains
Young, rugged mountains

Natural boundaries between Europe and Asia

144

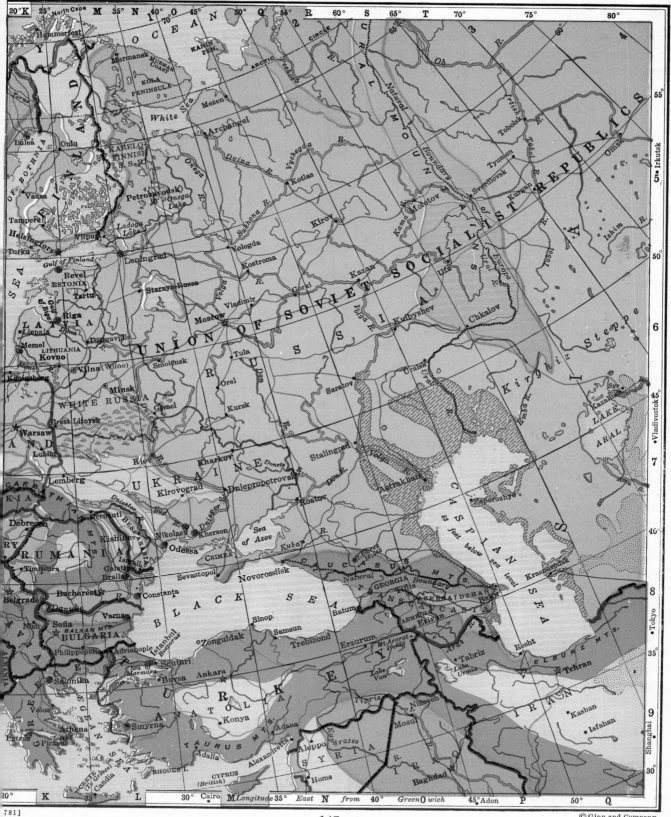

145

Reminders of home. Name one or more places in France where each person described below would find something to remind him of home.

1. A dairy farmer from New England.
2. A steel-manufacturer from Pittsburgh.
3. A rubber-manufacturer from Akron.
4. A Gloucester fisherman.
5. A cotton-manufacturer from Georgia.
6. A coal-miner from Pennsylvania.
7. A sugar-beet grower from Utah.
8. A farmer from the corn belt.
9. A California grape-grower.
10. A glove-manufacturer from New York State.
11. A silk-manufacturer from Paterson, New Jersey.
12. An automobile-manufacturer from Detroit.

A manufacturing test. 1. Use the map on pages 140–141 to point out the three leading cotton-manufacturing districts of France. Explain what advantages each district has for this industry. Tell which one of them is also a woolen-and-linen manufacturing district.

2. Point out the great silk-manufacturing district of France, and explain why the industry has developed there.

3. Point out the chief iron-and-steel manufacturing districts of France. Tell which ones have grown up where iron ore is mined, and which ones where coal is mined.

4. Point out the great glove-manufacturing center of France, and explain why the industry has developed there.

Finding likenesses. Tell of at least one way in which the following pairs of cities are alike: (1) London and Paris; (2) Southampton and Cherbourg; (3) Manchester and Rouen; (4) Liverpool and Le Havre; (5) Dover and Calais; (6) Birmingham and St. Étienne; (7) Leeds and Lille; (8) Stoke on Trent and Limoges.

Facts about Paris. 1. Tell how Paris ranks in population among (1) the cities of France; (2) the cities of Europe. 2. Name the different ways in which Paris is a great transportation center. 3. Tell why American women are especially interested in Paris.

Some comparisons to explain. In the three statements below you will find some comparisons between France and Great Britain. Explain what each comparison means by answering the questions that follow it.

1. France is nearly two and a half times as large as Great Britain, and has three million fewer people. (1) Which country is more densely populated? (2) Which one needs more food?

2. In Great Britain $\frac{4}{10}$ of the people who work are engaged in manufacturing, and less than $\frac{1}{10}$ are farmers. In France $\frac{3}{10}$ of the workers are engaged in manufacturing, and $\frac{4}{10}$ are farmers. (1) In which country is farming more important? (2) In which country is manufacturing more important? (3) Which country must import more food?

3. The total value of the exports and imports of Great Britain is more than twice that of the exports and imports of France. In which country is foreign trade more important?

Giving reasons. The comparisons which you have just studied show that farming is more important in France than in Great Britain, and that manufacturing and foreign trade are more important in Great Britain than in France. Prove that you understand the reasons for these facts by completing the sentences below:

1. The French people carry on more farming than the British because they have more _ _ _ _ _ land suitable for raising _ _ _ _ _ _.

2. The British carry on more manufacturing than the French because their country is not so well suited to _ _ _ _ _ _ _, and because they have larger supplies of _ _ _ _ for power.

3. The British have a greater import trade than the French because their farms produce less _ _ _ _, and because they need more _ _ _ _ _ _ _ _ _ _ for their factories.

4. The British have a greater export trade than the French because they carry on more _ _ _ _ _ _ _ _ _ _ and therefore have a greater surplus of _ _ _ _ _ _ _ _ _ _ goods to sell.

Special credit work. Find out all you can about the Louvre, the Eiffel Tower, the Arc de Triomphe, and the Cathedral of Notre Dame, and tell your classmates about them.

Figure 141. A view of Algiers, the capital and chief seaport of Algeria, as it looks from a boat in the harbor. Notice how the white buildings of the city shine in the brilliant Mediterranean sun. The sailboat is a fishing boat, and the steamer tied up at one of the wharves is a freight and passenger ship.

II. THE POSSESSIONS OF FRANCE

Foreword. Use the maps on pages 42–43 and 148–149 to compare the French possessions in distant lands with those of the British. Which country controls more land in the Americas? in Asia? What should you say about the extent of the French lands in Africa compared with the extent of the British lands in that continent?

You have learned that the British possessions are very valuable as sources of raw materials and foodstuffs and as markets for manufactured goods. As you study about the possessions of France, watch to see if they serve the French people in the same ways.

1. FRENCH LANDS IN AFRICA

If we include the island of Madagascar, the French control about the same amount of territory in Africa as do the British. Using the map on pages 148–149 as a help, locate the French possessions in Africa on Figure 42 (p. 49). Where among them do you find the fewest people? What reason does Figure 41 suggest for this very sparse population? What reason does it suggest for the larger numbers of people farther north and south in the French possessions? What parts of the French lands in Africa do you think are most valuable? Why?

The Coastal Possessions in Northern Africa

Algeria, Tunisia, and Morocco. The French find it easy to visit their lands in northern Africa, for it is only about 400 miles across the Mediterranean from Marseille to Algiers, the capital of Algeria. *See Figure 141.*

Locate Algeria, Tunisia, and Morocco on the map on pages 226–227. Algeria is a French colony with a French governor. Tunisia and Morocco have native rulers; but they are under French protection, and French officials direct the government.

FRANCE, BELGIUM, THE NETHERLANDS, AND THEIR POSSESSIONS

	AREA IN SQUARE MILES
France	212,659
Algeria, Tunisia, and Morocco	1,061,600
Madagascar	241,094
Other possessions in Africa	2,783,516
French possessions in Asia	286,196
French possessions in America	35,800
Total	4,620,865
Belgium	11,775
Belgian Congo	902,082
The Netherlands	13,203
Netherlands Indies	735,268
Dutch possessions in America	54,670

	POPULATION
France	41,907,056
Algeria, Tunisia, and Morocco	16,500,000
Madagascar	3,797,936
Other possessions in Africa	19,044,000
French possessions in Asia	24,324,000
French possessions in America	586,000
Total	106,158,992
Belgium	8,386,553
Belgian Congo	10,381,700
The Netherlands	8,728,569
Netherlands Indies	60,727,233
Dutch possessions in America	305,000

FRANCE, BELGIUM, THE NETHERLANDS
AND THEIR POSSESSIONS
Scale of miles along the Equator

[782]

The map shows that these French lands include the Atlas Mountains, which border the southern coast of the western Mediterranean. What does Figure 41 (p. 49) show about the rainfall on the seaward slopes of these mountains? Judging from the map on pages 226–227, what kinds of work do you think the people of these French lands do?

The climate of the Atlas region is of the Mediterranean type, like that of the Riviera coast. The summers are hot and dry, and most of the rain falls during the mild winter. The winter weather is so delightful that Algiers has become a winter resort.

Natives and European colonists. The native people of Algeria, Tunisia, and Morocco are mostly Arabs and Berbers, and they are believers in the Mohammedan religion. You learned about the Arabs in your study of "Home Life in Far-away Lands." They are people of the white race, and those in northern Africa are descended from Arabs who came from Arabia long ago. The Berbers are descended from tribes who entered northern Africa from southwestern Asia even earlier than the Arabs.

Many of the native people live and work in the cities and towns, and some are farmers.

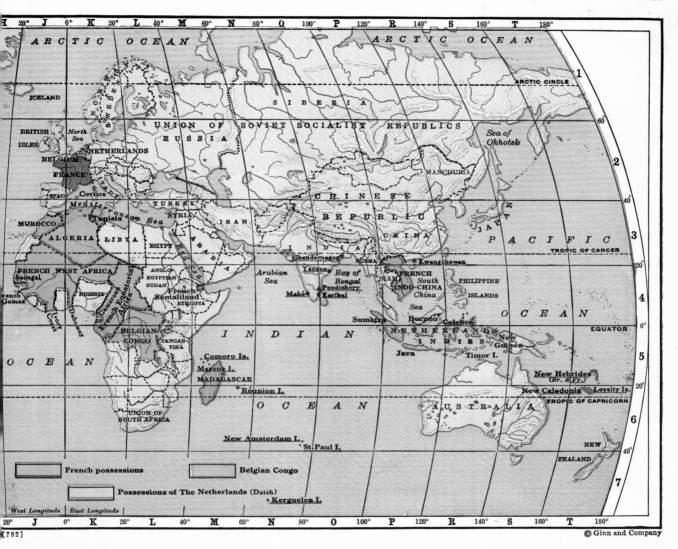

© Ginn and Company

Large numbers, however, live a half-nomadic life farther inland, where they raise cattle, sheep, and goats. *See Figure 142.*

Many of the natives are skillful in weaving rugs, and others in making fancy leather goods such as slippers, purses, and small handbags. These products of native handwork are displayed in the bazaars in Algiers (Alger), Tunis, and other coastal cities, where they find an excellent sale among the tourists.

In addition to the native people in these French possessions there are considerable numbers of colonists from France, Spain, and Italy. Why is it natural that the colonists should come chiefly from those countries? Many of them are farmers, and others carry on business in the cities.

The farm lands. The best farm lands of this northern part of Africa are the narrow, fertile lowlands near the coast and between the mountain ranges. Farming suffers somewhat from the summer drought; but the people overcome this handicap by raising crops such as grapes and olives, which are able to stand the dry weather, and by irrigating other kinds of fruit crops from streams and wells. They also raise large crops of winter wheat and barley. *See Figure 143.*

Figure 142. A Berber shepherd and his sheep in Morocco. The sheep raised by the Berbers and Arabs in northern Africa provide considerable quantities of wool for export to other lands.

Metal ores. In both Algeria and Tunisia iron ore, lead, and zinc are mined. Since very little lead and zinc are mined in France, these metal ores are exported chiefly to the home country. The iron ore, on the other hand, goes chiefly to Great Britain. You should be able to give two reasons for this fact. What are they?

Another mineral product of the French possessions in northern Africa which is very valuable is phosphate. Tunisia, Algeria, and Morocco together rival the United States in the production of phosphate rock, and large quantities are exported to France and other European countries. You will remember that phosphate rock is one of the three principal raw materials used in the manufacture of fertilizers. What have you learned about work in France which explains why the home country provides a good market for phosphate from the mines of northern Africa?

A forest product. Among the trees that grow on the slopes of the Atlas Mountains is the cork oak, the bark of which furnishes cork. Some of the natives make their living by stripping the bark from the trees and preparing it for export to France and other countries. *See Figure 144.*

The seaports and their trade. Algiers (Alger), the capital and chief seaport of Algeria, is one of the most picturesque cities on the Mediterranean Sea. The French call it *une ville étincelante* — a shining city — because nearly all the buildings are white, and they fairly shine in the brilliant Mediterranean sun. They cluster closely around the harbor, and climb the green, wooded slopes of the bordering hills.

Algiers has many fine hotels and public buildings, but visitors find their greatest interest in the beautiful old Mohammedan mosques, and in the native bazaars where Arab merchants in white robes and turbans sell their wares. *See Figure 145.*

Special credit work. Find out all you can about how cork is grown, how it is prepared for market, to what countries it is sent, and how it is used.

By Burton Holmes from Ewing Galloway

Figure 143. A European colonist and his native helper harvesting wheat on a farm in northern Algeria. How is the climate in this part of Africa suited to the raising of winter wheat?

Figure 144. Algerian natives stripping the bark from a cork oak. Cork oaks live to be very old, and the bark can be stripped off at intervals of from six to ten years during the lifetime of the trees.

Tunis, the capital and chief seaport of Tunisia, is much like Algiers. In the harbors of both these ports you will see ships from many distant lands; but you are likely to see more French flags than British or American, for more than half the trade of Algeria and Tunisia is with France. Locate Algiers and Tunis on the map on pages 226–227 (*D3* and *F3*). What foodstuffs do they export? What two raw materials are among their leading exports? If there were room to print more exports on the map, what metal ores would be among them? What do ships bring to Algiers and Tunis from France?

The work of the French. After studying the trade of Algiers and Tunis you will not need to be told that the French possessions in northern Africa are of great value to the home country as sources of foodstuffs and raw materials, and especially as markets for manufactured goods.

Since more people mean greater markets, the French are doing many things to make these colonies attractive to European settlers.

They have built thousands of miles of good roads and many hundreds of miles of railroads; they have introduced the telephone and the telegraph; they have improved the harbors; and they have opened up new lands for farming by drilling artesian wells. All these improvements are helping greatly in the development of the north African possessions of France; and as farming, mining, and other kinds of work increase in these lands, they become more and more valuable to the home country.

Some things to explain. Explain why

1. Grapes, olives, wheat, and barley are crops well suited to the climate of the French possessions in northern Africa.

2. Wool is one of the raw materials exported from these possessions of France.

3. The people of France take most of the lead and zinc ores exported from these possessions.

4. The people of France take much less of the exports of iron ore.

5. The French are spending much money to make their possessions in northern Africa attractive to European colonists.

6. The European colonists in these possessions are largely from France, Italy, and Spain.

© Publishers Photo Service, Inc.

Figure 145. A street bazaar in northern Africa. In Algiers, Tunis, and all the larger cities of northern Africa goods are sold out of doors in open markets. This street is the furniture market in Tunis.

Photograph by John A. Boardman

Figure 146. Camels resting at Touggourt, an oasis town on the northern margin of the Sahara Desert. Touggourt is a large oasis and can be reached from Algiers by railroad and motor road.

The Sahara

A vast desert. The map on page 50 shows that the French control a large portion of the great Sahara Desert. This, as you know, is the greatest desert in the world. It stretches all the way across northern Africa from the Atlantic Ocean to the Red Sea, a distance greater than that from New York City to San Francisco. The eastern half of it extends to the Mediterranean Sea, but the western half is cut off from the Mediterranean by the Atlas Mountains. Far to the south the desert gradually gives way to the grasslands of the Sudan.

In the Sahara, as in the desert of Arabia, the summer days are very hot and the winter days are very warm. But at night, even in the summer, the air cools off quickly.

Vast stretches of the Sahara are a windswept waste of sand and gravel, and here and there bare, rocky hills rise above its surface. In places the wind has piled the sand up in great dunes which at a distance look like the waves of the sea. Because this great desert is so dry, most of it is useless. What does Figure 42 (p. 49) show about its population?

Life in the oases. The only inhabited spots in the Sahara are the oases, where the water from springs and wells makes possible the growth of crops. Find the oases of the Sahara Desert on the map on page 46.

Some of the oases are large and support good-sized towns; others are small and contain only a few hundred people. The people are chiefly Arabs, and they live in houses with thick walls of sun-dried mud bricks which help to keep out the heat. In gardens which they irrigate from springs and wells, they raise grain, vegetables, and fruits. *See Figures 146 and 147.*

In the oases you will see many groves of date palms, for these trees grow especially well

Figure 147. A street in an oasis town in the Sahara. The trees are date palms, and beyond them are some of the mud-brick houses in which the people live.

under the hot desert sun, provided that their roots can reach water. Dates are the only export product of any importance from the oases, and large quantities of them are dried and sent to Mediterranean ports for export.

Transportation in the desert. Turn to the map on page 50 and find the railroads which the French have built across the Atlas Mountains to oases on the northern margin of the desert. What reasons can you give for the absence of railroads elsewhere in the Sahara?

Until quite recently anyone wishing to travel in the desert had to join a camel caravan. The caravans move slowly over long-used routes leading from one oasis to another, and from ports on the Mediterranean to Timbuktu and other trading towns in the northern part of the Sudan.

Camel caravans are still used in the desert, but along some of the old caravan routes the French have opened roads for passenger automobiles and motor trucks. Newest of all is the airway from the Mediterranean coast to the Gulf of Guinea. Passengers and mail leaving Algiers by plane reach the Niger River, in French West Africa, the next day. *See Figure 148.*

French Lands South of the Sahara

Well-populated lands. On the map on page 48 find Timbuktu (*C3*) and notice its location near the big northern bend of the Niger River. What does Figure 42 show about the population of the part of French West Africa south of the latitude of Timbuktu compared with the population of the Sahara region farther north? What reason does Figure 41 suggest for this difference? Turn to the map on pages 148–149 and find the places where

Photograph by Burton Holmes from Ewing Galloway, N. Y.

Figure 148. Old and new means of transportation in northern Africa. The good roads built by the French make possible the use of automobiles in some places, but the natives still use donkeys in and near the oases, and camels in the open desert.

French West Africa reaches the Atlantic coast and the Gulf of Guinea. Judging from the map on page 50, what kinds of work do you think are most important in the well-populated part of French West Africa?

The Sudan. Timbuktu is in the northern part of the region of Africa known as the Sudan. This region, as you already know, borders the Sahara on the south, and has enough rain for the growth of grass with scattered clumps of trees. On the west it extends to the Atlantic coast, where the French colony known as Senegal is located. Most of the people of the Sudan are native Negroes who make their living by raising cattle and by farming in a simple way. *See Figure 149.*

Hides and skins are exports of some importance from this region, but the products in which the people of France are most interested are the peanuts and the cotton which the natives raise. Peanuts, you will remember, are valuable oilseeds, and large quantities of them are exported to Marseille. To encourage more cotton-growing the French have built

Courtesy of French Colonial Government

Figure 149. One of the native villages in the Sudan region of French West Africa. The people of these villages carry on farming and raise cattle.

canals to carry irrigation water from the Niger River to farm lands in the western part of the Sudan.

Timbuktu is an old trading town which long ago became important as a meeting place for caravan routes from the north. From its port on the Niger, goods can be sent down the river to the coast of the Gulf of Guinea.

For many years the export products of the interior of the French Sudan were either carried northward across the desert by camel caravan to the Mediterranean or were sent down the Niger River to the Gulf of Guinea. Today most of these products are exported through the port of Dakar in Senegal, for the French have built a railroad to connect that port with the town at the head of navigation on the Niger River. Find this railroad on the map on page 50. What advantages has it over the older routes as a means of exporting goods from the Sudan to France?

The French share of the Guinea coast. What did you learn on page 66 about the climate of the coast of the Gulf of Guinea? The French lands here are the Ivory Coast and the coastal portion of Dahomey. The people of these hot, rainy coast lands are mostly native Negroes who carry on farming in a simple way, raising foodstuffs for themselves and cacao for export. They also collect the kernels of the wild oil palm and cut mahogany logs in the forests. As in the neighboring British colonies on the Guinea coast, the leading exports are cacao, palm kernels, and palm oil. These go chiefly to France, and in return the French supply the natives with cotton goods which they need for clothing.

French Equatorial Africa. Only the southern part of this French colony is truly "equatorial," for it stretches northward to the margin of the Sahara Desert. The equatorial part is a tropical forest, while the part farther north belongs to the Sudan. The people are Negroes, and they are so backward that they produce very little for export.

French Somaliland and Madagascar

Somaliland. This little colony on the strait known as Bab-el-Mandeb is too small and too hot and dry to have any important products. To the French it is valuable chiefly because its port of Jibuti provides a coaling station for ships on the waterway between the Mediterranean Sea and the Indian Ocean.

Madagascar. On the map on page 50 find Madagascar (*H6–7*). This island is more than twice as large as New Zealand and has between two and three times as many people. In spite of these facts it is at present less valuable to France than New Zealand is to Great Britain because it has but few white people. Most of the people are dark-skinned natives who are more like the people of southeastern Asia than like the Negroes of the neighboring part of Africa.

The map on page 50 shows that Madagascar may be divided into three regions: the mountains in the east, the interior plateau, and the coastal plain on the west. Because of the southeast trade winds the eastern coast and the eastern slopes of the mountains are rainy and covered with tropical forests. The rest of the island, which has less rain, is chiefly grassland.

Along the hot, moist eastern coast the people raise large quantities of rice and other food crops, while the people of the grasslands farther west raise large numbers of cattle. Among the special products of the island are vanilla beans from which vanilla flavoring is made. Many of the European colonists, who are mostly French, are interested in developing plantations of coffee, cacao, and sugar cane, and in time plantation agriculture may make the island very valuable to France.

Madagascar has much mineral wealth, but as yet mining is carried on in only a few places. At present the most valuable mineral product is graphite. More than three fourths of all the trade is with France. From the map on page 50 name the leading exports and imports.

A product test. 1. Below is a list of some of the products which the French import from their possessions in Africa. Name the colony or region from which each one comes, and point to it on the map.

cork	wool
cacao	dates
wines	wheat
graphite	peanuts
olive oil	phosphate
vanilla beans	cattle hides
lead and zinc ores	palm oil and kernels

2. Now arrange the products correctly under the following headings:

a. French possessions in northern Africa
b. French lands in the Sudan
c. French lands on the Guinea coast
d. Madagascar

3. Make a statement telling which of the four groups of possessions in Africa you think is most valuable to the French as a source of foodstuffs and raw materials.

From Ewing Galloway

Figure 150. A glimpse of some of the street bazaars in Damascus. In this street woven baskets and household utensils of metal are offered for sale.

2. FRENCH LANDS IN ASIA

Compared with the British lands in Asia, the lands under French control in that continent are very small. Find them on the map on pages 148–149.

Syria and Lebanon. Syria was once part of Turkey but came under French protection after the First World War. Later Syria was divided into two states: Syria and Lebanon. In 1944 France agreed to transfer all powers to the Syrian and Lebanese governments, and in 1946 French troops were withdrawn. Find Syria and Lebanon on the map on pages 226–227 (*L 3–4*).

In Lebanon and along the coast of Syria the yearly rainfall is over 20 inches, but most of the rain falls in winter, and the summers are hot and dry. Here, as in other borderlands of the Mediterranean, the people raise grapes, olives, oranges, and other fruits, and winter crops of barley and wheat. In certain places tobacco and cotton are grown. One of the most important kinds of work is the raising of silkworms and the preparation of raw silk for export. This is work in which the French have given the native people much help. Can you explain why?

Figure 151. Native coolies, or laborers, working in a rice field on the delta of the Sonkoi River in French Indo-China. In what ways is this delta plain well suited to rice-growing?

Figure 152. Coolies carrying coconuts gathered from the trees on a plantation in French Indo-China.

Farther inland there is much less rain, and much of Syria is desert land. There most of the people are nomads who wander about with their flocks of sheep, goats, and camels.

On the map on pages 226–227 find Damascus (Esh Sham) and Beirut (*L 4*). Damascus, the capital of Syria, is an old Arab trading town, with bazaars like those in Algiers and Tunis. Beirut is the capital of Lebanon and an important seaport. *See Figure 150.*

French Indo-China. On the map of the Far East (p. 298) find French Indo-China (*B 5*). Notice that this French colony shares with the neighboring country of Siam the lowland plain of the Mekong River. Find the delta plain of another river farther north in Indo-China. What does Figure 64 (p. 71) show about the rainfall in these plains? In what zone is French Indo-China? What kinds of work do you think the people do there?

French Indo-China is a monsoon land like India, and its plains will remind you of the plain of the lower Ganges. Like that plain, they are among the great rice-growing regions

of the world. Rice is the principal food of the people, and it makes up about half of all the exports. The rice that is exported goes chiefly to China, Japan, and the Netherlands Indies, neighboring lands crowded with millions of people who, like the Indo-Chinese themselves, depend on rice as their principal food. *See Figure 151.*

Other crops which are raised in various parts of the country are corn, cotton, sugar cane, tea, coffee, pepper, and coconuts. The French have established rubber plantations, and the exports of rubber are increasing. The leading import is cotton cloth, which the natives use for clothing.

The French officers in charge of the government of this colony make their headquarters at Hanoi, the capital, and at Saigon, the chief port. Besides the government officials there are a good many French and other Europeans who are interested in the development of tropical plantations. *See Figure 152.*

The native people, who make up most of the population, are of the Mongolian race, like the Chinese and the Japanese. Most of the settlements are along the rivers near the seacoast, and besides the people who live on the land there are many who live in boats on the rivers. In this colony the French have a very valuable possession, for it is well suited to plantation agriculture, and the natives make good plantation workers.

East of Indo-China the French hold a small area on the Chinese coast known as Kwangchowan. This is a center for French trade with China.

French towns in India. On the map on pages 148–149 find the five towns on the coast of India which belong to the French. These possessions are very small, but they are important to the French as centers for trade with India.

Pacific islands. Like the British, the French own many small islands in the South Pacific Ocean. You learned on page 92 how easily the native people of these tropical islands make their living. The French islands are useful to the people of France in the same ways that the British islands are useful to the people of Great Britain.

A check. Check your knowledge of the lands which France owns or protects by naming the places described below:

1. An island in the Mediterranean Sea.
2. Three French possessions in northern Africa.
3. A large area of French lands lying mostly in the Sudan.
4. French lands bordering the coast of the Gulf of Guinea.
5. The French possession in Africa through which the equator passes.
6. Two Arab states in the Near East formerly under the protection of France.
7. The French colony on the strait called Bab-el-Mandeb.
8. A large island off the east coast of Africa.
9. The French colony in the Far East.
10. The French colony in South America.

11. The tiny country in the Pyrenees under the protection of France.

Giving reasons. Complete each of the following sentences by giving reasons:

1. Algeria, Tunisia, and Morocco are the most valuable of the French possessions because - .

2. A large section of the French lands in Africa is almost useless because - - - - - - - - - - - - - - - .

3. Although Madagascar is more than twice as large as New Zealand, it is less valuable to France than New Zealand is to Great Britain because - .

4. As a whole, the French possessions are less valuable than the British possessions because - .

5. The French want more European settlers in their possessions in northern Africa because - .

A picture test. Below is a list of pictures which a traveler took in the French possessions, and a list of the places where he took them. The number after each place tells how many pictures were taken there. Name the pictures taken in each place.

LIST OF PICTURES

Rice fields	A cacao plantation
A phosphate mine	Stripping cork bark
Harvesting wheat	Raising silkworms
A field of peanuts	A graphite mine
Date palms	A rubber plantation
A lead mine	Vineyards
An olive grove	An artesian well
A camel caravan	Cutting mahogany logs
Vanilla beans	Palm kernels

LIST OF PLACES

Syria (1)	Madagascar (2)
The Sahara (2)	French Indo-China (2)
French Sudan (1)	The Guinea coast (3)

French possessions in northern Africa (7)

Map work. On an outline map of Africa color all the British possessions in red. Then color all the French possessions in purple. Keep this map and add to it as you study the possessions of other European countries in Africa.

Figure 153. Dairy cows grazing on the island of Zealand, in Denmark. There are more than two millions of dairy cows in Denmark, and butter is one of the most valuable exports of the country. What industrial country bordering the North Sea do you think probably provides a good market for butter from Denmark?

THE SMALL NORTH SEA COUNTRIES

I. BELGIUM, THE NETHERLANDS, AND DENMARK

Foreword. Bordering the North Sea, opposite Great Britain, are three small kingdoms — Belgium, the Netherlands, and Denmark. The Netherlands is often called Holland, but Holland is simply the name of one section of the country. The total area of these three countries is little more than that of the state of Ohio, yet they have about three times as many people. One of the countries owes its prosperity chiefly to agriculture, the second chiefly to manufacturing, and the third chiefly to agriculture and commerce.

Find these three countries on the map on pages 22–23. From what you can learn of them from the map, write down their names in the order in which you think they are described above. Keep your list for checking when you finish studying this chapter.

Turn to the map on pages 148–149 and find the distant possessions of Belgium and the Netherlands. How do the possessions compare in size with the homelands? Which of the two countries has possessions in the Americas? What is the name of the largest of those possessions?

From Figure 168 on page 171 tell what large island belongs to Denmark. Do you think this is a valuable possession? Give a reason for your answer.

As you study about Belgium, the Netherlands, and Denmark, find answers to these questions:

1. How do so many people make a living in these small countries?

2. Of what use to them are their distant possessions?

1. FARMING AND FISHING

In all three of these North Sea countries there are large numbers of farmers, and along the coast of the Netherlands and Denmark there are many people who carry on fishing. Can you suggest reasons for the importance of farming and fishing in these countries?

The land and the climate. The map shows that all of Denmark and the Netherlands and more than half of Belgium are in the Central Plains of Europe. Thus most of the surface is well suited to farming. The climate too is favorable, for the westerly winds from the Atlantic bring rain at all seasons.

Along the North Sea coast of these countries there is a narrow belt of sand dunes. Farther inland much of the land is covered with glacial soils which are not very fertile, but they can be made to produce good crops by the use of fertilizers. The richest soils are in the western part of the Netherlands, south of the Zuider Zee, for this region is the delta plain of the Rhine and the Meuse rivers.

The land of the Danes. The map shows that Denmark occupies the peninsula of Jutland and the islands between that peninsula and Sweden. It has no coal or oil, no metal ores, and no water power. Its soils are almost its only natural resource, and even those are

Photograph by James Sawders

Figure 155. A coöperative creamery in Denmark. All over the country there are creameries where cream purchased from the farmers is used to make butter.

rather poor. Yet Denmark is a prosperous country, for the people make the best possible use of their land.

Danish farmers and their work. One third of all the workers of Denmark are farmers, and another third are engaged in work connected in one way or another with the marketing of farm products. By using fertilizers and cultivating their land carefully the Danish farmers have turned three fourths of their country into valuable farm lands, and they have made Denmark famous for its dairying industry. *See Figures 153 and 154.*

On nearly every Danish farm you will see not only cows but pigs and poultry, and on many you will see beef cattle. Part of the cultivated land is used for food crops, — chiefly rye, wheat, potatoes, and sugar beets, — but even more for oats, barley, and other crops grown chiefly to feed the live stock. The products that bring in the most money are cream, eggs, and pigs. The pigs can be raised cheaply because they are fed partly on skimmed milk.

Photograph by James Sawders

Figure 154. Threshing grain on a farm in Denmark. Danish farmers use modern machinery in their farm work. What reason can you suggest for the fact that they raise large quantities of grain?

Royal Dutch Airlines Photograph from OROC

Figure 156. A glimpse of the Dutch polder land from an airplane. Notice the strips of cultivated land separated by ditches into which the water drains. The windmills are used to pump the water into canals which carry it to the sea. Pumps run by steam power and by electric power are also used for this purpose.

Working together. One of the chief reasons for the prosperity of the Danish farmers is that they coöperate, or work together, to market their products. Nearly every farmer belongs to one or more of the many hundreds of coöperative societies which own creameries, cheese factories, egg-packing plants, and bacon factories. He sells his products to the societies to which he belongs. The societies, in turn, prepare the products for use and carry on the business of marketing them at home and in other countries. *See Figure 155.*

By selling to their coöperative societies instead of trying to market their products separately, the Danish farmers have a better chance of getting good prices; and since Denmark is almost wholly an agricultural country, the prosperity of the farmers means the prosperity of the entire nation.

Many cities in England depend largely on Denmark for their butter, eggs, and bacon. In fact, more than half of all the foodstuffs exported from Denmark go to Great Britain. What reasons can you give for this?

The Dutch polders. The best farm lands in the Netherlands are the polders on the great delta built by the Rhine and the Meuse rivers just as the great Mississippi delta in our own country was built. The polders are low, flat lands which the Dutch have drained by building dikes around them and pumping the water out. The larger canals, which carry away the water, are used for transportation. *See Figures 156 and 157.*

K. L. M. Photo from OROC

Figure 157. Another view of the polder land from an airplane. This is a Dutch town on a river near Amsterdam. Notice that the town lies between the railroad tracks and the river, and that the surrounding land is divided into polders. Across the river, at the left in the picture, are some small factories.

The low, moist polders make rich pastures, and therefore the principal work of the polder farmers is dairying. Butter is exported to Germany and other neighboring countries, and Dutch cheeses find markets in distant lands as well as in those close by.

Some of the polder farmers have market gardens where they raise fresh vegetables for the people of the cities and for export to neighboring countries. Many of the market gardeners have hothouses so that they can raise vegetables in winter as well as in summer. This is profitable business, for fresh vegetables bring high prices in the winter.

If you visit the polder land in the spring, you will see acres and acres of beautiful flower gardens filled with tulips, hyacinths, and narcissi. These flowers are grown not for the blossoms but for the bulbs, which are sold to florists and seed merchants in many different parts of the world.

Adding to the polder land. The higher land east of the polders has much poorer soil; but in spite of this it is used for raising rye and other grains and for pasturing cattle. But the Dutch want more of the rich polder land, and they are getting it by draining a large part of the Zuider Zee. Find the Zuider Zee on the map on pages 22–23 (*K4*).

The Zuider Zee used to be a large inlet from the North Sea, but it has been closed by a great dike across its entrance. The dike keeps out the sea waters, and makes the Zuider Zee a fresh-water lake called the

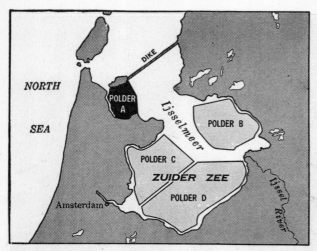

Figure 158. New polder land from the Zuider Zee. Polder A has been completed and is being used for farming. Polders B, C, and D will be added later.

Ijsselmeer. The Dutch are now at work diking and draining enough of the lake to uncover more than half a million acres of its level bottom for farming. Figure 158 shows the new polder land already made in this way, and the much larger polders that will be added when the project is completed.

Farming in Belgium. As you would expect, the best farm land of Belgium is in the lowland region. The farms are very small, but the land is used intensively; that is, every acre is made to produce all it possibly can. Mixed farming is the rule, and the leading crops are rye, wheat, potatoes, and sugar beets for food, and forage crops for live stock.

On the map on pages 22–23 find the place in the lowland of Belgium where flax is a special crop. This district is in the valley of the Lys River. What kind of manufacturing do you think is carried on in this valley?

Study the map again and see if you find any foodstuffs among the leading exports of Belgium. Do you know of any reason why the Belgians do not export foodstuffs, as the Dutch and the Danes do?

Dutch and Danish fishermen. Since the North Sea is one of the best fishing grounds in the world, many people along the coast of Denmark and the Netherlands make their living from the sea. The Dutch and Danish fishermen catch many kinds of fish, but herring, cod, and mackerel are the most important.

On the map on pages 22–23 find the canal which connects Amsterdam with the North Sea (K4). At the entrance to this canal is the Dutch fishing port of Ymuiden, which will remind you of the fishing ports along the east coast of England and Scotland. It has a large fleet of trawlers which bring in great quantities of fresh fish from the North Sea. Express trains, waiting near the wharves, rush the fish to Amsterdam and to cities in Germany.

Fishing and seamanship. In the Netherlands, as in England, fishing long ago led many men to follow the sea; and the Dutch very early became explorers and settlers of distant lands. Today the Dutch have a large fleet of merchant ships, and they carry on trade in all parts of the world.

Proving statements. What facts can you give to prove each of the following statements?

1. The Danes are skillful, businesslike farmers.
2. The Dutch are more fortunate in their soils than the Danes.
3. The Dutch wish to add to their better farming lands.
4. The Belgians need all the food they can produce.

Special credit work. Find out what the Dutch have had to do to make the low polder land safe from river floods, and tell your class about it.

2. SEAPORTS AND MANUFACTURING CITIES

Turn to the map on pages 22–23 and find the chief seaports of Belgium, the Netherlands, and Denmark. Which country has two large ports? What port is at the mouth of the Rhine? Judging from the exports, which one of the three countries do you think carries on the most manufacturing?

The capital of Denmark. On the map find Copenhagen, the capital and chief seaport of Denmark (*O3*). Notice that it has an excellent location for trade with the neighboring countries. The Danish name for this city is Köbenhavn, which means "Merchants' Harbor." Ships can reach it easily from the Baltic Sea on the east, and by two routes from the North Sea on the west, one around the northern end of Jutland, and the other through the Kiel Canal. Find this canal on the map (*M3*).

Copenhagen can also be reached by train from all parts of Denmark, from Sweden, and from Germany. Through train service is made possible by ferries which carry freight and passenger cars across the bodies of water which separate the Danish islands from one another and from Jutland, and across those which separate Denmark from Sweden and Germany.

Because of its location, its shipping, and its railroad connections, Copenhagen is the largest city and the leading business center of Denmark. It also carries on some manufacturing, especially shipbuilding, but it is much more important as a commercial center than as an industrial center. *See Figure 159.*

Manufacturing and trade in Denmark. The lack of coal, oil, and water power in Denmark is a great handicap to manufacturing, and the principal industries are those which have to do with agriculture, such as the making of butter, cheese, and condensed milk, meat-packing, sugar-refining, and the manufacture of dairy equipment.

The trade of Denmark shows clearly how largely the people depend on agriculture. The leading exports, as you know, are foodstuffs from the farms. Among the imports

Photograph by James Sawders

Figure 159. Looking eastward over part of Copenhagen. In the distance you can see the entrance to the harbor. The open water beyond is the strait which separates Denmark from Sweden.

are millions of dollars' worth of oil cake and grain for cattle feed, and large quantities of fertilizers. The rest of the imports show Denmark's lack of fuel and its small industrial development. Turn to the map on pages 22–23 and prove that this is true.

Rotterdam — gateway for the Rhine Valley. On the map on pages 22–23 find Rotterdam (*K5*). This great seaport is on the Meuse River (or the Maas, as the Dutch call it), a short distance below the point where that river is joined by one of the distributaries of the Rhine. On the map on pages 144–145 trace the Rhine upstream from its mouth to Basel, in Switzerland.

The Rhine is navigable for barges and river steamers all the way from Basel to Rotterdam, and its valley is an important railroad route. The Rhine Valley is also a rich agricultural region, and in and near it in western Germany are many great industrial centers. Much of the commercial importance of the Netherlands is due to the fact that it controls the mouth of the Rhine, and Rotterdam is one of the greatest seaports of Europe because it is the ocean gateway for the Rhine Valley.

K. L. M. Photo from OROC

Figure 160. An airplane view of one of the many docks, or deep-water basins, for ships along the Maas at Rotterdam. Notice the many ocean freighters and river barges, and the long storage warehouses which border the dock. The large ship nearest you, with two smokestacks, is a transatlantic passenger liner.

Large ocean ships come to Rotterdam through a deep waterway which the Dutch have dug from the North Sea, and they load and unload in huge docks on both sides of the river. Many of the bulky imports, such as grain, oil, and coal, are loaded on barges at Rotterdam and sent upstream to the industrial centers of the Rhine Valley in Germany. *See Figure 160.*

Of course Rotterdam imports and exports goods for the Dutch people; but when you think of this great seaport, you will want to remember that it not only handles trade for the Netherlands but is also important to the trade of the neighboring part of Germany.

Amsterdam. The map shows that Amsterdam is farther north, near the Zuider Zee (K 4). This is the largest city of the Netherlands, and the official capital of the country.

The Zuider Zee is much too shallow for ocean-going ships, but the Dutch have made Amsterdam a great seaport by digging a deep canal connecting it with the North Sea. Ships come to it from all over the world, and it is the port through which much of the Dutch trade with the East Indies is carried on.

Amsterdam and Rotterdam are connected not only by railroads but also by a canal, and large quantities of goods are carried back and forth between them by barges. In both cities there are many small canals for the transportation of goods in small barges. *See Figure 161.*

The Hague ('s Gravenhage). On the map (pp. 22–23) find The Hague (K 4). Although The Hague is not the capital of the Netherlands, it is the city where the queen lives and the work of the government is carried on. It is a very attractive city with many parks and boulevards and many beautiful public buildings.

The trade of the Netherlands. The map shows that the Dutch people import a great variety of goods. Among them you will find foodstuffs and raw materials from the Netherlands Indies and other tropical lands. Grain and flour also are important, especially corn and wheat; for the Netherlands is too cool for the best growth of corn and too damp for the best growth of wheat. The imports of coal and oil suggest a shortage of fuel in the Netherlands, and the high rank of iron and steel goods among the imports indicates that there are no great iron-and-steel-manufacturing centers in the country.

Philip D. Gendreau N. Y.

Figure 161. A canal in Amsterdam. Amsterdam has a network of canals on which goods are carried in small boats and barges. The boats in this picture have come in from the countryside loaded with plants to be sold in the flower market.

The map shows that the principal exports of the Netherlands are dairy products and other foodstuffs. Notice, however, that cotton goods are among the leading exports. To what part of the world do they go?

Manufacturing in the Netherlands. The Dutch have but one small coal field in their country, and they have no iron or other metal ores. Some of their leading manufactures, such as butter and cheese, depend on raw materials produced at home, but more of them are connected in one way or another with foreign trade.

As you would expect, Rotterdam and Amsterdam are the leading manufacturing cities, and both are shipbuilding centers. Can you explain why? Imports of tropical products have made Amsterdam a center for cigar-making, coffee-roasting, and the manufacture of cocoa and chocolate. Amsterdam is also well known for the cutting of diamonds. Where do the rough diamonds come from?

Another important industry in the Netherlands is the manufacture of vegetable oils from imported oilseeds. Large quantities of vegetable oils are exported, and large quantities are used in the making of soap and of margarine, a substitute for butter.

As you would expect, the Dutch people also manufacture goods to supply the needs of the people in the Netherlands Indies. Chief among these is cotton cloth. Can you explain why?

Do you see how important commerce is to the Dutch people? Long ago their seamanship made them traders and won them the rich East Indies. Their location at the mouth of the Rhine also has increased their commerce greatly; and commerce, in turn, has played a large part in the growth of manufacturing.

Antwerp and its trade. On the map on pages 22–23 find Antwerp (Anvers), the seaport of Belgium (*K5*). This city is located not far from the mouth of the Scheldt River and is connected with all parts of Belgium by railroads and canals. Many of its imports go to western Germany, but it is a somewhat less important gateway for that region than is Rotterdam. Like Amsterdam, Antwerp is a shipbuilding center, and is well known for the cutting of diamonds. *See Figure 162.*

Philip D. Gendreau, N.Y.

Figure 162. A glimpse of the water front on the **Scheldt River** at Antwerp, showing the old castle known as The Steen. The lower course of the Scheldt has been deepened by dredging so that large ocean ships can come upstream to Antwerp.

How many things do you find among the imports and exports of Antwerp to prove that Belgium is a manufacturing country? Belgian trade is much like British trade; for the leading imports are foodstuffs and raw materials, and the leading exports are manufactured goods. Do you know why Belgium is a greater manufacturing country than the Netherlands?

The Belgian coal field and its manufactures. Turn to the map again and you will see that the coal field of northern France continues eastward along the margin of the upland region of Belgium. The coal mined here has led to the growth of a great iron-and-steel industry. At Liége and other cities along the coal field there are blast furnaces, steel mills, and many factories for the manufacture of iron and steel products. *See Figure 163.*

A little iron ore is mined near the coal field, but most of the ore comes from the neighboring duchy of Luxembourg. Find Luxembourg on the map (K–L 6), and you will see that its iron field is a northern extension of the Lorraine field of France. Luxembourg has an independent government, but in its business affairs it is closely associated with Belgium.

Other important industries of the Belgian coal field are the manufacture of glass and chemicals and the refining of zinc and copper. Crude zinc and copper are imported from distant lands.

East of Liége, in the upland region, is a district where woolen goods have been manufactured for over five hundred years. The upland has always been a sheep-raising region, but today it supplies only a small part of the raw material needed by the mills. Most of the wool now comes from Argentina.

Textile-manufacturing in Flanders. The western part of the plain of Belgium is called Flanders, and for hundreds of years it has been a famous textile-manufacturing region. Flax grown in the valley of the Lys long ago led to the manufacturing of linen goods, but the industry has now outgrown the home supply of raw material. Later, cotton-manufacturing was begun in this region. Today all the larger cities have linen mills or cotton mills, or both. The largest of the textile centers is the old city of Ghent (Gand). Much of the flax and most of the cotton for its mills come by barge from Antwerp.

The capital of Belgium. On the map on pages 22–23 find Brussels (Bruxelles), the capital and largest city of Belgium (K 5). Its central location in the country has made Brussels an important railroad and business center. It is also a beautiful city, with many parks and playgrounds and fine public buildings. Its chief manufactures are laces, rugs, and carpets, and it is a center for the sale of lace which Belgian women make by hand.

Photo Nels, Brussels

Figure 163. Charleroi, the most important coal-mining center in Belgium. Charleroi is one of the many mining and industrial cities located on the coal field which extends from northern France across Belgium. Besides its coal mines, the city has iron-and-steel plants, glass factories, and many other kinds of manufacturing plants.

A check. 1. Look at the list which you were asked to make at the beginning of this chapter and see if it reads as follows: Denmark, Belgium, the Netherlands. If it does, it is correct.

2. Complete the following sentences by giving reasons.

a. Farming is the most important kind of work in Denmark because _____.

b. Manufacturing is more important in Belgium than in Denmark or the Netherlands because _____.

c. The Netherlands is a greater commercial country than Denmark or Belgium because ___ _____.

Explaining differences. In the following sentences certain differences between Belgium, the Netherlands, and Denmark are stated. Give the principal reasons for the differences.

1. Denmark has about 225 people to each square mile, while Belgium has about 710.

2. The Netherlands is not quite so densely populated as Belgium.

3. The Belgians need all the food they can produce, while the Danes have large quantities of food for export.

4. The Dutch have a much larger fleet of merchant ships than the Danes or the Belgians.

5. In proportion to the population the Danes import more manufactured goods than the Dutch or the Belgians.

6. There are many more miners among the Belgians than among the Danes or the Dutch.

7. The Belgians import greater quantities of cotton and wool than the Dutch.

Naming ports. Name the port in Belgium, the Netherlands, or Denmark where you would be most likely to see each ship described below, and explain why.

A ship (1) unloading wool from Argentina; (2) loading butter and bacon for England; (3) unloading goods bound for western Germany; (4) loading iron and steel goods; (5) unloading oil cake and fertilizers; (6) loading vegetable oils; (7) unloading coffee and cacao.

II. COLONIAL POSSESSIONS

Foreword. You have learned that the Dutch carry on much trade with their possessions in the East Indies. The trade of the Belgians with their colony in Africa is very much less, and Danish trade with Greenland is exceedingly small. Can you suggest any reasons for these great differences in trade?

K. N. I. L. M. Photo from OROC

Figure 164. One of the many sugar factories in Java. In the factories the cane stalks are crushed to squeeze out the juice, and the juice is boiled and evaporated to obtain the raw sugar. Notice the little settlement of overseers' houses in the picture.

THE NETHERLANDS INDIES[1]

Tropical islands. The Netherlands Indies include the Dutch parts of Borneo and New Guinea, the large islands of Sumatra, Java, and Celebes, and many smaller islands. Their area is over fifty times as large as the Netherlands, and they have about seven times as many people. These East Indian islands are in the heart of the tropics, and are hot and rainy the year round. Many parts are mountainous and covered with tropical forests.

[1] In 1947 the people of the Netherlands Indies became self-governing partners with the Dutch in a Netherlands Indonesia Union in which Java, Sumatra, and Madura form the Republic of Indonesia. This republic and the other parts of the Netherlands Indies make up the United States of Indonesia.

Plantation products. The East Indies are very valuable possessions because they produce tropical products needed in the temperate countries of Europe and America. The Dutch and other groups of white people have established plantations of rubber, sugar cane, coffee, tea, tobacco, coconut trees, and oil palms on the islands, and large quantities of the plantation products are exported, chiefly to Europe and the United States. *See Figures 164 and 165.*

The Netherlands Indies stand next to British Malaya in the production of crude rubber, furnishing about a third of the world's supply. Java stands high in cane-sugar production, and it exports more coffee than any other part of the Old World. The native people of the East Indies are intelligent, and they make excellent plantation workers. Many thousands of them work on the plantations, where they live in huts provided by the owners.

The chief crop which the natives raise for their own use is rice, for this grain is their principal food. In Java, where the population is so dense, additional supplies of rice are imported from the neighboring countries of southeastern Asia.

Mineral wealth. Borneo, Sumatra, and Java have valuable oil fields. In all three islands there are petroleum refineries, and gasoline, kerosene, and fuel oil are exported to the Netherlands, Great Britain, and other European countries, and to China and Japan. The islands of Banka and Billiton, near Sumatra, have such rich tin mines that the Netherlands Indies rank next to British Malaya and Bolivia in the production of this metal.

Batavia and its trade. On the map on page 298 find Batavia (*B7*). On what island is it? Batavia is the largest city and chief seaport of the Netherlands Indies. It is also the capital, where the Dutch officials who have charge of the government make their headquarters.

Batavia serves as a collecting and distributing center for the Netherlands Indies, just as Manila serves the Philippine Islands. Besides the large ocean ships in its harbor, you will see the small boats which bring in products of the other islands for export and carry back supplies for the people. Turn to the map on page 298 and prove that the trade of these islands is like that of other tropical lands, — an exchange of foodstuffs and raw materials for manufactured goods.

In normal times the export and import trade of the Netherlands Indies is chiefly with the Netherlands and other European countries, and with Japan and the United States. The leading export to our country is rubber, for we use more rubber than any other nation in the world.

The Netherlands and Japan supply many of the manufactured goods used in the islands, especially cotton goods. Great Britain also has a share in the import trade of the Netherlands Indies, because the British are better able to supply machinery and other manufactures of iron and steel than are the Dutch. Explain why.

BELGIAN CONGO

Another tropical land. Turn to the map of Africa on page 50 and find Belgian Congo. What great river basin lies wholly in this possession of the Belgian people? How can you prove by the map that this basin is another tropical land?

The Congo Basin is hot and rainy, and much of it is covered with thick, tropical forests. Railroads are so hard to build in such a region that the Congo River and its tributaries are the chief highways of travel and transportation. Ocean ships go up the Congo as far as the town of Matadi, but they cannot go farther upstream on account of rapids in the river. From Matadi to Leopoldville, the capital, a railroad has been built. From Leopoldville the Congo is navigable for 980 miles to Stanleyville, where there are more rapids and another railroad.

The native people. The natives of Belgian Congo are Negroes who live in little villages along the rivers and get their food by raising a few vegetables and fruits, and by fishing. They also gather the fruit of the oil palms which grow wild in the forests, and sell the kernels to European traders. *See Figure 166.*

Handicaps to plantation farming. The Belgians have found it difficult to establish plantations in the Congo Basin because it is almost impossible to get the natives to work steadily. Their needs are so few that they

By Ewing Galloway, N.Y.

Figure 165. A native laborer at work on a rubber plantation in Java. He goes from tree to tree, setting the cups in place and cutting a thin shaving of bark to start the flow of the latex.

Figure 166. A glimpse of a village in Belgian Congo, showing the thatched-roofed houses of the native people.

Figure 167. A smelting plant in the southern part of Belgian Congo where crude copper is smelted from the ore for export. Belgian Congo ranks high among the copper-producing countries of the world.

care very little about earning money, and they prefer the easy life in their villages.

At present the most important plantations are those where oil palms are grown and the kernels crushed to extract the oil. Palm kernels gathered from the wild trees by the natives and palm oil from the plantations are valuable exports.

Congo mines. From the map on page 50 name the mineral products of Belgian Congo. By far the most important is the copper that is mined in the south. *See Figure 167.*

The ores are smelted near the mines, and the crude metal is exported in the form of bars. Most of it is shipped from a port on the coast of Angola. Study the map and explain why the copper is shipped from there instead of from the ports of Belgian Congo.

The trade of Belgian Congo. As you might expect, about half the trade of Belgian Congo is with Belgium. Copper is by far the most valuable export, and palm oil and palm kernels are next. Among the imports, cotton goods hold a high place. What reason can you give for this fact?

Looking forward. Belgian Congo is much larger than the Netherlands Indies; it is not yet crowded with people; its mineral wealth is great; and it can be made to produce large quantities of plantation products, such as rubber, cacao, and cotton. Its development has only just begun, and in time it may prove as valuable to the Belgians as the East Indies are to the Dutch.

GREENLAND AND THE FAROE ISLANDS

The largest island. If we except the island continent of Australia, Greenland is the largest island in the world. It is also an almost useless island; for nearly all of it is north of the arctic circle, and most of it is covered with ice and snow which never melt away.

A cold, frozen land. The interior of Greenland is a vast plateau of ice. At places the surface is 9000 feet above the sea, and the ice is probably thousands of feet thick. This great ice cap is like those which once covered the northern parts of North America and Europe. The ice moves slowly outward from the center of the island, and at places where it reaches the sea it breaks off in huge blocks, forming icebergs.

Off the east coast of Greenland there is a current of water from the Arctic Ocean which makes the climate of that coast so cold that no one can live there. On the west coast there is a narrow belt of tundra which is covered with green grass during the short summer. Perhaps this explains why Eric the Red, the Icelander who discovered the island, called it Greenland.

The people of Greenland. There are less than twenty thousand people in this cold, frozen island, and nearly all of them are Eskimos. They live along the west coast and get their living by fishing and by hunting seals, walruses, blue foxes, and other animals. The few hundred Danes who live among them are traders and the officials who carry on the business of the government.

In the summer, ships from Denmark carry supplies to the Greenlanders and take back considerable quantities of furs and fish. But the population of the island is so small that trade between the colony and the mother country does not amount to much.

The Faroe Islands. Small as these islands are, they have more people than Greenland, and they are of greater value to Denmark. Some of the people raise sheep, and wool and mutton are exported. Most of the people, however, are fishermen, and salted codfish and cod-liver oil are the leading exports of the islands.

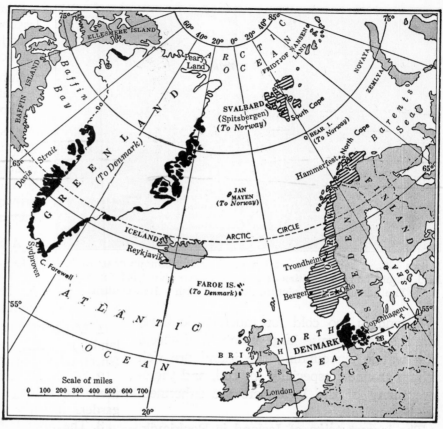

Figure 168. Denmark and Norway and their possessions.

ICELAND

Relations with Denmark. For hundreds of years Iceland belonged to Denmark. In 1918 the Danes gave Iceland full self-government, but the Icelanders agreed to recognize the Danish king as their king for a period of years. In 1944, after the agreement had run out, they voted to break this last tie with Denmark and to set up an independent republic.

The island and its people. Iceland is a mountainous island close to the arctic circle. Because of its location and the height of its mountains, much of the island is covered with ice and snow, and there are not many trees. Many of the higher mountain peaks are volcanoes, and the island also has geysers and hot springs. Nearly all the people live in the small lowland regions in the southwest.

Figure 169. A cod-fishing station on the mountainous coast of Iceland, where large quantities of cod are salted and dried for export. The barrels in the picture are filled with salted codfish.

Iceland is too cold for much agriculture, but the people raise large numbers of sheep. The waters surrounding the island are rich fishing grounds, especially for cod, and therefore many of the Icelanders are fishermen. *See Figure 169.*

The largest town of Iceland is Reykjavik, the capital and seaport. The leading exports of Reykjavik are wool and fish, and the leading imports are lumber, foodstuffs, fuels, and manufactured goods. Most of the trade is with Denmark and Great Britain. Can you think why?

Some things to explain. Explain why

1. The East Indies are possessions which any European country would be glad to own.

2. At present Belgian Congo is less valuable to the Belgians than the Netherlands Indies are to the Dutch.

3. Belgian Congo will probably become a more valuable possession in the future.

4. Greenland is of very little value to the Danes.

5. Belgium and the Netherlands export large quantities of cotton goods to their colonies.

Map work. Color Belgian Congo on the map of Africa which you are making.

Finding reminders. 1. Name at least one export product of the Netherlands Indies which reminds you of each country listed below:

Cuba	Ceylon
Brazil	Puerto Rico
Mexico	British Malaya

2. Name a river basin in South America of which the Congo Basin reminds you. Why can ocean ships go much farther upstream on the principal river of that basin than they can go on the Congo River?

A combination test. In each sentence you are to choose the correct word or phrase from those in parentheses, and then complete the sentence by giving reasons.

1. Much of the polder land in the Netherlands is used for (fruit-growing) (dairying) (sheep-raising) because _____.

2. Much of the farm land in Denmark is used for (forage crops) (orchards) (market gardens) because _____.

3. The abundant (zinc) (coal) (iron ore) in Belgium is of great value to the people because _____.

4. The Dutch and the Danes carry on much (lumbering) (mining) (fishing) because _____.

5. The seaport of greatest importance in the small North Sea countries is (Copenhagen) (Rotterdam) (Antwerp) because _____.

6. The principal crop raised by the natives of the Netherlands Indies for their own use is (rice) (sugar) (coffee) because _____.

Can you name these cities? Name each city described below:

1. The capital of Belgium.

2. The chief seaport of Belgium.

3. The capital and chief seaport of Denmark.

4. An important port which is the official capital of the Netherlands.

5. The city in the Netherlands where the work of the government is carried on.

6. The capital and chief seaport of the Netherlands Indies.

Courtesy Norwegian Travel Information Office

Figure 170. One of the many beautiful fiords on the western coast of Norway. Notice how steeply the mountains rise from the water. The fiords are narrow, but they are so deep that large ships can sail far inland on them. Where in the Americas do you think you could see coasts somewhat like this fiorded one of Norway?

SCANDINAVIA AND FINLAND

I. NORWAY AND SWEDEN

Foreword. The two countries which occupy the Scandinavian Peninsula of northwestern Europe are the kingdoms of Norway and Sweden. Find these countries on the map on pages 144–145. How do they compare in size with Belgium, the Netherlands, and Denmark?

The two Scandinavian countries are more than seven times as large as the three small North Sea countries, yet they have less than half as many people. In Sweden there are less than 40 people to the square mile, and in Norway less than 25. Although the population has always been sparse, thousands of people have left Norway and Sweden to make new homes in the United States. Our north-central states, especially, have large numbers of people of Swedish and Norwegian descent.

All these facts suggest that Norway and Sweden cannot support so many people as the countries farther south in Europe. Do you know why? Watch for the reasons as you study this chapter.

Map work. Before you read further, turn to page 177 and work out the map studies in Group I there.

The mountains of Scandinavia. The mountains which make up a large part of the Scandinavian Peninsula are very old. For long ages streams and glaciers have been wearing down their summits and deepening their val-

Figure 171. A boat passing through the Göta Canal. The trip across southern Sweden by the river, lake, and canal route takes two and a half days. The boats carry passengers and small freight.

leys. The snow fields and glaciers which you can see in the Scandinavian highlands today are reminders of the great ice cap which formed there long ago and spread over the northwestern part of Europe.

The fiord coast of Norway. Along the western coast of Norway the mountains rise steeply from the sea. Long ago this coast sank, and the sea entered the lower parts of the river valleys. Many of the valleys were steep-walled canyons, and today they form deep, winding fiords which lead far into the land. *See Figure 170.*

The coast is fringed with thousands of rocky islands, and between the islands and the coast there is a deep "inside passage" for ships, like the one along the coast of southeastern Alaska. This waterway is the principal highway of travel and transportation between the cities and towns along the coast, for there is no railroad connecting them.

Thousands of tourists visit western Norway every summer, for the scenery along the coast is beautiful. Among the sights which they enjoy are the waterfalls which tumble down the steep, rocky walls of the fiords.

A "**land of the midnight sun.**" Many of the tourists go to North Cape to see the midnight sun. Find North Cape on the map on page 176 (*H 1*). In that latitude the sun remains above the horizon continually for nearly three months during the summer. Day after day it appears to swing around the earth, rising highest in the southern part of the sky at noon, and sinking lowest in the northern part of the sky at midnight; but it does not set.

The length of time during which the sun does not set varies from one day on the arctic circle to six months at the north pole. In the winter there is a period of equal length during which the sun does not rise. This period is called the "winter night."

The lowlands of Scandinavia. Turn to the map on page 176 and notice how little of the lowland region of Scandinavia is in Norway. What does that suggest about the importance of farming in Norway compared with Sweden?

The Scandinavian lowlands have a rolling surface with many small hills. Some of the hills are of hard rock, and others are made up of loose rock materials left by the great ice sheet of long ago. There are also many lakes which occupy hollows left when the ice melted away.

Use the map on page 176 to show how you might travel by boat from Göteborg (*D 4*) across southern Sweden to the Baltic Sea. Through what two lakes should you pass? through what canal? This inland waterway is too shallow for large ships, but it is used by boats such as you see in Figure 171.

Some differences in climate. Because of their latitude, the Scandinavian countries have a cool climate; but they are not so bitterly cold in winter as the part of Europe

Photograph by James Sawders

Figure 172. Harvesting grain in southern Sweden. In this part of Scandinavia the surface is level enough to permit the farmers to use farming machinery.

Photograph by James Sawders

Figure 173. Haying on the west coast of Norway. Here the land is so mountainous and the patches of level ground so small that farm work is done by hand.

farther east. That is because the peninsula is so nearly surrounded by water. The western coast of Norway is warmed by the westerly winds that blow over the Gulf Stream Drift, and its harbors do not freeze over in the winter. This coast is also very rainy. Explain why.

Sweden has colder winters and warmer summers than Norway because it is on the leeward side of the peninsula, or the side away from the westerly winds. Figure 8 (p. 13) shows that it also has less rain than Norway. Give a reason for this.

Waste land. More than half of Norway is waste land — too rough for farming and too cool for the growth of valuable trees. Sweden also has much waste land, but not so large a part of the country is useless. Explain why.

Farming in Sweden. Since nearly all the lowland region of the Scandinavian Peninsula is in Sweden, more people can make a living by farming in that country than in Norway. Most of the farms are in the broader, southern part of the lowland. Why?

The Swedish farmers carry on mixed farming, raising cattle and growing crops suited to the cool, moist climate. For winter feed for the cattle large quantities of hay and of root

crops such as carrots and turnips are grown. The chief grain crop is oats, but the farmers also raise wheat, rye, and barley. Potatoes, too, are an important crop. See Figure 172.

The southernmost part of Sweden is an important dairying section, and the farms there will remind you of Denmark. Most of the dairy farmers keep pigs as well as cows, and many raise sugar beets as a money crop.

Farming in southern Norway. Norway is so mountainous that less than four per cent of the land is used for crops. The best farm lands are in the lowland region and in the valleys in the southern part of the country. There the people carry on farming much as their neighbors in Sweden do.

West-coast farms. Along the deep fiords of western Norway the people live on little farms, with the water almost at their front doors and the mountains rising behind them. They keep a few cattle, sheep, and goats. In the summer the older girls take the cattle to pastures high in the mountains. The men and boys stay at home, raising grain, potatoes, and forage crops on the farms. They also cut every bit of hay they can find, and store it in the barns for winter feed for the live stock. See Figure 173.[1]

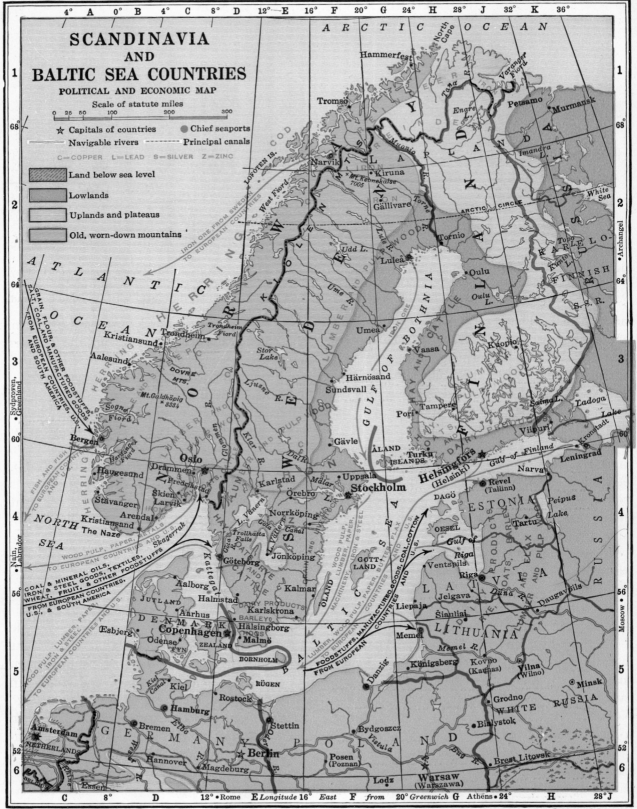

SCANDINAVIA
AND
BALTIC SEA COUNTRIES
POLITICAL AND ECONOMIC MAP

Scale of statute miles

0 25 50 100   200   300

★ Capitals of countries ● Chief seaports
— Navigable rivers ---- Principal canals

C=COPPER L=LEAD S=SILVER Z=ZINC

Land below sea level
Lowlands
Uplands and plateaus
Old, worn-down mountains

© Ginn and Company

Figure 174. One of the many pulp-and-paper mills in Sweden. In these mills large quantities of pulp-wood logs are used to make wood pulp. Much Swedish wood pulp is exported to other countries, and much is used in Sweden itself to make newsprint (paper for printing newspapers), wrapping paper, and cardboard.

Photograph by James Sawders

Map discoveries. Now work out the map studies in Group II on this page and you will discover some other kinds of work in Scandinavia.

Scandinavian resources. If the people of Norway and Sweden had to depend on farming alone, both countries would be poor; for not even Sweden has any large surplus of farm products for export. Fortunately, both countries have other resources besides their farm lands. In Norway these resources are fisheries and forests; and in Sweden, forests and mines.

Forests and forest work. About a fourth of Norway and more than half of Sweden are covered with valuable forests. The trees are largely pines, spruces, and other softwoods which are valuable for lumber and pulp wood. In both countries thousands of men work in the forests in the winter, cutting down the trees and getting the logs to the rivers. In the spring, when the ice melts, the logs are floated down the streams to sawmills and pulp mills. *See Figure 174.*

Turn over to page 178.

MAP STUDIES

Group I

1. Which of the two Scandinavian countries borders the Atlantic Ocean? 2. Which one borders the Baltic Sea and the Gulf of Bothnia? 3. Which country is almost entirely mountainous? 4. How should you describe the coast line of that country? 5. Which Scandinavian country has a considerable extent of lowland?

6. Trace the arctic circle across Norway and Sweden. 7. What does that suggest about the climate of the two countries? 8. In which country do you think more people can make a living by farming? Why? 9. In which country do you think the people make greater use of the sea? Why?

Group II

1. What do you find among the imports of Norway and Sweden to show that the farms of those countries do not provide all the food that the people need? 2. What do you find among the exports to prove that forest work is very important in both countries? 3. In which country do you think fishing is very important? Why? 4. Which country exports a product of its mines?

Figure 175. Cod-fishing boats at a little port in the Lofoten Islands. Winter is the season for fishing in this part of Norway, and no matter how cold or stormy the weather may be, the fishermen go out to the fishing grounds every day in their small boats.

Industries depending on forest work. Sawmills, pulp mills, and paper mills are found all through southern Norway and Sweden, and along the Swedish coast of the Gulf of Bothnia. From these mills large quantities of lumber, wood pulp, and paper go to the leading ports for export to Great Britain, France, and other European countries where the forests have been largely cut down. Our own country is a good customer for Scandinavian wood pulp. Can you explain why?

Another Scandinavian industry which depends on forest work is the making of safety matches. Millions of boxes of these matches are exported each year to many different countries of the world.

Norwegian fisheries. In Norway, fishing is more important than any other kind of work, and fish and fish products are the most valuable exports. There are several reasons for this: (1) the land is so poor for farming that the people are forced to make use of the sea; (2) the neighboring waters are rich in fish; (3) the irregular coast line provides many good harbors; and (4) fishing can be carried on the year round because the harbors do not freeze over in the winter.

The chief kinds of fish caught by the Norwegians are herring, cod, mackerel, and salmon. The best cod-fishing grounds are near the Lofoten Islands. Find these islands on the map on page 176 (*E1*). Herring are caught all along the coast, mackerel chiefly in the south, and salmon in the fiords. *See Figure 175.*

Preparing fish for export. Some of the fish are exported fresh, but much greater quantities are frozen or preserved in other ways. Cod are salted and dried, as they are in New England. The larger herring are salted or smoked, and the little ones are preserved in olive oil or other vegetable oils and sold in tins as Norwegian "sardines." All this work gives employment to large numbers of people.

The center of the fishing industry. On the map on page 176 find Bergen (*C3*). This is the second largest city in Norway, and the business center of the fishing industry. It is also the great port of export for Norwegian fishery products. *See Figure 176.*

Great Britain and the other densely populated countries of Europe provide excellent markets for Norwegian fish. Can you explain why? Large quantities of preserved fish, such as smoked herring and Norwegian sardines, are also sent to the United States and other distant countries.

Why fishing is less important in Sweden. The Swedish people carry on much less fishing than the Norwegians because the Baltic Sea and the Gulf of Bothnia are less salty than the Atlantic Ocean, and the fish that live in their waters are not the best kinds for food. Furthermore, these inland waters freeze over for several months each winter, and therefore fishing can be carried on only part of the year.

Photograph by James Sawders

Figure 176. The outdoor fish market at Bergen. The people are crowding round the little counters where fresh fish which have just been brought in by the fishing boats are being sold. Study the imports of Bergen on the map on page 176. What do you find among them that is used in the preserving of fish?

Sweden's wealth of iron ore. On the map on page 176 find the two parts of Sweden where iron ore is mined. In the Lapland district, north of the arctic circle, Sweden has one of the best iron-ore fields of Europe. Unfortunately, Sweden has no coking coal, and so the greater part of the iron ore that is mined there is exported to Great Britain and other European countries where such coal is plentiful. *See Figure 177.*

On the map on pages 144–145 find the railroad which connects the iron mines of northern Sweden with the Atlantic coast and the coast of the Gulf of Bothnia. During the summer the ore is sent to the Swedish port of Luleå (*K2*) for shipment to southern Sweden or for export to other countries. But in the winter, when the Gulf of Bothnia is frozen over, the ore is shipped from the Norwegian port of Narvik (*J1*). Explain why.

Iron-and-steel manufacturing. In spite of the lack of coal, the iron-mining district which is located in southern Sweden has many blast furnaces and steel mills. The manufacture of iron began here long ago because the ore was abundant and the forests supplied charcoal for fuel. Coking coal is now imported from Germany and Great Britain, but some of the finest Swedish iron is still made with charcoal.

Much of the Swedish iron and steel is exported to the great manufacturing countries of Europe, and much is used at home for the manufacture of machinery and other iron and steel products. Great Britain is the best customer for Swedish steel, and large quantities are used in making cutlery at Sheffield.

Norway's mineral resources. Norway, like Sweden, has no coal within its boundaries, and in metal ores it is poorer than its neighbor.

Swedish State Railways Travel Information Bureau

Figure 177. Mining iron ore in an open-pit mine in the Lapland district of Sweden. The steam shovel shown in the picture was manufactured in our state of Ohio.

Iron and other metal ores are mined in a few places, but the total production of the mines is not very great.

Figure 168 (p. 171) shows that the islands known as Svalbard or Spitsbergen belong to Norway. They are too far north to have many people, but they are valuable to the Norwegians because they have abundant coal. Unfortunately, however, the coal can be shipped only in the summer, for during the rest of the year no boats can reach the islands on account of the ice. For this reason most of the coal used in Norway is imported from other European countries.

Using water power instead of coal. Because Scandinavia is mountainous and has much rain, it has many swift-flowing streams which furnish water power for making electricity. Both Norway and Sweden have large numbers of hydroelectric plants, which provide electricity for light, for telephones, and for power to run street cars, railroads, and manufacturing plants. Thus the streams make up in part for the lack of coal. *See Figure 178.*

In both countries far more hydroelectric power than steam power is used for manufacturing, and much electricity is used in the making of chemicals and fertilizers, the smelting of ores, and the refining of metals.

Do you remember the desert in Chile where nitrate is mined for fertilizer and other purposes? In Norway and Sweden an electrical process is used to take from the air a gas called nitrogen and transform it into nitrate.

In Norway, especially, electricity is used for smelting and refining ores of aluminum and other metals. Ores and crude metals are imported, and refined metals are exported.

Three important cities. On the map (p. 176) find Oslo (*D4*), Göteborg (*E4*), and Stockholm (*F4*). Which of these cities is the capital of Norway? Which is the capital of Sweden? In what way are they all alike?

Oslo is the capital and largest city of Norway. It has an excellent harbor at the head of a fiord and is the leading seaport of the country. How does its location help to explain why it is a larger city than Bergen?

Stockholm, the capital and largest city of Sweden, is an important seaport and one of the most beautiful cities of Europe. The center of the city is located where a number of short waterways lead from Lake Mälar to the Baltic Sea, and part of the city has been built on peninsulas and islands. *See Figure 179.*

Figure 178. A hydroelectric plant near Trondheim in Norway. Electricity from power plants like this is sent over wires to many cities and towns in Norway.

Photograph by James Sawders

Figure 179. A view of the oldest part of Stockholm, which has been the capital of Sweden for 700 years. This picture shows the island where the city began its growth. The large building at the left of the picture is the royal palace, where the king of Sweden lives. The winding harbor of Stockholm is lined with stone wharves, and small steamers, ferryboats, and launches carry people from one part of the city to another.

Stockholm has docks for ocean ships, and wharves for smaller steamers which run to other ports along the coast. In the winter, ice-breakers are used to keep the harbor open for shipping.

From Stockholm small boats go down the coast to the entrance to the Göta Canal and from there through the inland waterway to Göteborg. This city is the leading port of Sweden. What reason can you give for the fact that more Swedish trade passes through this port than through Stockholm?

Norwegian dependence on the sea. What reasons can you give for the fact that more people can make a living on the land in Sweden than in Norway? Why have the Norwegians been forced to make greater use of the sea than the Swedish people?

From the earliest days the Norwegians have been famous seafaring people. Their country is so poorly suited to farming that long ago they turned to the sea in order to obtain part of their food by fishing. Fishing led them to build boats and to venture farther and farther from land. Thus they became skillful seamen. Before the year 900 the Norsemen had made settlements in Iceland, and before the year 1000 Eric the Red had established a settlement in Greenland. It is interesting to remember that that was five hundred years before Columbus made his first voyage of discovery.

Today, as you know, Norway is famous for its fisheries. In addition to all its fishing boats Norway has the largest fleet of whaling ships in the world. These ships go to the Far South to catch whales in the icy waters near Antarctica, and they obtain millions of dollars' worth of whale oil each year. Whale oil is obtained by heating with steam the blubber, or fat, of whales. This work is done on the whaling ships. The oil is used for dressing leather, for lubricating, or oiling, machinery, and for many other purposes.

Norway has a large fleet of merchant ships also. Some of these ships carry goods back and forth between Norway and other countries, but many of them are carriers for other nations. They are owned by shipping companies in Norway, and they earn money for their owners by carrying goods between ports of various foreign countries. *See Figure 180.*

A trade test. 1. From the map on page 176 prove that (1) the leading exports of Sweden come directly or indirectly from its forests and mines; (2) that all but one of the leading exports of Norway come directly or indirectly from its fisheries and forests.

2. Explain why the Scandinavian people import (1) wheat and other foodstuffs; (2) coal and mineral oils; (3) many kinds of manufactures.

Making comparisons. The four sentences below make comparisons between Norway and Sweden. Complete each sentence by naming Norway and Sweden in the proper places and giving reasons for the fact stated.

1. Farming is more important in _____ than in _____ because _____.

2. Fishing is more important in _____ than in _____ because _____.

3. Mining is more important in _____ than in _____ because _____.

4. Lumbering is important in _____ and even more so in _____ because _____.

By Ewing Galloway, N. Y.

Figure 180. The harbor at Oslo with some of the ships which make up the large and well-known Norwegian fleet of merchant ships. These ships will be going to ports all over the world, carrying the goods of many nations. Why would you expect shipping to be such an important means of making a livelihood for the Norwegian people?

Photograph by James Sawders

Figure 181. Cows grazing on a farm in the southern part of Finland. The cool, moist climate of Finland is well suited to dairy farming, for the grass remains fresh and green all summer long, and hay grows well. Can you name a part of the United States which is well suited to dairy farming for much the same reasons?

II. FINLAND

Foreword. East of the Gulf of Bothnia is the republic of Finland. Find it on the map on page 176. Judging from the products and exports, what two kinds of work seem most important in Finland?

Handicaps to farming. The map shows that much of Finland is an upland region. The surface of this region is so hilly and rocky that it is not good farming land. Along the coast there are lowlands, but even these are not very well suited to farming because they have coarse glacial soils and a short growing season. But the Finns are intelligent and energetic people, and they make the best possible use of their agricultural land. Their chief crops are hay and oats, and they keep a good many cattle. In the southern part of the lowland region dairying and poultry farming are important, and butter and eggs are exported. *See Figure 181.*

The greatest resource. When you were studying the map, did you notice the large number of lakes in the southern part of the upland of Finland? The land in this lake region is covered with thick forests of pine and spruce trees, which are the greatest natural resource of Finland. Thousands of men work in the lumber camps, and many others in the sawmills, pulp mills, and paper mills. Lumber of various kinds is by far the most valuable export of Finland, and wood pulp and paper are next. *See Figure 182.*

Helsingfors. On the map on page 176 find Helsingfors, or Helsinki, as the Finns call it (*H3*). This is the capital, the largest city, and the chief seaport of Finland. In what part of the country is it located? On what body of water?

The harbor of Helsingfors freezes over during the winter, but except when the ice is unusually thick, the port is kept open for shipping by ice-breakers.

Lapland. The map (p. 176) shows that the northern part of Finland, Sweden, and Norway is called Lapland. This is a bleak, almost treeless land inhabited mostly by the people known as the Lapps. Many of the Lapps are nomads who keep herds of reindeer which provide them with food, clothing material, and means of transportation.

Photograph by James Sawders

Figure 182. A sawmill at one of Finland's lumber ports. The man in the boat is trying to free some logs with his pole so that they will not jam together but can move into the mill. Notice the wooden runways going into the mill building in the distance. The runways support moving belts which carry logs into the mill.

Can you give these names? Give the name of each of the following:

1. The gulf between Finland and Sweden.
2. The islands near the best cod-fishing grounds of Norway.
3. The canal which forms part of the inland waterway across southern Sweden.
4. The name given to the northern part of Finland, Sweden, and Norway.
5. The sea between Sweden and the Soviet Union.
6. The gulf south of Finland.
7. The group of islands in the Far North belonging to Norway.

A ship test. Five ships are steaming away from ports of Scandinavia and Finland. The country which each ship has just left is given in the first column below, and the ship's cargo is given in the second column, opposite the name of the country. Name the port where each ship was loaded.

		(Port)
Norway	fish	―――――
Finland	newsprint	―――――
Sweden	iron ore	―――――
Sweden	machinery	―――――
Norway	wood pulp	―――――

Special credit work. 1. Look at home and in the stores to see how many things you can find that came from Sweden, Norway, and Finland. 2. Try to make a collection of safety-match boxes from these various countries.

Sentences to complete. Complete each sentence below by giving reasons:

1. The greater part of the land in Norway, Sweden, and Finland is not well suited to farming because ――――――――――――――――――.
2. These countries export large quantities of lumber, wood pulp, and paper because ――――――.
3. Norway and Sweden have much water power because ――――――――――――――――――.
4. Water power is especially valuable in these countries because ―――――――――――――――.
5. The Norwegians make much use of the sea because ――――――――――――――――――.
6. Norway, Sweden, and Finland cannot support so many people as the countries farther south in Europe because ―――――――――.

Matching countries and capitals. Match correctly the countries and capital cities below:

Finland	Oslo
Norway	Stockholm
Sweden	Helsingfors

By Ewing Galloway, N.Y.

Figure 183. Plowing land for winter wheat on a large farm in the Plain of Hungary. Notice how level the surface is in this region of central Europe. Find the Plain of Hungary on the map on page 12. What is its elevation? What does Figure 8 show you about the rainfall of the plain with reference to farming?

THE COUNTRIES OF CENTRAL EUROPE

I. GETTING ACQUAINTED WITH CENTRAL EUROPE

Foreword. The map on pages 140–141 shows that the central part of Europe is divided among six countries: Germany, Poland, Czechoslovakia, Switzerland, Austria, and Hungary. Which two of them are the largest? What can you say about the location of the other four with reference to outlets to the sea?

Switzerland was the only central European country which was not drawn into the war in one way or another. Except in Switzerland the war years made great changes in the economy, or use of the resources, in the central European countries. The Germans turned their country into a huge arsenal for the production of the fighting equipment which was to make them masters of all Europe. In Austria and Hungary the people coöperated in putting their resources and industries to work for Germany.

In conquered Poland and Czechoslovakia the people were forced against their will to do likewise.

Great changes in political boundaries in central Europe resulted from the war. The largest transfers of territory were the area which Poland gave up to the Soviet Union and the parts of Germany which Poland received in exchange.

Central Europe is faced with years which must be devoted to reconstruction before either the aggressor nations or their victims can hope to live as well as they did before the war. Just what each country will be like when the reconstruction has been completed, no one can say. The best we can do, therefore, is to find out what each one has in the way of resources upon which to build.

Some differences in surface. As we study about the countries of central Europe we shall find that differences in the surface of the land have much to do with the life and work of the people. For example, what differences in the land and its use are shown in Figures 183 and 184?

In order to picture to yourself the many differences in surface in central Europe, use the map on pages 140–141 to answer the following questions:

1. What two of the central European countries have a large share of the Central Plains of Europe? 2. What kind of work is important in those plains? 3. How does the surface in southern Germany and Poland differ from the surface of the northern plains? 4. What country of central Europe has an upland region surrounded by a ring of old, worn-down mountains? 5. What do you find on the map to show that the uplands of Germany, Czechoslovakia, and Poland are not too rough for farming? 6. What reason have you to think there may be industrial centers in these upland regions?

7. What mountain region does Poland share with Czechoslovakia and Russia? 8. What mineral wealth have those mountains? 9. In what country is the central portion of the Alps? 10. What part of central Europe is made up largely of an eastern extension of the Alps? 11. What mineral wealth have the mountains of Austria?

12. Which of the central European countries lies almost wholly in a lowland region which is surrounded by rugged mountains? 13. How do you think most of the people of the Plain of Hungary get their living?

The northern plain of Germany and Poland. The map shows clearly that farming is very important in the northern plain of Germany and Poland. This plain has a gently rolling surface, with many low hills and many lakes, ponds, and marshes. It is a region covered with glacial soils left by the great European ice sheet of long ago. For the most part these soils are sandy and poor, and in order to make them produce good crops the farmers have to enrich them with large quantities of fertilizers. Study the map (pp. 140–141) and see if you can discover a mineral resource of Germany which is of help to the farmers.

In Germany and western Poland large areas which were once marshes have been drained and turned into good farm lands. The area that was eastern Poland and is now part of the Soviet Union has great stretches of land too wet for farming where swamps and marshes have not been drained.

Higher regions in the south. South of the northern plain is a belt of uplands and old, worn-down mountains. The soils of the uplands are good; and although these regions are rougher than the northern plains, they have broad valleys which provide excellent farm lands.

Turn to the map on pages 140–141 and find some names in central Europe which suggest that the mountains are forested. Almost all the land that is level enough for farming has been cleared, but there are forests on the mountain slopes and in the rougher parts of the uplands. These are cared for so that they produce regular "crops" of timber.

The Alps and the Carpathians. South of the uplands of Germany are the Alps, which extend from southeastern France through Switzerland and northern Italy into Austria. These are higher than any mountains of Europe except the Caucasus, and there are snow fields and glaciers among their summits. Farther northeast are the Carpathians. They are much lower than the Alps, and they are forested nearly to their summits.

The slopes of these rugged mountains are for the most part too steep for farming, and the higher parts of the Alps are too cool for any crops. The lower slopes of the Alps are covered with forests, and above the tree line there are grassy pastures where cattle, sheep, and goats graze during the summer.

Courtesy of Swiss Federal Railroads

Figure 184. Cattle grazing on the high pastures in the Swiss Alps. What reason can you give for the fact that far more land in the Alps is used for grazing than for the raising of crops? The snow-capped mountain peaks shown in the picture rise to elevations of more than 13,000 feet above the level of the sea.

The Plain of Hungary. The Plain of Hungary will remind you of our prairies; for it is a grassland with few trees except along the streams, and it is one of the best farming regions of Europe. What other countries share this plain with Hungary?

The rainfall of central Europe. Figure 8 on page 13 shows that very little of central Europe has less than 20 inches of rain a year. That is because there are no ranges of mountains running from north to south in western Europe as there are in the western part of our country, and therefore there is nothing to prevent the westerly winds from carrying moisture far inland from the Atlantic Ocean. Central Europe, then, has plenty of rain for farming.

The heaviest rainfall is in the mountainous regions, especially in the Alps. Explain why.

The Alps are so high that much of the annual, or yearly, rainfall comes in the form of snow. That accounts for the snow fields and glaciers which never melt away.

Temperature conditions. Central Europe has greater extremes of temperature than western Europe because it is farther from the Atlantic Ocean. For example, the summers are hotter and the winters colder in Berlin, the capital of Germany, than in London, and there are still greater differences between the summer and winter temperatures at Warsaw, the capital of Poland.

Wherever you travel in the temperate zones you will find that inland regions have greater extremes of temperature than coastal regions. That is because they do not have the warming influence of the oceans in winter or the cooling influence in summer.

Length of growing season. The growing season in the northern plain of central Europe is long enough for grains such as wheat, oats, and rye to ripen. The uplands have a growing season of about the same length as the northern plain; for while they are somewhat farther south, they are higher.

The longest growing season in central Europe is in the Plain of Hungary, and the shortest growing season is in the higher parts of the Alps in Switzerland and Austria. Give reasons for these facts.

Central Europe as a source of rivers. The maps will show you that several of the longest and most important European rivers rise in the higher parts of central Europe. You already know that the Rhine and the Rhône rise in the Swiss Alps. Which of these two rivers flows northward to the North Sea? In what country is the mouth of this river?

On the map on pages 140–141 find each of the following rivers and trace them from source to mouth: the Weser (*L2*), the Elbe (*M2*), the Oder (*O2*), the Vistula (*R2*), and the Danube (*L4*). In order to trace the lower course of the Danube, you will need to use the map on pages 226–227. As you trace each river, name the country in which it rises and the country where it reaches the sea.

Inland waterways. In studying the important rivers that rise in central Europe did you notice that they are all navigable? Turn to the map again, and you will see that many of their tributaries are also navigable and that the different river systems are connected by canals. This great network of inland waterways furnishes slow but inexpensive means of transportation.

In order to understand why transportation by river and canal is so important in central Europe, we must remember that this part of the continent was thickly populated long before railroads were dreamed of. In those early days the rivers were the chief routes of travel and transportation, and the inland towns that grew the fastest were those which had the best locations for trade by water. To make it possible for towns on different rivers to trade with one another, canals connecting the various river systems were built.

The map on pages 144–145 shows that today central Europe is covered with a network of railroads. Nevertheless, here, as in France, rivers and canals continue to be used for transporting large quantities of bulky goods, chiefly because transportation is cheaper by water than by rail. In fact, in recent years old canals have been deepened and new canals have been built.

Countries without seacoasts. When you were studying the map, you must have noticed that some of the countries of central Europe have no seacoast. What countries are they? We say that such countries are landlocked. What disadvantage is it to them to have no land bordering the sea?

Internationalized rivers. In order to give the landlocked countries of central Europe means of shipping goods cheaply by water to the seaports of neighboring countries, the more important navigable rivers are *internationalized*. That means that they are open and free for the use of all nations on equal terms.

The Danube is internationalized all the way from Ulm, in southern Germany, to the Black Sea. This river has always been an important highway of transportation and trade, and it is a great help to Hungary to be able to use it. The map on pages 226–227 shows that Czechoslovakia too can make use of the Danube. Find its river port of Bratislava (*G1*). How may ships reach the Mediterranean Sea from the mouth of the Danube?

The Elbe and the Oder rivers are internationalized as far as they are navigable, giving Czechoslovakia free water routes to the North Sea and the Baltic Sea.

The Rhine, which you already know is a great highway of trade, is internationalized all the way from its mouth to Basel, in Switzerland, giving that little country a free navigable waterway to the port of Rotterdam. *See Figure 185.*

Highways and airways. Like France, the countries of central Europe have an excellent system of automobile highways, and are served by a network of airlines. Turn to the map on page 128 and study the central European airways. Notice how thick the network is in Germany, and how that country is connected by air lines with all its neighbors.

Figure 185. A view of the water front on the Rhine at Basel, in Switzerland. The long, low boats nearest you are barges for transporting freight. The steamer farther away is a passenger boat.

Something to prove. Prove that you are getting acquainted with central Europe by giving the names called for below:

1. The two largest countries of central Europe.
2. The landlocked countries.
3. The two countries that have a large share of the Central Plains of Europe.
4. The countries of central Europe which share the Alps.
5. The country in which the Bohemian Plateau is located.
6. The country which is almost wholly a plain.
7. The principal river of Poland.
8. The river that rises in the Black Forest and flows to the Black Sea.
9. The river that rises in Switzerland and flows to the North Sea.
10. The river that rises in the Bohemian Plateau and flows to the North Sea.
11. The river that rises in Switzerland and flows to the Mediterranean Sea.

A shipping test. Use the map on pages 140–141 to show how goods may be shipped by water between each pair of places named in the next column:

1. From Danzig ($R1$) to Warsaw ($S2$).
2. From Stettin ($O2$) to Breslau ($P3$).
3. From Hamburg ($M2$) to Berlin ($N2$).
4. From Hamburg ($M2$) to Prague ($O3$).
5. From Rotterdam ($J3$) to Basel ($K5$).
6. From Cologne ($K3$) to Vienna ($P4$) and Budapest ($R5$).

A map to make. 1. On an outline map of Europe trace the boundaries of the countries of central Europe with a colored pencil, and print their names neatly.

2. Add the names of the following rivers: the Rhine, Danube, Weser, Elbe, Oder, Vistula.

3. Find the capital cities of the central European countries on the map on pages 140–141. Show their locations by stars on your map and print their names.

4. Add red dots to show the locations of the seaports of Bremen, Hamburg, Stettin, and Danzig, and print their names.

Some things to prove. Prove by the map you have made that

1. All but one of the capital cities of central Europe are on navigable waterways.

2. The four leading seaports are at the mouths of navigable rivers.

By Ewing Galloway, N.Y.

Figure 186. Harvesting potatoes in Germany. Notice that the farmers are using a potato-digger. Where in the United States could you see sights like this?

Photograph by Ewing Galloway, N.Y.

Figure 187. A sugar-beet field in northern Germany. The beets have been dug from the ground and their tops cut off, ready to be sent to a sugar factory.

11. GERMANY

Foreword. Today the Germans are paying the penalty for starting the Second World War. What is left to them of their country is under strict control by occupation forces of the United States, Great Britain, the Soviet Union, and France, and it seems likely that this control will continue for many years.

Before the war Germany was the second greatest manufacturing country in Europe, outranked only by Great Britain. Now its industries are being controlled and greatly restricted by the Allies. This means that for a long time Germany will be a much less important industrial and commercial country than it was before the war, and farming will play a greater part in the over-all life of the nation.

The clearing up of the war wreckage and the necessary rebuilding in their country are only part of the task facing the Germans. Their manufacturing and foreign trade will be less than they have ever had. These are facts to keep in mind if you wish to understand what is going on in Germany now and how it makes out in the future.

1. THE NORTHERN PLAIN AND THE BORDERING UPLANDS

If we should fly in an airplane over the northern plain of Germany, we should look down on a vast number of farms, many cities and towns, and a close network of railroads, rivers, and canals. Along the seacoast at the north we should see large seaports, and along the southern margin of the plain and in the neighboring uplands smokestacks would tell us of industrial districts.

From the map on pages 140–141 tell what you expect to see on the farms of northern Germany. What reason does the map suggest for the industrial districts along the southern margin of the plain and in the neighboring uplands?

The Farm Lands of Northern Germany

Getting good crops from poor soils. Although the northern plain of Germany has rather poor glacial soils, the German farmers produce larger quantities of foodstuffs per acre than almost any other farmers in the world. The reason for this is that they use the best methods of work. They add plant food to the soils by using large quantities of fertilizer; they sow the best of seed and tend the growing crops carefully; and they rotate their crops in such a way that the soil never becomes "worn out." You will remember from your study of the United States that crop rotation means planting different crops in each field from year to year.

Germany's wealth of potash. You will also remember that the principal raw materials used in manufacturing fertilizers are potash, nitrate, and phosphate. Germany has the richest deposits of potash salts in the world. Turn to the map on pages 140–141 and find the places where the potash is mined. These mines help to provide the German farmers with fertilizers at prices they can afford to pay, and they make Germany the leading producer and exporter of potash.

The leading crops. The leading crops of northern Germany are rye, oats, and potatoes, because they grow well in the sandy soils and the cool climate. Wheat is also raised, but in much smaller quantities, for most of the soils are too sandy to make good wheat lands. Oats are grown chiefly for live stock. Rye is the principal bread grain, and rye and potatoes are the chief food crops. Large quantities of potatoes also are grown for making alcohol and starch. *See Figure 186.*

On the map find the parts of the northern plain where the farmers raise large quantities of sugar beets. In normal times Germany's refineries turn out more beet sugar than those of any country except the Soviet Union. *See Figure 187.*

Live stock and dairying. On the farms of the northern plain you will see large numbers of cattle, pigs, and poultry, and many sheep. Since the climate is too cool for corn, the farmers raise carrots, turnips, and other root crops to feed their live stock. They also feed potatoes to their pigs, and beet tops and beet pulp to their cattle.

Photograph by James Sawders

Figure 188. Making butter in a creamery in Germany. One man is pressing the butter into pound blocks and the other is wrapping the blocks in paper.

Near all the larger cities there are market gardens and dairy farms, but the principal dairying section is in the northwest. This portion of the German plain is part of the great dairying region of northwestern Europe which extends from western France to southern Sweden. *See Figure 188.*

Small farms and many workers. Because Germany is so densely populated, most of the farms are small, and the need for food leads the farmers to make every acre of land produce all it possibly can. Farm workers are plentiful, for the women and children work side by side with the men in the fields. This is true in all the central European countries.

The growth of cities in the northern plain. As you would expect, the German plain has a number of large cities and many smaller cities and towns. Most of the cities began as trading centers for the surrounding farm lands. Today they are also manufacturing centers, and in many of them you will find flour mills, sugar refineries, factories for making starch and alcohol from potatoes, and plants for the manufacture of farming tools and machinery. Those that have become railroad centers have many different industries.

Photograph by James Sawders

Figure 189. A Saar coal mine. The big wheel at the top of the steel framework runs the elevator "cage" which lifts small carloads of coal from the mine.

Some things to explain. Give an explanation for each fact stated below:

1. The farmers of the northern plain of Germany do not raise corn. (Remember what kind of weather corn needs while it is growing.)

2. Rye, rather than wheat, is the chief bread grain grown in northern Germany.

3. In spite of rather poor soils the German farmers raise large quantities of foodstuffs per acre.

4. Flour-milling and the manufacture of sugar, starch, and alcohol are important in northern Germany.

Industrial Districts

Foreword. Under the rules which the Allies have laid down and are enforcing, Germany has lost its former high rank in manufacturing. The three great industrial districts which you will read about in this section were very important before the Second World War. They are much less so now, but they are still the chief areas for such manufacturing as the Germans are allowed to carry on. All over the country, in the leading industrial areas and elsewhere, there are food-processing plants and factories which manufacture consumer goods.

Germany's wealth of coal. On the map on pages 140–141 find the coal fields of Germany. These are bituminous coal fields, and the northwestern one is the richest in the continent of Europe. Before the war Germany was mining so much coal that it had a large surplus for export. Its great prewar industrial growth was due in large measure to its wealth of this fuel.

How the Germans use lignite. Besides bituminous coal, Germany has large beds of lignite. This, as you may remember, is brown coal, much softer and poorer in quality than bituminous coal. Nevertheless, the Germans use large quantities of it for making steam power and steam-electric power for manufacturing, and they press it into egg-shaped lumps called briquets, to be used as household fuel for heating and cooking. They also use much lignite in the manufacture of dyes, chemicals, and fertilizers.

Getting oil from coal. Germany has very small petroleum resources, but the German scientists have found ways of getting oil from both lignite and bituminous coal, and refining it. To a certain extent the oils which are obtained in this way take the place of petroleum products which otherwise would have to be imported.

Coal fields and industrial districts. Germany has many manufacturing centers, but its three greatest industrial districts are located on and near the three great coal fields. As you read about each one, locate it on the map on pages 140–141.

The Saar Basin. The map on pages 140–141 shows that the coal mines of the Saar Basin (*K4*) are not far from the French iron mines in Lorraine. For this reason the Saar Basin is an important iron-and-steel-manufacturing district. Among its other industries, glassmaking and the manufacture of porcelain products hold high rank. *See Figure 189.*

because the carthage wanted to keep
the trade of Mediterr. there for.
they wanted to keep the emperor
Rome.

Taurus

1) Anatolia

2) Iran

3) Tibet

4) Tarim basin

5) Gabi Desert

Takis Constandinides.

1) what is a Republic; what is the
different between an Aristocratic Republic
and a Democratic one Republic

2) who was Rome's arrival in the
western Mediterranean.
   why did the Rome want to conquer

---

1) A republic is a form of government
where every year or every three
years the comes and vote together
and elect a president to rule the
country.

2) The difference between is that
in aristocratic republic only the
nobles or the rich people. have
the rights to voted and to be elect
But in Democracy everyone people
can voted.

2) The Carthagians who lived
   at Med. Sea. side of Africa
and controlled the trade of Med.

Photograph from R. I. Nesmith and Associates

Figure 190. Part of one of the great steel plants in the Ruhr Valley. The round-topped towers in the center of the picture are blast furnaces.

Photograph by James Sawders

Figure 191. A mill in the Rhine Valley where rayon fiber is made from wood pulp. The barges are loaded with pulp wood imported from Sweden.

The Ruhr district. The best coking coal in Germany comes from the rich coal field in the valley of the Ruhr River, a small tributary to the Rhine. Before the war the Ruhr Valley was one of the greatest iron-and-steel manufacturing districts in the world. The city of Duisburg, at the junction of the Ruhr with the Rhine, had become the world's greatest inland port.

Visitors in those days found the valley crowded with cities for forty miles eastward from Duisburg, and the whole area dotted with coal mines, blast furnaces, steel mills, and plants for the manufacture of heavy products of iron and steel. The products varied from all kinds of hardware and cutlery to locomotives, heavy machinery, steel rails, and huge steel plates to be used in building ships. *See Figure 190.*

The cities and coal mines are still there; but the area looks very different today, for Allied bombing in the war destroyed many of the manufacturing plants in this region. For this reason and because German manufacturing is now strictly limited and controlled by the Allies, the Ruhr Valley is no longer the great manufacturing area that it formerly was.

You will want to remember that the Ruhr Valley is simply the chief center of such "heavy industries" as the Germans are now allowed to carry on.

Industrial centers in the Rhine Valley. The abundance of coal in the valley of the Ruhr has led to the growth of many manufacturing centers in the neighboring part of the valley of the Rhine. Many different kinds of manufacturing are carried on, but the textile industries are the most important.

Large quantities of cotton, woolen, linen, and silk goods are manufactured from raw materials imported through Rotterdam and Antwerp. Krefeld, west of the Rhine, is the leading silk-manufacturing city of Germany. Another important branch of the textile industry in this part of the Rhine Valley is the making of rayon and rayon goods. Many kinds of chemicals, too, are manufactured, and among them dyes for coloring yarn and cloth are very important. *See Figure 191.*

Photograph by E. M. Newman from Wide World Photos, Inc.

Figure 192. A view of Cologne from across the Rhine. The cathedral with its tall spires is one of the most beautiful churches in Europe. The long building with the rounded roof at the right is the central railroad station. Besides being a great railroad center, Cologne is one of the most important river ports in Germany.

The largest city of the Rhine Valley. Among the industrial cities of the Rhine Valley is Cologne (Köln), the third largest city of Germany. Find Cologne on the map on pages 140–141 (*K 3*), and notice its location near the place where the Rhine leaves the upland region and enters the plain.

The valley of the Rhine is the principal railroad route through the upland region, and Cologne is the place where railroads from the east, north, and west meet to pass southward. This makes Cologne a great railroad center. It is also a busy river port; and since it is a meeting place for routes of transportation by river and rail, it had become before the war a great business and industrial center. *See Figure 192.*

The Saxony industrial district. Turn to the map on pages 140–141 and trace the Elbe River (*N 3*) downstream from the boundary between Germany and Czechoslovakia to Magdeburg. The part of Germany drained by this stretch of the Elbe and its tributaries is called Saxony.

The coal of Saxony is not good for coking, but iron and steel from western Germany are used to manufacture many kinds of machinery and other iron and steel products. Even more important are the textile industries, especially cotton manufacturing, for which raw cotton is imported from the United States and other distant lands. Saxony has also great chemical industries.

Leipzig and Dresden. The largest cities of Saxony are Leipzig and Dresden. Find them

Figure 193. An airplane view of part of Dresden, on the Elbe River. The large building nearest you at the left is the Opera House, and the building at the right of it is a famous museum which contains many beautiful paintings, sculptures, and other works of art. Dresden is one of the great centers of art in Europe.

on the map on pages 140–141 (*N3*). Which one is on the Elbe River? Both cities are important industrial centers, and Dresden is a busy river port.

Dresden was a beautiful city before it was wrecked by bombs in the war, and it was visited by thousands of tourists because of its museums and its art treasures. Dresden china, the best-known product of Saxony, is not made in Dresden, but in a neighboring town. The industry began there long ago because of deposits of fine clay close by. *See Figure 193.*

Leipzig ranks among the ten largest of the cities of Germany. Its central location near the southern margin of the plain makes it a gateway city between that region and the southern uplands, and it is one of the great commercial centers of Europe. Twice each year a great fair is held at Leipzig, and merchants from all over Europe come to this city to display and sell their goods. Leipzig is also one of the world's greatest fur markets.

German leadership in making chemicals. In each of the great industrial districts and in many other places in Germany there are factories for making dyes, drugs, medicines, acids, and other chemical products. The Germans are famous for their skill in this kind of work, and they have long been leaders in the chemical industries.

One of the leading chemical industries is the manufacture of dyes from coal tar, which is a product left over in the making of coke from coal. The coal-tar dyes are made in

Figure 194. A view in the Rhine Gorge. In many places the steep slopes are covered with vineyards, and on some of the hilltops there are castles which were built hundreds of years ago. The Rhine Gorge is one of the most beautiful valleys in the world, and the Germans have written many songs and stories about it.

thousands of tints and shades and are exported in large quantities. Other kinds of work closely connected with the chemical industries are the making of nitrate from nitrogen extracted from the air by electricity, and the manufacture of fertilizers.

A coal test. You have learned that Germany's industrial growth is due largely to its wealth of coal. Prove that you understand this statement by completing the sentences below:

1. The coal fields of Germany are in the valley of the ____ River, in the ____ Basin, and in the state of _____.

2. These fields provide large quantities of ____ suitable for use as fuel for making _____ power and also for making _____ power for manufacturing.

3. In the Ruhr district Germany has large supplies of coal suitable for making ____ for smelting ____ ___.

4. The plants which make coke from coal also furnish ____ ___ for use in making ____.

5. In addition to its bituminous coal, Germany has large quantities of _____ which is used for _____.

2. THE VALLEY OF THE MIDDLE RHINE AND THE BAVARIAN UPLANDS

Turn to the map on pages 140–141 and find Cologne (*K3*) again. Trace the Rhine upstream from Cologne to Mainz (*L 4*). Through what kind of land does the Rhine flow in this part of its course?

If you should take a boat trip up the Rhine from Cologne, you would first pass through the part of the Rhine Valley which is so narrow and steep-walled that it is called the Rhine Gorge. Figure 194 shows the kind of sights you would see there.

On reaching Mainz you would enter the broad valley of the middle Rhine, where the river flows through a fertile lowland some 15 to 20 miles wide. South of Karlsruhe the part of this valley west of the river is in France. What kind of work do you think you might find the people of this valley lowland doing?

East of the valley lowland are the uplands of Bavaria, so called because Bavaria is the name of the largest state in this part of Germany. Judging from the map on pages 140–141, what kind of work do you think is important in this region?

The valley of the middle Rhine. This lowland region is sheltered from cold winds by the bordering uplands and mountains, and therefore spring comes early and the growing season is long. The rich soils and the climate combine to make it one of the best farming regions of Germany.

The sunny hillsides bordering the lowland are covered with vineyards and fruit trees, and the people make wines as famous as those of France. On the lower lands of the valley grain, sugar beets, tobacco, and hops are raised, and many of the farmers keep beef cattle, dairy cows, and pigs. *See Figure 195.*

In the cities and towns of the plain there are creameries, sugar factories, cigar factories, and breweries where barley and hops are used to make beer. Beer is the national drink of the Germans, just as light wines are the national drink of the French.

The largest city of the middle Rhine plain is Frankfurt on Main. Find this city on the map on pages 140–141 (*L3*) and notice its location near the junction of the river Main with the Rhine. This location long ago made Frankfurt an important river port, and today it is also a busy industrial center. Among its many manufacturing plants are chemical works, breweries, machine shops, and cotton mills. What else can you discover about Frankfurt from the map on page 128?

The Black Forest. This mountain region lies across the Rhine Valley from the Vosges Mountains of France; and as its name suggests, it has valuable forests. The abundance of wood has made this region a center for the manufacture of many small wooden articles, such as toys, wooden clocks, and musical instruments. Much of this work is carried on in the homes of the people.

In the valleys of the Black Forest much land has been cleared for farming. The people raise rye, barley, and potatoes and keep cattle, many of which are driven to

Photograph from Black Star

Figure 195. Gathering grapes in a vineyard in the Rhine Valley. Strapped on the man's back is a wooden basket for carrying the grapes.

pastures on the higher mountain slopes to graze in the summer.

In this region, as in the Vosges, there is abundant water power, and this has helped the growth of manufacturing. Among the industries the manufacture of paper and the making of shoes are important. Can you suggest any reasons for this?

Farming in the Bavarian uplands. The Bavarian uplands, with their wooded hills and fertile valleys, are quite different in appearance from the northern plain of Germany. Although their surface is rougher, their soils are better, and the lower parts of the region provide rich farm lands. The greater part of Germany's wheat is grown here, as well as large quantities of rye, oats, and barley. Tobacco and hops are money crops on many of the farms, and vineyards cover the sheltered hillsides along the tributaries of the Rhine. *See Figure 196.*

By Ewing Galloway, N.Y.

Figure 196. Threshing wheat in a farmyard in Bavaria. Notice that the women of the family are helping the men with the threshing. Notice also how neat and well-kept the house and the barn look.

Courtesy of German Railroads Information Office, N.Y.

Figure 197. Workers in a German toy factory. They are trimming the fur on Teddy bears.

The farmers of this region keep cattle, pigs, and sheep, but cattle are by far the most important. At the south, where the uplands meet the lower slopes of the Alps, there is a rich dairying section.

Advantages for manufacturing. The Bavarian uplands have no coal or metal ores, but, nevertheless, manufacturing is important in all the larger cities and towns. That is partly because the region is densely populated and produces certain valuable raw materials, and partly because of the railroads and waterways which connect it with other parts of Germany and with neighboring countries. Use the map on pages 140–141 to show how coal may be brought to the Bavarian uplands from western Germany by water.

Some important industries. The northeastern part of the uplands has valuable deposits of clay and sand which have led to the manufacture of porcelain and glass. This is the leading glass-manufacturing district of Germany. Glass-making has led, in turn, to the manufacture of fine lenses and all kinds of optical instruments.

In the same part of the uplands toy-making is an important industry. This work began long ago, when all the toys were made by hand from wood obtained from the forests of the region. Today there are many factories where toys of metal as well as of wood are made. Thousands of the toys that fill our shops at Christmas time come from this part of Germany. *See Figure 197.*

The center of the toy-making is the city of Nürnberg, on the canal which connects the river Main, a tributary of the Rhine, with the Danube. Besides its toy factories, Nürnberg has glass works, pulp mills, machine shops, and many factories where optical instruments and fine metal goods are made. The manufacture of jewelry and other metal goods which require much skill is important in several other cities of the region.

Because hops and barley are important crops of Bavaria, this region has many breweries. Among the industries which depend on imported raw materials, cotton-manufacturing is especially important. The center of this industry is the large city of Stuttgart.

Georg Grebe, Munich

Figure 198. A square in Munich where street-car lines from all directions come together. The old gateway which you see straight ahead leads into the principal business district of the city. Besides being a great business center, Munich is an important manufacturing city. What explanation can you give for this fact?

Munich. On the map on pages 140–141 find Munich, or München, as the Germans call it (*M 4*). In what part of the Bavarian uplands is it located? Munich is one of the largest cities of Germany, and the great railroad and commercial center of the southern part of the country. To the people of other countries, however, it is best known not for its business and industry but for its wonderful art collections and museums of science.

In order to understand the growth of Munich, turn to the map on pages 140–141 and find the Brenner Pass through the Alps (*M5*). Notice that Munich is directly north of it. Through this pass runs the main railroad line from Berlin to Rome, the capital of Italy.

Find the railroad from Berlin (*H5*) to Rome (*H7*) on the map on pages 144–145. Find, also, the main east-west railroad which connects Paris (*F6*) with Vienna (*J6*). Notice

that these two railroad lines cross at Munich. Notice also that other railroads meet the one from Berlin at Munich to cross the Alps by way of the Brenner Pass. You can see now that the location of Munich has made it a great railroad center, and from what you know of other railroad centers you should be able to explain why it has become one of the largest cities of Germany and one of the great cities of Europe. *See Figure 198.*

Some lists to make. Below is a list of some of the important products manufactured in the regions of southern Germany which you have just been studying. Divide them into two lists: (1) those made with the use of raw materials produced in that part of Germany, and (2) those made with the use of raw materials from outside.

wooden toys	cotton goods	porcelain
glass	metal toys	machinery
jewelry	butter	cigars

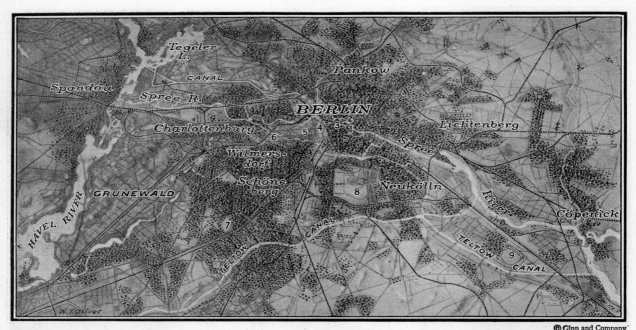

© Ginn and Company

Figure 199. A relief map of Berlin and its surroundings. The numbers show the locations of the following places of interest: 1, the former royal palace, now a museum; 2, the National Gallery, containing paintings and sculpture; 3, the University of Berlin; 4, Unter den Linden (a boulevard); 5, the Tiergarten (a beautiful wooded park); 6, Zoölogical Garden; 7, Botanical Garden; 8 and 9, landing fields for airplanes.

3. BERLIN AND THE GERMAN SEAPORTS

The largest city of Germany is Berlin, the capital, and the second largest is Hamburg, the leading seaport. Find these two cities on the map on pages 140–141 (*N2, M2*). In what region is Berlin located? Between what two rivers is Hamburg located? Find the other important German seaport. On what river is it located?

Germany's capital. Before the war Berlin was the second largest city in Europe, outranked only by London in population. Berlin is not a young city, for the first settlement was made several years before the discovery of America. But it grew more slowly than London or Paris, and it did not become a really great city until after it was made the capital of Germany in 1871. *See Figure 199.* American travelers in Europe before the war used to be surprised to find that Berlin looked very new compared with London and Paris. The reason it looked so modern was that many of its public and private buildings had been erected in the last

fifty years. Everyone admired its magnificent buildings, its broad streets, and its parks, gardens, and homes. *See Figures 200 and 201.*

The map (pp. 144–145) shows that Berlin (*H5*) ranks with Paris and Moscow as one of the three greatest railroad centers of Europe. It is in the eastern part of Germany, about halfway between the Elbe and Oder rivers, and it is connected with both of these navigable waterways by barge canals. As you can see from the map on page 341, Berlin is also one of the chief airway centers of Europe. Largely because it is a great center of transportation, it is normally an important manufacturing center.

Because of Berlin's importance as a transportation and industrial center it was one of the principal German targets for Allied bombers in the war. The bombing left it half in ruins, and before the war ended about half its population had moved away. Whether or not it will ever regain its former importance among the cities of Europe, only time can tell.

Photograph by E. M. Newman from Wide World Photos, Inc.

Figure 200. A view of one side of Unter den Linden in Berlin. Lining this famous avenue before the war were some of the most fashionable shops, hotels, and restaurants of the German capital.

Otto Junga, Berlin

Figure 201. The Brandenburg Gate in Berlin, at the entrance to the Tiergarten from Unter den Linden.

Berlin now serves as the headquarters of the commanding officers of the Allied forces of occupation in Germany.

The location of the German seaports. You already know that Germany controls the mouths of two of the navigable rivers of central Europe. At the heads of the estuaries of these rivers stand the leading German seaports: Hamburg on the Elbe and Bremen on the Weser. Turn to the map on pages 140–141 and study their locations (*L–M2*).

Vast quantities of goods move to and from these seaports in barges on the rivers, and each port is well supplied with railroads. In a general way each port serves its own river basin; but of the two Hamburg attracts by far the greatest amount of foreign trade, and is one of the very great seaports of the world. *See Figure 202.*

Why Hamburg leads. Bremen is somewhat handicapped by the fact that the Weser does not flow through any great industrial district. A canal connects the Weser with the Ruhr district, but that does not greatly increase Bremen's trade, because the Rhine is the natural river outlet for the Ruhr.

The map will show you the advantages which Hamburg has over Bremen. Because of its location at the mouth of the Elbe this port is the ocean gateway for the trade of two great industrial districts: Saxony in Germany and the Bohemian Plateau of Czechoslovakia. Furthermore, the Elbe is connected by canals with Berlin and the Oder River. Because of this and the fact that Hamburg is a North Sea port, it handles some of the foreign trade of the German capital and even of Silesia. But, although Hamburg handles more trade than Bremen does, Bremen is also very important.

Harbor sights. At each of the German ports there are miles of wharves and docks along both sides of the river, and in normal times large ocean ships continually come and go, bringing in cargoes from distant lands and carrying away German products. Both Hamburg and Bremen are ports for transatlantic liners. Hamburg is also one of the

Photograph from R. I. Nesmith and Associates

Figure 202. Part of the harbor of Hamburg, showing an ocean liner in dock. At this great German port you will see all kinds of boats: ocean liners and freighters flying the flags of many different countries, coastal vessels, and barges and steamers which carry passengers and goods up and down the Elbe.

chief airway centers of Germany. *See map, page 128.*

Manufacturing at the seaports. Both Hamburg and Bremen are manufacturing cities with a variety of industries. Before the war they were great shipbuilding centers; but Germany is not allowed to build ocean-going ships now, and the industry is limited to the construction of small craft: tugboats, river steamers, and barges. Imports of raw materials from distant lands have led to the growth of textile industries, such as cotton-manufacturing at Bremen and jute-manufacturing at Hamburg.

German trade. You have learned enough about Germany to know that it was a great manufacturing country before the war. What, then, do you expect its chief exports and imports were? Check your answer by the map on pages 140–141.

After studying the map, you will not be surprised to learn that before the war about three fourths of all Germany's exports were manufactured goods and that about half its imports were raw materials. Like Great Britain, Germany sought raw materials for its industries and markets for its manufactured goods in all parts of the world. In normal times Great Britain, the Netherlands, France, Italy, Switzerland, and Belgium bought the largest quantities of German exports. Our own country ranked high in supplying Germany's imports. Can you explain why?

Today Germany is an occupied nation. What do you think has happened to its trade? It is impossible to say when Germany will be released from Allied control, but it does seem certain that the industrial leadership in continental Europe which Germany has lost will not be rewon. What will this mean to Germany's trade in the future?

A list to make. Write down the names of the cities described below. When you have finished, you will have listed some important German cities.

1. The capital of Germany.
2. A great commercial center in Saxony.
3. The leading seaport of Germany.
4. The great river port and railroad center on the Rhine.
5. The important railroad center in Bavaria.

Giving reasons. Complete each sentence below by giving reasons for the fact which it states.

1. Farming is a very important kind of work in the northern plain of Germany because ____.

2. German farmers are able to buy fertilizers at reasonable prices because _____.

3. The leading industrial districts of Germany are in the uplands bordering the northern plain because _____.

4. Lignite plays a much greater part in manufacturing in Germany than in any other country because _____.

5. Toy-making is an important kind of work in Bavaria because _____.

6. Hamburg is the leading seaport of Germany because _____.

7. Shipbuilding and textile-manufacturing are important at the German seaports because ____.

8. Part of the foreign trade of Germany is carried on through the Dutch port of Rotterdam because _____.

Some things to explain. 1. Explain why Germany had become such a great industrial country before the war. The questions below will help you.

(1) What important raw materials do the Germans produce for certain of their manufacturing industries?

(2) What mineral resources have they which provide power for manufacturing?

(3) Why has Germany plenty of factory workers and large home markets for manufactures?

(4) What advantages have the Germans for getting raw materials from near and far, and for marketing manufactures in foreign countries?

2. Explain why Germany is no longer the great industrial country that it formerly was.

III. AUSTRIA

Austria was an independent country until 1938, when it was annexed by Germany. For seven years Austria was part of Germany, and it shared its defeat in the war. Then, by agreement among the Allies, it was separated from Germany and again became an independent country.

Find Austria on the map on pages 140–141 and study its natural regions. Notice (1) that the mountains of Austria are an eastern extension of the Swiss Alps; (2) that the Danube River flows through the northern part of Austria, and (3) that Austria has a share in the rich Plain of Hungary. Judging from the map, what kinds of work do you expect to see going on in Austria?

Work in the mountains. In the mountains of Austria there are many small valleys dotted with little farms where the people raise a few food crops and keep dairy cows and sheep. The mountain sides are forested, and much

wood is cut for lumber and the making of wood pulp. *See Figure 203.*

In the eastern part of the mountains Austria has abundant iron ore, and in the northern foothills coal is mined. The iron ore and the coal have led to the growth of iron-and-steel manufacturing in several of the cities on the margins of the mountains. *See Figure 204.*

As a whole, the mountains of Austria are but thinly populated, and in the western part, especially, the people depend on the entertainment of visitors for a considerable part of their income. The beautiful scenery and the cool mountain air attract large numbers of tourists in the summer, and opportunities for skiing, skating, and other winter sports bring many visitors in the winter.

The best farm lands. As you would expect, the best farm lands of Austria are in the

By Ewing Galloway, N. Y.

Figure 203. A little village in a valley in the Austrian Alps. The level land is used for crops and the grassy slopes for pasture. Notice the forests on the mountains, and the bare, rocky peaks above the tree line. The swift-flowing streams in the mountains supply the villages and towns with hydroelectricity.

Danube Valley and the Austrian part of the Hungarian plain. In these regions the people carry on mixed farming, raising wheat, rye, oats, and other grains, and keeping cattle and other live stock. The farm lands are dotted with cities and towns, and are much more thickly populated than the mountainous regions.

Manufacturing. About a third of the people of Austria are engaged in farming, and another third in manufacturing. The importance of manufacturing is due chiefly to the abundance of coal and iron ore, and to the fact that the streams in the mountains provide water power from which abundant hydroelectricity is made.

The industries best developed are the manufacture of iron and steel and their products, textiles, wood pulp and paper, and leather and shoes. Cotton-manufacturing is the leading textile industry, and much raw cotton is imported for the spinning mills.

The farms play an important part in Austrian manufacturing, for they provide wool for the making of woolen goods, and hides and skins for the leather industries. The forests, too, play an important part, for they supply pulp wood for the making of wood pulp, paper, and rayon, and lumber for the manufacture of many different products of wood.

Vienna (Wien). More than a fourth of all the people in Austria live in Vienna—so many that Vienna is one of the six largest cities of Europe. Long ago its location made it one of the great centers of Europe for business, trade, and manufacturing.

Find Vienna on the map on pages 140–141 (*P4*). Notice its location on the Danube at the place where that great river leaves the uplands and enters the plain. Notice also that Vienna is located at the southern end of a natural "corridor" between the mountains of Czechoslovakia. This corridor and the Danube Valley have long been great routes

Austrian Federal Railroads

Figure 204. A mountain of iron ore in eastern Austria. The ore is dug by steam shovels from the huge steplike terraces cut in the mountain side.

of travel and transportation, and Vienna, at the meeting place of these routes, is one of the "crossroads" of Europe. Prove by the map on pages 144–145 and the map on page 128 that railroads and airways from all directions meet and cross at Vienna.

This crossroads location has attracted so many people that more than a fourth of all the Austrians live in Vienna. Large numbers of people find work in Vienna's banks and business offices, and in its mills and factories. Its busy wharves along the Danube tell of its river trade, and its large freight yards tell of its trade by land.

Vienna is a beautiful city, with broad streets, many parks and gardens, and many fine public buildings. Like so many of the large European cities, it is a center of learning and culture, and it has some wonderful art galleries. *See Figure 205.*

Some questions to answer. 1. Why are the Austrians not able to produce as much grain and meat as they need?

2. Why is Austria able to export lumber?

3. Why has Austria an abundance of water power?

4. What other resources has Austria for carrying on manufacturing?

5. Why is Vienna a much more important city than you might expect the capital of so small a country to be?

James Sawders

Figure 205. A glimpse of the beautiful city of Vienna. Notice how broad the streets are and how many trees there are. You can see some of the many fine public buildings which face a famous avenue that is known as The Ring. The building shown in the background which has the tall central tower is the city hall.

From Ewing Galloway, N. Y.

Figure 206. Unloading sugar beets at a sugar factory in Poland. Poland, like Germany, has many factories where sugar is made from sugar beets from the farms.

From Ewing Galloway, N. Y.

Figure 207. Cattle in a farmyard in Poland. Why are the crops and live stock raised in northern Poland like those raised in the northern plain of Germany?

IV. POLAND AND CZECHOSLOVAKIA

Foreword. Poland and Czechoslovakia are countries which became independent after the First World War of 1914–1918, when many changes in political boundaries were made in Europe. For many years before that war Czechoslovakia had been united with Austria and Hungary, and Poland had been divided among Germany, Austria, and Russia.

Czechoslovakia was taken by the Germans in 1938–1939, and Poland was invaded by them in September, 1939. Poland was liberated by the Russians in the last year of the Second World War, and freedom came to Czechoslovakia when Germany surrendered.

Find Poland and Czechoslovakia on the map on pages 140–141. How do they compare in size? Which one has more land suitable for farming? Which one appears to have more mineral wealth?

A note about names. As you continue your study of the countries of central Europe and then go on to study the countries of southern Europe, you will find many cities referred to by two names, as, for example, Prague (Praha). In every case the first name is the one we commonly use, while the second, in parentheses, is the name used by the people of the country

themselves. It is well to know the national names as well as the names we commonly use; for the national names sometimes appear in our newspapers, and they should always be used in directing letters to foreign countries.

POLAND

Farming in Poland. Poland is first and foremost an agricultural country, and before the war about two thirds of the people were farmers. In general the farm products are like those of Germany. The leading crops are rye, oats, wheat, barley, potatoes, and sugar beets, and the farmers keep large numbers of cattle, pigs, and poultry. Another important crop is flax, grown for both the fiber and the seed. In Poland, as in Germany, the better soils are in the southern uplands, and it is there that most of the country's wheat is grown. *See Figures 206 and 207.*

Normally, agricultural products make up the leading class of Polish exports, and large quantities cross Poland's land boundaries to markets in Germany, Czechoslovakia, and Austria. Among them ham and bacon are especially important, and for these Great Britain is an excellent customer.

Figure 208. One of the iron-and-steel plants in Polish Silesia. What mineral resources for the manufacture of iron and steel has this part of Poland?

Poland's forests. Before the war the forests of Poland supplied the home needs for lumber and a large surplus for export. The lumber came chiefly from the northeastern part of the country and from the Carpathian Mountains in the south. The northeastern forests are largely in the territory which now belongs to Russia.

Mineral wealth. The map (pp. 140–141) shows that the western part of the southern uplands of Poland is rich in mineral resources. This area, with the adjoining part of the Oder valley, is known as Silesia. It is one of the important coal-mining districts of Europe, and it also produces iron ore, zinc, and lead. The coal is good for coking as well as steam power, and the area as a whole is a great mining, smelting, and manufacturing section. *See Figure 208.*

Before the war this great industrial area was divided between Poland and Germany. In both parts there were blast furnaces, steel mills, factories for the manufacture of heavy machinery and

a great variety of lighter metal products, and chemical plants.

Another source of mineral wealth in Poland is the petroleum which is found in the Carpathian region. This mineral resource was one of Poland's greatest losses in the transfer of land in this section to the Soviet Union. The most important of Poland's oil fields became Russian, the one oil field left to the Poles having contributed only about a fourth of their petroleum production before the war. *See Figure 209.*

Breslau and Krakow. The largest city of southern Poland is Breslau, in the former German part of Silesia. Breslau is beyond the main industrial area, but it is a busy river port and an important commercial and manufacturing center.

Southeast of the Silesian industrial area is Krakow, on the Vistula River. Krakow is one of the old commercial centers of Europe, and it now has a variety of modern industries. In a town a few miles away are some famous salt mines which have been worked for about nine hundred years.

Warsaw. On the map (pp. 140–141) find Warsaw (Warszawa), the capital and largest city of Poland (S2). Notice its central location

Figure 209. A view in one of the oil fields of Poland. This field produces its own power, for steam power made by burning fuel oil is used for pumping the petroleum from the deep wells.

Figure 210. Harvesting grain in the Bohemian Plateau of Czechoslovakia. The men are using machines which mow the grain and leave it lying on the ground. Other workers gather up the grain, tie it in bundles, and stack the bundles in shocks to dry in the sun. Notice the broad stretch of cultivated fields in the distance.

on the Vistula River. The map on pages 144–145 shows that Warsaw (*K5*) is also the hub of Poland's railroad system, which links up with those of all the bordering countries. Because of its railroads and its outlet to the Baltic Sea by way of the Vistula, Warsaw is an important commercial and manufacturing city.

Warsaw suffered terribly in the war. Before the people finally gave up its defense, large areas of the city were nothing but heaps of rubbish.

Poland's textile industries. Turn to the map (pp. 140–141) again and find Lodz (*R 3*) and Poznan (*P2*). These two cities and Warsaw are Poland's leading textile centers. All kinds of textiles are produced, and for their manufacture large quantities of raw materials are imported. Poznan and Lodz manufacture both cotton and woolen goods, and Warsaw manufactures linens as well as cotton and woolens. All three cities combine rayon-manufacturing with their other textile industries.

The Polish seaports. You can see from the map (pp. 140–141) that Poland has three important seaports. The westernmost one is the former German port of Stettin (*O2*), at the mouth of the Oder River. Stettin (Szczecin) owes its importance chiefly to the fact that it is the Baltic gateway to the Silesian industrial area.

The other two Polish ports are close together: Danzig (Gdansk), at the mouth of the Vistula River, and Gdynia, a few miles to the north (*R1*). Danzig is a very old port, but during the period between the two world wars it was a free city, with a government of its own.

The Poles were unwilling to depend on a port over which they had no political control, especially as the majority of the people of Danzig were Germans. So, in order to have a port in their own territory, they transformed a little fishing village into the city and port of Gdynia, modern in every way. Gdynia is now the more important of the two ports, but Danzig has a generous share in handling Poland's foreign trade.

Prospects for the future. Poland of today is the new Poland which moved westward after the Second World War; and it is too soon to say exactly how its gains in territory from Germany balance against its losses in territory to the Soviet Union.

On the whole Poland seems to have gained more in resources than it has lost, and it appears to be headed toward greater industrialization.

THE COUNTRY OF THE CZECHS AND SLOVAKS

Czechoslovakia. In studying the map you must have noticed what a strangely shaped country Czechoslovakia is. The people who live in the western part are mostly Czechs, and those who live in the eastern part are mostly Slovaks. This explains the name of the country.

Czechoslovakia is made up of three parts: the Bohemian Plateau, the Moravian corridor, and the mountainous region of Slovakia. Find these three parts of Czechoslovakia on the map on pages 140–141. The Moravian corridor is the strip of upland in the central part of the country.

Farming in the Bohemian Plateau. The map shows that the Bohemian Plateau is an upland surrounded by a ring of old, worn-down mountains. The streams that rise on the inner slopes of the mountains flow toward the center of the plateau, where they join to form the Elbe River. The broad valleys of the streams have rich soils which make the plateau an important farming region. The farmers raise excellent crops of rye, oats, barley, wheat, potatoes, and sugar beets, and keep many cattle and pigs. *See Figure 210.*

A great industrial region. About two fifths of all the workers in the Bohemian Plateau are engaged in manufacturing, for this region is one of the busiest industrial districts of central Europe. What reasons for this can you discover from the map?

The abundance of coal in the plateau has led to the development of many kinds of manufacturing. Most important of all are the textile industries, for which large quantities of cotton, wool, silk, flax, and rayon yarn are imported. Large quantities of hides and skins also are imported, and the making of shoes and gloves is very important. *See Figure 211.*

Photograph from Wide World Photos, Inc.

Figure 211. Making summer shoes for women in a factory in Czechoslovakia. Czechoslovakian shoes are exported to many different countries.

The iron ore mined near the coal fields has helped the growth of iron-and-steel industries, and additional supplies of iron and steel are purchased from other countries for use in the factories which manufacture machinery and other products of these metals.

Many raw materials produced in the plateau itself and the neighboring mountains also help to make this region a great industrial district. The forest-covered mountains supply pulp wood for the manufacture of wood pulp and paper, and the farms supply large quantities of sugar beets for making sugar.

Valuable deposits of clay provide the raw material for making porcelain ware, and beds of sandstone provide sand for the manufacture of glass. Bohemian glassware is famous for its beauty of color and design, and finds markets in many parts of the world. Perhaps you have seen some of it, for it is sold in many of our stores.

The Moravian corridor. The narrow belt of land known as the Moravian corridor is a small but important part of Czechoslovakia. Like Bohemia, it is an agricultural and industrial region because it has fertile farm lands and good coal fields.

Figure 212. The palace and the beautiful cathedral at Prague. The palace, which was built long ago when Bohemia was an independent kingdom, is now used for the offices where government business is carried on. What reasons can you give for the fact that Prague is one of the leading cities of central Europe?

The northern end of the corridor is Czechoslovakia's greatest iron-and-steel center, for there is excellent coking coal close at hand. Most of the iron ore is imported from Sweden. The coal mined in the south has helped to make Brünn (Brno) a busy industrial city, with textile mills and many other manufacturing plants. Find Brünn on the map on pages 140–141 (P4). It is the second largest city of Czechoslovakia.

Slovakia. East of the Moravian corridor is Slovakia, the part of Czechoslovakia which lies mostly in the Carpathian Mountains. In many ways this is a rich region, but it is not nearly so well developed as the rest of the country. That is partly because it is so mountainous and partly because the Slovaks are mostly simple peasants. The Czechs are well educated, and they have made much greater use of their resources than have the Slovaks.

The mountains of Slovakia are covered with valuable forests, and lumbering is of some importance. The region is known to be rich in iron and other metal ores, but as yet mining is carried on only in a few places.

Most of the Slovaks are farmers. The best farm lands are in the parts of the Plain of Hungary which extend into Slovakia, but there are also many farms in the valleys among the mountains.

Prague (Praha). The capital of Czechoslovakia is the fine old city of Prague. Find Prague on the map on pages 140–141 (O3), and notice that it has an outlet to the sea by way of the Elbe River.

Prague is the railroad center of Bohemia, and one of the great airway centers of central Europe. Because of its location in the heart of the busiest region of Czechoslovakia, it is the largest city and the leading industrial and commercial center of the country. *See Figure 212.*

Raw materials from distant lands come to Prague from Hamburg by way of the Elbe and are distributed to other parts of the country, and manufactured products from Czechoslovakian mills and factories are collected here for export. Among the manufacturing plants in Prague itself are cotton mills, machine shops, glass factories, and chemical works.

Czechoslovakia's trade. The exports and imports of Czechoslovakia show clearly how greatly the people depend on manufacturing. Among the imports raw cotton and wool are by far the most valuable, and many other raw materials are imported. Wheat and other foodstuffs also are purchased from other countries, showing that although farming is well developed in Czechoslovakia, the people produce less food than they need. The most important exports are textiles. Others are iron and steel, machinery, glassware, and leather goods, especially shoes.

For a landlocked country Czechoslovakia has unusual advantages for trade. It extends east and west for about 450 miles through central Europe, and is crossed by several of the main north-south railroads of the continent. These railroads, with others that run east and west, connect it with all parts of Europe. Although it has no seacoast, its location is such that it can use three of the internationalized rivers: the Elbe leading to the North Sea, the Oder leading to the Baltic Sea, and the Danube leading to the Black Sea. *See Figure 213.*

Much of Czechoslovakia's trade is with the neighboring countries, but it obtains from many distant lands raw materials for its textile and leather industries. Our own country supplies much of the cotton, and purchases Czechoslovakian textiles, shoes, and glass.

Naming cities. 1. Give the name which we commonly use for each of the following cities:

Brno   Praha   Warszawa   Szczecin

2. Complete each sentence below correctly:

a. _____, the capital of Czechoslovakia, is located in the Plateau of _____.

b. _____, the capital of Poland, is located on the _____ River.

c. _____ is the second largest city of Czechoslovakia.

d. _____ is the largest city in southeastern Poland.

Figure 213. A view of the water front at Bratislava, Czechoslovakia's river port on the Danube. Find Bratislava on the map on pages 144–145 (*J6*) and show how barges reach this port from the Black Sea.

Giving reasons. Complete each sentence below by giving reasons for the fact which it states.

1. There are more and better farms in the western part of the plain of Poland than in the eastern part because _____.

2. Poland's wheat lands are largely in the southern uplands because _____.

3. The upland of Silesia is very valuable because _____.

4. The Carpathian region is valuable to Poland because _____.

5. The Bohemian Plateau is well suited to farming because _____.

6. The Bohemian Plateau is one of the great industrial regions of Europe because _____.

7. Both Poland and Czechoslovakia have many sugar factories because _____.

8. Glassware is one of the important manufactures of Czechoslovakia because _____.

9. For a landlocked country Czechoslovakia has unusual advantages for trade with distant lands because _____.

10. The Poles have built wharves, docks, and warehouses at Gdynia because _____.

Figure 214. Mountain-climbers looking into a deep crevasse, or crack, in a glacier in the Swiss Alps.

Figure 215. A hockey match at Davos, one of the famous winter resorts in Switzerland. At these resorts the skating rinks are lighted by electricity at night, and workmen keep the ice in perfect condition night and day.

V. SWITZERLAND AND HUNGARY

Foreword. Switzerland and Hungary are two of the landlocked countries of Europe. In that way they are alike, but in surface and resources they are almost exact opposites. Find them on the map on pages 140–141 and tell how they differ in surface. Which one do you think is the more important agricultural country, and why?

Life in the high Alps. The people of the Swiss Alps have little farms in the valleys and on the lower mountain slopes, and they depend chiefly on dairying. One or two of the men or older boys in each family take the cows to the high pastures above the tree line to graze during the summer. While they are there they make butter and cheese, which they send down to the valleys to be sold.

In the meantime those who remain on the farms are busy raising forage crops and cutting hay to feed the cows during the long, cold winter, when the ground is covered with snow. In the autumn the herdsmen return from the mountain pastures with the cows, and the out-of-door farm work is over for the year.

These mountain people usually spend the winter months doing some kind of handwork. Many of the men carve toys and small ornaments of wood, and many of the women make laces and embroideries. Most of these articles are beautifully made, and their sale adds considerably to the income of the people.

A world playground. The Alps attract large numbers of visitors from all over the world, both in summer and in winter. These rugged mountains, with their forest-clad slopes, their sharp, rocky peaks, their glaciers and waterfalls, provide some of the most wonderful scenery in the world, and this alone brings thousands of people to the Alps. In summer many of the visitors come to tramp over the glaciers and climb the mountain peaks. In the winter the Alps become a great playground for people who enjoy skating, skiing, and tobogganing. *See Figures 214 and 215.*

Courtesy of Swiss Federal Railroads

Figure 216. In a watch factory in Switzerland. Swiss watches are well known the world over, and thousands are sold each year in our own country.

Many hotels have been built, and thousands of people in Switzerland make part or all of their living by caring for the needs and wants of the guests. The visitors also provide much business for the railroads, the motor-bus companies, and the shops and stores.

A manufacturing country. Switzerland is too mountainous to be an important farming country; and since it has no coast line, the people cannot turn to the sea as the Norwegians have done. So, although they have almost no coal or iron ore, the Swiss have found ways to become a manufacturing nation.

To make up for the lack of coal, the Swiss use their swift-flowing mountain streams to make electricity. Most of the railroads and nearly all the factories are run by electric power. Few raw materials are produced in the country, and so the Swiss specialize in the manufacture of products which require much skill in the making rather than large quantities of bulky raw materials. *See Figures 216 and 217.*

Among the manufactures are watches and clocks, jewelry, laces and embroideries, fine cotton and silk goods, light machinery, delicate tools and instruments, chocolate, and condensed milk. How do you explain the importance of the last two items in this list?

How the Swiss trade with the world. The highest ranges of the Alps are in the south of Switzerland, and there the Swiss people have built wonderful tunnels by means of which railroads from the north cross the mountains to the seaports of Italy. These tunnels make Switzerland a meeting place for several of the railroads which connect northern and southern Europe, and the railroads provide the country with excellent means of transportation for carrying on trade. Switzerland can also use the internationalized waterway of the Rhine. Swiss trade with distant lands is carried on through Rotterdam, Antwerp, and Le Havre in the north, and through Genoa and Marseille in the south. On the map on pages 144–145 point out the railroads and waterways which connect Switzerland with these ports.

Courtesy of Swiss Federal Railroads

Figure 217. Part of the Swiss city of Zürich, with the Lake of Zürich and the snow-capped Alps in the background. The picture shows some of the factories that make Zürich a center for the weaving of fine silk goods and cotton goods.

© Publishers Photo Service, Inc.

Figure 218. Cattle grazing on the Plain of Hungary. The cattle are watered from wells such as you see in the picture. Why is Hungary an important stock-raising country?

Pix-Ace Williams

Figure 219. Hungarian shepherds cooking a meal out of doors. Notice the shaggy sheep-skin capes which they are wearing.

Cities of the Swiss plateau. Most of the people of Switzerland live in and near the plateau region in the northwest. In this region, surrounded by the best farm lands of the country, are the largest cities: Zürich, Basel, Geneva, and Bern. Find these cities on the map on pages 140–141 (*K–L5*). Which one is the capital of Switzerland? Which one is on the Rhine?

All these cities are busy industrial centers with textile mills, factories for making metal goods, and many other manufacturing plants. Bern is the capital of Switzerland, and Zürich is the largest city of the country. Basel is Switzerland's port on the Rhine, and Geneva, on a beautiful lake of the same name, is an important business center.

Hungary — an agricultural country. Hungary is entirely different from Switzerland, for it is almost wholly a plain, and its greatest resource is its soils. It has a little coal and iron ore, and these are being used to build up an iron-and-steel industry. It also has bauxite deposits, and in recent years the manufacture of aluminum has become important. To a large extent, however, the Hungarians depend upon agriculture.

The Plain of Hungary is a fertile grassland like our prairies, and three fifths of all the people of the country are farmers. They raise large quantities of grain and large numbers of pigs, cattle, and sheep. Shut in by mountains, the plain has hot summers, and chiefly because of this, it is one of the few regions of Europe where much corn is grown. Even more land is used for wheat, the leading money crop, than for corn, and much is used for rye, barley, and potatoes. In certain areas sugar beets are grown, and in the northeast tobacco is an important money crop. *See Figures 218 and 219.*

Farm products for trade and manufacture. The Hungarian farmers produce much greater quantities of grain and meat animals than are needed for the home markets. Because of this, there is a large surplus of wheat, flour, and other foodstuffs for export to the more densely populated industrial countries of Europe.

Manufacturing is of much less importance than farming, and most of the leading industries are kinds which make use of farm products. Among them flour-milling, sugar-refining, tobacco manufacture, and the making of leather are important.

Hungary's capital. Hungary's only large city is its capital, Budapest. Find this city on the map on pages 140–141 (*R5*). Notice its location in the north-central part of the country, near the sharp bend in the Danube. What advantages for trade has this location? Turn to the map on pages 144–145 and see if Budapest is a railroad center.

Budapest is a beautiful city, made up of two parts: Buda on the hills on the west bank of the Danube, and Pest on the lowland on the east bank. A great bridge connects the two parts. Budapest is sometimes called the "Minneapolis of Europe" because of its many large flour mills. It has other kinds of manufacturing plants also, and is the leading industrial and commercial city of Hungary.

Explaining differences. This test will help you to prove that you understand some of the differences between Switzerland and Hungary. Start each sentence with the name that makes it correct, and complete it by giving reasons.

Of these two countries

1. _____ is the one which is not well suited to farming because _____.

2. _____ is the one which is chiefly a farming country because _____.

3. _____ is the one which exports farm products because _____.

4. _____ is the one which carries on much manufacturing because _____.

5. _____ is the one which has a large tourist business because _____.

Can you name these rivers? Name each river described below:

1. The river which provides a waterway from Warsaw to the Baltic Sea.

2. The river which gives Czechoslovakia a waterway to the German seaport of Hamburg.

3. The river which provides a waterway from Silesia to the port of Stettin.

4. The river which provides a waterway from Switzerland to the Dutch port of Rotterdam.

5. The river which gives Czechoslovakia and Hungary a waterway to the Black Sea.

Giving reasons. Give as many reasons as you can why

1. Prague has become the greatest city of Czechoslovakia.

2. Vienna is one of the great cities of Europe.

3. Hamburg is a much more important port than Danzig.

A population test. Below is a table showing the density of population in the countries of central Europe. Study the table carefully, and then answer the questions following it.

COUNTRY	POPULATION PER SQUARE MILE
Germany	472
Czechoslovakia	272
Switzerland	267
Hungary	253
Poland	231

1. Of these five central European countries, which three lead in manufacturing? What relationship does the table above show between manufacturing and density of population in these countries?

2. What reasons can you suggest for the fact that Germany stands at the head of the list in density of population?

3. What reasons can you give for the fact that Hungary and Poland have fewer people per square mile than Czechoslovakia and Switzerland?

Matching countries and capitals. Match correctly the countries and capital cities listed below:

Germany	Bern
Poland	Berlin
Czechoslovakia	Budapest
Switzerland	Prague
Hungary	Warsaw

Special credit work. 1. Hunt in old magazines for pictures taken in the Alps, and make a collection of them to show your class.

2. Try to find a book which tells some of the interesting old legends connected with the Rhine. Perhaps your teacher will let you tell one of these stories to your classmates.

Figure 220. A view of Cadiz, an old city on the southern coast of Spain. For many years after the discovery of America Cadiz was the headquarters of the ships which brought gold and silver from the New World.

Figure 221. The house in Genoa where Columbus is believed to have lived when a boy.

SOUTHERN EUROPE AND ANATOLIA

I. MEDITERRANEAN BORDERLANDS

1. FOREWORD

The largest inland sea. The Mediterranean Sea is the largest inland sea in the world. From the Strait of Gibraltar it extends eastward for 2200 miles, and it touches three continents — Europe, Asia, and Africa. Toward its eastern end it is connected with the Black Sea by the Sea of Marmara and the narrow straits of the Dardanelles and the Bosporus. What canal connects the Mediterranean Sea with the Red Sea?

The Mediterranean peninsulas. On the map on pages 226–227 find the three great peninsulas of southern Europe. The westernmost one is the Iberian Peninsula, between the Atlantic Ocean and the Mediterranean Sea. What two countries occupy this peninsula? Which country is the larger?

Farther east, extending into the central part of the Mediterranean Sea, is the boot-shaped peninsula of Italy, bordered by two arms of the Mediterranean — the Tyrrhenian Sea on the west and the Adriatic Sea on the east. What country borders the Mediterranean between Spain and Italy?

Toward the eastern end of the Mediterranean is the Balkan Peninsula, which includes the land between the Adriatic and Ionian seas on the west and the Ægean and Black seas on the east. Lying wholly or partly within the Balkan Peninsula are six countries — Greece, Albania, Yugoslavia, Rumania, Bulgaria, and Turkey. Find each one of them on the map.

The map shows that only a small part of Turkey is in the Balkan Peninsula. Much the greater part of this country is in the peninsula of Anatolia, between the Black Sea and the Mediterranean. Anatolia is part of Asia, and is often called Asia Minor, which means "smaller Asia."

Mediterranean peoples of long ago. Long before any strong nations had grown up in central and northern Europe, there were groups of very advanced people living in some of the lands bordering the Mediterranean Sea. The earliest of these peoples were the Egyptians, who lived in the Nile Valley in Africa. More than five thousand years ago they were carrying on agriculture and trade, and some of their pharaohs, or rulers, built the wonderful pyramids which you will see when you visit Egypt.

At the eastern end of the Mediterranean, on what is now the Syrian coast, lived the Phœnicians. They became great traders, and were the first seafaring people of the Mediterranean. Later the Greeks came into power, and for a time their capital city of Athens was the greatest center of art and learning in the world. Still later the Romans conquered the Greeks. The Romans, who lived in what is now Italy, were great soldiers and lawmakers, and at one time they controlled all the lands bordering the Mediterranean.

A training school for seamen. Because the Mediterranean is an almost landlocked sea, it is calmer and safer for ships than the open oceans. Therefore, long before men living along the Atlantic coast of Europe ventured far from shore, Mediterranean sailors were crossing and recrossing their inland sea on trading trips which took them out of sight of land. Thus the Mediterranean became the first training school for European seamen, and the Mediterranean countries furnished the earliest of the world's great explorers.

You will recall that Columbus was born in Genoa, on the shores of Italy, and that he made his voyages of discovery in the service of Spain. At that time the Spanish and the Portuguese were among the foremost nations of Europe, and they took a leading part in exploring and settling distant parts of the world. *See Figures 220 and 221.*

You will also recall that Vasco da Gama, who discovered the route around Africa to India, was a Portuguese sea captain. Another great Portuguese explorer was Ferdinand Magellan, who planned the first trip around the world. Magellan died in the Philippine Islands, but his voyage was completed by one of his captains, a Spaniard named Del Cano. Trace the route of this famous voyage on the map on pages 334–335.

Lands won and lost. On the map on pages 334–335 find the lands explored by the Spanish and Portuguese. How does the location of Spain and Portugal explain the fact that the Spanish and Portuguese played a greater part in the early explorations than the other Mediterranean nations?

You learned in your study of the Americas how Spain and Portugal lost their colonies in the New World. Turn to the map on page 234 and find the colonial possessions of Spain and Portugal today. Find also the possessions of Italy. In what continent are nearly all of these possessions located?

Can you answer these questions? Review some of the facts which you have learned about the Mediterranean lands in earlier chapters of this book by answering the following questions:

1. Why is the Mediterranean Sea a great highway of travel and transportation? 2. What nation controls the gateways to the Mediterranean? 3. What Mediterranean lands of Africa belong to France? 4. What Mediterranean islands belong to Great Britain? 5. What Mediterranean island belongs to France? 6. What country at the eastern end of the Mediterranean is under, British protection?

Something to do. If any members of your class were born in southern Europe or if any of their families came from there, point out their European homelands on the map.

By Burton Holmes from Ewing Galloway

Figure 222. A mountainside in Italy which has been terraced to make strips of level land for vineyards and gardens. Only by terracing can slopes as steep as this be used for raising crops.

2. FIRST GLIMPSES OF THE MEDITERRANEAN PENINSULAS

The various nations of southern Europe speak different languages and have somewhat different customs, yet there are many likenesses in the ways in which they use the lands in which they live. In order to understand why they live and work as they do, we need to picture to ourselves the great peninsulas which are their homelands. With the three European peninsulas we shall also study the peninsula of Anatolia.

As you read further, ask yourself this question: Are the Mediterranean peninsulas more favorable, or less favorable, for the growth of strong nations than the lands of central and northwestern Europe?

The Natural Regions

The mountain regions. In studying the map on pages 226–227 did you notice how much of southern Europe and Anatolia are mountainous? As you read the next few paragraphs trace the mountain ranges on the map.

First find the place where the Alps border the beautiful Riviera coast of France and Italy. Near Genoa the Alps join the Apennines, which make up most of the peninsula of Italy. The Apennines are lower than the Alps, and there are no glaciers or snow fields among their summits. *See Figure 222.*

From the "toe" of Italy the mountains extend westward through Sicily, and appear again in northern Africa. Beyond the Strait of Gibraltar they curve eastward, forming the rugged Sierra Nevada of Spain. Farther north the Pyrenees rise like a great wall between Spain and France.

From the eastern end of the Alps in Austria the mountain ranges swing southeastward, joining other ranges which stretch southward through the Balkan Peninsula. The Carpathians too make a great curve to the south, joining the Transylvanian Alps of Rumania. These mountains, in turn, join the Balkan Mountains, which extend eastward through Bulgaria to the Black Sea. The mountains of the Balkan Peninsula continue eastward through the peninsula of Anatolia, and the many islands in the Ægean Sea are peaks of mountain ranges which long ago connected Greece with Asia Minor.

The plateaus. You will see from the map that most of the Iberian Peninsula is a plateau. This plateau is called the Meseta, and its highest parts are from 3000 to 5000 feet above sea level. The northern and southern margins are mountainous, and through the center there are east-west mountain ranges and river canyons which make travel from north to south difficult.

Figure 223. Mediterranean borderlands. Lands of "Mediterranean climate" are shown by slanting lines.

The map also shows that there is a plateau region in Rumania and another in Anatolia. The one in Rumania is called the Plateau of Transylvania, and the other is called the Plateau of Anatolia. Notice that both of them are encircled by mountains.

The lowlands. Turn to the map on pages 226–227 and find the few lowland regions of southern Europe. Notice especially the Plain of the Po in northern Italy, the plain of the lower Danube in Rumania and Bulgaria, and the part of the Plain of Hungary which extends into Rumania and Yugoslavia. These are the best farm lands in southern Europe.

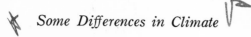

Some Differences in Climate

The Mediterranean climate. Figure 223 shows the parts of the Mediterranean borderlands which have what is called the "Mediterranean climate." In such a climate the summers are hot and dry. The winters are mild and rainy, but between the storms there are days of clear, bright sunshine.

During the northern summer, when all the wind belts of the earth move northward, the Mediterranean basin is in the belt of the northeast trade winds. These winds, blowing from the lands of eastern Europe toward the southwest, have little or no moisture, and therefore summer is a season of drought. During the northern winter, when the wind belts move southward, the Mediterranean basin is in the belt of the rain-giving westerly winds from the Atlantic Ocean. That is why winter is the rainy season.

During the hot, dry summer the earth is parched and dusty, the grasses wither and turn brown, and even the leaves on the trees look dry and lifeless. With the coming of the winter rains new grass springs up, flowers begin to bloom, the trees take on new life, and the landscape changes from brown to green.

Other kinds of climate. The parts of southern Europe and Anatolia which lie outside the limits of the Mediterranean climate have colder winters. Among these regions the Plateau of Anatolia and the interior of the Spanish Meseta have the most unfavorable climate for farming, for they have very dry summers as well as cold winters.

Photograph by Alfred F. Loomis from R. I. Nesmith and Associates

Figure 224. A Greek farmer threshing wheat. The cattle drag a thick rocker-shaped board round and round over the wheat stalks to knock off the seeds. The farmer's wife and baby ride on the rocker to give it weight.

Elsewhere, most parts of southern Europe beyond the limits of the Mediterranean climate have rain at all seasons, usually more in summer than in winter. Their climate is much like that of central Europe, and is favorable for farming because rain falls during the growing season.

Farm Lands and Pasture Lands

Lands where farming is difficult. In spite of the fact that most parts of the Mediterranean peninsulas are hilly and mountainous, far more than half of all the people are farmers. The rougher regions make poor farming lands, but the people use them as best they can. In these regions most of the farmers work much as their ancestors did hundreds of years ago. They plant and harvest their grain by hand, and many of them do their threshing by the method shown in Figure 224.

These farming people of the rougher regions manage to make a living, but most of them are very poor. Their poverty is not their own fault, for most of them are hard workers. It

is due, rather, to the fact that they are trying to live by farming in lands not well suited to that use.

The better farm lands. The better farm lands are the lowland regions along the coasts and in the valleys of the larger rivers. The largest and most important of these regions are the Plain of the Po in Italy and the plains of Yugoslavia and Rumania.

These lowlands are beyond the limits of the Mediterranean climate and do not suffer from summer drought. Thus in climate as well as surface they are better suited to farming than most parts of southern Europe.

Farming in the Mediterranean climate. In the lands of Mediterranean climate farming goes on the year round. During the summer the farmers are busy raising fruits — chiefly grapes, olives, figs, oranges, and lemons. Most of the citrus-fruit groves are irrigated, but the grapevines and the olive and fig trees can stand the summer drought and therefore do not need irrigation. In certain places nuts of various kinds are also important crops.

The principal winter crops are wheat and barley. They are planted in the autumn just before the first rains are expected, and they grow steadily during the mild, rainy winter. After the winter rains are over, they ripen quickly in the hot sun and are ready to be harvested in the late spring. Earlier in the spring, while the moisture from the winter rains is still in the ground, the farmers plant crops of vegetables which they harvest before the hottest and driest part of the summer begins.

How the Mediterranean crops are used. From the grapes and olives the people make large quantities of wine and olive oil. Wine is the principal drink of the Mediterranean nations, and olive oil takes the place of butter at meals and of lard and other fats for cooking. Both wines and olive oil are produced in such large quantities that there is a surplus for export. Oranges and lemons are also valuable exports, as well as dried figs, raisins, currants, and nuts.

There is no surplus of the winter crops of grain; for the Mediterranean people need all that they can raise, and they even have to import additional supplies of wheat. Most of the vegetables also are used at home, though a few special varieties are grown in sufficient quantities for export.

The pasture lands. There are no great ranches in southern Europe and Anatolia, but many of the people make at least part of their living by keeping live stock. In the rougher regions many of the farmers keep sheep or goats, pasturing them on the slopes that are too steep and rocky for crops. In the driest regions, such as the Plateau of Anatolia and parts of the Spanish Meseta, the raising of sheep and goats is more important than farming. *See Figure 225.*

In certain other regions, especially in the Balkan Peninsula, large numbers of pigs are pastured in the forests of oak and beech trees, where they eat the acorns and beechnuts which fall to the ground.

Mediterranean Fisheries

Making a living from the sea. Along the shores of the Mediterranean peninsulas there are little villages where many of the people make their living by fishing. Visitors always enjoy watching the fishermen as they start out in the early morning in their little boats with colored sails, or as they come sailing home with their day's catch.

James Sawders

Figure 225. A Bulgarian shepherd tending his sheep. The sheep are grazing on land that is used in some years for crops and in others for pasture. In the background are the Balkan Mountains.

The principal kinds of fish caught along these coasts are sardines and tunny. There is always a good market for them, for fish is a very important food in these Mediterranean lands — so important that the people also import large quantities of salted codfish, chiefly from Norway and Newfoundland.

Along the shores of Sicily, Italy, and Greece many men make a business of dredging or diving for sponges. Others prepare the sponges for use by washing, bleaching, and drying them.

Some things to explain. Explain why

1. The Mediterranean borderlands of southern Europe have winter rains and summer drought.

2. Farming goes on the year round in the lands of Mediterranean climate.

3. Wheat and barley are winter crops in those lands.

4. Grapes and olives are crops well suited to the Mediterranean climate.

A check. Turn back to page 218 and read again the question in the second paragraph of this section of the text. From what you have learned thus far, how should you answer it? What reasons can you give for your answer?

U. S. Department of Commerce

Figure 226. One of the iron mines in northern Spain, near Bilbao. The deposits of iron ore in this part of Spain are among the richest in Europe, and they have been worked ever since the days when the Romans ruled the Mediterranean lands. Bilbao exports iron ore to many of the great manufacturing countries.

II. SPAIN AND PORTUGAL

Foreword. As you know, in the days of Columbus Spain and Portugal were among the leading countries of Europe. Little by little, however, they have lost the high rank which they once held, and other European countries farther north have outstripped them in prosperity and power. These facts suggest that Spain and Portugal must suffer from handicaps which have hindered their growth in modern times. Try to discover what these handicaps are as you study this chapter.

1. A VISIT TO THE IBERIAN PENINSULA

Let us imagine that we have chartered a boat for a visit to Spain and Portugal. We shall stop at the more important seaports, and take time to make some trips inland. This will give us an opportunity to find out why these countries are less prosperous than those farther north in Europe. On this trip keep the following questions in mind and try to find answers for them:

1. What natural resources have Spain and Portugal, and how do the people make use of them?

2. What do these countries export and import, and why?

Spain's iron-and-coal district. We shall sail first for Bilbao, a port on the northern coast of Spain. There we shall probably see some British ships unloading coking coal and taking on iron ore. Spain is rich in metal ores, and the iron ore in the north is one of its most valuable resources. *See Figure 226.*

Find Bilbao on the map on pages 226–227 (C2). Notice that northern Spain has coal as well as iron ore. At Bilbao there are blast furnaces and steel mills which use ore from

Figure 227. A boat on the Douro River, loaded with kegs of wine. Kegs of port wine are sent down to Oporto in river boats, in trains, and in oxcarts.

the neighboring mines. But instead of using Spanish coal, the manufacturers find it cheaper to buy British coking coal brought in the ships that come to get iron ore.

In spite of the wealth of iron ore, Spain's iron-and-steel industry is not very great, for the Spanish have been slow in developing manufacturing industries on any large scale. At present much more iron ore is exported than is used at home, and iron and steel goods are imported.

Northwestern Spain. As we sail westward from Bilbao and swing around the northwestern corner of Spain, we shall be passing a hilly coast with many fishing villages which will remind us of Brittany. Very likely we shall see some sardine fishermen in their boats.

This northwestern corner of Spain is in the path of westerly winds the year round, and therefore its climate is mild and moist. The land is hilly, but the valleys are fertile and there is a large farming population. This is Spain's "land of cattle and corn," for it is the only part of the country

where the pasturage is rich and there is rain enough in summer for the growth of corn. Rye and potatoes are other important crops, and many of the farmers keep pigs as well as cattle.

A stop at Oporto (Porto). Our next stop is at Oporto, the seaport of northern Portugal. Find Oporto on the map on pages 226–227 (*B2*) and notice its location at the mouth of the Douro River. As we approach the mouth of the river we catch glimpses of vineyards and olive groves in the distance. The olive groves are a sign that we have reached the part of the coast of the Iberian Peninsula where the "Mediterranean" climate begins.

On the wharves at Oporto we shall see barrels and kegs of wine ready for export, for this city is the shipping point for the "port" wines for which Portugal is famous. These wines come from vineyards in the sunny valley of the Douro River, where tons and tons of grapes are grown each year, and in value they make up about a fourth of all Portugal's exports. *See Figures 227 and 228.*

By Ewing Galloway, N. Y.

Figure 228. A view of Oporto, showing the steel bridge over the Douro River. Fair-sized ocean ships can come up the river to Oporto; but since the Douro is not very deep, a harbor for larger ocean ships has been built three miles north of the mouth of the river.

Figure 229. Portuguese fishermen pulling up a net full of sardines. Sardines are caught all along the coast of Portugal, and they form one of the most valuable export products of the country.

From the map on pages 226–227 tell what you expect to see being unloaded from ships from distant lands at Oporto. The cotton goes to mills in the city, for Oporto is a textile-manufacturing center of some importance. Can you prove by the Portuguese imports that the people do not manufacture sufficient cloth for their needs?

Portugal's capital. Steaming southward from Oporto, we soon reach Lisbon (Lisboa), the capital and largest city of Portugal. Find Lisbon on the map on pages 226–227 (B3). Near the mouth of what river is it located? What are its leading exports?

Lisbon is an attractive city, built on hills which slope down to the Tagus. It has an excellent harbor, and it became a busy seaport in the days when the Portuguese were among the great exploring and trading nations of the world. It is still the leading seaport of Portugal, but it has lost the high rank which it once held among the ports of the world.

A trip inland from Lisbon. If we travel north or south from Lisbon, or up the valley of the Tagus, we shall see why fruits and nuts are among the exports of Portugal. We shall find the hillsides, as well as the lowlands, dotted with vineyards and with groves where olives, figs, oranges, almonds, and other fruits and nuts are grown. You already know how well the Mediterranean climate is suited to these crops, and why, therefore, there is a surplus for export.

In southern Portugal we shall discover where the cork that is exported comes from. Cork oaks, like olive and fig trees, can withstand summer drought, and they grow wild in southern Portugal. Some of the cork is gathered from the wild trees, but even more from trees in planted groves. The sheets of cork are sent to factories in Lisbon, where they are dipped in hot water, pressed flat, and dried. Some of the cork is exported in this form, but from much of it bottle corks are cut by machinery, and these too are exported in large quantities. Portugal is one of the leading countries of the world in the production and exportation of cork.

Perhaps we can plan to have our boat meet us at the fishing port of Setubal, south of Lisbon. There we shall see canneries where large quantities of sardines caught by Portuguese fishermen are packed in tins and sent to Lisbon for export. *See Figure 229.*

Resources that are not fully used. During our travels in Portugal we shall find the people raising corn, wheat, rye, and other crops in various places. We shall notice, however, that most of the farmers do their work in simple, old-fashioned ways. As a result, most of them are poor, and they do not raise enough grain to supply the needs of the country.

We shall also find that as yet not much use is made of Portugal's mineral resources. Coal is mined, but not enough for the needs of the people. Tungsten ore, mined for export, is the only metal ore of which Portugal is an important producer. Its chief use is in making certain kinds of very hard steel.

Figure 230. One of the narrow streets in old Seville. The canopies over the street are put up to protect the passersby from the heat of the sun.

Figure 231. A Spanish cart bringing a load of cork bark to a factory in Seville. This is a common means of transportation in southern Spain.

Finally, we shall discover that Portugal is not very well supplied with first-class railroads, and that many of the roads are very poor. For this reason the commonest means of transportation in many parts of the country is the slow-moving oxcart. Poor transportation is perhaps the greatest of the handicaps to the development of the resources of Portugal.

A trade test. From the map on pages 226–227 make a list of the leading exports of Portugal and another of the leading imports. Then answer the following questions:

1. Why are wines, cork, and fruits among the leading exports of Portugal?

2. How are the imports of tin plate connected with the exports of sardines?

3. Which of the imports shows that the Portuguese farmers do not raise enough grain to supply the needs of the people?

4. What imports suggest the fact that Portugal is not an important manufacturing country?

5. What imports suggest the trade of Portugal with its African colonies?

6. What reason can you give for the fact that the Portuguese carry on a considerable trade with Brazil?

"Sunny Spain." Have you ever heard people speak of "sunny Spain"? They mean southern and eastern Spain, with its brilliant sunshine and its bright blue skies. This part of Spain has a "Mediterranean" climate.

Up the Guadalquivir to Seville. We shall get our first glimpse of "sunny Spain," with its vineyards and its fruit groves, as we steam up the Guadalquivir River to Seville (Sevilla). Find Seville on the map on pages 226–227 (*B3*). Although it is about 70 miles inland, it is a seaport, because the Guadalquivir River has been made deep enough for good-sized ocean-going ships.

Seville is a very old city, with narrow, winding streets and some beautiful public buildings. Most of the buildings are only two or three stories high, and many of the houses are built around open courts, or *patios*, planted with flowers and small trees. Where in the Americas did we find houses of this style?

Seville is the business center of the Guadalquivir Valley, and the chief port of export for the wines, olive oil, and fruits which are the leading products of that region. The city also has a few manufacturing plants, among which cork factories are important. Southwestern Spain, like southern Portugal, has many groves of cork oaks. *See Figures 230 and 231.*

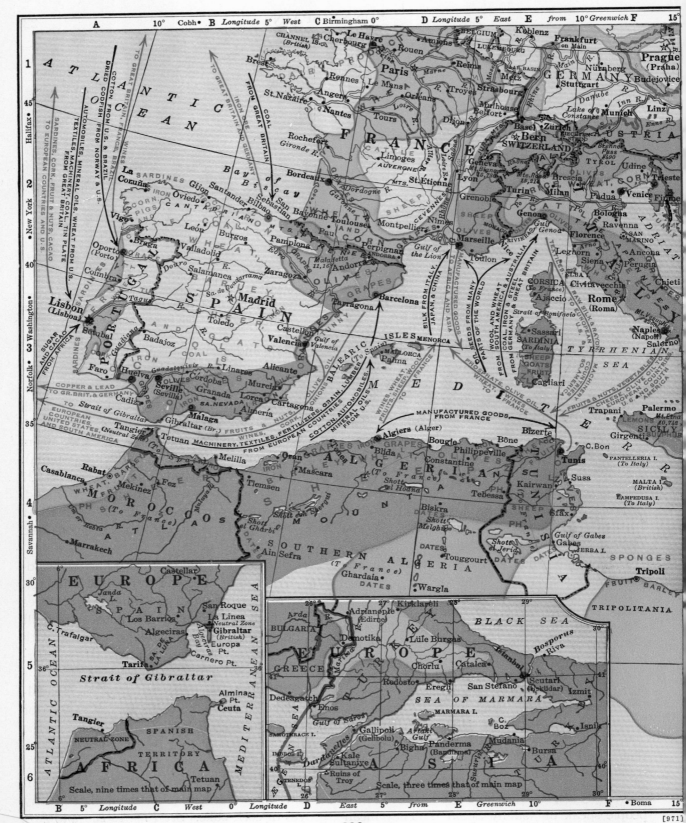

[971]

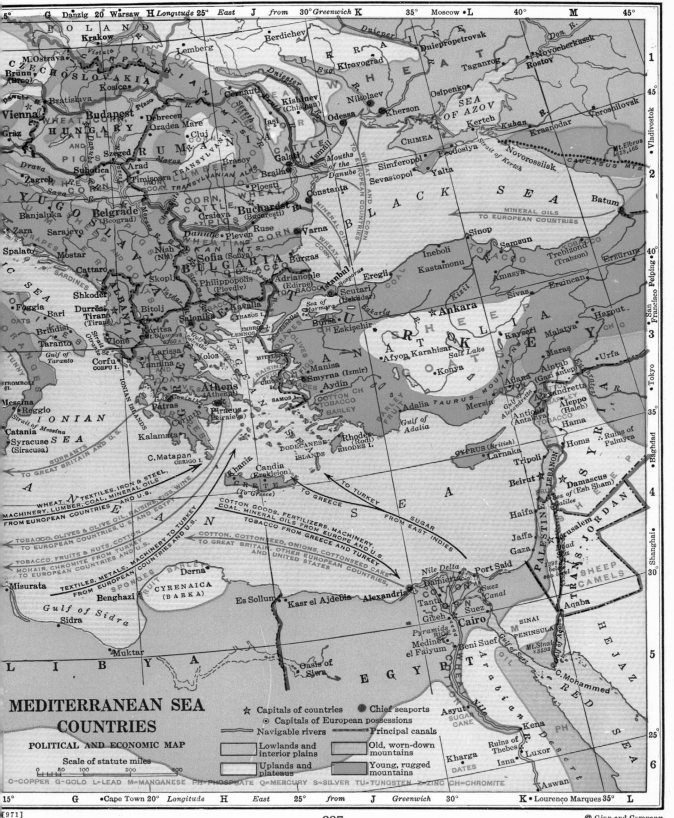

MEDITERRANEAN SEA COUNTRIES

POLITICAL AND ECONOMIC MAP

Photograph by Burton Holmes from Ewing Galloway

Figure 232. Terraced farm lands on the hilly coast near Málaga. On terraces of this kind the people of southern Spain plant vineyards, orchards of fruit trees, and crops of winter wheat and barley.

Mineral wealth in southern Spain. On the map on pages 226–227 find the mining centers in the southern part of the Meseta which we might visit by train from Seville. Notice that there are other mining centers in the Sierra Nevada. The iron mines in this part of Spain are small producers, but the copper, lead, and zinc mines are very valuable. Since Spain is not an industrial country, large quantities of its metals are exported to the manufacturing countries of western and central Europe. The port of Huelva is the shipping point for most of the exports of copper.

In studying the map did you notice where mercury, or quicksilver, is mined? In some years Spain is the world's leading exporter of this mineral product. Mercury, as you probably know, is used in thermometers and in "silvering" the backs of mirrors. It also has several other less well-known uses.

From Seville to Valencia. Leaving Seville, our boat steams down the Guadalquivir and turns eastward, passing the old Spanish port of Cadiz with its fine natural harbor. What did you learn about Cadiz on page 216? Today is a much less important port than Seville.

Passing through the Strait of Gibraltar, we cruise along the coast of southeastern Spain, and in the distance we see the snow-capped peaks of the Sierra Nevada outlined against the clear blue sky.

The Sierra Nevada is the highest of the many ranges of mountains in southeastern Spain. In the sheltered valleys among these mountains the people raise grain, and grapes, olives, and other fruits. Málaga, the chief seaport of the region, is the center of a district where large quantities of grapes are sun-dried to make raisins. *See Figure 232.*

Passing by the coastal lowland in which the city of Murcia is located, we round the eastern end of the mountains and soon reach Valencia, the third largest city of Spain. The map on pages 226–227 shows that Valencia (*C3*) is located in another coastal lowland.

"Garden spots" of Spain. The lowlands of Murcia and Valencia are very dry, and yet they are among the richest and most productive regions of Spain. For many centuries they have been irrigated from rivers that rise in the mountains, and they are the "garden spots" of the country. All kinds of Mediterranean crops are grown, both on the level lands and on terraced hillsides. Much land is also used for raising onions and other vegetables, and in many places hundreds of acres are flooded for the growing of rice.

The lowland of Valencia is one of the chief orange-growing regions of southern Europe, and as we visit its great orange groves we shall be reminded of southern California. The oranges are exported in large quantities, chiefly to the countries of northern Europe.

The city of Valencia is the business center of the lowland, and the shipping point for its

Figure 233. A view of Barcelona, showing the inner end of the harbor and one of the docks for ships. Barcelona has a large natural harbor which has been made deep enough for the largest ships, and passenger liners, as well as ocean freighters, come to its wharves. Prove by the map on pages 226–227 that the leading exports of Barcelona are chiefly "Mediterranean" products. How do you explain this fact?

oranges and other products. It also carries on some manufacturing. Here and in Murcia there are silk mills which use raw silk from places close by where some of the people grow mulberry trees and raise silkworms.

Barcelona. Leaving Valencia, we shall sail northeastward to Barcelona, the largest city and the leading seaport of Spain. Find Barcelona on the map on pages 226–227 (*D2*), and study its exports and imports.

Barcelona is the center of the only important industrial district of Spain, and is the leading manufacturing city of the country. Coal for its mills and factories comes from the mines of northern Spain, and electricity from hydroelectric plants in the neighboring mountains provides additional power.

The leading manufactures of Barcelona are cotton, woolen, and linen goods. What does Barcelona import from the United States for its textile mills? The making of cotton goods is the most important manufacturing industry, not only at Barcelona but in Spain as a whole, and raw cotton is the most valuable import of the country. Much of it comes from the United States. *See Figures 233 and 234.*

The Ebro Valley. The map shows that the Ebro Valley is cut off from the coast by mountains. It is a dry, treeless region, but along the river wheat and other cereals are grown on irrigated lands. In many parts of the valley grapes and olives are grown without irrigation, and wines and olive oil are exported through Barcelona.

Figure 234. A cotton mill in the foothills of the Pyrenees, north of Barcelona. The machinery used in this mill was manufactured in our state of Massachusetts, and is run by hydroelectric power.

harvesting the grain with sickles and scythes, and threshing it by trampling.

Spain's capital city. You would hardly expect to find a large city in the midst of the dry Meseta, yet Madrid has more than a million people, and is the second largest city of Spain. It began its growth long ago when a Spanish king made it the capital of the country because of its central location. When railroads were built, the capital was made the center of the Spanish railroad system, and that helped its growth still more.

Today Madrid is a busy, modern commercial center, with fine business buildings and streets crowded with traffic. To the visitor the strangest sights are the creaking oxcarts and the heavily loaded donkeys that are seen in the market centers of the city. They are constant reminders that almost within a stone's throw of the city there are many people who are living and working much as their ancestors did a long time ago.

Spanish trade. You have already discovered that the leading exports of Spain are (1) "Mediterranean" products — fruits and nuts, olive oil, wines, and cork — and (2) ores and metals. Among the imports manufactured goods have the greatest total value, although raw cotton is the largest single import and the people buy considerable quantities of grain from other countries. These facts show that Spanish mills and factories do not supply the needs of the people, and that the farms do not provide all the grain that is needed.

Looking forward. The Spanish have been slow to adopt modern methods of agriculture, mining, and other work, and as a result they have not made the best use of their natural

Across the Meseta to Madrid. The map on pages 144–145 will show you that from Barcelona or any of the other Spanish ports where we have stopped we can take a train to Madrid, the capital of Spain. No matter what port we start from, we must cross a long stretch of the bleak, dry Meseta, for Madrid is located almost exactly in the center of Spain. Most of the Meseta is a grassland with but few trees, cold and wind-swept in winter and hot and dusty in summer.

The southern part of the Meseta is so dry that the chief use of the land is for pasturing sheep and goats. In the spring many of the herdsmen take their animals into the mountains, where there is fresh green grass after the snow melts away. In this way the grass of the plateau is saved for winter pasturage. *See Figures 235 and 236.*

The northern part of the Meseta has a little more rain, and many of the people raise wheat and barley. Much more grain could be grown here if it were not for the fact that most of the farmers work in old-fashioned ways,

Figure 235. A Spanish shepherd tending his sheep on the Meseta. Why are many parts of the Meseta used for grazing rather than for raising crops?

Photograph by Burton Holmes from Ewing Galloway

resources. In recent years, however, conditions have been changing. Manufacturing has increased, and better methods of farming and mining have been coming into use. In time, if Spain can continue this progress, it will be a much more prosperous country.

But in 1936 the worst thing that can happen to any country happened in Spain. The people quarreled among themselves, and a terrible civil war broke out. The war lasted nearly three years, and it interrupted Spain's progress and made the country much poorer. Thousands of people were killed, and Madrid and many of the other cities were left half in ruins. It will take the Spanish years to repair all the damage and make another start toward prosperity.

Naming ports. See if you can name each port described below:

1. The leading port of Spain in the export of iron ore.
2. A Portuguese port famous for its exports of wine.
3. Spain's copper-exporting port.
4. The leading port of Spain.
5. A Spanish port which exports large quantities of oranges.
6. The leading port of Portugal.

Giving reasons. Complete each of the following sentences by giving reasons for the fact which it states:

1. The coastal regions of Spain are more densely settled than the Meseta because _____
_____
2. Parts of the Meseta are better suited to grazing than to farming because _____.
3. Spanish and Portuguese farmers grow large quantities of grapes, olives, oranges, and other fruits because _____.
4. Northwestern Spain is the only part of the country where large quantities of corn are grown because _____.
5. Wheat is the leading grain crop of Spain and Portugal because _____.
6. Mining is important along the northern and southern margins of the Meseta because
_____
7. Large quantities of the ores and metals produced in Spain are exported because _____
_____
8. Barcelona has greater advantages for manufacturing than Madrid because _____.
9. Spain's iron-and-steel industry is located on the northern coast because _____.
10. Spain and Portugal import foodstuffs because _____.

Photo by Hugo Miller

Figure 236. Irrigating a field of vegetables in the Meseta. The horse walks round and round, turning a wheel that lifts water from a well. Small fields in the Meseta are often irrigated in this simple way.

Figure 237. Part of Funchal, the capital and chief port of the Madeira Islands. Notice the terraced vineyards. The first grapevines were brought to the Madeiras by the Portuguese, who discovered the islands in 1419. How long ago was that?

2. OTHER SPANISH AND PORTUGUESE LANDS

On the map on page 234 find the lands outside the Iberian Peninsula which belong to Spain, and those which belong to Portugal. Judging from their location and extent, which country's possessions do you think are the more valuable?

Spanish and Portuguese islands. In the Mediterranean Sea are the Balearic Isles, which are part of Spain. They have fertile soils and the Mediterranean type of climate, and their chief products are fruits, wines, and olive oil.

Off the northwestern coast of Africa are the Canary Islands, which belong to Spain, and the Azores, the Madeira Islands, and the Cape Verde Islands, which belong to Portugal. The Canaries, the Azores, and the Madeiras all have a mild, moist climate, and the people raise fruits and early vegetables for European markets. The Cape Verde Islands are drier, and therefore they have fewer agricultural products for export.

The chief ports of all these groups of islands are coaling stations for ships and have cable stations for receiving and sending messages. *See Figure 237.*

Islands in the Gulf of Guinea. The Spanish and Portuguese also hold a number of small tropical islands in the Gulf of Guinea. Because of their hot, moist climate, these islands have many plantations where cacao and other tropical crops are grown. The Portuguese island of St. Thomas is especially noted for its large production of cacao, most of which is exported to Lisbon.

Spanish possessions on the mainland of Africa. The map on page 234 shows that Spain holds a very small portion of northern Morocco. Farther south on the coast of Africa is the Spanish colony of Rio de Oro. This colony has no commercial importance; for it is too dry for farming, and its mineral resources have not been developed.

On the coast of the Gulf of Guinea Spain holds the small area of Rio Muni, a hot, rainy, densely forested land. The native people, who are Negroes, collect a few forest products such as rubber and palm kernels, which they sell to Spanish traders.

Portuguese Guinea. Find this little Portuguese colony on the map on page 50 (*B3*). The coastal lowland is forested, and the people there gather palm kernels and export palm oil. Farther inland there are grasslands, where the natives raise cattle which provide small quantities of hides for export.

Angola. Much farther south in Africa is the large Portuguese colony of Angola. From the map on page 48 and Figure 41 (p. 49) describe the surface and rainfall of Angola.

The dry coastal belt of Angola will remind you of the coastal desert of Peru, for farming is carried on only where water for irrigation can be obtained from streams, and the chief crops of the irrigated lands are sugar cane and cotton. Irrigated farming, however, is much less important here than in Peru, and the exports of sugar and cotton are very small.

Of somewhat greater importance is the coffee which is grown on plantations farther east in the northern half of Angola, where the rainfall is greater. From these plantations coffee is exported to Portugal, but not in very large quantities.

Much of Angola is savanna, or tropical grassland, and because of this more of the natives are engaged in raising cattle than in any other kind of work.

Mozambique. The most valuable of the Portuguese possessions is Mozambique, on the eastern coast of Africa. Use the map on page 48 and Figure 41 (p. 49) to compare Mozambique and Angola in surface and rainfall. What reason can you suggest for the greater importance of Mozambique?

Mozambique has plentiful rainfall for farming, because the southeast trade winds bring rain to it from the Indian Ocean. The climate is warm as well as moist, and on the coastal lowland the Portuguese have established plantations of sugar cane, cotton, coconuts, and other tropical products. As yet, however, they have not done so much to develop plantation agriculture as the British have farther north, and the exports of tropical products are small. The leading export is sugar, much of which goes to Portugal. *See Figure 238.*

The interior of Mozambique is part of the grassy plateau region of East Africa. It is known to have coal and other mineral wealth, but as yet very little mining is carried on.

In Mozambique the Portuguese have a colony which could be made much more valuable than it is today. But in their possessions, as

By Burton Holmes from Ewing Galloway

Figure 238. Freighters from Europe taking on cargoes at Lourenço Marques, the capital and chief seaport of Mozambique. This Portuguese port handles some of the trade of the Union of South Africa. What reason for this can you discover from the map on page 50?

in the home country, the Portuguese have been much slower to develop the resources than have the British and the French.

Portuguese possessions in Asia. On the west coast of India the Portuguese have three tiny possessions, and in China they hold the island and city of Macau near the British island of Hong Kong. These possessions are trading centers, and with the eastern half of the little island of Timor in the East Indies are the only Portuguese lands in Asia. What country owns the western half of Timor?

Can you answer these questions?

1. Why are the possessions of Spain less valuable than those of Portugal?

2. Which possession of Portugal is the most valuable, and why?

3. Why does Portugal export cacao to other countries of Europe?

4. What reasons can you give for the fact that the Spanish and Portuguese discovered the small islands off the northwest coast of Africa?

5. In what countries of the Americas do the people speak Spanish, and why?

6. In what country of the Americas do the people speak Portuguese, and why?

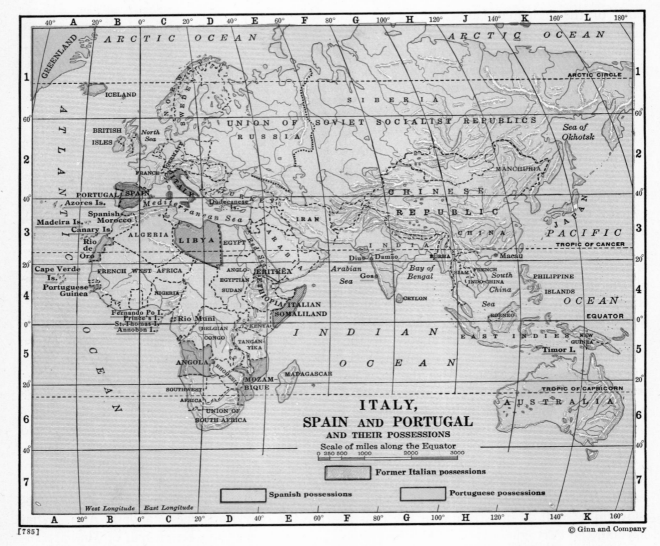

ITALY,
SPAIN AND PORTUGAL
AND THEIR POSSESSIONS
Scale of miles along the Equator

Former Italian possessions

Spanish possessions   Portuguese possessions

[785]   © Ginn and Company

Testing yourself. Test your knowledge of the Iberian Peninsula by giving the right name to match each phrase below:

1. The plateau shared by Spain and Portugal.
2. The river at the mouth of which Oporto is located.
3. The mountains which separate Spain from France.
4. The river on which Seville is located.
5. The highest of the mountain ranges of southern Spain.
6. The river at the mouth of which Lisbon is located.
7. An important river valley in the northern of Spain.

Some things to explain. Explain why

1. Madrid was chosen as the capital of Spain.
2. It is now the second largest city of Spain.
3. Barcelona imports large quantities of raw cotton from the United States.
4. The dry lowlands of Murcia and Valencia are "garden spots" of Spain.
5. Silk-manufacturing is important in Murcia and Valencia.
6. More land is used for crops in the northern part of the Meseta than in the southern part.
7. Seville and Lisbon have many cork factories.

Map work. Color the possessions of Spain and the possessions of Portugal on the map of Africa which you are making.

Photograph by James Sawders

Figure 239. Haying on a farm in the southern part of the Plain of the Po. This part of the plain is an important dairying section, and the cheese that is made there is exported to many parts of the world. Notice how level the land is in this region. What other advantages has the Plain of the Po for agriculture?

III. ITALY

Foreword. Of the countries of southern Europe, Italy is the most densely populated, and before the Second World War it was by far the most important. Today Italy is finding reconstruction a slow, hard task. As you study this chapter see what resources Italy has to help it to become important again.

1. NORTHERN ITALY

The map on pages 226–227 shows that Italy may be divided into two sections: the northern, or continental, part, and the southern, or peninsular, part. What mountains form the northern margin of Italy? What plain lies between those mountains and the Apennines?

The Plain of the Po is one of the most thickly settled regions of Europe, and within it live two fifths of all the people of Italy. What reasons can you suggest for the great density of population in this plain?

A river-made plain. Long, long ago what is now the Plain of the Po was a great arm of the Adriatic Sea. Year after year the rivers from the bordering mountains washed mud and sand into it until at last it was filled with these fine rock materials and became dry land. The delta at the mouth of the Po shows that even now the plain is being extended into the Adriatic Sea.

In places the surface of the plain is remarkably level, and the river-laid soils are fine, deep, and fertile. The summer weather is hot, and the growing season is long, but snow sometimes falls in the winter. The plain is beyond the limits of the Mediterranean climate, and has rain in the summer.

A great farming region. As you might expect from its surface, soils, and climate, the Plain of the Po is a great farming region. It

Figure 240. The cathedral in Milan. Because of its location in the Plain of the Po, Milan has been an important city for hundreds of years. The building of the cathedral was begun in 1386.

is one of the leading wheat-and-corn regions of Europe, and by far the most important rice-growing region of the continent. All three of these crops provide large quantities of food for the Italian people, but even so, the country is so densely populated that much wheat and some corn are imported.

Most of the farmers of the plain use farming machinery and do much of their work in modern ways. Many irrigate their fields so that their crops get exactly the right amount of moisture, and some get as many as three crops a year from the same land.

On the northern and southern margins of the plain much of the land is used to pasture cattle, and in the south, especially, dairying is very important. Among the dairy products are Gorgonzola and Parmesan cheeses, for which Italy is famous and which are exported in large quantities. *See Figure 239.*

Mulberry trees and silk. Along the western and northern margins of the plain mulberry trees are grown and large numbers of silkworms are raised. The cocoons are sent to factories where the delicate fibers are unwound by machinery and then twisted together to make the strands of raw silk.

A great manufacturing region. Besides being a rich farming region, the Plain of the Po is one of the leading manufacturing regions of Europe. It has no coal or iron ore, — in fact, all Italy is poor in these mineral resources, — but the large population provides abundant labor, or workers, for factories, and the location of the plain makes it easy for the manufacturers to market goods in all parts of Europe. To help to make up for the lack of coal, the Italians have built great hydroelectric plants on the swift-flowing rivers from the Alps. In fact, they use more hydroelectricity than any other nation of Europe. Nevertheless, large quantities of coal are imported, chiefly from Germany and Great Britain.

Textile-manufacturing. In all the larger cities of the plain there are textile mills, and textile-manufacturing is the leading industry. This work began long ago with the manufacture of silk goods from raw silk produced in the plain, but today there are large numbers of cotton, woolen, and rayon mills as well as silk mills. For the making of rayon fiber the Italians use pulp wood from the poplar trees of their country. In rayon-manufacturing, as in silk-manufacturing, Italy ranks high among the countries of the world.

The leading textile centers are the two largest cities of the plain, Milan (Milano) and Turin (Torino). Find these cities on the map on pages 140–141 (*L6* and *K6*). Notice how conveniently they are located to obtain supplies of raw materials and to market manufactured goods through the port of Genoa. To this port come large quantities of cotton from the United States, Egypt, and South America, and much wool from South America and Australia.

Figure 241. Bellagio, a town on the shore of Lake Como in the Italian Alps. The blue water, the green wooded hills, and the snow-capped mountains make this one of the beauty spots of Europe.

cities, providing work for more farmers in the country districts. An increasing farm population, in turn, means larger home markets for manufactured goods. Thus manufacturing and farming have grown together, each helping the other.

The Alpine region. From the Plain of the Po the Alps rise on the west and the north, reaching heights of over 15,000 feet in the peaks of Mont Blanc and Monte Rosa. Find these peaks on the map on pages 140–141 (*K6*). Find also Lake Como, Lake Maggiore, and Lake Garda, farther east. The district of the Italian lakes is one of the most beautiful parts of Europe, and thousands of tourists from all over the world visit it each year. *See Figure 241.*

In the valleys among the Italian Alps and on the sunny hillsides along the northern margin of the plain the people raise grapes and olives and make wine and olive oil. Many of the vineyards and olive groves are on terraces on the mountain slopes. *See Figure 242.*

Other kinds of manufacturing. Although textiles are the most important manufactured products of the plain, many other kinds of manufacturing are carried on. Large quantities of iron and steel are imported and used in the manufacture of many different products. For example, Milan makes locomotives and many kinds of machinery, and Turin turns out large numbers of steel railroad cars and of automobiles. Still other important manufactures are chemicals and glass.

The growth of cities in the plain. The largest cities of the Plain of the Po are Milan, with more than a million people, and Turin, with more than half a million. Turn to the map on pages 144–145 and notice that both these cities (*G6*) are on railroad lines which pass through tunnels in the Alps, connecting northwestern Europe with the Mediterranean. Milan has become the larger city chiefly because it is the place where two of these north-south railroad lines meet and cross the main east-west railroad line through the Plain of the Po. *See Figure 240.*

In this plain, as in all industrial regions, manufacturing has greatly increased the population and the demand for foodstuffs in the

By Ewing Galloway, N. Y.

Figure 242. One of the many Italian boys who work in the vineyards at harvest time picking the grapes. He is waiting for a ride home in one of the oxcarts which carry the grapes down to the valley.

Photograph by James Sawders

Figure 243. The Grand Canal in Venice. In the distance is one of the churches, and at the left is an old Italian palace. The posts in front of the palace are for tying gondolas.

Figure 244. One of the smaller canals, or "water streets," in Venice, bordered by houses and shops.

On the higher slopes of the Alps the people make a living mostly by keeping cows and goats, as many do in neighboring parts of Switzerland.

Trieste. The map (pp. 144–145) shows that its location makes Trieste (*H6*) more important as an outlet for landlocked Austria and Hungary than for Italy. After the war Trieste and its neighborhood were made a free territory under United Nations control so that all nations needing to use this port might do so freely.

Venice (Venezia). There is no other city in the world quite like Venice. It is built on a large number of small islands in a shallow lagoon, or bay, just north of the delta of the Po. One railroad, passing over a long bridge, connects the city with the mainland.

Most of the islands are too small to have many streets, and the canals, or waterways, between them are the main highways of the city. Most of the houses face the canals, and many of them rise directly from the water. Hundreds of bridges connect the various islands, but the principal means of transportation in the city are long, narrow boats called *gondolas. See Figures 243 and 244.*

Long ago, before the route to the Orient around the southern tip of Africa was discovered, Venice was a great commercial port, serving as a gateway for trade between Europe and eastern Asia. Venetian merchants sent their ships to the eastern end of the Mediterranean, loaded with European goods to be exchanged for those which came overland by camel caravan from India and the Far East. This "carrying trade" brought wealth and power to Venice, and the people built beautiful palaces and public buildings, many of which are standing today.

Venice is now a much less important port than it once was, for much of the trade of Europe with the Orient is carried on by ships which sail directly from northern ports through the Mediterranean and the Suez Canal to India and the Far East. It is, however, an important Italian port, serving as the eastern gateway for the Plain of the Po. From the map (pp. 140–141) name its leading exports. The lace and the glassware which you find among them are manufactures for which Venice has long been famous.

Photographs by James Sawders

Figure 245. Two pictures which suggest the commercial importance of Genoa. At the left you see the place where trains enter the great railroad station. At the right is a glimpse of the water front, with a large grain elevator in the background. Genoa is one of the leading ports on the Mediterranean Sea.

Venice is so beautiful and so interesting that thousands of tourists visit it each year. Perhaps you can find a book which tells about the fine old palaces, the art museums, and the beautiful churches there.

Genoa (Genova). In the days when Venice was a great commercial port, Genoa was its only rival. Today Genoa has outstripped Venice in trade and population and is the leading seaport of Italy. Find Genoa on the map on pages 140–141 (*L6*) and see if you can discover any reasons for its growth.

Because of its location, Genoa serves as the ocean gateway for the western part of the Plain of the Po — the part where Milan and Turin are located and where manufacturing has developed to the greatest extent. For this reason it imports far more of the raw materials, fuels, and foodstuffs needed in the Plain of the Po than does Venice, and exports much larger quantities of the manufactured products. *See Figure 245.*

Another reason why Genoa is a more important port than Venice is that its location is such that it handles much of the foreign trade of Switzerland. Use the map on pages 144–145 to show why this is so.

As you would expect, Genoa is also a busy industrial city, with cotton mills, shipbuilding yards, and many other manufacturing plants. Like Marseille, it imports large quantities of oilseeds for making vegetable oils and soap.

The Riviera. Extending westward from Genoa is the warm, sunny Riviera coast which Italy shares with France, and which attracts such large numbers of winter visitors. What do the people of this region do for a living besides caring for the needs of visitors?

An export and import test. From the maps on pages 140–141 and 226–227 make a list of the exports of Genoa and another of the imports. Then answer the following questions:

1. Among the imports, what two are for use in the textile mills of northern Italy? 2. What two suggest that Italy is poor in fuel resources? 3. What one proves that Italy needs more grain than the farmers produce?

4. Among the exports, which ones prove that Italy produces a surplus of certain foodstuffs? 5. Which ones suggest Italy's importance as a manufacturing country? 6. What raw materials for textile-manufacturing does Italy produce in sufficient quantities to supply the home needs and provide a surplus for export?

By Burton Holmes from Ewing Galloway, N. Y.

Figure 246. An Italian shepherd driving his sheep and goats to pasture in the Apennines. The sheep of the Italian peninsula help to supply wool for manufacturing, and the goats help to provide the people with milk. Why are there more sheep than cattle in Italy?

2. THE ITALIAN PENINSULA AND SICILY

From the map on pages 226–227 describe the surface of the Italian Peninsula and Sicily. What does Figure 223 (p. 219) tell about their climate? How do you think the work of the people in the "Mediterranean" lands of Italy differs from work in the Plain of the Po? As you study this section, find out whether or not your answer is correct.

Farm lands and pasture lands. Although the Italian Peninsula and Sicily are largely mountainous, more of the people are engaged in farming than in any other kind of work. The farms are small, and many of the farmers are very poor; but altogether they produce large quantities of wheat, vegetables, and the usual "Mediterranean" fruits.

Much of the wheat grown in this part of Italy is especially well suited to the manufacture of macaroni, which is one of the principal foods of the Italian people. In Naples and other cities there are factories where macaroni is made for home use and for export.

On the map on pages 226–227 find the places where Italian farmers raise large quan-

tities of citrus fruits. Lemons from Sicily and oranges from the "toe" of Italy are among the important exports of the country, going chiefly to markets in northern Europe.

Nearly every farmer of southern Italy has a small vineyard and makes wine for family use, and many have olive groves and press their own olive oil. In certain places fine qualities of olive oil are made on a large scale for export. The rougher lands and those with the poorer soils are used largely for pasturing sheep and goats. See Figure 246.

Mineral products and water power. In the northern part of the Apennines are the famous marble quarries of Carrara. Carrara marble is pure white and very fine, and it is shipped to many distant lands. A little farther south there are mercury mines. These, with others north of Trieste, make Italy the rival of Spain in the production and export of mercury.

In metal ores and fuels Italy is very poor. Iron ore is mined, chiefly in the island of Elba, but not nearly enough to meet the needs of the Italian iron-and-steel industry. Petroleum is almost lacking, and what coal there is happens to be a kind that cannot be used for coking. Lignite is mined in the Apennines, but it is of poor quality.

Fortunately, Italy has much water power, and, as you know, more and more hydroelectricity is being used for manufacturing power. The Italians are trying also to make up for the lack of petroleum by getting oil from lignite and from certain kinds of oil-bearing rocks which are quarried in the Apennines. In time they may be able to solve their fuel problems in these ways, but for iron, copper, and other metals they will always have to depend chiefly on imports.

Figure 247. The Ponte Vecchio, or "Old Bridge," in Florence. The bridge is lined with little shops, and forms part of a passageway connecting two famous art galleries on opposite sides of the Arno.

By Burton Holmes from Ewing Galloway

Figure 248. Two famous sights in Rome. In the foreground is part of the Forum, and in the distance the Colosseum.

Florence (Firenze) and the Arno Valley. Almost every visitor to Italy goes to Florence, for this old city has some of the most wonderful art galleries in the world. Find Florence on the map on pages 140–141 (*M7*), and notice its location on the Arno River. The valley of the Arno is not large, but it is one of the richest farming regions in the Italian Peninsula. Its people have always been prosperous, and that is one reason why Florence long ago became a center of art and learning. *See Figure 247.*

Rome (Roma). On the map on pages 226–227 find Rome, the capital of Italy (*F2*). Notice its location on the Tiber River, about halfway between the northern and southern ends of the Italian Peninsula. From this central location the Romans of long ago conquered all Italy and then extended their power, little by little, until they controlled all the Mediterranean borderlands.

For more than two thousand years Rome has been one of the most famous cities of the world, first as the capital of the Roman Empire, and later as the headquarters of the Roman Catholic Church. For many hundreds of years it has been the home of the Roman Catholic Popes.

Rome is built on a group of low hills bordering the Tiber, and on the margin of a small coastal plain. In the days of the Roman Empire the plain was thickly settled by farmers who helped to provide the great city with food. In the course of many centuries it became marshy and unhealthful, and for a long time it was almost deserted. Now the Italians have drained it and are cultivating it again.

Rome is the largest city of Italy and one of the chief airway centers of southern Europe. Its people are engaged in many kinds of work connected with business, government, and the entertainment of thousands of visitors who come to the city each year. One may spend weeks visiting the beautiful churches of Rome and the ruins of buildings which go back to the old Roman times, and still not see all that this famous Italian city offers of religious and historic interest. *See Figure 248.*

Figure 249. An airplane view of the Vatican City, in Rome. The large domed building is St. Peter's Church, and beyond it, at the left, is the Vatican. Both build- ings contain many wonderful works of art. The tall column in the open *piazza* in front of St. Peter's was brought to Rome from Egypt about 1900 years ago.

The Vatican City. Within the boundaries of Rome is the small independent Vatican City, which the Italian government in 1929 placed entirely under the control of the Roman Catholic Church. Within this city is St. Peter's Church and the palace of the Vatican, which is the home of the Pope. *See Figure 249.*

A famous volcano. Many visitors to Europe get their first glimpse of Italy as their ship steams into the beautiful Bay of Naples. Long before the ship moves into one of the docks that line the water front, the passengers are on deck with field glasses, looking at Vesuvius, the great volcanic mountain a few miles east of Naples. Usually there is a cloud above the mountain, for Vesuvius is an active volcano. The cloud is due to the water vapor which rises in the throat of the volcano, passes into the air, and is cooled. *See Figure 250.*

At times the hot liquid lava in the crater of Vesuvius rises and overflows the rim. As it creeps down the mountain slope it spreads over fields, highways, and even villages, and sometimes the people have to flee for their lives. For centuries Vesuvius has been more or less active, and at times it has caused much damage. In the year 79 a great eruption from this volcano buried the cities of Pompeii and Herculaneum at its base in a huge shower of hot mud and ashes. For a long, long time these cities were almost forgotten. Now they have been excavated, or uncovered, and the streets and houses tell much of the life and work of the Romans of long ago.

Naples (Napoli). Locate Naples on the map on pages 226–227 (*F 2*). We shall find this seaport of southern Italy a busy, crowded city, surrounded by farm lands where the people raise the "Mediterranean" crops. It is the third largest city of Italy in population, and it handles much of the foreign trade of the southern part of the country. In recent years Naples has become an important industrial city. The growth of manufacturing has been due in large measure to the development of hydroelectric power from streams in neighboring parts of the Apennines.

Sicily. The map shows that Sicily is separated from the "toe" of Italy only by the very narrow Strait of Messina. In the crust of the earth beneath this strait there are deep fissures, or cracks, and along these cracks movements of the crust which result in earthquakes frequently take place.

On the map on pages 226–227 find Mount Etna in Sicily (*F 3*), and give its height. This great mountain peak is a volcano, and, like Vesuvius, is active from time to time. Near the base of Mount Etna there are valuable sulphur deposits, and the mining and preparation of sulphur for export provides work for many people.

Figure 9 on page 13 shows that Sicily is crowded with people. Most of them are farmers, and, as you would expect, their principal crops are wheat and Mediterranean fruits. Palermo, the largest city, exports large quantities of Sicilian lemons.

Sardinia. Turn to the map on pages 226–227 and find the island of Sardinia, which belongs to Italy (*E 2–3*). Like its neighbor, Corsica, Sardinia is a mountainous island with the Mediterranean type of climate, and most of the people are farmers. Sardinia has considerable quantities of lead, zinc, and other metal ores, but the roads are so poor that only a few mines are worked.

Photograph by E. M. Newman from Wide World Photos, Inc.

Figure 250. The Bay of Naples, with Mount Vesuvius in the background. Notice the cloud of steam rising from this famous volcano. The Bay of Naples is one of the most beautiful spots in the world.

Italy's trade in normal times. Italy is the only Mediterranean country where manufacturing is important enough to require large imports of cotton, wool, iron, and other raw materials. Lack of fuel resources makes necessary large imports of coal and mineral oils, and the dense population requires more wheat and corn than are produced in the country.

In return for these and other imports, Italy has a variety of products for export. First come its surplus manufactures, especially textiles, rayon fiber, iron and steel goods, machinery, and automobiles; next its surplus agricultural products, chiefly fruits and nuts, vegetables, cheese, and olive oil; and finally, its surplus mineral products — marble, sulphur, and mercury.

With such a large and varied trade, it is natural that Italy should buy and sell in many parts of the world. From our own country Italy buys large quantities of cotton, wheat, mineral oils, and metals, and in return we buy many Italian products, especially cheese and olive oil. Other countries which have a large share in Italian trade are Germany, France, Great Britain, and Switzerland.

Some points to remember. In summing up the points which help to explain why Italy had become such an important country before the war we should remember

1. The northern plain, with its advantages for farming and manufacturing.

2. The Mediterranean climate of Sicily and most of the Italian Peninsula, which makes it possible for the people to carry on farming the year round.

3. The water power, which makes up in part for the lack of coal.

4. The dense population, which provides abundant labor for all kinds of work and large home markets for manufacturers.

5. The central location of Italy in the Mediterranean Basin, making it easy for the people to trade with all parts of the world.

We cannot, however, explain Italy's development by these facts alone, for the country has several serious handicaps, the greatest of which is its lack of coal and its small resources of iron ore. We have seen that the Italian people have been quick to make good use of the resources which they have, and to find ways to overcome their handicaps. This resourcefulness, perhaps more than anything else, was the reason why Italy became one of the leading countries of Europe.

By Burton Holmes from Ewing Galloway

Figure 251. A native Libyan boy climbing a date palm to pick the dates.

3. ITALY'S FORMER POSSESSIONS

Use the map on page 234 to locate the lands in Africa which were Italian colonies before the war: Libya (*C–D3*), Eritrea (*D–E4*), and Italian Somaliland (*E4*). Which was the largest Italian colony? Which one is on the Red Sea? Which one borders the Indian Ocean?

Now turn to the map on pages 226–227 and find the Dodecanese Islands (*J3*). After the war these islands were taken away from Italy; and they have been given to Greece, because their people are mostly Greeks.

Libya, Eritrea, and Italian Somaliland were taken away from Italy as colonial possessions and will probably be governed under an arrangement known as international trusteeship. If so, some one country (perhaps Italy itself) or a group of countries will have charge of these lands and will be responsible to the United Nations for governing them well.

Libya. Directly across the Mediterranean Sea from Italy is Libya. Most of it is desert land, but along the coast there is a little more rainfall, and it is here that most of the people live. Among them are a good many Italian colonists who raise Mediterranean crops.

Vast stretches of the Libyan desert are uninhabited, but here and there widely scattered oases support good-sized towns. The oases produce dates of fine quality for export. *See Figure 251.*

For thousands of years the oases could be reached only by camel caravan, but in recent years the Italians built motor roads to connect them with Tripoli and other ports on the coast. The newest motor road is one which runs all the way across Libya from Egypt to Tunisia.

Eritrea and Italian Somaliland. As you discovered from the map, Eritrea and Italian Somaliland are very dry lands, and for this reason they are of little commercial value. The Italians encouraged irrigated farming, but most of the people are nomadic herdsmen.

Map work. Color the former possessions of Italy on the map of Africa which you are making.

Making choices. Choose the ending which makes each sentence below correct:

1. Rome, the capital of Italy, is located on the

Po River.   Arno River.   Tiber River.

2. The leading seaport of Italy is

Genoa.   Naples.   Venice.

3. The city of Italy which is located on islands and has "water streets" is

Florence.   Venice.   Milan.

4. The largest manufacturing city of the Plain of the Po is

Milan.   Turin.   Palermo.

5. The Vatican City is in

Venice.   Rome.   Florence.

6. The famous mountain near Naples is

Mt. Etna.   Mt. Vesuvius.   Mont Blanc.

7. Italy shares the Riviera coast with

Yugoslavia.   Switzerland.   France.

8. The two large islands in the Mediterranean which are parts of Italy are

Corsica and Sardinia.   Sardinia and Sicily.
          Sicily and Crete.

9. Most of the former Italian possessions are in

Africa.   South America.   Asia.

Sentences to complete. Complete the following sentences by giving reasons:

1. The Plain of the Po is one of the best farming regions in Europe because _____.

2. This plain is one of the few important corn-growing regions of Europe because _____.

3. The farms are smaller and the farmers poorer in peninsular Italy than in the northern plain because _____.

4. Peninsular Italy and Sicily are the parts of the country where most of the "Mediterranean" crops are grown because _____.

5. Grapes and olives can be grown on the south-facing slopes of the Alps in northern Italy because _____.

6. Far more cattle are raised in the Plain of the Po than in peninsular Italy because _____.

7. Sheep and goats are the kinds of live stock raised in largest numbers in peninsular Italy because _____.

8. The Plain of the Po is one of the important industrial districts of Europe because _____.

9. Textile-manufacturing made an early start there because _____.

10. The growth of manufacturing in the Plain of the Po has increased the prosperity of the farmers because _____.

Something to discuss. It is rather unusual for countries which are poor in coal and iron ore to carry on manufacturing on a large scale. Italy and Switzerland are exceptions to this rule. Discuss with your classmates the reasons why these two countries have so many important manufacturing industries. In this discussion you will find it helpful to answer the following questions:

1. What advantages have Italy and Switzerland for obtaining raw materials and marketing manufactured goods?

2. Why are both countries well supplied with labor for manufacturing?

3. How do they both make up in part for their lack of coal?

A possessions test. 1. Name each of the former Italian possessions described below:

a. The islands in the Ægean Sea inhabited mostly by Greeks.

b. The colony in Africa most of which is in the Sahara Desert.

c. The colony on the Red Sea.

d. The colony on the east coast of Africa, bordering the Indian Ocean.

2. Explain why the former Italian lands in Africa are less valuable than the British and French lands in that continent.

Special credit work. 1. Try to find a book which tells about the destruction of Pompeii, or about the ruins of this old Roman city as they look today. Report to your class on one of these subjects.

2. Find out all you can about the manufacture of rayon fiber and report to your class.

Keystone View Company

Figure 252. An improved road in one of the country districts of Greece. This road has been widened and smoothed for motor traffic, but heavily laden donkeys and oxcarts are common sights on it because the country people cannot afford automobiles.

By Burton Holmes from Ewing Galloway

Figure 253. How the poorer lands are used in Greece. These sheep are grazing where the soil is too coarse and stony to make good crop land.

IV. THE BALKAN COUNTRIES

1. FOREWORD

A bridge land. The map on pages 6–7 shows that the Balkan Peninsula forms a bridge between Europe and southwestern Asia. Across this bridge people have passed back and forth for many centuries. As you know, the first civilized people in the Balkan Peninsula were the Greeks, who occupied the southernmost part. Later other peoples moved into the peninsula from the northeast.

Because the Balkan Peninsula is so mountainous, no one group of people has succeeded in keeping control of it, and so it has come to be divided among several different countries. The people of each country speak a language of their own, and even within some of the countries themselves there are differences of language which make it hard for the people of one section to understand those of another.

You already know that the six countries which lie partly or wholly in the Balkan Peninsula are Greece, Albania, Yugoslavia, Rumania, Bulgaria, and Turkey. Locate these countries again on the map on pages 226–227. Which ones border the Mediterranean Sea? the Black Sea? Which one occupies the peninsula of Anatolia, with only a small part of its area in the Balkan Peninsula?

Hindrances to development. As a whole, the Balkan nations have been slow in developing the resources of their countries. One reason is that for many years they suffered from wars and weak governments. Another is that so much of the land is mountainous that even today some sections are without railroads or motor highways. In recent years, however, means of transportation have been improved, and much progress in the use of resources has been made. *See Figure 252.*

Most of the people of the Balkan Peninsula and Anatolia are farmers or herdsmen. Many of the farmers do their work in the simple ways of long ago, and some of the herdsmen wander about with their flocks and herds, living a half-nomadic life.

Albania. Albania, the smallest of the six Balkan countries, borders the Adriatic Sea.

It is a land of rugged mountains, with no railroads, only a few good roads, and but little foreign trade. Along the coast there is a lowland where the people carry on farming of the Mediterranean type. Tirana (Tiranë), the capital, and Durazzo (Durrës), the chief seaport, are in this lowland. The people of the interior of the country are mountaineers who make their living chiefly by raising sheep and goats.

European interest in the Balkans. Although the Balkan countries are rather poorly developed, they are of great interest to the larger and stronger countries farther northwest in Europe. As you study this chapter, find reasons for this interest.

2. GREECE

Turn to the map on pages 226–227 and explain why Greece is sometimes called "a peninsula of peninsulas." The long, irregular coast line, with its many gulfs and bays, long ago led the Greeks to make use of the sea. Today, as in olden times, many of the Greeks are sailors and many are merchants. Greek ships carry on much of the trade of the eastern Mediterranean region, and are seen in all the great ports of the world.

The map shows that Crete and most of the small islands in the Ægean Sea belong to Greece, as do Corfu and the Ionian Islands off the west coast of the country. What can you say about the surface of these islands?

From the products and exports of Greece, what can you tell about the use of the land? about the climate?

Mediterranean climate and products. Figure 223 (p. 219) shows that nearly all of Greece has the Mediterranean climate. The land is hilly and mountainous, but in the sunny valleys the people raise Mediterranean fruits and winter wheat and barley.

Along the Gulf of Corinth and the west coast of Greece the farmers grow a special variety of small, black, seedless grapes which are dried in the sun and called currants. Large quantities of currants are shipped to distant lands from the seaport of Patras, and they hold second place among the exports of Greece. Raisins, figs, wines, olives, and olive oil are also exported.

Although many Greek farmers raise wheat, the total production falls far short of the needs of the country, and wheat is one of the leading imports.

An important export crop. In the part of Greece bordering the northern end of the Ægean Sea there are several fertile lowlands where, in addition to grain and fruit, large quantities of tobacco are grown. Tobacco is by far the most valuable export of Greece, and it is shipped to many other countries for use in making cigarettes.

Sheep and goats. Large numbers of sheep and goats are pastured among the mountains of Greece, for these animals can graze on slopes that are too steep and rocky for farming, and on lands where the soils are too poor and stony for crops. They provide the people with milk, cheese, and wool. *See Figure 253.*

Mining and manufacturing. Greece has a variety of metal ores, but mining is not nearly so important as it might be. The chief reasons for this are that Greece has no coal for the smelting of ores, and that as yet not much of the water power has been harnessed to supply electricity. As a result, most of the ores are exported. Among them are iron ore, bauxite, and ores of lead, zinc, and nickel.

The lack of coal and the failure to develop hydroelectricity have also hindered the growth of manufacturing in Greece. Except for cotton-manufacturing, the only industries of importance are those which use raw materials produced in Greece itself. Among these industries are flour-milling and the making of cigarettes, olive oil, and woolen cloth, rugs, and carpets. Since manufacturing is so little developed, manufactured goods are among the leading imports of Greece.

Photograph by Ewing Galloway, N. Y.

Figure 254. The busy harbor of Piræus. Because of its importance as a port, Piræus has yards where ships are built and repaired, and engineering plants where ships' engines are manufactured.

Athens (Athenai) and its seaport. On the map on pages 226–227 find Athens, the capital and largest city of Greece, and its seaport of Piræus (Peiraievs) (*H3*). Today, as in ancient times, Piræus is the chief port of Greece and the gateway to Athens, the city which was once the greatest center of art and learning in the world. Thousands of tourists from all parts of the world pass through Piræus every year on their way to Athens. *See Figure 254.*

Piræus and Athens are only about five miles apart, and the trip from the port to the capital can be made quickly by railroad or automobile. Visitors watch eagerly for their first glimpse of the Acropolis, a rocky, flat-topped hill on which are the ruins of some of the most beautiful temples ever built anywhere in the world. They are built of marble, and the most famous is the one called the Parthenon. The ancient city of Athens clustered closely round the base of the Acropolis, and here, as on the hill, are the ruins of some very old buildings.

Surrounding the old part of Athens is the Neapolis, as the Greeks call the newer part of the city. Here the streets are wide, and the buildings are much like those in other European capitals. In this part of the city is the National Museum, which is a treasure house of statues and other objects of art made by the Greeks of long ago. *See Figure 255.*

Hundreds of students from western Europe and America go to Athens to spend a year or two studying the art and architecture of the ancient Greeks, or reading Greek plays and poetry in the very same surroundings in which they were written, many hundreds of years ago.

The airway map on page 128 will show you that Athens is one of the three great

Keystone View Company

Figure 255. The buildings of the University and the National Academy in the newer part of Athens. These are modern buildings, but they are designed in the Greek style of long ago.

Photograph by Ewing Galloway, N.Y.

Figure 256. Threshing wheat in Rumania. The plains of Rumania and northern Yugoslavia are the only parts of the Balkan countries where many of the farmers are prosperous enough to have farming machinery. What reason can you suggest for this fact?

airway centers of southern Europe. How does its location help to explain its importance as an airway "crossroads"?

Salonika — a gateway city. Turn to the map on pages 144–145 and find the Greek port of Salonika (*K7*). Notice that it is the southern terminus, or end, of a railroad from Berlin and Vienna. This railroad is the chief route of travel and transportation between central Europe and the eastern part of the Mediterranean Sea. Because of this, Salonika is a gateway city, where ships from eastern Mediterranean ports and from Asiatic ports meet trains from the countries of central Europe and an exchange of goods takes place. Compared with Genoa or Marseille, however, Salonika's export and import trade is small because it serves a part of Europe which is rather poorly developed.

The Greek islands. Crete and the smaller islands which belong to Greece are mountainous, but most of the people are farmers who raise grain and Mediterranean fruits and keep sheep and goats. The islands off the west coast of Greece share the currant industry with the neighboring mainland, and Corfu is especially noted for its fine olives.

Sentences to complete. Sum up what you have learned about Greece by completing the following sentences:

1. Sun-dried fruits are important products of Greece because _____
-------------------------------------.

2. The leading export of Greece is
-------------------------------------.

3. There are large numbers of sheep and goats in Greece because
-------------------------------------.

4. Mining and manufacturing have developed slowly in Greece because _____
-------------------------------------.

5. Thousands of people from all parts of the world visit Athens because _____.

6. Salonika is a gateway city because _____
-------------------------------------.

3. YUGOSLAVIA AND RUMANIA

The map on pages 226–227 shows that Yugoslavia and Rumania are the largest of the Balkan countries and extend the farthest north. Which of these countries borders the Adriatic Sea? the Black Sea? In which one of them is the mouth of the Danube River?

If we study the foreign trade of these countries, we shall find that they both export corn and other grains, live cattle and pigs, and meat. What explanation for these exports can you discover from the map on pages 226–227? from Figure 223 on page 219? Before you read further, study Figure 256.

Some rich farm lands. The regional map shows that Yugoslavia and Rumania both have a share in the rich Plain of Hungary, and that Rumania has within its borders the greater part of the plain of the lower Danube. Figure 223 (p. 219) shows that these lowland regions are outside the limits of the Mediterranean climate. What did you learn about their rainfall on page 220?

These plains, with their hot, moist summers and their cold winters, will remind you of our

Figure 257. A group of shepherds near Sarajevo, in the part of Yugoslavia known as Bosnia. Notice how they are dressed. Bosnia is one of the mountainous parts of Yugoslavia, where many of the people still follow the customs of their forefathers.

Lumbering. The mountains of Yugoslavia are covered with forests, — chiefly beech trees on the lower slopes, and spruce and pine higher up. So too are the Carpathian Mountains and the Transylvanian Alps in Rumania, and lumbering is carried on in many places in both countries. So important is this work that lumber leads among the exports of Yugoslavia and stands high among those of Rumania. It goes mostly to the countries of western Europe. *See Figure 258.*

Mineral wealth in Yugoslavia. Yugoslavia has coal and ores of iron, copper, lead, zinc, and other metals, and the people are trying to make their country a large producer of metals and metal products. Mining is carried on in many places, and the iron-and-steel industry is growing steadily. Ores are exported to some extent, but each year more smelting is being done within the country itself, and the production of metals and metal products is increasing. The newest mineral industry in Yugoslavia is the mining of bauxite and the production of aluminum.

Rumanian oil fields. On the map on pages 226–227 find the oil fields in the mountains of Rumania. Find also the city of Ploesti and the seaport of Constanța (*J2*).

The oil fields are so rich that Rumania is one of the leading countries of the world in petroleum production. There are oil refineries in more than a dozen cities and towns near the oil fields, but the greatest refining center is Ploesti. From there and from other refining centers large quantities of gasoline and other petroleum products go to Constanța on the Black Sea, where they are pumped into tank steamers for export. Mineral oils are the most valuable exports of Rumania,

own Central Plains, for the farmers grow large quantities of corn and winter wheat and raise large numbers of cattle and pigs. They also raise other grain crops, and in certain sections tobacco, sugar beets, and grapes and other fruits. Plums are a special crop in northern Yugoslavia, and large quantities of them are sun-dried to make prunes.

Rumania has other rich farm lands in the Plateau of Transylvania and in the regions east of the Carpathians. Because it has much more land well suited to farming than Yugoslavia has, its exports of grain are greater. The exports of foodstuffs from both countries go chiefly to the densely populated industrial countries farther northwest.

Work among the mountains of Yugoslavia. Among the mountains which make up the greater part of Yugoslavia there are many small but fertile valleys where the people carry on farming. Cattle-raising is not important in these mountainous lands, but large numbers of pigs feed on acorns and beechnuts in the forests, and sheep and goats graze on the rougher and poorer lands. *See Figure 257.*

From Ewing Galloway, N.Y.

Figure 258. Logs being floated down a river to a saw-mill in the Carpathian Mountains in Rumania. Why are the Carpathian Mountains thickly forested?

From Ewing Galloway, N.Y.

Figure 259. A glimpse of one of the oil fields in Rumania. Why does Rumania find good markets for its mineral oils in other countries of Europe?

and they go to many different countries of Europe. *See Figure 259.*

The coast of Yugoslavia. In studying the map you discovered that Yugoslavia has a long, mountainous coast line on the Adriatic Sea. The coastal region is the only part of the country which has the Mediterranean climate, and, as you would expect, the people raise grapes, olives, and other fruits. Fishing is also important in the coastal towns and villages.

Handicaps to the growth of ports. Although the coast of Yugoslavia has many good harbors, it has no large seaports. The reason for this is that the coast is bordered by long mountain ranges which form an almost unbroken barrier between the interior of the country and the sea. These mountains have hindered railroad-building, and at present only three railroads reach the coast. Find them on the map on pages 144–145.

The central and southern railroads wind through the mountains, making transportation so slow and expensive that the ports to which they lead are of little importance. The northern railroad leads to the Italian port of Fiume, and is more direct. Wishing to have a port of their own at this railroad end, the

Yugoslavs have built piers and docks at Susak, a town which adjoins Fiume but is just inside the boundary of Yugoslavia.

Some of the trade of Yugoslavia by sea passes through the Greek port of Salonika, where the Yugoslavs are allowed to use a certain section of the water front. The map (pp. 144–145) shows why it is helpful to the Yugoslavs to be able to use this port.

The Danube and the Rumanian seaports. The map on pages 226–227 shows that the Danube has built a great delta at its mouth. Notice that it has three main distributaries. The middle one has been deepened so that good-sized ocean ships can go upstream to the Rumanian ports of Galati and Braila.

You will remember that the Danube has been internationalized, and that all the countries through which it flows may use it freely. Therefore Galati and Braila export not only Rumanian grain and lumber, but some of the products of Yugoslavia, Bulgaria, and the landlocked countries of central Europe.

During the winter, navigation on the Danube stops on account of the ice, and the harbors of Galati and Braila are usually frozen over. Constanţa, farther south, is ice-free in

By Ewing Galloway, N.Y.

Figure 260. Two of the newer business buildings in Bucharest. This city owes its growth to its location in the rich plain of southern Rumania.

By Ewing Galloway, N.Y.

Figure 261. The University buildings in Belgrade. On this side of the street is an open-air vegetable market with the morning crowd of customers.

winter, and for that reason the Rumanians have made it their petroleum port, with large storage tanks for oil and a special basin for oil tankers. Some of the Rumanian exports of grain also pass through Constanţa.

Two capital cities. On the map on pages 226–227 find Belgrade (Beograd), the capital of Yugoslavia (*H2*), and Bucharest (Bucuresti), the capital of Rumania (*J2*). Which one is on the Danube?

Of the two capital cities, Bucharest is the larger and the more modern. It is the home of most of the wealthy people of Rumania, and the better part of the city has many fine public buildings and beautiful homes. Both cities are important business centers and carry on manufacturing to some extent. Both have flour mills, and Bucharest has oil refineries. *See Figures 260 and 261.*

Belgrade owes much of its importance to its location on the Danube at the point where the railroad from Berlin and Vienna crosses that river. Find Belgrade on the map on pages 144–145 (*K7*) and trace the railroad southward from there. Notice that at Nish the railroad divides, one branch running to Salonika and the other to Istanbul.

The railroad which runs through Belgrade to Istanbul is the great route of travel and transportation by land between central Europe and southwestern Asia. The fact that a railroad of great commercial importance runs through the Balkan Peninsula is one of several reasons why many of the other European countries are deeply interested in the Balkan countries.

Trade and manufacturing in Rumania and Yugoslavia. Both Rumania and Yugoslavia are chiefly agricultural countries, and four fifths of the people are farmers. Farm products, as you know, are among their leading exports. Manufactured goods, especially textiles, iron and steel goods, and machinery, are the leading imports of both countries, showing that neither one has as yet become a great manufacturing country.

At present the only manufacturing industry of importance in either country which depends on imported raw materials is the making of cotton goods. The leading industries are chiefly those which make use of raw materials produced at home, such as oil-refining in Rumania, smelting in Yugoslavia, and grain-milling in both countries.

James Sawders

Figure 262. A view over the rooftops of Istanbul. You are looking toward the Bosporus and the Asiatic shore of Turkey. Istanbul is a great center of the Mohammedan religion, and the domed buildings with the tall, slender towers which you see in the picture are mosques, or Mohammedan places of worship.

Sentences to complete. Complete each of the following sentences by giving reasons:

1. Yugoslavia and Rumania are much more important farming countries than Greece because _____.

2. Rumania's exports of grain are greater than those of Yugoslavia because _____.

3. Both Yugoslavia and Rumania export lumber because _____.

4. Large numbers of pigs, sheep, and goats are raised in the mountains of Yugoslavia because _____.

5. The mineral resources of Yugoslavia are of much value because _____.

6. There are no large seaports on the coast of Yugoslavia because _____.

7. Constanța is an important oil-exporting port because _____.

8. The Rumanian ports of Galați and Braila are of interest to several other countries besides Rumania because _____.

9. Manufactured goods are the leading imports of Rumania and Yugoslavia because _____ _____.

4. BULGARIA AND TURKEY

The map on pages 6–7 shows that the bridge between Europe and southwestern Asia is narrowest in the southeast, between the Ægean Sea and the Black Sea. In this part of the Balkan Peninsula are Bulgaria and the European part of Turkey. Although only a very small part of Turkey is in Europe, that part is of much interest to the other European countries. What reasons does the map on pages 144–145 suggest for this fact?

Farming in Bulgaria and European Turkey. The map shows that in the north Bulgaria shares part of the plain of the lower Danube with Rumania. It is here that Bulgaria's corn, wheat, and cattle lands are located. These lands provide some of the leading exports of the country. This plain has two outlets to the Black Sea. One is by way of the Danube River, and the other is by way of the Bulgarian port of Varna.

Photograph by Margaret Willis, sold by R. I. Nesmith and Associates

Figure 263. A narrow street in one of the older parts of Istanbul. Many of the people live and have their little workshops on streets like this.

Bordering the plain on the south are the Balkan Mountains, where farming is limited to the valleys, and the rougher lands are used to pasture sheep and goats. In the western part of the mountains is Sofia (Sofiya), the capital and largest city of Bulgaria, through which runs the railroad from Belgrade to Istanbul.

The Balkan Mountains shut out the cold winter winds from the north, giving the lowlands of southern Bulgaria and European Turkey a warmer climate. Tobacco is one of the leading crops in these lowlands, and is the most important export of Bulgaria. Silkworms also are raised here, and in the foothills of the Balkan Mountains there are gardens where roses are grown for the manufacture of a perfume known as attar of roses.

Istanbul — a crossroads city. Istanbul is the Turkish name for the old city which was long known as Constantinople. It is by far the largest city of the Balkan Peninsula, and for many years it was the capital of Turkey. After the First World War the capital was changed to Ankara, in Anatolia.

Find Istanbul on the map on pages 144–145 (*L7*). Notice that it stands at the point where the main highway of overland travel

by railroad between central Europe and southwestern Asia crosses the narrow strait known as the Bosporus. The Bosporus breaks the overland route, but from Scutari, across the strait from Istanbul, the railroad continues southeastward. *See Figure 262.*

After studying the map you can understand why Istanbul has so long been a large and important city. It has a "crossroads" location at the meeting place of two continents and two seas. The overland route between Europe and southwestern Asia passes through it, and all the shipping between the Black Sea and the Mediterranean must pass by it.

Although, as people say, "Turkey sits astride the straits," the Turks allow the waterway between the Black Sea and the Mediterranean to be used freely by the ships of all nations for purposes of trade. This free use of the Dardanelles, the Sea of Marmara, and the Bosporus is of special value to the countries which border the Black Sea.

Where " East meets West." In some ways Istanbul is more like an Oriental city than a European city. The Mohammedan mosques, with their slender towers, or minarets, give it an Oriental look, and visitors to the old Turkish quarters of the city feel as if they were in some far-away part of Asia. Here the narrow streets are crowded with carts, heavily loaded donkeys, and swarms of people on foot. Merchants in little booths opening on the streets bargain with customers in the Oriental fashion, and craftsmen work at their trades in tiny shops. *See Figure 263.*

The "foreign quarters," where people from central and western Europe carry on business, are very different. Here automobiles move along well-paved streets, business is carried on in modern stores and office buildings, and work of all kinds is done in Western ways. Because of these strange and interesting contrasts, Istanbul is often called a city where "East meets West."

Anatolia

The map on pages 226–227 shows that the European part of Turkey is very small in comparison with the Asiatic part in the peninsula of Anatolia. It is in the Asiatic part that most of the Turks live, and about four fifths of them are farmers and herdsmen. *See Figure 264.*

The "Mediterranean hem" of Anatolia. The most densely populated part of Anatolia is the "hem" of the peninsula, where the climate is of the Mediterranean type. Most of the people live on little farms where they raise winter wheat and barley and Mediterranean fruits. The most valuable "export" fruits are sun-dried figs and raisins which are grown in the neighborhood of Smyrna (Izmir), the chief port of Anatolia.

In several localities tobacco-growing is very important — so important that tobacco is the leading export of Turkey. Turkish tobacco is used in our own country and in many others for making cigarettes.

On the map on pages 226–227 find the places in Anatolia where cotton is an important crop. Cotton-growing is increasing, and cotton is exported. The leading cotton-growing district is in the lowland around Adana, and in that city there are cotton gins, cottonseed mills, and a few cotton factories.

The interior of Anatolia. The rainfall in Anatolia grows less from the coasts toward the interior, and the central plateau is a rather dry grassland. For this reason the plateau and the bordering mountain slopes are chiefly grazing lands for sheep and goats. Anatolia is the native land of the famous Angora goats, from which mohair is obtained.

The sheep's wool and the mohair produced in this region have led many of the people to become weavers of carpets and rugs. This work is carried on in the homes and in workshops in many of the villages and towns. Perhaps you have seen Anatolian rugs, for they are sold

James Sawders

Figure 264. A country merchant in Anatolia. Riding a donkey and leading two pack camels, he travels from one village to another selling his wares.

in our country as one of the less expensive grades of Oriental rugs.

On the map on pages 226–227 find Ankara (*K 3*), the capital of Turkey. Explain why it has a better location for its purpose than Istanbul, the former capital. Ankara is a very old city which the Turks have changed into a modern center of business and of work connected with the government.

Mining and manufacturing. Anatolia has considerable mineral wealth, but only recently have the Turks made much use of it. Now they are mining more than enough coal for their needs, and a number of different metal ores. Among the metal ores is chromite, which Turkey exports in large quantities.

The Turks are also making progress in manufacturing by building up industries which use raw materials produced in Anatolia. Among the industries which are growing each year are flour-milling, tanning and the making of leather goods, and the manufacture of cotton and woolen goods.

Matching countries and capitals. Match correctly the countries and capital cities listed below:

Spain	Ankara
Portugal	Athens
Italy	Belgrade
Greece	Bucharest
Albania	Lisbon
Yugoslavia	Madrid
Rumania	Rome
Bulgaria	Sofia
Turkey	Tirana

A population test. Below is a table showing the density of population in the countries of southern Europe and Anatolia. Study the table carefully, and then answer the questions following it.

COUNTRY	POPULATION PER SQUARE MILE
Italy	377
Portugal	220
Rumania	175
Yugoslavia	164
Bulgaria	164
Greece	142
Spain	138
Turkey	60

1. Compare this table with the one on page 215 showing density of population in the central European countries. As a whole, how do the countries of southern Europe compare in density of population with those of central Europe? What reasons can you suggest for the difference?

2. Which Mediterranean country has the most people per square mile? What reasons can you give for its dense population? How does its population density compare with that of the most densely populated country of central Europe?

3. What have you learned about the surface and climate of the various countries of southern Europe and Anatolia which helps to explain why Spain and Turkey stand at the foot of the list in density of population?

4. What reasons can you suggest for the fact that Yugoslavia is somewhat more densely populated than Greece? for the fact that Rumania is somewhat more densely populated than Yugoslavia?

Naming countries. The blank space at the beginning of each sentence below stands for the name of some one of the countries of southern Europe and Anatolia. Give the correct name to begin each sentence, and complete the sentences which need endings.

Of these countries

1. _____ carries on the most foreign trade because _____.

2. _____ is the one with the most mineral wealth, yet it is not a great manufacturing country because _____.

3. _____ is the one which makes most use of hydroelectric power because _____.

4. _____ is the one which exports the most grain because _____.

5. _____ is the one which depends most largely on its forest resources.

6. _____ is the only one which exports petroleum.

7. _____ is the one well known for its exports of tobacco and currants.

8. _____ is the one which depends most largely on its fisheries.

9. _____ is the least important because _____.

10. _____ is the one which is largely in southwestern Asia.

Some things to explain. Explain why

1. Istanbul is the largest city of the Balkan Peninsula.

2. The countries farther northwest in Europe are interested in the Balkan countries.

3. The fact that the Dardanelles, the Sea of Marmara, and the Bosporus may be used freely by the ships of all nations is a great help to Rumania and Bulgaria.

4. People say that Istanbul is a city "where East meets West."

Addressing letters. Imagine that you have a friend who is traveling in Italy and who has asked you to send him a letter at each of the cities listed below. Give for each city the Italian name which you should use in addressing the letters.

Florence	Naples	Venice	Genoa
Rome	Turin	Milan	

© Publishers Photo Service, Inc.

Figure 265. A picture taken in a village on the Nile. Why are the houses built with flat roofs? What do the palm trees show about the climate of Egypt?

Figure 266. Egyptian sailboats on the Nile at Cairo. Boats of this kind are used to carry goods up and down the Nile between the towns along its banks.

INDEPENDENT COUNTRIES OF AFRICA AND SOUTHWEST ASIA

I. EGYPT — LAND OF THE NILE

Foreword. Study the map of the possessions of the European countries in Africa which you have been making, and see how many political divisions of that continent are still uncolored. If your map is correct, it should show three such divisions, — Egypt, Liberia, and Ethiopia, which are the only independent countries in Africa. Of the three, Egypt is by far the most important. Do you know any reasons for this fact?

People say that "Egypt is the Nile, and the Nile is Egypt." This saying is a true one, for Egypt lies in the Sahara Desert, and without the Nile it would be as useless as the rest of that dry, barren region. But because of the Nile, Egypt has within its borders the most densely populated area in all Africa. Figure 42 (p. 49) shows that this area is a narrow strip of land bordering the river, and that the rest of Egypt is as thinly populated as the other parts of the desert. *See Figures 265 and 266.*

Egypt is a very old country, and the Nile Valley has been the home of civilized people for thousands of years. Today the valley has over 1000 people per square mile, and is as crowded as some of the industrial districts of western Europe and the United States. The surprising thing about this crowded valley is that most of the people make their living by farming. How do you suppose this is possible in a land where for months at a time not a drop of rain falls?

One of the world's great rivers. The Nile is one of the great rivers of the world. It is longer than any other river except our own Missouri-Mississippi, and about one fourth of its course is in Egypt. On the map on page 48 find Khartoum (*G3*), in Anglo-Egyptian Sudan, where the White Nile from the Lake Plateau of East Africa joins the Blue Nile from the Ethiopian Highlands. Trace the Nile northward from Khartoum to its mouth, and

Figure 267. The Aswan Dam, over a mile long. This great dam holds back part of the water of the Nile. When water is needed downstream, it is let out by opening gates in the lower part of the dam.

© Publishers Photo Service, Inc.

notice that there are six *cataracts* in its course. These are places where the river tumbles over rock ledges, forming rapids and falls.

The first cataract, or the one farthest downstream, is at Aswan, in southern Egypt. There the great dam which you see in Figure 267 has been built across the Nile. Can you suggest any reason for the building of this dam?

Picturing the Nile Valley. Figure 268 will help you to picture the Nile Valley in Egypt. Notice the narrow, flat-bottomed trough through which the Nile flows northward to Cairo, and the great delta which begins at Cairo and spreads out in fan shape to the Mediterranean. Use the scale of miles to estimate the width of the valley and the length and width of the delta.

If you should fly in an airplane from Aswan to Cairo, following the course of the Nile, you would see that the valley is a narrow green band of cultivated fields in the midst of the bare, reddish-brown desert. Scattered through it are many little villages of mud-brick houses and a few good-sized towns.

Continuing your flight from Cairo across the delta, you would look down on a broad stretch of very low land divided into thousands of small farms, and crisscrossed by distributaries of the river, canals for irrigation and drainage, and a network of railroads. You would also see that the delta is dotted with towns and villages.

A great oasis. By now you will know that the Nile Valley is a great oasis, where farming is made possible by use of the waters from the river. In fact, it is the greatest oasis in all the world. Here, for thousands of years, the Egyptians have carried on irrigated farming, making an almost rainless region produce large quantities of grain and other crops.

The winters are warm in Egypt, and therefore farming can be carried on the year round. The principal winter crops are wheat, barley, and beans, onions, and other vegetables; and the principal summer crops are cotton, corn, rice, and sugar cane.

Using flood waters for irrigation. From ancient times until less than a hundred years ago the Egyptians depended chiefly on the annual, or yearly, flood of the Nile for water to irrigate their farm lands. Newer methods of irrigation are now used in the delta and the lower Nile Valley, but the "flood method" is still common in the upper part of the valley.

The annual flood comes in September and October and is due to the heavy rains which fall in the Ethiopian Highlands during the summer. Because of these rains, the Blue Nile pours huge quantities of water into the main stream. This causes the Nile to rise and overflow its banks, flooding the bordering lands to a depth of several feet.

In order to hold the flood waters long enough for the soil to be thoroughly soaked, the lands irrigated in this way are divided into basins surrounded by low dikes, and the basins are connected by shallow canals which carry the water from one to another. When the flood waters finally drain off, a thin layer of fertile mud is left on the fields, which enriches the soil. While the land is still wet, the farmers plant their wheat, barley, beans, and other winter crops. These crops grow quickly during the warm winter and are ready to be harvested in February or March.

So long as the flood method was the principal means of irrigation in Egypt, the only places where the farmers could raise summer crops — that is, crops planted in the spring and harvested before the flood season — were the fields immediately bordering the river and its distributaries. For these fields water was lifted from the streams by *shadoofs* and water wheels. These simple methods of irrigation are still used in some places in Egypt even today. *See Figure 269.*

Year-round irrigation. Although Egypt is an independent country, the British have long been interested in it because the Suez Canal and the northern section of the Cape to Cairo Railway are in Egyptian territory. Furthermore, Egypt was at one time under British control. During that period the British built the great dam at Aswan and several smaller dams at other places along the river to give the Nile Valley year-round irrigation.

The dams hold back the waters of the Nile, storing them up for use all through the year. Water for irrigation can be let out whenever it is needed, and canals carry it to the farm lands in the lower valley and the delta. Thus these lands can be irrigated throughout the whole year, and the farmers can raise crops in summer as well as in winter.

© Ginn and Company

Figure 268. A relief map of the valley and delta of the Nile.

From the map on pages 226–227 name the leading crops grown in the lower valley of the Nile and on the delta. The farms are very small in these crowded lowlands, and most of the farmers work in the old-fashioned ways of long ago; but, cultivating their lands intensively both summer and winter, all together they produce millions of bushels of wheat, corn, and other food crops, and large quantities of very high-grade cotton.

Although the Egyptian farmers raise foodstuffs in large quantities, the population is so great that nearly all these products are needed

Figure 269. Lifting water for irrigation from the Nile by means of a shadoof. Explain how the shadoof works.

Figure 270. Picking cotton in Egypt. Egyptian children work in the cotton fields with their fathers during the picking season. Where in the United States do we raise the Egyptian variety of cotton?

for home use. Therefore, in spite of being almost entirely an agricultural country, Egypt is not a great exporter of foodstuffs. From the map on pages 226–227 name the one food product which ranks high among the exports. What crop supplies all the other leading exports?

Egyptian cotton. It is clear from the map that cotton is the great export crop of Egypt. The exports of cotton fiber alone are worth about three times all the other exports combined, and cottonseed and cottonseed cake and oil are also shipped to distant lands.

Egyptian cotton has a long, silky fiber, and because of its fine quality it is in great demand in all the important cotton-manufacturing countries. Nearly all the farmers in the delta and the lower valley of the Nile raise cotton as a money crop. They sow the seed in February or March, pick the cotton in September or October, and send it to towns where it is ginned and baled for export. *See Figure 270.*

Great Britain usually buys more than half of the yearly crop of cotton from Egypt. Can

you explain why? Our own country is also a good customer for it, because the amount of "Egyptian" cotton which we raise on irrigated lands in the Southwest is not sufficient to supply our needs.

Alexandria — the seaport of Egypt. On the map on pages 226–227 find Alexandria, the leading seaport of Egypt (*J4*), and notice its location at the western end of the Nile delta. Can you think of any reason why Egypt's chief seaport should have grown up here, rather than at the mouth of one of the distributaries of the Nile?

Study the map more closely, and you will see that the mouths of most of the distributaries of the Nile are almost cut off from the sea by sand bars along the outer margin of the delta. The distributary mouths and the openings between the sand bars are choked with shifting mud and sand washed down by the Nile, and are much too shallow for ocean-going ships. Since these waterways can be used only by small boats, the towns located on them are unimportant as ports.

Photograph by Gardner Wells from R. I. Nesmith and Associates

Figure 271. An American ship being loaded with raw cotton at the Egyptian port of Alexandria. Explain why our country, which is a large producer of cotton, buys cotton from Egypt.

Alexandria is located on a sand bar; but since it is beyond the westernmost of the distributaries of the Nile, its harbor is free from shifting sands. It is not a good natural harbor, however, and has to be protected by breakwaters. *See Figure 271.*

Alexandria was founded over two thousand years ago, and today it is the second largest city in Africa. At its busy wharves ships from distant lands load and unload cargoes, and in its cotton exchange the business arrangements are made for selling cotton to manufacturers in England, the United States, and other countries. What do you find among the imports of Alexandria which shows that the Egyptians do not use much of their cotton for manufacturing?

Cairo — the largest city of Africa. On the map on pages 226–227 find Cairo, the capital of Egypt (*K5*). This is the only city in Africa with over a million people. Notice that it is located on the right bank of the Nile, at the head, or inner end, of the

delta. Because of its location where the narrow valley of the Nile ends and the delta begins, Cairo is the point where the railroad from Aswan meets the railroads from Alexandria, Port Said, and other parts of the delta. It is chiefly this "crossroads" location in the midst of the richest agricultural region of Africa which has made Cairo the largest city of the continent. *See Figure 272.*

If you visit Cairo in the winter, you will find many visitors from Europe and America there, for the winter weather is delightfully mild. The hotels where the visitors stay, the government buildings, and the better stores are in the "European quarter" of the city, where the streets are well paved and broad enough for automobiles.

Very different are the old "native quarters" of the city, with their many Mohammedan mosques and their Oriental bazaars full of life and color. There you will find a tangle of streets so narrow and crooked that

Photo by Lionel Green

Figure 272. A view of Cairo from the wall of the old citadel, showing a large Mohammedan mosque in the foreground. Notice the even sky line, which shows how level the surface of the Nile delta is.

Figure 273. The pyramids near Cairo. These wonderful monuments are built of huge blocks of stone, and are over 5000 years old. Each one was built as a tomb for an Egyptian king and queen.

sand years ago, is located. Many of the wonderful things taken from his tomb are in the museum at Cairo.

Mineral resources and manufacturing. Egypt is not a country of great mineral resources, and there are but few places where mining is of any importance. One is in the Sinai Peninsula, where manganese ore is mined; and another is on the desert shore of the Red Sea, where there are phosphate mines. Along the western margin of the Gulf of Suez there are oil wells, from which the crude oil is sent in tank steamers to refineries in the port of Suez. The chief product of these refineries is fuel oil, which is stored at Suez and Port Said to supply ships which need refueling as they go through the Suez Canal.

Since Egypt is so largely an agricultural country and has no coal, manufacturing is of little importance. There are, of course, a few manufacturing plants where Egyptian products are prepared for use, such as the cotton-ginning plants and cottonseed-oil mills in some of the delta towns and the oil refineries at Suez. Except for work of this kind, the only important manufacturing industry is the making of cigarettes. The tobacco comes from Greece and Turkey, and many of the men who make the cigarettes are Greeks.

Egyptian trade. Since nearly all the people of Egypt are farmers, it is not surprising that the leading exports are agricultural products. An interesting fact about Egyptian trade is that the exports consist largely of a single agricultural product. In foreign trade, cotton is more important to Egypt than coffee is to Brazil. Chiefly with its cotton and cottonseed products, Egypt pays for a variety of imports from distant lands.

it is clear they were laid out long before anyone dreamed of automobiles, — streets lined with little shops where workmen carry on their trades and with tiny booths where merchants sell their wares. From daylight until long after dark endless streams of people move through these Old World streets, elbowing their way among carts and heavily loaded donkeys and camels, and stopping now and then to chat with one another or to bargain with the merchants.

While you are in Cairo you will surely visit the National Museum, where the Egyptians have preserved many of the treasures which have been taken from the tombs of the kings and queens of long ago. Among these treasures are paintings, clothing, jewelry, and many objects of daily use which tell of the life and work in Egypt in ancient days. You will also make a trip by automobile, or on camelback if you choose, to the great pyramids which stand on the edge of the desert, five miles beyond the Nile from Cairo. *See Figure 273.*

At Cairo you can take passage on a comfortable steamer and go up the Nile to Luxor, where the tomb of Tutenkhamon, a young king who ruled Egypt more than three thou-

Giving reasons. Complete each sentence below by giving reasons for the fact which it states.

1. Nearly all the people of Egypt are crowded into an area which makes up less than one twenty-fifth of the country because _ _ _ _ _ _ _ _ _ _ _ _ _ .

2. The prosperity of the Egyptian people depends on the rain which falls farther south in Africa because _ _ _ _ _ _ _ _ _ _ _ _ _ _ _ _ _ .

3. Since the British first became interested in Egypt, more and more land in the delta and lower valley of the Nile has been used for growing crops the year round because _ _ _ _ _ _ _ _ _ _ _ _ .

4. The Nile is not navigable throughout its entire course in Egypt because _ _ _ _ _ _ _ _ _ _ .

5. The Egyptian farmers build their houses of sun-dried mud bricks instead of wood because _ .

6. Although Egypt is almost wholly an agricultural country, it is not a great exporter of foodstuffs because _ _ _ _ _ _ _ _ _ _ _ _ _ _ .

7. Great Britain has a larger share than any other country in the export trade of Egypt because _ .

8. Cairo is the largest city of Egypt because _ .

9. The seaport of Alexandria is west of the mouths of the Nile because _ _ _ _ _ _ _ _ _ _ _ _ _ _ .

10. The British hold Port Said and Suez because _ .

An import test. Below is a list of some of the leading imports of Egypt. Explain why the Egyptians need each one of them.

| cotton goods | coal | lumber |
| machinery | fertilizers | tobacco |

A model to make. If you have a sand table or can get some modeling clay, make a good-sized model of the portion of Egypt shown in Figure 268. Show the locations of Cairo, Alexandria, the Aswan Dam, and the ports at either end of the Suez Canal. Perhaps you can think of ways to show some of the chief crops of Egypt, the pyramids near Cairo, a ship passing through the Suez Canal, and some boats on the Nile.

Special credit work. Try to find a book which tells about the Egyptian pyramids, or the temples at Karnak, or the discoveries in the tomb of Tutenkhamon. Report to your class on one of these subjects.

II. LIBERIA

Foreword. On the map on page 50 find the independent country of Liberia on the west coast of tropical Africa. Do you think it probable that this country is densely populated? Check your answer to this question by Figure 42 on page 49.

The people of Liberia are Negroes. Have you any idea how their country happens to be independent, surrounded as it is by possessions of European countries?

A Negro republic. Liberia was founded over a hundred years ago as a homeland for freed slaves from the United States, and ever since that time it has been an independent Negro republic. Its name means " liberty." Some of its people are descendants of the freed slaves, and the rest are African Negroes. The capital city, Monrovia, was named for President Monroe of the United States, who helped to establish the republic.

Tropical products. As you would expect from its location on the west coast of tropical Africa, Liberia has a hot, rainy climate. The people grow their own foodstuffs in small gardens, and for export products they raise a little coffee and cacao and gather palm kernels and rubber in the forests. In recent years an American rubber company has established large rubber plantations in Liberia, which provide work for several thousand people. At present, palm kernels and palm oil are the leading exports, but in time rubber may be much more important than it is at present.

Special credit work. Try to find a book which tells about the establishment of Liberia and make a report to the class.

III. ETHIOPIA

Foreword. The map on page 50 shows that Ethiopia is a plateau and mountain country with no seacoast. The mountains are high and rugged, and the plateau is crossed by deep canyons carved by rivers. The rough surface has hindered the development of the country; but in the days when Europeans were gaining control of one part of Africa after another, it helped the Ethiopians to keep them out and to remain an independent nation.

In 1936 Ethiopia was conquered by Italy and became an Italian colony. But in 1941, during the Second World War, a British army drove the Italians out and Ethiopia again became independent.

Three " work " zones. Like Mexico, Ethiopia may be divided into three zones, or belts, according to the elevation of the land above sea level. The lowest zone includes the lands not over 5000 feet in elevation. Because the country is so near the equator, the climate in this zone is hot the year round, and the people raise tropical and subtropical crops. Chief among them is coffee, which is one of the few exports of Ethiopia.

The second zone is the land between 5000 and 8000 feet, where, because of greater elevation, the climate is mild, but not hot, the year round. This is the zone where most of the people live, and where Addis Ababa, the capital, is located. The principal crops are temperate-zone cereal grains and fruits, but the work of greatest importance is the raising of cattle. *See Figure 274.*

The third and highest zone is the land over 8000 feet, where the climate is still cooler. Little farming is carried on in this zone, and most of the people get their living by keeping sheep and goats. Hides and skins from the middle zone and the highest zone are the leading exports of Ethiopia.

A country awaiting development. The mineral resources of Ethiopia are almost untouched, farming is less important than it might be, and the foreign trade of the country is small. One of the chief reasons for this backwardness is poor transportation. The only railroad in the country is the line connecting Addis Ababa with Jibuti, the port of French Somaliland on the Red Sea. Most of the roads are little better than trails, and goods are carried largely on the backs of donkeys, mules, and other pack animals.

The Ethiopians are freedom-loving people, and they found the years under Italian control hard to bear. Now that they are free again, they have one worth-while souvenir of that period — several thousand miles of motor roads that the Italians built. This is the beginning of a highway system which, when completed by the Ethiopians themselves, will help greatly in the development of the country and its trade.

Can you explain these facts? 1. Addis Ababa is in the tropics, yet it is seldom uncomfortably warm. What is the reason for this?

2. Ethiopia is a difficult country in which to build roads and railroads.

Salisbury from Ewing Galloway, N.Y.

Figure 274. An Ethiopian farmer pounding grain in a hollow log to make flour. His house is built of sticks of wood, and the roof is thatched with straw.

By Ewing Galloway, N. Y.

Figure 275. A view near the mountainous margin of the Plateau of Iran in southwestern Asia. The parts of the plateau which cannot be irrigated can be used only for pasturing sheep and goats. Where there are streams for irrigation, the people raise crops of grain and vegetables, and many different kinds of fruits.

IV. ARABIA, IRAQ, IRAN, AND AFGHANISTAN

Foreword. On the map on page 70 find the Plateau of Arabia, the lowland of Mesopotamia, the Plateau of Iran, and the Hindu Kush Mountains. What does Figure 64 show about the rainfall in these regions of southwest Asia? What does Figure 65 show about their population?

The countries in this southwest part of Asia which are independent of European control are Iraq, Arabia, Iran,[1] and Afghanistan. Arabia is made up of several more or less independent states, but all the smaller states recognize Saudi Arabia, the largest one, as their leader. Before you read further, locate Arabia, Iraq, Iran, and Afghanistan on the map on page 75, and use that map to work out the map studies in the next column.

[1] Iran is the official name of the country long known as Persia. The people are commonly called Persians.

Map studies. 1. What country once under British control borders Arabia? 2. What one once under French control borders Iraq? 3. What gulfs separate southern Iran from Arabia? 4. In what country does most of the lowland of Mesopotamia lie? 5. What two rivers drain that lowland? 6. What kind of land makes up most of Afghanistan? 7. What kind of land borders the Plateau of Iran? 8. What kind of work seems to be most important in the plateau regions of Arabia, Iran, and Afghanistan?

9. In which two countries does farming seem to be more important, — Arabia and Afghanistan, or Iran and Iraq? 10. What crop in the lowland of Mesopotamia reminds you of the Nile Valley? 11. How do you explain the production of dates in dry Arabia? 12. What mineral product is important in Iran and Iraq? 13. How do you explain the noticeable lack of railroads in Arabia, Iran, and Afghanistan? 14. Which country has no railroads and no seacoast?

© Publishers Photo Service, Inc.

Figure 276. A Bedouin family encamped outside an oasis town. Why is it that the only houses the Bedouins have are tents of woolen cloth?

High lands and dry lands. The plateaus of Arabia and Iran are fairly high, rising to elevations of from 3000 to 5000 feet above sea level. The mountains which surround the Plateau of Iran are still higher, and the ranges of the Hindu Kush are some of the highest and most rugged mountains in the world.

These regions of southwestern Asia are so dry that large stretches of Arabia are desert lands, and many parts of the Plateau of Iran have but the scantiest covering of poor grass. The mountains have a little more rainfall than the plateaus, and in Iran and Afghanistan snow falls on the higher mountain slopes in the winter. This is a great help to the people, for the waters from the melting snow drain off in streams which provide water for irrigation on the lower lands in the spring and summer. *See Figure 275.*

The lowland of Mesopotamia. This lowland is another very dry region, but its soils are deep and fertile. It has hot summers and mild winters, and so, except for the lack of enough rainfall, it is well suited to agriculture. Fortunately, two rivers flow through it,—the

Tigris and the Euphrates,—and they provide water for irrigation. The map on page 75 shows that the Tigris and Euphrates join to form a single stream before reaching the Persian Gulf. What city is near their junction?

Nomadic life. Groups of nomadic Bedouins wander about in the dry Plateau of Arabia, in search of grass and water for their flocks and herds. They measure their wealth in the number of camels, sheep, goats, and horses which they own, for these animals provide them with most of their food and clothing materials and with their only means of transportation. Now and then the Bedouins stop at one of the oasis towns to exchange some wool, skins, and cheese for small supplies of flour, dates, and coffee, or perhaps a saddle or a few cooking pots. *See Figure 276.*

In the drier parts of Iran and Afghanistan there are other groups of people who wander from place to place with their flocks and herds. All these nomadic people make a very poor living and often suffer great hardships in their wanderings. *See Figure 277.*

Towns and farm lands. The number of nomads in these countries is small compared with the number of people who live in and near the towns. The towns have grown up at places where water for irrigation can be obtained from wells or streams and the people can make a living by farming. These "garden spots" are found along the margins of the deserts, in the oases, and in the valleys among the mountains.

Arabian crops. The oasis towns of Arabia will remind you of those in the Sahara. They are clusters of mud-brick houses surrounded by gardens which are irrigated with water from wells, and the size of each town depends on the amount of water that can be obtained. The people raise fruits, vegetables, and grain, and forage crops for the camels and donkeys which are used to lift water from the wells and to carry burdens.

By Ewing Galloway, N.Y.

Figure 277. Persian nomads and their tent. Their clothing and their tent differ from those of the Bedouin Arabs, but they live in much the same way.

In all these oases there are groves of date palms, for these trees grow better in hot, sunny deserts than anywhere else, provided, of course, that their roots can reach water. The people dry the dates in the sun, pack them in wooden boxes, and send them to the coastal towns for export.

The map on page 75 shows that coffee is grown in the Arab state of Yemen on the coast of the Red Sea. There the mountains cause a little more rain to fall, and the fogs from the sea provide additional moisture. Most of the coffee is used in Arabia, for the Arabs are great coffee-drinkers.

Arabian towns. On the map on page 75 find Mecca, the largest town of Arabia, and Medina, farther north (*D 6*). Mecca is the place where Mohammed, the founder of the Mohammedan religion, was born, and Medina is his burial place. Every year thousands of Mohammedans from near and far make pilgrimages to these two cities, both of which depend largely on the selling of food and other supplies to the pilgrims.

There are no railroads in Arabia, but in some parts motor roads have been built connecting the more important towns. Elsewhere in

Arabia travel and transportation are chiefly by camel caravan over routes which connect the oasis towns with one another and with the small seaports.

The "Mediterranean" crops of Iraq, Iran, and Afghanistan. In the upper part of the lowland of Mesopotamia, in the mountain valleys and along the margins of the plateau in western Iran, and in the valleys among the mountains of Afghanistan, crops like those of the Mediterranean lands are raised. The light rainfall of these sections comes in the winter, making it possible for the people to raise winter wheat and barley.

The summer crops are irrigated with water from streams and wells, and among them fruits and nuts are especially important. A great variety of fruits are raised, including grapes, peaches, plums, apricots, melons, and figs of unusually fine quality, and in Iran considerable quantities of some of the fruits are sun-dried for export. In both Iran and Iraq cotton is another summer crop, but it is grown chiefly for home use. *See Figure 278.*

The mulberry trees which are grown in some of the sheltered valleys in northern Iran

James Sawders

Figure 278. Spinning cotton yarn in the native way in Iraq. What have you learned about Iraq which explains why this work can be done out of doors?

By Ewing Galloway, N.Y.

Figure 279. Persian boys weaving a rug. It takes many months to make one of these beautiful rugs, for every knot is tied separately by hand.

and in Afghanistan are another reminder of the Mediterranean lands. They are cultivated to provide leaves to feed silkworms, which, in turn, supply the raw material for the weaving of silk goods.

The lower part of the lowland of Mesopotamia, from Baghdad to the Persian Gulf, is the driest and hottest part of Iraq. Here, in irrigated groves, large quantities of dates are grown for export.

Baghdad and Basra. The capital of Iraq is the old city of Baghdad, which has been a trading center for thousands of years. The chief port is Basra, which is located near the place where the Tigris and Euphrates rivers join to enter the Persian Gulf. Find these two cities on the map on page 75 (*D–E4*). Notice that Baghdad is on the Tigris River and is connected with Basra by a railroad.

Persian rug-makers. Perhaps you know that the finest of our Oriental rugs come from Iran. In every village and town you will see Persian women and children sitting at looms, patiently tying the knots of colored wool which

make the patterns that we admire so much. Rug-making is a very old industry in Iran, for wool is plentiful and rugs have always been the principal furnishings in Persian homes. For many years all the rugs were made in the homes, and for home use; but now that so many are wanted by the people of other countries, workshops have been established where many weavers work together. *See Figure 279.*

Some valuable oil fields. Years ago the British obtained permission to develop what have proved to be rich oil fields in both Iran and Iraq. Pipe lines carry the crude oil from the fields in Iran to Abadan, at the head of the Persian Gulf, where there are large refineries. The refined oils go chiefly to Europe, and they are the leading exports of Iran. From the fields in northern Iraq pipe lines have been built to carry the crude oil all the way to ports on the eastern coast of the Mediterranean Sea. There are other oil fields on Bahrein Island, in the Persian Gulf. Bahrein is a British possession, but the oil is produced and refined by American companies.

Cities of Iran. The largest cities of Iran are Tehran, the capital, and Tabriz. Locate them on the map on page 75 (*E–F3*) and notice their railroads. For many years the only railroad in Iran was the one from Tiflis, in Transcaucasia, and it went no farther than Tabriz The lines linking Tehran with Tabriz and with Bandar Shahpur, on the Persian Gulf, have been built recently, and are helping greatly in the development of the country.

Afghanistan and its capital. Afghanistan is so mountainous that far more of the people are engaged in raising sheep, goats, camels, and other live stock than in farming, and hides and skins, with a little silk, are the chief exports. The country has no railroads and no seacoast. Therefore the people have little to do with the outside world, and their trade with other countries is small.

Kabul, the capital, is the only city of any importance. Find it on the map on page 75 (*J4*) and notice that it is directly west of the Khyber Pass. This narrow pass is the only route across the mountains to India, and the one by which most of Afghanistan's trade is carried on. Kabul, therefore, is the center where goods are collected to be sent out of the country and from which goods that come into the country are distributed. *See Figure 280.*

A city test. Name each city described below and answer the questions concerning it.

1. The largest city of Africa. Of what country is it the capital? Why does it entertain many visitors from distant lands each year?

2. The chief seaport of Egypt. Why is it an important cotton market? Why is much of its trade with Great Britain?

3. The capital of Liberia. For whom was it named?

4. The capital of Ethiopia. In what zone of the country is it located? What reason can you suggest for its location in that zone?

5. The city where Mohammed was born. In what country is it located? Why does it have thousands of visitors every year?

6. The capital of Iran. In what part of the country is it located? What kind of workshops should you expect to see in this city?

7. The capital of Afghanistan. Why is it the chief commercial center of the country?

8. The capital of Iraq. What advantages has it for carrying on trade?

Giving reasons. Complete each sentence below by giving reasons.

1. Egypt is by far the most important of the three independent countries of Africa because _____

2. Egypt is of special interest to Great Britain because _____.

3. People say that "Egypt is the Nile, and the Nile is Egypt" because _____.

James Sawders

Figure 280. A camel train on the road that leads from Kabul through the Khyber Pass to India. The British use light motor trucks on this road, but the Afghans use camels.

4. The United States is a good customer for Egyptian cotton because _____.

5. The export trade of Egypt consists largely of agricultural products because _____.

6. Manufacturing is of little importance in Egypt because _____.

7. Liberia helps to supply one of the great manufacturing industries in the United States with raw material because _____.

8. Some of the people of Arabia and Iran live nomadic lives because _____.

9. The size of the towns in Arabia depends largely on the amount of water that can be obtained because _____.

10. In certain parts of southwest Asia the people raise crops like those of the Mediterranean lands because _____.

11. The British have a special interest in Iran and Iraq because _____.

12. Rug-making has long been an important industry in Iran because _____.

13. The people of Afghanistan have little to do with the outside world because _____.

14. There is abundant water for irrigation in the lowland of Mesopotamia because _____.

Special credit work. Find out all you can about Persian and other Oriental rugs — their patterns and how they are woven — and tell your classmates about them.

Sovfoto

Figure 281. Harvesting wheat with a "combine" on a plain in the Soviet Union. The combine is a machine which cuts and threshes the grain as it moves back and forth across the field. Before the First World War the Russian farmers did most of their work by hand, but now many use farming machinery.

THE UNION OF SOVIET SOCIALIST REPUBLICS

I. THE LARGEST COUNTRY IN THE WORLD

Foreword. The Union of Soviet Socialist Republics is often called Russia, for it includes most of the land which belonged to the Empire of Russia before the First World War. The largest of its various republics is the Russian Soviet Republic.

The word *soviet* means a council of delegates of workers. Each village, town, and city, each province of each republic, and each republic itself is governed by a soviet. All the republics are parts of the Soviet Union, and each one sends representatives to the All-Union Congress which meets in Moscow (Moskva), the capital city.

The Soviet Union has rich farming lands, vast forests, coal, iron ore, and much water power. It has long been a great farming country, but only in recent years has it become an important manufacturing country.

Map Studies. Before you read further, use the two maps on page 276 to work out the following map studies:

1. What can you say about the size of the Soviet Union? 2. Is it a European country or a Eurasian country? 3. What bodies of water does it border? 4. What kind of land makes up most of the western half of the country? 5. What part of the country is best supplied with railroads? 6. What use do you think the people make of many of the rivers?

Now turn to page 71 and locate the Soviet Union on Figure 65. What part of the country is most densely populated? What reason does the rainfall map suggest for the fact that the European part is so much more densely populated than most of the Asiatic part? Compare the population map with the lower map on page 276 and see if you can discover any relationship between the distribution of population and the railroads.

First Glimpses of the Soviet Union

A giant country. You have discovered from the maps that the Union of Soviet Socialist Republics stretches from east-central Europe all the way across Asia to the Pacific Ocean. This is the largest country in all the world. The European part is usually called European Russia, and it is nearly as large as all the other European countries combined. The Asiatic part of the Union is nearly four times as large as the European part, and the country as a whole is over two and a half times the size of the United States without Alaska.

On the lower map on page 276 trace the railroad route from Leningrad (*C3*) to Chita (*L3*), and from there along the southern boundary of the Soviet Union to Vladivostok (*N4*). The Asiatic part of this railroad is called the Trans-Siberian Railroad because it crosses the vast stretch of Asia known as Siberia. The distance by train from Leningrad to Vladivostok is about 5500 miles, or nearly twice the distance by train across our country from New York to San Francisco.

Use the maps on page 276 to describe the regions that you would cross on the railroad trip from Leningrad to Vladivostok. The names of the regions are on the upper map.

The plains of the Soviet Union. You have discovered that the western half of the Soviet Union is made up largely of lowland plains. Turn to page 276 again and name the three divisions of these plains. Notice that they extend from the Arctic Ocean to the Black and Caspian seas in Europe, and to the high mountains in central Asia. Great stretches of these vast plains are less than 500 feet above sea level, and there are but few places more than 1000 feet above the sea.

Photo by Hugo Miller

Figure 282. Milking cows on a large farm in the southern part of European Russia. Notice how level the land is. How can you tell from the picture that the rainfall is not heavy here?

Figure 12 (p. 18) shows that the great continental ice sheet of long ago spread over the northern and western parts of European Russia. There, as in northern Germany and Poland, the plain is rolling or hilly, with many lakes, ponds, and marshes. Elsewhere the plains of the Soviet Union are more nearly level, and in places they are very flat. *See Figures 281 and 282.*

A sunken sea. What does the map on page 277 show about the level of the Caspian Sea? What does it show about the elevation of much of the land bordering that sea? The Caspian Sea and Lake Aral, farther east, have no outlets. Because of this, they are much saltier than the Black Sea, for all the salts which the rivers bring to them are left behind as the water evaporates from their surfaces. What great lake in the United States has become very salty because it has no outlet?

Higher and rougher lands. On the upper map on page 276 find the mountainous regions of the Soviet Union. Notice that the Ural Mountains and the Caucasus Mountains form parts of the natural boundary between Europe and Asia. The young, rugged Caucasus Mountains are higher than the Alps, and their

Photo by Hugo Miller

Figure 283. Harvest time on a small farm in the Caucasus region of the Soviet Union. Notice how steeply the slopes rise from the level ground which is used for raising grain. In the background you can see the outline of the mountains against the sky.

The basin of the Lena River in Siberia has the coldest winters of any inhabited part of the world, and it is not uncommon for the temperature to drop to 50° F. or 60° F. below zero there. Yet in the summer this same region often has temperatures well above 70° F.

In the European part of the Soviet Union the extremes of temperature are somewhat less, but even so, the winters are very cold and the summers often very warm. At Moscow, for example, the temperature often drops below zero in winter, and rises above 80° F. in summer. *See Figure 284.*

Some differences in rainfall. Turn to Figure 64 (p. 71) and study the distribution of rainfall in the Soviet Union. What parts of the country have over 20 inches of rain a year? Judging from the rainfall, which one of the three regions of plains do you think is best suited to farming?

summits are covered with ice and snow the year round. The old, worn-down Urals are much lower, and they do not form a serious barrier to travel and transportation between Europe and Siberia. *See Figure 283.*

The map shows that the largest stretches of mountains, uplands, and plateaus in the Soviet Union are in the far eastern part of the country. There you will find young mountains and old mountains, and the great stretch of uplands and plateaus known as the East Siberian Uplands. These regions are mostly a forested wilderness, and are thinly populated.

Some differences in temperature. As you would expect in such a huge country, there are great differences in climate within the Soviet Union. The very fact that the country extends from the Arctic Ocean to the parallel of 35° north latitude (the latitude of Memphis, Tennessee) means that there are great differences in temperature and length of growing season from north to south.

Furthermore, Eurasia is such an enormous mass of land that the interior becomes very cold in winter and very warm in summer.

The map shows that vast stretches of the Soviet Union have less than 20 inches of rain. The lands which have less than 10 inches are deserts or semi-deserts, where farming can be carried on only by irrigation. Fortunately, many parts of the lands which have between 10 and 20 inches of rainfall receive much of their rain in the spring or early summer. For this reason they are well suited to the growth of spring-sown wheat and other grains, which need moisture during the early part of the growing season and dry weather during the period when they are ripening.

The rivers and their use. On the upper map on page 276 find the following rivers of the Soviet Union: Dnieper (*C 4*), Don (*D 4*), Volga (*D 4*), Dvina (*D 2*), Ob (*F–G 2*), Yenisei (*H 2*), and Lena (*M 2*). Name the body of water into which each one flows.

As in many countries of Europe, so in the Soviet Union, the rivers have long been important routes of travel and transportation. Unfortunately, however, they cannot be used for navigation all the year round, for they are frozen over from three to six or more months every year, according to their location. Another handicap to the use of some of the rivers for commercial navigation is that they flow northward to the Arctic Ocean.

The rivers that are used most for the transportation of goods for export are those which flow southward to the Black Sea. Can you explain why? The Volga, which is the longest river of European Russia, is used extensively for travel and transportation between the cities along its banks, but it is of little importance in the transportation of goods for export. Give a reason for this.

Disadvantages of the coasts. The Soviet Union borders two seas and two oceans; yet its outlets to the great ocean trade routes of the world are poor. The short strip of western coast is at the inner end of the Baltic Sea, hundreds of miles from the Atlantic Ocean. The Pacific coast is thousands of miles from European Russia, where most of the people live; and the southern coast, on the Black Sea, is a poor one for trade because it is so far distant from both the Atlantic and the Pacific oceans.

The northern coast, longest of all, borders the Arctic Ocean, which is frozen over for many months each year. Only at the extreme western end is there an ice-free port on this coast. At present the Soviet government is trying the experiment of keeping the Arctic waters open for shipping in winter by using giant ice-breakers.

"U. S. Official" Photograph

Figure 284. A winter scene in the north-central part of European Russia. For many months the snow lies deep on the ground, and in the places where there are no railroads, sledges and sleighs are the only means of transportation and travel over the land.

Some things to do. 1. Use the lists on pages 330–331 to make the following comparisons:

a. Compare European Russia in size with France, the largest of the countries which lie wholly in Europe.

b. Compare the size of the Asiatic part of the Soviet Union with that of the Chinese Republic, the largest of the countries which lie wholly in Asia.

2. Find out the average temperatures for January and July where you live. Compare these temperatures with those in central Siberia.

3. Use the map on page 277 to show how goods may be transported by water from

a. Gorki (*H3*) to Leningrad (*F3*), on the Gulf of Finland.

b. Gorki to Astrakhan (*J5*), on the Caspian Sea.

c. Kiev (*F4*) to Warsaw (*D4*), and Danzig (*C4*).

Special credit work. 1. Find out all you can about the building of the Trans-Siberian Railroad and report to your class on it.

2. Make some graphs comparing the Union of Soviet Socialist Republics in size and population with the Chinese Republic, Canada, Brazil, and the United States.

Figure 285. A herd of reindeer in the tundra of northern Europe. The reindeer have sharp hoofs with
which they can dig down through the snow and get at
the grass buried beneath it. The men who own the
herd shown in the picture are Lapps who wander over
northern Finland and the adjoining part of Russia.

II. WORK IN THE GREAT BELTS OF THE SOVIET UNION

Foreword. The upper map on page 276 shows that the Soviet Union may be divided into four great vegetation belts. The two northern belts are the tundra and the taiga, which run all the way across this vast country. Farther south is the grassland, which extends only part way across the country. Still farther south is the belt of steppe and desert, which grows drier and drier from north to south.

Make a list of these four belts of the Soviet Union. Then, with the help of the lower map on page 276 and the map on page 277, write opposite the name of each belt the kinds of work that you think are most important there. Keep this list and add to it as you study this chapter.

The Tundra

The Far North of Eurasia. When you were studying North America, you learned about the cold, frozen tundra of the Far North. What did you learn about the people of that region of North America and the ways in which they make their living?

Eurasia too has its tundra, and this region forms the northernmost belt of the Soviet Union. The upper map on page 276 shows that the tundra borders the Arctic Ocean all the way from Finland to Bering Strait. How should you describe the surface of the land in most of this region?

There are but two seasons in the tundra: a long, dark winter when the temperatures are far below zero, and a short, warm summer of almost unbroken daylight. After the snow disappears in the spring the ground thaws, but the melting extends less than two feet below the surface.

The tundra is overgrown with mosses, li-chens, and many small shrubs which are dwarfed in their growth because the weather is so bitterly cold most of the year. Even full-grown trees are seldom more than two feet high in this cold region, and many are less than a foot in height. During the short sum-mer berries are plentiful, and many bright-colored flowers bloom for a few weeks.

Reindeer-herders. The few people of the tundra are mostly reindeer-herders who live in small groups widely scattered across the entire country. They live chiefly on reindeer milk and meat, though they also catch fish and birds and gather berries. During the summer they follow their bands of reindeer to the shores of the Arctic Ocean. As the cold weather approaches, they move southward to the margin of the forest belt, where they live in little huts of rocks or wood covered with sod during the coldest months of the winter. *See Figure 285.*

The Taiga

One of the greatest forests in the world. Bordering the tundra on the south is the taiga, which is one of the greatest forests in the world. The forests of Scandinavia, Finland, and the Baltic Sea countries form the westernmost part of this belt, and it stretches all the way across the Soviet Union to the Pacific Ocean. The trees in the northern part of the taiga are mostly evergreen softwoods, while those farther south are mixed hardwoods and softwoods.

Farming and lumbering in the taiga of European Russia. The upper map on page 276 shows that the taiga covers half or more of the European part of the Soviet Union. South of the parallel of 60° much of the land has been cleared for farming, but north of that line the climate is so cool that but little farming is carried on.

In the sections where much land has been cleared the farmers raise large quantities of rye, oats, flax, and potatoes. These crops, as you know, grow well in cool temperate lands because they do not need a long growing season. Many of the farmers in this part of the Soviet Union keep cattle and various other kinds of live stock, but in the region as a whole the raising of crops, especially grain and flax, is the most important kind of work. *See Figure 286.*

Lumbering is important in many places in the European part of the Russian taiga. Large numbers of trees are cut for lumber and pulp wood, and the logs are sent to sawmills and pulp and paper mills on the streams. Like the countries farther west in the taiga, European Russia plays an important part in supplying the densely populated countries of western Europe with lumber and pulp wood.

The Baltic republics. The three small Baltic republics of Estonia, Latvia, and Lithuania are in the part of the taiga where agriculture is important; and for their size they are large producers of grain, flax, and dairy products, as well as lumber and wood products. During the period between the two world wars they were independent countries, but in 1940 they were taken into the Soviet Union. Together they added about 1000 miles to the coast line of the Union and gave it two additional ports of importance: Riga, in Latvia, and Revel, in Estonia. Find these ports on the map on page 176 (*G–H4*).

Sovfoto

Figure 286. A group of Russian peasant women eating their noonday meal in a grainfield. The women of the farming families in the Soviet Union work side by side with the men in the fields.

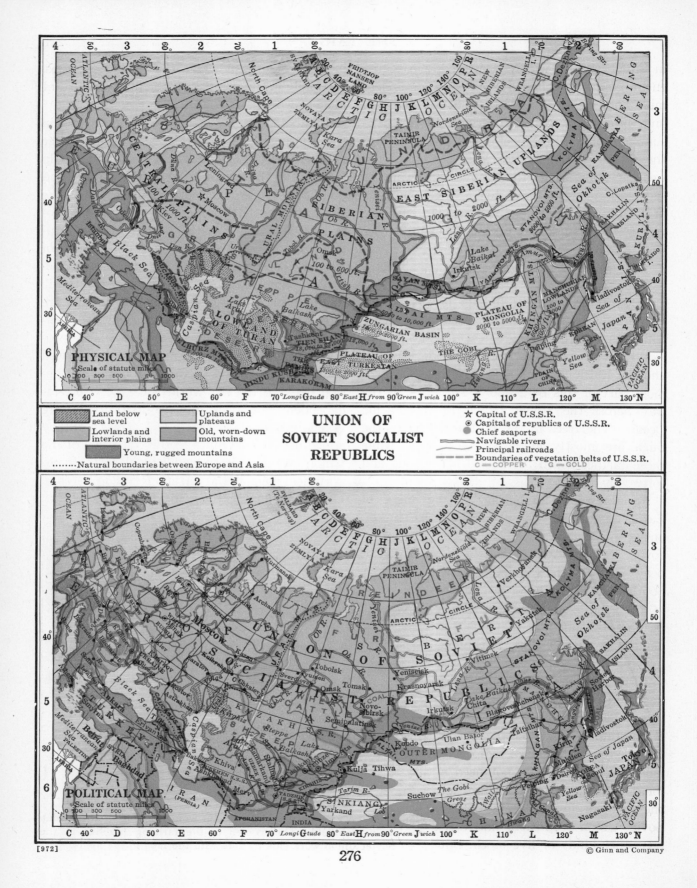

UNION OF SOVIET SOCIALIST REPUBLICS

PHYSICAL MAP

Scale of statute miles
0 100 300 500 1000

Legend:
- Land below sea level
- Lowlands and interior plains
- Young, rugged mountains
- Uplands and plateaus
- Old, worn-down mountains
- ······ Natural boundaries between Europe and Asia
- ☆ Capital of U.S.S.R.
- ⊙ Capitals of republics of U.S.S.R.
- ● Chief seaports
- Navigable rivers
- Principal railroads
- ── Boundaries of vegetation belts of U.S.S.R.
- C = COPPER   G = GOLD

POLITICAL MAP

Scale of statute miles
0 100 300 500 1000

© Ginn and Company

EASTERN EUROPE
POLITICAL AND ECONOMIC MAP

Scale of statute miles

0   100   200   300   400

★ Capitals of countries   ● Chief seaports
⊙ Capitals of Soviet republics
Navigable rivers   ------ Principal canals
C=COPPER G=GOLD M=MANGANESE P=PLATINUM
B=BAUXITE
•••••• Natural boundaries between Europe and Asia

▨ Land below sea level

Lowlands and interior plains
Uplands and plateaus
Old, worn-down mountains
Young, rugged mountains

Photograph by E. M. Newman from Wide World Photos, Inc.

Figure 287. A view of Moscow. At the left, in the distance, is part of the walled Kremlin, or inner city. Within the Kremlin are many beautiful buildings, some of which are used as the offices of the central government of the Soviet Union.

Moscow is one of the largest cities of Europe. Before the war only London and Berlin outranked it in population. Long ago, when Moscow began its growth, the forest provided wood for fuel and building, and the rivers provided means of carrying on trade. Today most of the land around Moscow has been cleared for farming, and trade is carried on chiefly by means of the railroads which spread out from the capital city like the spokes of a great wheel.

Chiefly because of its location and its railroads, Moscow is the center of a densely populated industrial district. The leading products of this district are textiles, and it turns out about four fifths of all the cotton, woolen, linen, silk, and rayon goods manufactured in the Soviet Union. The raw materials for the linen and rayon industries come from the neighboring taiga. Cotton and wool also are produced in the Union itself, but additional supplies are imported. Before the war nearly all the raw silk was imported from Japan.

The Moscow district also has many factories for the manufacture of leather goods, particularly shoes; and many plants where iron and steel from other parts of the country are used in the manufacture of machinery, engines, and other iron and steel products.

Leningrad—the gateway to the Baltic. Figure 288 is a picture of Leningrad, the second largest city of the Soviet Union. After you have studied the picture, find Leningrad on the map on page 277 (*F3*). At the head of what gulf is it located?

Leningrad was founded long ago by a Russian czar so that his country might have a port on the Baltic Sea, and for many years it was the capital of the Russian Empire. During those years it grew to be a large city, and the government helped to establish ship-

Metal industries in the Urals. The map on page 277 shows that the Ural Mountains are a storehouse of mineral wealth. Because of the coal, iron, and manganese in this region, the southern half of it has become a great metal-manufacturing district. It has modern blast furnaces and steel mills, and many factories for the manufacture of machinery and other heavy products of iron and steel.

Copper, lead, and zinc also are mined and smelted in the Urals, and the platinum mines make the Soviet Union one of the two leading countries of the world in the production of this valuable metal. The other leader is Colombia, in South America.

The Moscow industrial district. On the map on page 277 find Moscow (Moskva), the capital of the Soviet Union (*G3*). Notice that it is located in the central part of European Russia within easy reach of navigable rivers which flow north, south, east, and west. The maps on page 276 show that Moscow is near the southern margin of the taiga, and that it is the "hub" of the railroad system of European Russia. *See Figure 287.*

building and other industries there. Today Leningrad is an important manufacturing city.

Leningrad is the leading seaport of the Soviet Union, especially for imports. As an export port it is chiefly a gateway for the taiga of European Russia, and therefore lumber, grain, and flax are among its principal exports.

Arctic ports. The map on page 277 shows that the Soviet Union has two Arctic ports: Murmansk (*F1*) and Archangel (Arkhangelsk) (*H2*). Archangel has big sawmills and exports much lumber. For about four months during the winter, however, all shipping stops because the White Sea is closed by a thick cover of ice. Murmansk is a much newer port developed by the Russians because it can be used the year round. The reason for this is that a warm current of water from the Gulf Stream Drift keeps the seaway to Murmansk free from ice throughout the year.

The Siberian taiga. Much of the Siberian part of the taiga is a thinly populated wilderness. There are many small towns and villages in the "railroad belt" in the south and along the rivers, but vast areas between the streams have almost no people. The forests extend all the way from the Urals to the Pacific Ocean, and the uplands and mountains are rich in coal and metal ores. As yet, however, neither lumbering nor mining is well developed except in a few places in the south. The Soviet government plans to build more railroads to connect this vast forest with the outside world, and in time much greater use of its resources will be made.

Fur-trapping. The most valuable products of the Siberian taiga are the furs which are obtained by men who hunt and trap the wild animals which live in the forest. The hunters

Photograph by E. M. Newman from Wide World Photos, Inc.
Figure 288. A view of Leningrad, the Soviet Union's gateway to the Baltic Sea. The city is located at the mouth of the Neva River, which flows into the Gulf of Finland.

and trappers live in little settlements along the streams, and they kill large numbers of squirrels, hares, foxes, ermines, marmots, and other animals in the winter when the fur is thickest. In the summer traders come to the settlements in boats, and the hunters exchange their winter's "catch" of furs for food supplies, clothing, and other things that they need.

An Arctic experiment. In the Far North, beyond the arctic circle, the Soviet government is making a great experiment in the hope of developing the rich resources of northern Siberia. Towns have been built and people brought from other parts of the country to live and work in them. Coal is being mined, fishing encouraged, and ports are being developed at the river mouths for the export of furs, timber, and fishery products. Supplies are brought to the new towns by airplane in winter and by river boat in summer, and giant ice-breakers are being used to open lanes in the Arctic Ocean for shipping.

A far eastern port. On the lower map on page 276 find Vladivostok (*N4*). This city is the far eastern seaport of the Soviet Union, and it owes its growth chiefly to the fact that it is the eastern terminus of the Trans-Siberian

Sovfoto

Figure 289. How "wheat work" begins in the grass-land of European Russia. A tractor is being used to plow the wheat land.

Sovfoto

Figure 290. How "wheat work" ends. The wheat is being carried up a spout into a grain elevator, to be stored until needed.

Railroad. Since the most densely populated and most productive part of the Soviet Union is in Europe, and since much of the Soviet trade is carried on with other countries of that continent, the foreign trade of Vladivostok is much less than that of Leningrad.

Giving reasons. Complete each sentence below by giving reasons for the fact which it states.

1. The tundra of Eurasia is very thinly populated because _ .

2. Much more land has been cleared for farming in the southern part of the taiga of European Russia than in the northern part because _ .

3. Rye, oats, and flax are the leading crops of the taiga of European Russia because _ _ _ _ _ _ _ _ .

4. Far more lumbering is carried on in the taiga of European Russia than in the taiga of Siberia because _ _ _ _ _ _ _ _ _ _ _ _ _ _ _ _ _ _ .

5. The southern half of the Ural Mountains is well populated because _ _ _ _ _ _ _ _ _ _ _ _ _ _ .

6. Moscow is an important manufacturing center because _ _ _ _ _ _ _ _ _ _ _ _ _ _ _ _ _ _ _ .

7 The leading exports of Leningrad are lumber, grain, and flax because _ _ _ _ _ _ _ _ _ _ _ .

8. Leningrad is an important manufacturing center because _ _ _ _ _ _ _ _ _ _ _ _ _ _ _ _ _ _ .

9. Vladivostok is a less important seaport than Leningrad because _ _ _ _ _ _ _ _ _ _ _ _ _ _ _ _ .

The Grassland

A rich farming region. South of the taiga in European Russia and western Siberia is a region much like our prairies, for it is a rich grassland with trees only along the streams. From the upper map on page 276 what can you say about the surface of this grassland?

This belt includes most of the famous "black soil" region, and its deep, dark soils are wonderfully fertile. The rainfall is rather light, but fortunately much of it comes in the summer. Because of the climate, the fertile soils, and the level surface, this grassland is the best farming region of the Soviet Union. *See Figures 289 and 290.*

The farmers and their work. The farms will remind you of the plains of the Dakotas and the neighboring provinces of Canada, for the farmers raise immense crops of spring wheat and barley, and large quantities of rye, oats, and flax. Wheat is by far the most important money crop, and so much is raised that the Soviet Union ranks with the United States as one of the two leading countries of the world in wheat production. In the western part of the grassland, in the Soviet Republic of Ukraine, sugar beets and tobacco are very

Figure 291. A farmyard in Ukraine. Notice the ears of corn on the ground and on the pole hung from the eaves of the house. Why is this farmhouse built of different materials from the house shown in Figure 286?

important crops, and in the extreme southwest corn is grown. *See Figure 291.*

Not so very long ago Russia was one of the backward farming countries of the world. Even in Ukraine the farmers did their work with no help except the horse-drawn plow. In recent years the government has been supplying the farms with machines, and in a remarkably short time farming by hand labor has changed to farming with machinery.

In the Siberian part of the grassland some of the farmers specialize in dairying. The dairy farmers have coöperative creameries where butter is made. Much butter is sent to European Russia for use there or for export to other countries.

Market centers. Many of the larger cities and towns of the grassland are market centers for the surrounding farm lands. Chief among them is Kiev, the capital of Ukraine. Find Kiev on the map on page 277 (*F4*).

Like the great market centers in the plains of our own country, Kiev has become a manufacturing city. Among its industries flour-milling, sugar-refining, and the manufacture of tobacco are important. Explain why.

The largest cities of the Siberian grassland are Novosibirsk and Omsk, on the Trans-Siberian Railroad. Both are market centers. Near Novosibirsk is an area where coal and metal ores are mined. This area, known as the Kuznets Basin, has become the first great industrial district of Siberia.

The industrial district of Ukraine. On the map on page 277 find the coal field in southeastern Ukraine. This field produces about three fourths of all the coal mined in the Soviet Union. Farther west in Ukraine are mines which produce about three fifths of all the iron ore of the Union and much of the manganese. Because of its coal and the ease with which iron ore can be obtained, southeastern Ukraine has become a great iron-and-steel district and a center for the manufacture of machinery and other products of iron and steel. Among the many different manufactures, tractors and agricultural machinery are especially important. *See Figure 292.*

The leading cities of this great industrial district are Kharkov and Dniepropetrovsk. Find these cities on the map on page 277 (*G5*). Which one is located on the Dnieper River?

Sovfoto

Figure 292. Building a great machine in a Russian factory. There are large machine works in Ukraine and in the Ural region of the Soviet Union.

Sovfoto

Figure 293. An oil field on the edge of the Caspian Sea near Baku. This field was once under water, but the Soviet government diked and drained it so that wells could be drilled to obtain the petroleum. Little by little, more land along the shore of the Caspian Sea is being reclaimed for larger areas of oil fields.

About 60 miles downstream from Dniepropetrovsk, the Soviet government has built a giant dam across the Dnieper River, and a great hydroelectric plant. Besides this hydroelectric plant, a number of steam-electric plants have been built at Kharkov and several other places. Thus the industrial district of southeastern Ukraine has abundant electric power for its industries, as well as steam power from its coal.

Ports on the Black Sea. Turn to the map on page 277 again and name the ports of the Soviet Union on the Black Sea. The largest of these ports is Odessa, which has long been an important shipping point for Russian wheat. Nikolaev and Kherson share the grain trade with Odessa, and all three cities are important flour-milling centers. The exports of wheat from these seaports go chiefly to the industrial countries of Europe which find it necessary to import foodstuffs.

The Caucasus Region

A mountain and valley region. Between the Black Sea and the Caspian Sea the Caucasus Mountains rise more than 10,000 feet above the bordering plain. South of the Caucasus are other mountain ranges which stretch westward into Anatolia and eastward into Iran. Within this mountainous region of the Soviet Union are many fertile valleys where the people raise grain, fruits, and tobacco, and keep cattle, sheep, and goats. The region also has much mineral wealth. Name its mineral products from the map on page 277.

Some rich oil fields. By far the most valuable mineral product of the Caucasus region is the petroleum from the rich oil fields near Baku on the Caspian Sea, and from other fields on the northern margin of the mountains. On the map on page 277 find Baku (*J6*) and Batum (*H6*). Then study Figure 293.

Figure 294. Goats grazing on the poor grass on the Kirghiz Steppe. The wealth of the nomad families is measured by the number of animals which they own.

Why is life somewhat easier for these nomads of the steppe than it is for the nomads of the arctic tundra? Why do they keep a greater variety of animals?

At Baku there are large oil refineries from which kerosene and gasoline are sent to various parts of European Russia and southwestern Siberia, and which supply the boats which run on the Caspian Sea and the Volga River with fuel oil. Pipe lines carry crude petroleum from Baku to great refineries at Batum, on the Black Sea, and from there large quantities of mineral oils are exported to countries of western Europe. So rich are the oil fields of the Caucasus region that the Soviet Union is one of the greatest petroleum-producing countries of the world.

The Steppe and the Desert

A land of nomads. South of the grassland, and extending from the Caspian Sea to the mountains of central Asia, is the steppe, a belt of poor grassland where the rainfall is too little for farming. This is a land inhabited chiefly by nomadic peoples.

The nomads live in tents and have very little property except their horses, cattle, camels, sheep, and goats. They want little but the food and clothing needed from day to day because they have to move so often in search of fresh pastures for their flocks and herds.

They depend so largely on their animals that if there is an unusually dry season, when grass is scarce and many of the animals die, they suffer greatly. *See Figure 294.*

The desert of Turan. South of the Kirghiz Steppe there is a desert region where the rainfall is too little even for the growth of grass. Find this region on the upper map on page 276. In what lowland is it located? Fortunately, the mountains on the east receive more rain, and streams from these mountains provide water for irrigation in the southeastern part of the lowland.

Work in the irrigated lands. In the irrigated lands the people have long raised grain, fruit, and vegetables. More recently they have added cotton to their list of crops, for the Lowland of Turan is far enough south to have a long growing season. The Soviet government is encouraging cotton-growing, hoping that in time these irrigated lands may supply most of the raw cotton needed by the industrial cities of European Russia.

Mulberry trees grow well in this southern region, and the raising of silkworms is important in certain places. Many of the people are skillful in the weaving of silk goods and the making of silk embroideries. Others are rug-makers, using for this work wool from sheep which are raised in the region. In the bazaars of the old cities of Tashkent and Samarkand large quantities of these products of the hand loom and the needle are offered for sale.

On the lower map on page 276 find the railroad which connects the cities named above with Moscow. Before this railroad was built, the people of this southernmost part of the Soviet Union carried on trade with the outside world only by means of slow-moving camel caravans.

Transportation and Trade in the Soviet Union

Transportation within the country. The Soviet Union is such a huge country that the problem of providing means of transportation between all the various sections is a serious one. The lower map on page 276 shows that the European part of the country is well supplied with railroads which connect all the larger interior cities with one another, with the seaports, and with the countries farther west in Europe.

In addition to the railroads of European Russia, there are the many navigable rivers which serve as highways of transportation during the months when they are not frozen over. The map on page 277 will show you that canals have been built to connect the different river systems, providing almost unbroken waterways from the Black and Caspian seas in the south to the Baltic Sea and the Arctic Ocean in the north.

Conditions in the Asiatic part of the Union are quite different. The greater part of this vast section of the country is without railroads, and therefore the rivers must serve as the chief highways of transportation. But the longest rivers all flow northward to the icebound Arctic Ocean, and even their upper courses, in the south, are frozen from five to six months in the year. Lack of good means of transportation is the chief reason why the resources of Siberia are so largely unused. The greatest progress in Soviet transportation in recent years has been in the air. Airlines link Moscow with all the other large cities, and cross both the tundra and taiga to the Pacific.

Trade within the country. For the most part, trade between the different sections of European Russia is carried on in modern ways, the larger railroad centers and river ports serving as places of business and exchange. In some parts of the country the people follow an old custom of holding yearly fairs for the buying and selling of goods. At these fairs, which last about six weeks, not only Russian merchants but merchants from many other countries offer goods for sale. The greatest fair is the one held each year at Gorki, on the Volga River, from the first of August until the middle of September. Others are held at Kiev, Kharkov, and Baku at other times of the year.

Foreign trade. Since the Soviet Union is a great agricultural country, it is not surprising to find that among the exports farm products are important, especially wheat and other grains, flax, butter, and sugar. At the top of the export list, however, stand lumber, mineral oils, and furs. The exports go largely to the countries of western Europe.

Before the war, machinery for farming and manufacturing, and other kinds of iron and steel goods, formed the leading group of imports. With its industrial development of recent years Russia has begun to supply itself with many of the manufactures it needs. If the plans for even greater industrialization work out, we may expect the time to come when the Soviet Union will want to export surplus manufactures.

Raw materials for manufacturing are an important group of imports. Cotton, wool, hides and skins, rubber, and various metals are imported in large quantities.

An occupational test. This test will help you to review what you have learned about the occupations of the people in the various parts of the Soviet Union.

1. The belt of cold, frozen plains in the northern part of the Soviet Union is a thinly populated region called the _____. Most of the people who live there make their living by keeping herds of _____. They are wandering people, or _____, because _____ _____

2. South of the _____ is the great belt of forests known as the _____. In the European part of the _____ large numbers of trees are cut for _____ and ____ ____. Much less lumbering is carried on in the Siberian part of the _____ because _____

3. In the Siberian part of the taiga the trapping of wild _____ for their ____ is an important kind of work.

4. There are a number of important mining centers in the southern half of the ____ Mountains. This region makes the Soviet Union one of the two leading countries of the world in the production of _____. It has iron-and-steel plants because _____

5. The best farming land in the Soviet Union is in the belt of _____, south of the western portion of the taiga, because _____ _____ In this belt is the great _____ district of southeastern Ukraine. This district has ____ mines and ____ mines.

6. Extending from the Black Sea to the Caspian Sea are the _____ Mountains. In and near these mountains large quantities of _____ are obtained from beneath the ground.

7. The poor grassland extending eastward from the Caspian Sea is called the _____. The people of this region are _____ who live wandering lives because _____.

8. South of the steppe is a _____ region, too dry for the growth of grass. This region has very ___ people except in the southeast, where streams provide _____ for _____. On the _____ lands the people raise many

different _____. The Soviet government is encouraging the people of this part of the country to raise _____ because _____.

Some things to explain. Explain why

1. There are great differences in temperature and length of growing season in the Soviet Union.
2. The winter weather is much colder in Moscow than in Paris.
3. The long coast line of the Soviet Union on the Arctic Ocean is of little use to the people of the country.
4. The Black Sea is more useful to the Russians than the Caspian Sea.
5. The rivers of the Soviet Union cannot be used for navigation for as many months in the year as the rivers of France and Germany.
6. The waters of the Caspian Sea are salty.

Naming cities. Name each of the cities of the Soviet Union described below:

1. The capital of the Soviet Union.
2. The seaport on the Gulf of Finland.
3. The far eastern port of the Union.
4. The market center which is the capital of Ukraine.
5. The ice-free port on the Arctic coast of the Soviet Union.
6. Three ports on the Black Sea from which much wheat is exported.
7. The city on the shore of the Caspian Sea which is an oil-refining center.
8. The port on the Black Sea from which mineral oils are exported.

Finding reminders. Use the map on page 277 to show where in European Russia each person described below would find something to remind him of home.

1. A lumberman from our state of Washington.
2. A wheat farmer from North Dakota.
3. A tobacco-grower from Kentucky.
4. A sugar-beet-grower from Michigan.
5. A coal-miner from southern Illinois.
6. A potato-grower from Maine.
7. An "oil man" from Oklahoma.
8. An iron-miner from Minnesota.

Figure 295. A canal in Bangkok. Many of the houses in Bangkok face canals instead of streets, and the people use boats in getting from place to place. See the boatload of copper pots being paddled to market.

INDEPENDENT COUNTRIES OF THE ORIENT

Foreword. East of India and south of the far eastern part of Siberia is the part of Asia known as the Orient.

You have already learned about the countries of the Orient which have long been under European control. Now you are going to study the other Oriental countries: China, Japan, Outer Mongolia, Korea, and Siam. Find these countries on the map on page 295.

The end of the Second World War brought many changes to the Orient. The Chinese Republic has replaced the former Empire of Japan as the leading country. Formosa and Manchuria, which Japan conquered, have been restored to China. Outer Mongolia has received

its independence, Siam has regained its independence, and Korea has been promised independence.

In China, Japan, and the other countries which were battlegrounds, the reconstruction of ruined cities, ports, farms, and plantations will take many years. Trade with the outside world must be built up again, and this can be done only slowly as the people work their way back to the place where they again have large quantities of surplus products for export. You will want to remember that in the Orient, as in Europe, the people are now faced with the long, hard task of overcoming the setback of the war before they can even begin to go forward again.

I. SIAM

Find Siam on the maps on page 71. What can you say about its rainfall? about the density of its population compared with that of India and China? Like India, Siam is a monsoon land. At what season, then, does it have heavy rains?

Look at the map on page 298. What is the leading crop of Siam? What "climate reasons" can you give for this fact? Judging from the products shown on the map, what kinds of work besides farming are important in Siam?

A rice-growing country. The map on page 298 shows that there are mountains along the northern and western borders of Siam, but that most of the country lies in a lowland which it shares with French Indo-China. The lowland, with its year-round warmth and its monsoon rains, is well suited to the raising of rice, and in Siam, as in Indo-China, rice is by far the most important crop. The people depend on rice as their chief foodstuff, but they raise so much that they have a large surplus to export to the more densely populated lands of China, Japan, and Java.

The people raise other tropical crops, but none of them compares in importance with rice. In the part of Siam which extends into the Malay Peninsula rubber plantations have been started, and the exports of rubber are growing in importance.

Forest work. As you would expect, there are thick, tropical forests in this warm, moist country, and, like the forests of Burma and French Indo-China, they contain valuable teak trees. Large numbers of teakwood logs are cut in the forests, and elephants are used to carry them to the Menam River. The logs are too heavy to float, and so they are loaded on bamboo rafts to be sent downstream for export. *See Figure 296.*

Mineral wealth. Siam is fortunate in having coal and valuable ores of tin, zinc, iron, and other metals. Modern methods of mining are being introduced, and greater use of the mineral resources will certainly be made in the future. At present the most important mineral product is tin, which ranks next to rice among the exports. You will recall that the richest tin mines of the world are in the part of the Malay Peninsula which is under British control. Where in Siam, then, do you think the tin mines are located? Check your answer by the map on page 298.

Bangkok. Figure 295 is a picture taken in Bangkok, the capital, the largest city, and the seaport of Siam. Find Bangkok on the map on page 298 (*B5*). Near the mouth of what river is it located?

Although Bangkok is the port of Siam, large ocean ships do not go upstream to its wharves because the mouth of the Menam River is too shallow. Instead, they anchor as near the mouth of the river as possible, and their cargoes are transferred to smaller boats. The smaller boats carry the goods up to Bangkok and come back loaded with rice, tin, and other products for the ships to carry away. Because of this handicap to shipping, some of Siam's trade with distant lands is carried on through the great British port of Singapore.

By Ewing Galloway, N. Y.

Figure 296. Teakwood logs in the Menam River in Siam. Some of the men in charge of floating the logs downstream live in little huts on the rafts.

In what two ways may goods be sent back and forth between Bangkok and Singapore? What are the leading imports of Siam, and where do they come from?

A summary. The countries of southern Asia and the Orient which you have studied thus far are India and Burma, Ceylon, British Malaya, the Netherlands Indies, Siam, and French Indo-China. Summarize some of the important facts about these countries by completing the sentences in the next column.

1. Among these countries ____ and _____ are independent. The others belong to countries in _____.

2. In all these countries ____ is the chief grain crop and the chief foodstuff of the people.

3. The leading forest product of Burma, Siam, and French-Indo China is ____.

4. The important raw material produced on plantations in British Malaya, Ceylon, the Netherlands Indies, and Siam is _____.

5. The metal ore mined in the Malay Peninsula and shipped to many parts of the world is ___.

II. JAPAN

1. FOREWORD

An island people. You can see from the map on page 295 that Japan is made up of four main islands and the small ones close by. The largest island is named Honshu, and it is there that Tokyo, the capital, is located. The other main islands are Hokkaido, north of Honshu, and Shikoku and Kyushu to the south. In total area Japan is somewhat smaller than our state of California.

Less than a century ago the Japanese were a hermit nation. For two hundred years their doors had been closed to all Westerners, and they were living much as their forefathers had before any Europeans reached the Far East.

The opening up of Japan to trade. In 1853 a fleet of American naval ships was sent to Japan. The commanding officer had orders to try to make a treaty by which trade between the two countries might be carried on, and he took with him exhibits of American manufactures and inventions. He succeeded in his mission, and in 1854 the treaty was signed.

This treaty, and others with some of the European nations, opened Japan to world trade. Trade, in turn, opened the eyes of the Japanese to the advantages to be gained by adopting Western mechanical inventions, and in a remarkably short time Japan was transformed into an industrial and commercial country with a strong army and navy.

Japan and the war. As a result of the Allied victory in the Second World War nothing remains to the Japanese of the empire they had acquired but their home islands and the Ryukyus. Japan is now under the control of an Allied council, and it is occupied by American troops.

The problem of the future. You will find it helpful to compare the Japanese islands with the British Isles in order to understand why Japan, which less than a hundred years ago was almost unknown to the Western nations, had become one of the most important countries in the world before the war.

However, you will want to remember that Japan is not today as it was before the war or as it will be when the task of reconstruction has been completed. The thing to do is to learn what kind of country it is and what natural resources it has. Then you will have a good background for understanding how the Japanese make out in the future.

James Sawders

Figure 297. Fujiyama, thought by many people to be the most beautiful mountain peak in the world. It rises to a height of more than 12,000 feet above the level of the sea, and its summit is usually covered with snow.

2. THE JAPANESE AND THEIR COUNTRY

Map studies. Begin your study of Japan by working out the following map studies.

1. Turn to the map of Eurasia on page 295 and find the islands of Honshu, Shikoku, Kyushu (*M5*), and Hokkaido (*N 4*).

2. What statement can you make regarding the location of the islands of Japan and of the British Isles with reference to the great land mass of Eurasia? 3. What differences in the surface of the land do you find between the British Isles and the islands of Japan?

4. Now turn to page 71. Notice that Honshu, Shikoku, and Kyushu are among the most densely populated parts of Asia. 5. How do they compare with Great Britain and Ireland in density of population? in rainfall?

Some comparisons. You have discovered several interesting facts from the maps: (1) that the Japanese occupy a group of islands off the eastern coast of Eurasia, just as the British occupy a group of islands a little farther north off the western coast of Eurasia; (2) that both groups of islands have abundant rain for agriculture; (3) that the islands of Japan are much more mountainous than the British Isles; and (4) that Honshu, Shikoku, and Kyushu are even more densely populated than Great Britain and Ireland.

As you read further, find reasons why so many people are able to make a living in the mountainous islands of Japan.

The lands of Japan. Most travelers from our country to Japan sail from one of our Pacific seaports to the Japanese port of Yokohama, on the island of Honshu. If they are fortunate enough to enter the harbor of Yokohama on a bright, clear day, they see, off to the west, the beautiful mountain which the Japanese call Fujiyama, or Mount Fuji. *See Figure 297.*

Mount Fuji is the highest of the many volcanic peaks of Japan, which have been built up by great volcanic eruptions and by

Photo by Lionel Green

Figure 298. A cultivated valley in the wooded mountains of Japan. Here, as in most parts of Japan, all
the land level enough for farming is used for crops.
The flooded fields in the picture are rice paddies,
and at the right, surrounded by a high hedge, are
some of the thatched-roofed houses of the farmers.

outpourings of lava. Can you name some
peaks in Europe and the Americas which have
been built up in the same way? Many of the
Japanese volcanoes are still active, but there
has been no eruption of Fujiyama for over
two hundred years.

Most of the islands of Japan are mountainous, and the mountains are young, high, and
rugged. In many places they are so steep
that they can be used only for growing trees.
Because of this, and of the abundant rainfall,
forests cover about half of the surface in
Japan. *See Figure 298.*

You will remember that many regions of
young mountains suffer from earthquakes. In
the islands of Japan slight earthquakes occur
almost every day, and once in every few years
a very severe earthquake causes much damage
and loss of life.

Near the coast and in the valleys among
the mountains of Japan there are lowlands,
but most of them are very small. The only
large plain is the one in which Tokyo, the
capital of the country, is located. Since so
much of the country is made up of steep
mountain slopes, the lowland areas are greatly
overcrowded with people. In Honshu, for example, there are over 400 people to the square
mile, but they are so unevenly distributed
that the lowlands have more than 1000 people
to the square mile. What part of Africa is as
densely populated as that?

Figure 299. Transplanting rice in Japan. Both men and women work in the wet, muddy paddy fields, setting out the young rice plants. You can easily imagine what hard, tiresome work this is.

Farming in Japan

A land of very small farms. Because Japan is so mountainous, only about 15 per cent of the land is suitable for farming, yet more of the Japanese are engaged in farming than in all the other occupations combined. Since the amount of farm land is so limited, and the farming population is so large, the farms are very small. The average farmer has only two and a half acres of land on which to raise crops to support his family. Some farmers have five or six acres, while others have only one or two.

Since the farms are so small, the farmers cultivate every bit of land possible, and they tend their crops with the greatest care so that the land may produce all that it possibly can. Only in this way can such large numbers of people make a living by farming in this over-crowded country, and although they work hard, many of them are very poor.

In traveling through the farm lands of Japan you will notice that few of the farmers keep any cattle or sheep. That is because as much land as possible must be used to raise food for the people, and little can be spared for pasture or forage crops. For this reason meat and dairy products are expensive luxuries in Japan.

The chief crop. Rice is by far the most important crop in Japan, just as it is in the other Oriental countries. One reason for this is that the climate is well suited to rice-growing. Another reason is that in these densely populated countries the people must get as much food from the soil as possible, and an acre of land will produce a greater quantity of rice than of any other grain which they can raise, and at less cost. For these reasons the Oriental nations long ago came to depend on rice as their chief food.

Rice-growing. Early each spring the farmers plant the rice seeds in beds which have been enriched with fertilizers. In these seed-beds the plants are allowed to grow until they are a few inches above the ground. In the

Authenticated News Photo

Figure 300. Harvesting rice in Japan. The grain is cut by hand with sickles or knives, and tied in bundles. At harvest time, as at transplanting time, the women help the men in the fields.

Figure 301. Japanese children watching their mothers thresh rice. Notice that the women are pulling the grain through a large wooden comb which strips the seeds from the stalks.

How the rice crop is used. Every farmer tries to grow rice enough to supply his family, and, if possible, a little more. Those who have more than they need send their surplus to the cities, where there is always a good market for it. Altogether, the Japanese farmers raise many millions of bushels of rice on their little farms, yet they cannot fully supply the needs of the country, and rice is normally imported from Burma, Siam, and French Indo-China.

Although the Japanese raise rice chiefly for food, they make many different uses of the straw. The farmers thatch their houses with rice straw, and most of the country people wear straw sandals. The broad-brimmed hats such as you see in Figures 299 and 302 are also made of rice straw, and large quantities of mats and baskets are made of the same material. None of the rice straw is wasted, for all that is not used in other ways is put back on the fields as fertilizer.

Other food crops. In addition to rice, the Japanese farmers raise considerable quantities

meantime, the farmers plow the fields to which the rice plants are soon to be transplanted. These are called paddy fields.

When the time for transplanting comes, the young plants are carefully pulled from the seed-beds, tied in bundles, and set out in the paddy fields, which are flooded with water to a depth of six to twelve inches. Figure 299 shows how this work is done. During the early part of the growth of the rice, the paddy fields are flooded from time to time, for the plants need large quantities of water to grow well. Later, when the grain begins to ripen, the fields are drained.

Figure 300 shows how the rice is harvested. After it has been cut and tied in bundles, the bundles are hung up to dry in the sun, and in a few days the grain is ready for threshing. Figure 301 shows one of the ways in which the Japanese separate the seeds from the stalks, or straw. Some of the farmers have simple threshing machines like the one shown in Figure 302.

Figure 302. Japanese farmers tying up bundles of rice to be sent to market. The outer covering of the bundles is matting made of rice straw. At the right is a simple threshing machine.

James Sawders

Figure 303. A Japanese mother and baby enjoying the spring sunshine at cherry-blossom time. Across the lake you can see a Japanese temple.

© E. M. Newman from Publishers Photo Service, Inc.

Figure 304. Japanese women picking tea leaves on a steep hillside. Look carefully, and you will see a Japanese baby strapped on his mother's back.

of wheat, barley, oats, and millet. These are the chief grain crops in the northern parts of the country that are too cool for rice, and in the rice-growing lands they are winter crops, planted in September or October, after the rice has been harvested. The Japanese also raise large quantities of beans and other vegetables, and many different kinds of fruits, such as oranges, peaches, pears, and plums.

Japanese cherry trees. No doubt you have heard of the many cherry trees in Japan. The Japanese do not cultivate these trees for their fruit, but simply for their beauty. The Japanese are lovers of everything that is beautiful, and they look forward with the greatest pleasure to the springtime, when the cherry trees are covered with delicate pink blossoms. *See Figure 303.*

The tea crop. The food crops grown by the farmers of Japan are for use within the country, and there is no surplus for export. The chief crop grown partly for export is tea. The tea bushes are usually found on hillsides which are too steep for field crops and where the drainage is good. Two or three crops of tea leaves are picked by the women and girls each summer. Normally there is a surplus of tea for export, and much of it comes to the United States. After traveling through Japan you will understand why the greater part of the crop is used within the country, for all the Japanese, rich and poor, drink tea with every meal. *See Figure 304.*

Silk. Before the war raw silk was one of the leading exports of Japan, and our country was by far the best customer for it. At that time about one third of all the farming families raised silkworms, feeding them on leaves from cultivated mulberry trees.

During the war many of the groves of mulberry trees were cut down to provide more land for food crops, and the production of raw silk decreased accordingly. Whether or not it will ever regain its former importance will depend largely on the demand for raw silk in the United States and Europe, where nylon and rayon have become very popular as substitutes for silk.

Caring for the silkworms. Mulberry trees grow well in many of the warm temperate parts of the world, but the raising of silkworms requires so much care and handwork that raw silk is produced only in countries which, like Japan, are so densely populated that labor is cheap. For this reason the Oriental countries

Philip D. Gendreau, N.Y.

Figure 305. Japanese girls sorting cocoons in a filature. Their work is to separate the good cocoons from the poor ones.

James Sawders

Figure 306. Reeling silk in a filature. The man at the right brings buckets of cocoons from the sorting room, and the man at the left wheels away the reeled fiber.

of Japan and China produce far more raw silk than do any other countries in the world.

The raising of silkworms is carried on in the farmers' homes, and the women and children do the work. After the tiny worms hatch from the eggs, they are spread out on clean trays, and for a number of weeks fresh mulberry leaves are gathered several times a day to feed them. This is the period of growth for the worms, and at the end of it they stop eating and begin to spin the delicate silvery fiber which they wind around themselves, making cocoons about an inch long.

Preparing raw silk for market. Years ago all the reeling, or unwinding, of the fibers from the cocoons was done by hand by the Japanese women who raised the silkworms. Now most of the farmers sell their cocoons to dealers who, in turn, sell them to factories called *filatures*. In the filatures women are employed to do the reeling with the help of machinery. In the reeling several fibers are twisted together to form a single strand of raw silk. The strands are then made up in bundles called skeins, and the skeins are packed in bales to be sent to mills in Japan

or to the seaports for export. Some of the spinning mills have their own filatures. *See Figures 305 and 306.*

Sentences to complete. Prove that you have learned the more important facts about farming in Japan by completing the following sentences correctly.

1. Only a small proportion of the land in Japan is suitable for farming because _____ _____.

2. Japanese farms are very small because __ _____.

3. Rice is the chief food crop because _____ _____.

4. There are no surplus food crops for export because _____.

5. Few cattle or sheep are raised in Japan because _____.

6. The Japanese raise large quantities of tea because _____.

7. Japan is one of the two great silk-producing countries because _____ _____.

Special credit work. Find out what Oriental people discovered that the fibers of silkworm cocoons could be used to make cloth, and how the discovery happened to be made.

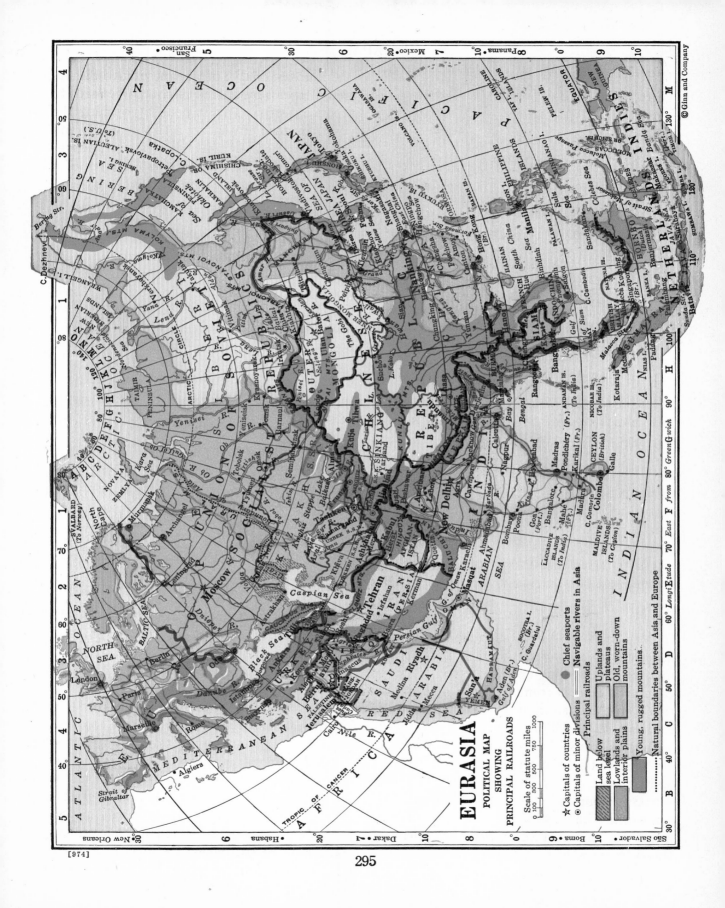

EURASIA

POLITICAL MAP
SHOWING
PRINCIPAL RAILROADS

Scale of statute miles

☆ Capitals of countries
◉ Capitals of minor divisions
Principal railroads
● Chief seaports
Navigable rivers in Asia
Natural boundaries between Asia and Europe

Land below sea level
Lowlands and interior plains
Uplands and plateaus
Old, worn-down mountains
Young, rugged mountains

© Ginn and Company

[974]

Figure 307. Japanese fishermen getting ready to go out to the fishing grounds. There are about three quarters of a million Japanese who depend entirely on fishing for their living, and as many more who depend partly on fishing and partly on farming.

Fisheries, Forests, and Mines

Japanese fisheries. Like the British, the Japanese have long depended on the sea for part of their food supply, and for the same reasons: (1) because the dense population demands large quantities of food, and the land that can be used for crops is limited; (2) because there are many good harbors along the coast; and (3) because the islands are bordered by waters rich in fish.

The Japanese carry on fishing along their entire coast line and off the coast of Siberia, even as far north as Bering Sea. Altogether, they catch huge quantities of herring, cod, tunny, mackerel, sardines, salmon, and other fish which help greatly in supplying the millions of people of Japan with food. Salmon-canning is an important industry, and in addition to the canned salmon used at home much is exported. *See Figure 307.*

Oysters, crabs, lobsters, and other shellfish are plentiful in the waters bordering Japan, and large quantities are gathered by the people who live along the coast. Much crab meat is canned, and most of it is exported. Our own country is one of Japan's best customers for this fishery product.

Culture pearls. The Japanese have discovered a process by which oysters can be made to produce pearls. This is done by opening the young oyster and placing a tiny grain of sand inside the shell. In time the oyster will cover the grain of sand with layer after layer of a milk-white substance which forms the pearl. Such pearls are called "culture pearls," and they bring high prices.

Forest products of Japan. All over Japan large numbers of trees are cut each year for firewood and for making charcoal, because wood and charcoal are the household fuels used by nearly all the people. The most valuable forests for timber are in Hokkaido and northern Honshu, where, because of the cool climate, the trees are mostly evergreen softwoods. In this northern part of the country there are pulp and paper mills which supply most of the needs of the Japanese for paper and its products.

About one third of the lumber cut in Japan comes from the beautiful cone-bearing trees known as *cryptomeria*. These trees belong to the same great tree family as the giant sequoias of California, and they grow to heights of nearly 200 feet. In many parts of Japan the government is reforesting cut-over areas, and the cryptomeria are the trees used most for this purpose. *See Figure 308.*

Another very valuable tree in Japan is the bamboo, which grows in the warmer parts of the islands. It grows rapidly and provides a light and exceedingly useful wood. The Japanese use much bamboo in building their houses, and much for making furniture.

Mineral resources. Judging from the map on page 298, what do you think are the most valuable mineral products of Japan? Do you think the Japanese are well supplied with the mineral resources that are most necessary for manufacturing? Give reasons for your answer.

The most valuable of Japan's mineral resources is the coal which is mined in Kyushu and Hokkaido, and which provides power for manufacturing. For coking, however, Japanese coal is poor, and before the war much coking coal was imported from China and Manchuria.

The chief oil fields of Japan are in Honshu; but they supply only a small part of the needs of the country, and large quantities of mineral oils were imported before the war.

Of the metal ores mined in Japan copper is by far the most valuable, making Japan an important copper-producing country. Gold and a few other metal ores are also mined, but in much smaller quantities.

Figure 308. Cryptomeria trees in Honshu. Notice the size of the tree trunks at the right. The road in the picture runs for forty miles through a cryptomeria forest.

Japan is poor in supplies of high-grade iron ore, and produces only a small part of the iron ore which it normally uses. For any iron-and-steel industry, then, Japan is forced to depend largely on iron ore and coking coal from neighboring parts of the continent of Asia.

Hydroelectric power. Since Japan is a mountainous country with abundant rainfall, it has many swift-flowing streams. Already the Japanese have harnessed about half their water power to make hydroelectricity, and much more hydroelectric power is likely to be developed in the future. Thus electric power, as well as steam power from coal, is at hand for use in manufacturing.

Cities, Manufacturing, and Trade

Foreword. The Japanese manufacturing centers were our chief bombing targets in the war; so in reading about them remember that they are now crippled and broken. Their reconstruction will take many years, and whether or not they will ever regain their former importance only time can tell. Today the Japanese are under strict control by the Allies, and their manufacturing is limited to products needed for peaceful purposes. In losing their empire the Japanese lost the outside sources from which they were getting iron ore, coking coal, and certain other key raw materials cheaply. Some people believe that for this reason alone Japan will never regain its former industrial importance. It would be safer to say that it probably will take the Japanese many years to make a full industrial comeback.

Contrasts between city and country. In the country districts of Japan the people live and work much as their ancestors have done for hundreds of years, cultivating the land with the same painstaking care, and content with the simplest of food, clothing, and houses. But in the cities before the war we could see another and newer Japan, where great changes have taken place since the Japanese have come in touch with the Western nations. Among the most important of these changes were the development of manufacturing and the growth of foreign trade.

The six largest cities of Japan are Tokyo, Osaka, Nagoya, Kyoto, Kobe, and Yokohama. Tokyo, with over six million people, is the largest city in Asia. Find these six cities on the map on page 298 (*E–F3*) and notice that they are all located in lowlands in Honshu,

THE FAR EAST
AND
EAST INDIES

POLITICAL AND ECONOMIC MAP

Scale of statute miles
0   100 200   400   600   800

Philip D. Gendreau, N. Y.

Figure 309. A glimpse of the business section of Tokyo. The picture shows a Japanese newspaper building, and to the left of it part of Japan's largest motion-picture theater.

The older sections of Tokyo are very different, for they have the narrow streets lined with little one-story and two-story wooden buildings which are common in all Oriental cities. Opening wide on many of these streets are little shops where all kinds of Japanese goods are sold, and little workshops where Japanese craftsmen are busy making many articles of wood, paper, metal, and pottery such as we saw in Japanese stores in this country before the war. *See Figure 310.*

Like all the larger cities of Japan, Tokyo offers a strange and interesting mixture of Eastern and Western sights. Bicycles, rickshaws, electric cars, automobiles, trucks, carts drawn by horses, and carts pulled by men pass back and forth through the main streets. In the crowds on the sidewalks one may see Japanese business men, clerks, and students dressed as men in our country dress, and laborers wearing the scanty native working clothes. Among the women there are many who have adopted Western fashions of dress, and many others who still

the largest and most important of the islands of Japan. Which one is the capital of Japan? What three are seaports?

Tokyo and its seaport. Tokyo, the capital and largest city of Japan, is located at the head of Tokyo Bay in the largest and most densely populated lowland region of Honshu. Its harbor is too shallow for ocean ships, and so Yokohama, farther down the bay where the water is deep, has become its seaport. In 1923 Yokohama was almost entirely destroyed by a great earthquake, and Tokyo was partly destroyed. This was a terrible calamity for the Japanese; but they started at once to repair the damage, and both cities were quickly rebuilt. In rebuilding Tokyo the people laid out broad streets and constructed modern stores, banks, business buildings, and government buildings. The Japanese were justly proud of their capital and its port, but both were badly wrecked during the war. *See Figure 309.*

James Sawders

Figure 310. A craftsman painting Japanese lanterns in one of the many little workshops in Toyko.

Figure 311. Some young Japanese women out shopping in their silk kimonos and their straw sandals.

By Burton Holmes from Ewing Galloway

Figure 312. A Japanese shipping picture. You can see bales of raw silk for export being transferred from a barge to an ocean freighter at Yokohama.

wear the long and beautiful kimonos with bright-colored sashes, which are their national costume. *See Figure 311.*

Business and manufacturing in Tokyo. Tokyo is the capital of Japan, and is the home of the emperor and the center of all the work of the government. In normal times it is also an important business and banking center, and the heart of a busy industrial district. Among the manufacturing industries of this district the making of textiles, clothing, iron and steel goods, electrical supplies, and paper products, and the refining of sugar are especially important. Study the imports of Japan on the map on page 298, and name some of the raw materials which normally the Japanese buy for their textile industries from other countries.

Yokohama and its trade. Yokohama is one of the leading seaports of the world, and the center of Japan's great export trade in raw silk. The leading silk-producing region of Ja-

pan is in the part of Honshu west of Tokyo and Yokohama, and therefore Yokohama is the center where raw silk is collected for shipment to distant lands. Before the war many business companies dealing in silk had their headquarters there. Cotton goods and many other Japanese products are exported from Yokohama, but raw silk was by far the most valuable item in its export trade before the war. *See Figure 312.*

The imports of Yokohama are many and varied, and they include raw materials such as cotton and wool, foodstuffs such as wheat, rice, and raw sugar, and manufactured goods, especially machinery of various kinds. Large quantities of the imports go to Tokyo for use there and for distribution to other parts of the country. Some of the raw materials are used in Yokohama itself, for this city, like most other large ports, is also an industrial center.

Nagoya and Kyoto. Southwest of the lowland in which Tokyo and Yokohama are located are two smaller lowlands, both of which are densely populated and open on bays. In one of these lowlands is the industrial city of Nagoya, which has modern cotton and silk mills and is the leading center for the manufacture of pottery and porcelain in Japan.

In the other lowland is Kyoto, one of the most beautiful cities in Japan. For a thousand years, until 1868, Kyoto was the capital of Japan, and the great center of the art and culture of the country. The ancient palaces of the rulers of long ago contain many beautiful works of art, and the temples, shrines, and gardens in and near the city are known throughout the Orient for their beauty.

Kyoto is noted for its manufacture of silk goods. Some of this work is done in factories, but many of the finest products are woven and embroidered by hand. Kyoto is also the great center for the finest of the old-time industries of Japan: the making of delicate porcelains, beautiful lacquer and bronze wares,

Courtesy of Saco-Lowell Shops

Figure 313. A Japanese girl tending a machine in a cotton-spinning mill in Osaka. The machine was manufactured in one of our New England cities.

exquisite fans and dolls, and the beautiful copper-and-enamel ware known as cloisonné.

Osaka and Kobe. Turn to the map on page 298 and study the location of Osaka and Kobe (*E 3*). Notice that they are at the northeastern end of the winding waterway which separates Honshu from Shikoku and Kyushu. This waterway is called the Inland Sea of Japan, and its mountainous shores and wooded islands make it one of the most beautiful bodies of water in the world.

Osaka is the second largest city of Japan and the leading industrial center. Before the war, people called it "the Manchester of Japan" because it was the leading cotton-manufacturing city of the country. Osaka was also an important center for the manufacture of iron, steel, and all kinds of iron and steel products, varying in size and value from locomotives and ships to wire and nails. *See Figures 313 and 314.*

Osaka is also an important seaport, but not so important as Kobe because its harbor is too shallow for the larger ocean ships. Kobe is an even greater port than Yokohama. It has a large, deep harbor, modern docks and wharves, and all the machinery necessary for

loading and unloading ships in the shortest possible time. In the business section of the city there are many large office buildings, and in normal times most of the business firms interested in Japanese foreign trade have headquarters or branch offices there.

Japanese railroads. One of the indications of modern progress in Japan are the many miles of railroads which have been built. Government railroads connect all the more important cities with one another, and railroads built by private companies reach many of the smaller places.

A summary of manufacturing. Fifty or sixty years ago there were very few factories in Japan, and nearly all the manufacturing was done by hand in the homes of the people and in small workshops. The Japanese had become very skillful hand workers, but they knew little or nothing of machine manufacturing.

Philip D. Gendreau, N. Y.

Figure 314. Department stores on one of the main streets in Osaka. Here, as in Tokyo, many modern buildings have been erected in recent years.

After the Japanese came in touch with Europe and the United States through trade, they saw that their country could make great progress by adopting Western methods of manufacturing. The government sent officials to the countries of western Europe and to the United States to study manufacturing methods, and in time factories were built and equipped with machinery purchased in those countries. From the very beginning Japan made steady progress in manufacturing. Its chief advantages for this work are its coal and water power, and its large and industrious population, which not only supplies abundant workers, but also provides large home markets for manufactured goods.

Among the factory products of Japan, cotton, silk, rayon, and woolen textiles were by far the most important before the war. Metal products and machinery came next, and for their manufacture large quantities of many different metals were imported.

Japanese trade before the war. Turn to the map on page 298 and prove by the exports that Japan manufactured a surplus of textiles. Large quantities of cheap cotton goods made in Japan were exported to China, India, and the East Indies, where they were sold in competition with cotton goods from Europe. Next

to textiles, raw silk was the most valuable of all the Japanese exports before the war, and it is becoming important again. The export of large quantities of manufactures was a fairly recent development in Japanese trade, and it showed that Japan had become one of the important manufacturing countries of the world.

Among the imports of Japan, cotton, wool, rayon pulp, metals, and other raw materials had the highest value,—another proof of the importance of manufacturing. The Japanese also imported certain manufactured products, such as machinery, which they did not as yet produce in sufficient quantities to supply their needs, and certain foodstuffs, especially wheat, rice, and raw sugar.

Twenty per cent or more of the exports of Japan, by value, came to the United States, chiefly because our country took such a large proportion of Japanese silk. The next largest share went to India, and the third largest to China, for those countries were the best customers for Japanese cotton goods.

In the import trade the United States held first place, followed by China and India, for these three countries supplied most of the raw cotton for the mills of Japan. Next came Australia, supplying Japan with much wheat and wool, and then Germany and Great Brit-

By Ewing Galloway, N. Y.

Figure 315. A power house seen from the Inland Sea in Japan. Notice how the mountains rise up in the background. The plant is located to receive the water from the swift-flowing streams of the mountains, and this water power is harnessed to make hydroelectricity. How is this natural resource an advantage to the Japanese?

ain, supplying many of Japan's needs for manufactured goods.

You will want to remember that the trade of Japan will be considerably changed from this prewar picture. Just how and to what extent it will develop will depend on what the Allied council permits Japan in the way of manufacturing and of imports and exports.

Making choices. Choose the word or phrase which makes each sentence below correct.

1. The leading food crop grown in Japan is

wheat.   millet.   rice.

2. The Japanese farmers produce much

raw cotton.   raw silk.   raw wool.

3. The most valuable mineral resource of Japan is

petroleum.   coal.   iron ore.

4. The most valuable metal ore mined in Japan is

copper.   iron ore.   gold.

5. The most valuable export product of Japan is

tea.   raw silk.   textiles.

6. The most valuable imports of Japan are

manufactured goods.   raw materials.   foodstuffs.

7. The country which normally buys the greatest quantities of raw silk from Japan is

the United States.   France.   Great Britain.

8. The country which held first place in supplying Japan with imports before the war was

China.   the United States.   India.

Giving reasons. Complete each sentence below by giving reasons.

1. Many of the people of Japan are very poor because _____.

2. Although Japan is one of the great rice-growing countries, the people import rice from other parts of the Far East because _____.

3. It is fortunate for the Japanese that the waters bordering their homeland are rich in fish because _____.

4. There are forests in many parts of Japan because _____.

5. Many of the forested lands will never be cleared for farming because _____.

6. Japan has many swift-flowing rivers because _____.

7. The rivers are of great value to the people because _____.

Naming cities. Name each city of Japan described below and answer the questions about it.

1. The capital of Japan. Why is it not a seaport? Why is it a manufacturing center?

2. The great seaport near Tokyo. Why is it the chief center for the export of raw silk from Japan?

3. The second largest city of Japan. For what manufacturing industries is it noted? What advantages has it for obtaining raw materials and fuel for its industrial plants, and for marketing manufactured goods?

4. The great seaport on the Inland Sea of Japan. Why is it a more important port than Osaka? Why did many foreign business firms have offices in this city?

Some things to explain. Explain why

1. The Japanese are one of the great fishing nations of the world.

2. The forests of Japan are a valuable resource.

3. Japan has plenty of workers for its mills and factories, and a large home market for manufactured goods.

4. The United States held first place in the export and import trade of Japan before the war.

5. India and China ranked high in the export and import trade of Japan before the war.

6. Yokohama is a great seaport.

7. Osaka was called "the Manchester of Japan" before the war.

8. The Japanese lived by themselves for many centuries, but finally came to take part in the trade of the world.

9. It is possible for the many millions of people to make a living in the mountainous islands of Japan.

James Sawders

Figure 316. This scene shows you a farmhouse and yard in Korea. Notice the straw roof on the buildings. What are some of the farm products which are raised in Korea? What reason can you give for the fact that the Korean farmers seldom have any difficulty in finding markets for the products which they raise?

III. KOREA AND OUTER MONGOLIA

Foreword. The defeat of Japan released Korea from thirty-five years of Japanese rule, and at present its affairs are being directed by the United States and the Soviet Union. The Russians have charge of the northern half of the country and we have charge of the southern half. Full independence has been promised the Koreans after a native government has been established and is running smoothly. With help from the Allies to start with, and by good management of its resources after independence, Korea has a chance to become a more prosperous nation.

Outer Mongolia is a landlocked country lying between the Soviet Union and the Chinese Republic. It was formerly an outlying territory of China, but the Chinese never had a very strong hold on it. After the First World War the people set up an independent government and renamed their country the Mongolian People's Republic; but their independence was not officially recognized by China until after the Second World War.

KOREA

Korean farming. The map on page 298 shows that Korea (*D3*) is a mountainous peninsula in about the same latitude as the Japanese island of Honshu. Most of the people live in the scattered lowlands, and all but about one fifth of them are farmers. The lowlands are a little less crowded than those of Japan; but the average Korean farm consists of only about $3\frac{1}{2}$ acres, and most of the farmers are poor. *See Figures 316 and 317.*

The food crops in Korea are much the same as in Japan, with rice holding top rank. For many years a large part of the yearly rice crop has been exported to Japan, and the Koreans have formed the habit of depending chiefly on crops of barley and millet for their own staple foods. Other important crops of the farms are soybeans, potatoes and other vegetables, and fruits.

Many of the farming families raise silkworms, and in the southern part of the country many use part of their cultivated land for raising cotton. Silk goods and cotton goods are manufactured in small factories, but during the period of Japanese rule a large part of the raw cotton was exported to Japan.

Korea's mineral wealth. Korea was worth much to Japan as a source of cotton and food, but much more as a rich source of minerals. Coal and iron ore are abundant, and the coal is good for coking and smelting. Korea is one of the world's leading producers of tungsten, and its mines also produce gold, copper, lead, zinc, molybdenum, and magnesite.

The development of the mineral resources has been chiefly the work of the Japanese. Korea has long furnished most of the coking coal for Japan's blast furnaces, and iron and other ores from its mines have helped greatly to make up for Japanese shortages. Korean blast furnaces and smelters, formerly owned and operated by Japanese companies, have supplied large quantities of metals to Japan's manufacturing plants.

In connection with the use of Korean resources the Japanese built many of the railroads in the country and developed its ports. During the period of Japanese rule most of Korea's trade consisted of an exchange of raw materials and foodstuffs for Japanese manufactures. For this reason Fusan, on the southeast coast, was the leading seaport. You can see from the map on page 298 how conveniently Fusan (*D3*) is located for handling this trade.

Sentences to complete. 1. Korean farms are small because __?__.

2. __?__ is the leading crop; but it is not the staple food of the Koreans, because __?__.

3. The raw materials for textile mills produced by Korean farmers are __?__ and __?__.

4. The Japanese built blast furnaces and steel mills in Korea during the years when they controlled the country, because __?__.

5. The steel alloy which Korea produces in large quantities is __?__.

6. The leading seaport of Korea is __?__.

OUTER MONGOLIA

A land of nomadic herders. The map (p. 295) shows that Outer Mongolia is in the part of Asia which is made up of plateaus encircled by mountains. Turn to Figure 64 (p. 71) and you will see that the rainfall over this entire area is very light. In the southern part of Outer Mongolia there is a desert known as the Gobi. The remainder of the country gets a little more rain and is mostly a poor grassland.

In view of these facts you will not be surprised to learn that Outer Mongolia is very thinly populated and that the people are mostly nomadic herders. Like all such peoples, they are dependent on pasturage for their flocks and herds; and when the grass around one camping place has been used up, they move to another.

Three Lions

Figure 317. A broom-maker working in the street of a Korean city. The brooms are made of reeds and the inner bark of bamboo.

If you should visit a Mongol camp in winter, you would find the people living in the kind of tents called yurts. A yurt has a latticelike framework of light wood which is covered with layers of felt made from wool. Tied on securely, the felt coverings keep out the wind and keep in the heat from a small fire built on the ground inside the yurt. In summer ordinary cloth tents are often used in place of some of the yurts.

Altogether the Mongolian herdsmen keep millions of sheep and goats, large numbers of cattle and horses, and a good many camels. From the sheep and goats they get the milk, cheese, butter, and mutton which are their chief foods, and the wool needed for clothing and for making the yurt coverings. *See Figure 318.*

The horses are small but strong, and are used as riding animals. The cattle and camels carry the yurt lattices, coverings, and furnishings which the herdsmen and their families take with them as they move from one camp to another. Both oxen and camels make good pack animals, or they can be harnessed to pull the simple two-wheeled carts which many of the Mongols use. *See Figure 319.*

Ties with the Soviet Union. The only country with which Outer Mongolia carries on trade or has any other relations is the Soviet Union. The trade is an exchange of animal products—chiefly wool, hides, and skins—for Soviet manufactures. It is carried on over motor roads built with Soviet help to connect Ulan Bator with Siberia. Ulan Bator is the capital and largest town of Outer Mongolia.

The Russians took part in setting up the independent government in Outer Mongolia, and they have been helping the Mongolians in many ways ever since. Among other things, they have helped to establish small manufacturing industries in Ulan Bator and a few other towns, and they operate an airline which connects Ulan Bator with southern Siberia.

Some questions to answer. 1. In your study of Asia you have found several regions besides Outer Mongolia where the people are mostly nomadic herders. Why are these regions not suitable for farming?

2. Why are they suitable for grazing?

3. Why do the herdsmen and their families lead wandering lives?

4. What can you say to prove that they depend largely on their flocks and herds for food, clothing, shelter, and transportation?

5. Do you think a country like Outer Mongolia is likely ever to be very densely populated? Why or why not?

Press Association, Inc.

Figure 318. Mongolian yurts in the background to the right. The herds of sheep are important to the Mongolians as the source of food and wool.

From Ewing Galloway, N. Y.

Figure 319. A Mongolian ox-cart caravan. The carts are loaded with the yurts and furnishings of the herdsmen to make the journey to another camp.

Philip D. Gendreau, N. Y.

James Sawders

Figure 320. Contrasts in China. The picture at the left shows a shopping street in the Chinese port of Shanghai. The one at the right, taken near one of the gates of Peiping, shows two men from the country selling vegetables. How many different means of transportation do you find in the two pictures?

IV. THE CHINESE REPUBLIC

1. FOREWORD

A very old nation. The Chinese are one of the oldest of the civilized nations of the world. For many centuries they were governed by emperors, and their lands formed the Chinese Empire. In 1912 the empire was overthrown, and the Chinese Republic took its place.

In area the Chinese Republic is the second largest country of the world. The Soviet Union is first, and after the Chinese Republic come Canada, Brazil, and the United States without Alaska. China has never had a careful census, or count, of population, but it is estimated that there are about 470 million people in the country, the largest number of people in any one country of the world.

The Chinese have always been a nation chiefly of farmers, and for thousands of years they lived so much by themselves that they knew little of what was going on in the rest of the world. Nevertheless, they made remarkable inventions and discoveries, and many of them became skillful craftsmen, talented artists, and great scholars.

A land of contrasts. Today China, like Japan, is a land of marked contrasts, where Eastern and Western civilizations are mixing, and the new and the old are found side by side. In the country districts millions of farmers live and work almost as simply as their forefathers did thousands of years ago, but in the cities the contrasts between the old and the new are very noticeable. Goods are transported in all kinds of vehicles, from wheelbarrows to modern motor trucks; people ride from place to place in rickshaws, taxicabs, and electric cars; skilled craftsmen work by hand in tiny shops, and factory workers tend machines in modern manufacturing plants. *See Figure 320.*

As you study the Chinese Republic, try to find out (1) why the people lived apart from the rest of the world so long; (2) how so many people can make a living in the country; (3) why farming has always been more important than manufacturing and commerce in China; and (4) what has led to the rapid changes that are taking place in the country today.

Political divisions. The Chinese Republic is made up of four principal political divisions. The eastern, and most important, division is China, or China proper, as it is often called to distinguish it from the rest of the country. China proper borders the Pacific Ocean. In the interior are the outer territories of Inner Mongolia, Sinkiang, and Tibet. Find these four main political divisions on the map (p. 295).

Map studies. 1. On the map on page 70 find the following regions of the interior of the Chinese Republic, and give their elevations: (1) Plateau of Mongolia; (2) Zungarian Basin; (3) Plateau of East Turkestan; and (4) Plateau of Tibet. 2. Which one of these regions is much higher than the others? 3. How do their elevations compare with the elevations of the surrounding mountains? 4. Now locate these interior plateaus on the map on page 68. 5. What can you say about their vegetation? 6. What explanation for their vegetation is suggested by Figure 64 (p. 71)? 7. On the map on page 70 locate (1) the Plain of China; (2) the Szechwan Basin; and (3) the East China Highlands. 8. What does Figure 64 show about their rainfall? 9. How do you expect their vegetation to differ from that of the interior plateaus? Check your answer by the map on page 68. 10. What does Figure 65 show about the number of people in China proper? in the interior plateaus?

The uneven distribution of population. You have discovered from the maps that the interior of the Chinese Republic is very thinly populated, while China proper is crowded with people. In fact, as Figure 3 on page 4 shows, China proper is one of the most densely populated parts of the whole world. It makes up less than half the area of the republic, yet it has over nine tenths of all the people.

Differences in surface. The maps have shown you that there are great differences in surface within the Chinese Republic. The interior is made up of plateaus surrounded by high, rugged mountains, while the eastern portion, bordering the coast, is made up of lowland plains and of mountains much lower than those of the interior. It is the lowland plains that are most crowded with people.

Differences in climate. Turn to the map on page 295 and notice that most of the Chinese Republic lies between the parallels of 20° and 50° north latitude. Thus it extends a little farther north than the United States does, and considerably farther south. As you would expect, then, there are very noticeable differences in the temperatures in the northern and southern parts of the country. In the north the poorer people often suffer greatly from the cold in the winter, while in the south the winter weather is never severe.

You have already noted the differences in rainfall in the republic. The interior has less than 20 inches of rain a year, and parts of it are so dry that they are deserts. Nearly all of China proper, on the other hand, has over 20 inches of rain a year, and much of it has between 40 and 80 inches.

The monsoon winds. The winds which bring most of the rain to China are the summer monsoons. They blow toward the interior of the great continent of Asia during the warmer part of the year, heavily laden with moisture from the Pacific and Indian oceans. The summer monsoons from the Pacific Ocean give China heavy rainfall in summer, just as those from the Indian Ocean give India heavy rainfall at the same season.

Since the interior of the Chinese Republic is bordered by high mountains on the south and east, little of the moisture brought by the summer monsoons reaches that part of the country. That is why the interior plateaus have so little rain, and the lack of sufficient rainfall for farming is the chief reason why those regions have so few people.

During the colder part of the year the winter monsoons blow outward from the dry interior of Asia, and therefore China, like India, has much less rain in winter than in summer. Northern China has bitterly cold winter winds from Siberia, which sometimes bring great clouds of dust with them. These cold dust storms are exceedingly unpleasant. In southern China the winter winds from the interior are cool, but that part of the country is so far south that the warmth of the sun makes the winter climate mild. In summer the weather in southern China is hot.

Giving reasons. Sum up some of the facts which you have learned thus far about the Chinese Republic by giving reasons to complete the following sentences:

1. China proper is much more densely populated than the interior plateaus, because _ _ _ _ _ _ _

2. China proper has sufficient rain for agriculture, because _

3. Much more of the rain comes in summer than in winter, because _

4. The interior plateaus suffer from too little rainfall, because _

2. MANCHURIA AND FORMOSA

From Dairen to Harbin. On the map on page 298 find Dairen (*D3*), the chief port of Manchuria. At Dairen you could take a modern streamlined train and travel northward through Mukden to Harbin. This trip would take you through the most densely populated part of Manchuria and would give you a good idea of the various resources and industries of this northernmost part of the Chinese Republic.

You would find Dairen a modern port which grew rapidly during the years when Manchuria was under Japanese control. Among the products awaiting export in its warehouses you would see large quantities of soybeans and soybean oil and cake. Someone would be sure to tell you that soybeans are the leading crop in Manchuria. *See Figure 309.*

Between Dairen and Mukden you would pass through the Manchurian iron-and-steel center which supplied the Japanese with large

Figure 321. Loading a freighter with bean cake at Dairen. Notice the stacks of "cakes" that are being lifted by one of the ship's cranes.

quantities of these metals before and during the war. The iron ore is mined close by, and the coking coal comes from east of Mukden.

On reaching Mukden you would be in the largest city of Manchuria, now rather badly damaged as a result of the war. Mukden is an important business and manufacturing center, with grain mills, bean-oil mills, cotton mills, and factories to make woolen carpets and rugs.

The old Chinese section of Mukden is walled, and many of its streets are narrow, crooked lanes lined with small shops and workshops. The new section was built by the Japanese, and it has broad streets and modern business buildings.

The next large city on your journey is Changchun, which was the capital of Manchuria during the period of Japanese control. On reaching Harbin you would find yourself in a city which looks more European than Oriental; for it was built by the Russians and has a considerable Russian population.

Manchurian agriculture. The mountains which border the Manchurian plain on the east are covered with temperate forests which make them the most valuable timberlands of

Figure 322. Harvesting wheat in Manchuria. The farmers are using a tractor which is drawing six harvesting machines. Manchuria is the only country of the Orient where sights like this can be seen. In China, as in Japan, the farms are too small and the farmers are too poor to have agricultural machinery.

China. The plain has lighter rainfall and is a temperate grassland with deep, fertile soils. The winters in this region are long and very cold, and the summers are short and hot. Fortunately, the rain comes mostly during the five or six months of the year when there is no danger of killing frosts.

To an American the tiny, intensively cultivated farms in the crowded lowlands of North China and South China are very interesting, but the larger ones on the less densely populated Manchurian plain seem more like home. By our standards even the Manchurian farms are small; but they are big enough for the use of machinery by farmers who can afford it, and land can be spared for pasture. Cattle, sheep, and goats are to be seen on many of the farms, and fodder crops are grown to feed them in the winter. *See Figure 322.*

Most of the crop land is used to raise grain and soy beans. Wheat is the leading grain crop, followed by kaoliang, millet, and corn. Altogether the Manchurian farmers produce a large surplus of food. During the period of Japanese control the exports went mostly to Japan. Normally they go partly to Japan and partly to North and South China. *See Figure 323.*

Some questions to answer. 1. Why would an American farmer feel more at home in Manchuria than in North or South China?

2. Why are the Manchurian farms larger than those elsewhere in China?

3. Why is Manchuria the most important industrial section of China?

4. Which of these cities is the largest in Manchuria, and which is the chief port?

Dairen   Harbin   Mukden

Keystone View Company

Figure 323. Chinese workmen weighing bags of soy beans in Manchuria. Soy beans, bean oil, and bean cake are the leading exports of Manchuria.

Formosa. Off the coast of South China is the island of Formosa, recently returned to the Chinese after fifty years of Japanese rule. Formosa is mountainous with a tropical climate, and it is famous for the beauty of its tropical vegetation, especially its wealth of flowering plants and shrubs.

Most of the people are farmers, and they raise a large variety of tropical and subtropical crops. During the years of Japanese rule Formosa was Japan's principal source of cane sugar, and of bananas, pineapples, and other tropical fruits. Rice is the chief food crop, and tea is grown for home use and export. The tea is the kind called oolong, and it is for sale in most of our grocery stores.

The most important forest product of Formosa is camphor, which is obtained from the wood of the wild camphor tree. Synthetic camphor is now manufactured by a chemical process, but Formosa supplies about three fourths of the world's demand for the natural product.

3. China Proper

For purposes of study it is helpful to divide China proper into three sections: (1) south China, which includes the lowland of the Si River; (2) middle China, which includes the lowlands bordering the Yangtze River; and (3) north China, made up largely of the Plain of China.

China proper is only about half as large as the United States, yet it has about three times as many people. Judging from the map on page 298, how do you think most of the people make their living? What products of China remind you of Japan? What mineral resources important in manufacturing has China? How well supplied with railroads does the country seem to be?

A land of farmers. The lowland regions of China proper are so densely populated that almost every acre of land which can be cultivated and which is not used for buildings or roads produces crops, chiefly foodstuffs for the millions of people. About four fifths of

Triangle Photo Service

Figure 324. Terraced rice fields in a hilly section of China. Each terrace, or step, is leveled off, and the soil is kept from washing away by a wall of earth. Hills and mountain slopes are terraced in all the rougher parts of southeastern China.

all the people make their living by farming, yet the average farm is only three and a half acres in size; and if a farmer has as many as five acres, he is considered well-to-do.

The Chinese farmers cultivate their little patches of land with the greatest care, for every square foot must be made to produce as much as it possibly can. Plowing is done with the help of oxen in the north and water buffaloes in the south, but the rest of the farm work is done by hand. In some places even the plows are pulled by men instead of by animals, for there are so many people in China that human labor is very cheap.

The better farm lands are, of course, in the lowlands, but the Chinese also terrace the hillsides and the mountain slopes for crops. Building terraces and keeping them in repair is hard work, but only by cultivating the

By Ewing Galloway, N. Y.

Figure 325. A Chinese cart of the kind commonly used in the northern part of China. Only a well-to-do Chinese farmer can afford to own a horse and cart.

hillsides and mountain slopes as well as the level lands can so many people manage to make a living by farming; and even so, most of the farmers are very poor. *See Figure 324.*

As you might expect, almost no land in China proper is used for pasture. The Chinese, like the Japanese, cannot afford to keep many cattle or sheep, because as much land as possible must be used to raise food crops, and little can be spared for pasture or forage crops. Pigs, chickens, and ducks, which can be fed cheaply, are abundant, and the farms supply large quantities of eggs for export.

Mineral wealth. China is a land of much mineral wealth. It has abundant coal and good supplies of iron and other metal ores. With these mineral resources it is well prepared to carry on manufacturing, but as yet its industrial growth has been slow. That is chiefly because the Chinese have only recently begun to carry on much manufacturing with machinery. As you visit different parts of China, you will see modern industrial plants here and there; but you will find that the greater part of the manufacturing is still done by hand in small workshops and in the homes of the people.

Means of transportation. The map shows that China is not well supplied with railroads. Altogether, there are less than 8500 miles of railroads in this great country — less than one twenty-eighth the number of miles of railroads in the United States. Furthermore, China is not well supplied with good roads. In recent years many miles of cart roads have been widened and smoothed for motor traffic; but even so, transportation by automobile and motor truck is difficult in many parts of the country, and in some parts impossible. In many sections the roads can be used only by slow-moving carts, and in others wheelbarrows and pack donkeys are the chief means of transportation. *See Figure 325.*

Fortunately, China has several long rivers which are navigable for good-sized boats, and in the eastern lowlands many canals have been built. But, as you know, transportation by boat is slow at best, and a country with few railroads and poor roads cannot make the best use of its resources.

China also has several thousand miles of airways, which are a great help in a country so large and so poorly supplied with railroads and motor roads. Remember, though, that only the well-to-do people can afford to travel by air, and that the great majority of the Chinese must continue to use the land or the rivers and canals in getting from one place to another.

Some things to explain. Give an explanation for each of the following facts:

1. Chinese farms are very small.
2. Chinese farmers do most of their work by hand.
3. The Chinese terrace hillsides which otherwise would be too steep for farming.
4. Compared with most farming countries, China has few cattle or sheep.
5. Transportation is slow in many parts of China.
6. Labor is cheap in China.

South China and Middle China

Mountains and plains. The map shows that much of south China and parts of middle China are mountainous. The mountains are not very high, however, and the people terrace many of the slopes for farming. The larger rivers are bordered by extensive lowland plains, all of which are overcrowded with people.

South China, as you know, has hot summers and mild winters, and even in middle China the winters are usually mild. For this reason most of the farmers of south China and middle China get at least two crops a year from their land.

Rice, silk, and tea. You may think of these two sections of China as lands of rice, silk, and tea, for rice and tea are the most valuable crops, and mulberry trees, both wild and cultivated, provide leaves to feed millions of silkworms. Tea bushes cover the hillsides in many places, and rice is grown in the lowlands and also on terraces on the hillsides. *See Figure 326.*

In all but the northern part of China proper, rice is the chief food of the people just as it is in Japan, and for the same reasons. Can you give the reasons? If not, review what you learned on page 291.

The Chinese cultivate their rice fields with the same painstaking care that the Japanese do, and the yearly production of rice is far greater than that of any other crop. Even so, it does not meet the needs of the huge population, and additional supplies of rice are imported from Indo-China and Siam.

The production of raw silk is carried on in China in much the same way as in Japan, except that there are fewer filatures and more of the reeling of the cocoons is done by hand

By De Cou from Ewing Galloway

Figure 326. Farmers plowing a rice field in south China. They are using water buffaloes to draw their plows. These animals are strong, and they work well in the mud and water of the rice paddies.

in the farmers' homes. In China, as in Japan, raw silk is normally an important export.

The Chinese, like the Japanese, are tea-drinkers, which accounts for the fact that tea is one of their leading crops. In addition to all the tea used within the country, there is a large surplus for export. The better qualities of tea are sent chiefly to Europe, while the poorer qualities are sold to the people in the interior regions of the Chinese Republic.

The lowland of the Si River. By far the most important part of south China is the densely populated valley and delta of the Si River. Find this lowland plain on the map on page 298 (*C4*). What Chinese seaport is at the mouth of one of the distributaries of the Si? What British port is located on an island beyond the delta?

This warm, moist lowland, with its subtropical climate, produces a great variety of crops. Rice is by far the most important, but much sugar cane and tobacco are grown, and many delicious kinds of fruit. This region is also one of the most important Chinese centers for the production of raw silk, for mulberry trees are abundant, and many of the farmers raise silkworms.

Photograph by Louis Tager from Lionel Green

Figure 327. A glimpse of the water front at Canton, showing some of the sampans, or small boats, in which so many of the people live. Most of the families who live in boats are very poor.

by carrying goods from one place to another. *See Figure 327.*

If you were to visit the warehouses along the water front in Canton, you would find some of them filled with Chinese goods for export, and you would notice especially the beautiful silk goods and silk embroideries. Canton is a great center for the reeling of silk, the weaving of silk goods, and the making of silk embroideries, shawls, and scarfs. Can you explain why?

Canton is a city of striking contrasts between the old and the new. Some of its streets are broad, well-paved, and lined with modern stores, banks, and office buildings. But in the older sections the streets are narrow lanes bordered by little one-story houses, shops, and workshops built as close together as possible. In many of the homes, as well as the workshops, people are busy weaving and embroidering, carving ivory, stone, and wood, and making jewelry, fans, lanterns, toys, and many other articles such as we see in Chinese stores in our country. There are modern cotton mills and other factories in Canton, but much of the manufacturing is still done by hand in the small workshops and in the homes.

The trade of Canton. Canton is the leading commercial center of south China and the chief port of that part of the country. Large ocean ships cannot come to its wharves, however, because the harbor is not deep enough. For this reason the goods for export are sent in small boats to the British port of Hong Kong, 78 miles away, and loaded on ocean-going ships there. Coming back to Canton, the small boats bring imported goods which have been unloaded from the ocean ships at Hong Kong. From the map on page 298 name the leading exports of Canton. Why is it

Among the native trees which grow on the hillsides in south China are tung trees, valuable for the oil which is obtained from the nuts. Tung oil is used in making paints and varnishes, and so much is needed in Europe and the United States that it is the most valuable of all China's exports.

Chinese tin mines. On the map on page 298 find the place in south China where tin is mined. Most of the mining is done in old-fashioned ways, but enough ore is produced each year to make tin one of the important exports of China.

Canton. Canton, the largest city of south China, is so overcrowded that more than one tenth of all the people live on the river in boats. Thousands of children are born and brought up on these boats, and never have any other place to live. When they are old enough to crawl about, their mothers put ropes around them and tie them to the boats to prevent their falling overboard. In some of the families both parents go ashore each day to work. Other boat families make their living

Figure 328. A small Chinese junk on the Yangtze River. Junks are important cargo boats in China, and many of them are much larger than this one.

natural that these products should be shipped from south China to distant lands?

The Szechwan Basin. Flowing from west to east through middle China is the Yangtze River. In its middle course it flows through the densely populated Szechwan Basin, a mountain-rimmed plain which is often called the Red Basin because of its red soils. These soils are very fertile, and the climate of the basin is mild and the growing season long. For these reasons it is one of the best farming regions in China, and the farmers raise a great variety of crops: rice, wheat, tea, cotton, sugar cane, and many others. Raw silk and tung oil are also very important products of the basin.

Down the Yangtze. Turn to the map on page 298 and trace the Yangtze downstream from Chungking (*B4*), the largest city of the Szechwan Basin. Notice that the river is navigable from some distance above Chungking all the way to the sea. What great seaport is located near its mouth?

There are no east-west railroads in this part of China, and therefore the Yangtze is the chief highway of travel and transportation between the Szechwan Basin and the sea. Chinese junks, such as you see in Figure 328, and river steamers carry passengers and all kinds of goods up and down the Yangtze between the cities along its banks.

East of the Szechwan Basin the Yangtze flows through another plain almost inclosed by mountains, and then winds across the great delta which it has built out into the East China Sea. Like the Szechwan Basin, these plains are rich farming regions and are densely populated. Rice and wheat are the chief grain crops, tea is grown on the inner plain, and large quantities of raw silk are produced on the delta. These lowlands bordering the Yangtze are also the chief cotton-growing regions of China. China stands next to the United States and India in the production of cotton.

An industrial center. On the map on page 298 find the cities of Hankow, Hanyang, and Wuchang (*C3*). Together these cities have over a million and a half people, and they

Figure 329. Part of the iron-and-steel plant at Hanyang. Study the map on page 298 and explain what advantages Hanyang has for the manufacture and distribution of iron and steel.

Figure 330. One of the narrower streets in Shanghai. The two-wheeled rickshaws are for hire like taxicabs.

Figure 331. A street scene near the water front in Shanghai. The men are Chinese coolies, or laborers, and they are pulling a cartload of goods to one of the wharves for shipment.

form one of the few modern industrial centers in China. Among their manufacturing plants are cotton mills, silk filatures, flour mills, and the iron-and-steel plant shown in Figure 329. The iron ore for this plant comes from mines a little farther south.

At Hankow you will find a plant for refining antimony, which is mined in the East China Highlands. Antimony is a cheap white metal which will not tarnish. It is used in making type metal, pewter, and certain other alloys, or mixtures, of metals.

Turn to the map on page 298 and find the place where the antimony is mined. Notice that there are tungsten mines in the same section of the mountains. China produces a considerable part of the world's supply of both antimony and tungsten. Tungsten, you know, is used chiefly in making certain kinds of very hard steel. It is also used in making the fine wires in electric-light bulbs.

The capital of the republic. Farther down the Yangtze is Nanking, the capital of the Chinese Republic. Nanking is also a commercial center, where many foreign companies which carry on business in China have offices.

Shanghai. On the map on page 298 find the city of Shanghai (*D3*). Shanghai is the largest city and the leading seaport of China. It is located on a small stream which flows into the estuary of the Yangtze River. This stream has been deepened so that good-sized ocean ships can reach Shanghai.

The new, or "European," portion of Shanghai has broad, well-paved streets and modern buildings. Along the *Bund*, as the water front is called, there are fine hotels and large stores, business buildings, and warehouses, most of which belong to foreign companies.

In Shanghai, as in Canton, the older part of the city, where the Chinese live, has the narrow, crooked streets and the crowded houses, shops, and workshops of old China. It is a fascinating experience to wander through this old city, to watch the craftsmen at their work, to visit the shops and tea rooms, and to see the jugglers who entertain the people for a small fee. *See Figure 330.*

A great shipping center. Just as Canton owes its growth to the fact that it is the ocean gateway for the rich lowland of the Si River, so Shanghai owes its growth to a location which makes it the ocean gateway for the rich lowlands of the Yangtze basin and the southern part of the Plain of China. Its harbor is always crowded with boats of all kinds, from Chinese junks and sampans to great ocean ships from distant lands. On both sides of the river there are docks where ships load and unload every day in the year. When the docks are full, as often happens, ships anchor in the river, and their cargoes are carried to shore in small boats. *See Figure 331.*

Turn to the map on page 298 and name the leading imports of Shanghai. Large quantities of imported goods are loaded on river boats at Shanghai and taken up the Yangtze to Hankow and other interior cities. Coming back down the river, the boats bring raw silk, cotton, tea, and other products from the farm lands in the Yangtze lowlands to be used in Shanghai or to be shipped to distant lands.

Manufacturing in Shanghai. In Shanghai there are cotton mills, silk mills, shipbuilding plants, flour mills, and many other industrial plants where thousands of Chinese are learning to carry on manufacturing in Western ways. Why is it natural that industrial plants of the kinds named above should be located at Shanghai?

Sentences to complete. Complete each sentence below by giving reasons:

1. Rice is grown on nearly every farm in south China and middle China because _____.
2. Tea is an important crop in these sections of China because _____.
3. The lowland of the Si River is well suited to the growing of sugar cane because _____.
4. Many farmers in south China and middle China cultivate mulberry trees because _____.
5. The Szechwan Basin is a rich farming region because _____.
6. The Yangtze River is an important highway of travel and transportation because _____.
7. Canton and Shanghai are great seaports because _____.

Figure 332. **Chinese farmers working in a field of soy beans. In the background is a field of kaoliang, which is grown extensively in north China for bread grain.**

North China

The Plain of China. North of the Yangtze lowlands, between the mountains and the sea, is the Plain of China, another rich farming region crowded with about one hundred million people. This plain has a cooler climate than the lowlands farther south, and so its crops are somewhat different.

Rice and cotton are grown in some parts of the plain, but wheat and other temperate grains are more important crops. Among these grains are kaoliang and millet, which provide food for large numbers of the poorer people. In the peninsula of Shantung, which extends into the Yellow Sea, the raising of silkworms is important.

In north China, and also in the Manchurian Lowlands, soy beans are grown both as a food crop and as a cash, or money, crop. The Chinese eat them as a vegetable, make a sauce from them to flavor their food, and use the oil in cooking as we use lard. In normal times there is a surplus of the beans and of bean cake from the oil mills for export. *See Figure 332.*

A river-made plain. The reason that the Plain of China is so fertile is that it is made up of fine sands and mud washed from the

Courtesy of Canadian Pacific Railway

Figure 333. One of the freight yards at Peiping, where goods are transferred from one railroad line to another. At the right in the picture is one of the outer gates of Peiping, built long ago.

mountains on the west and spread out in a series of deltas and flood plains. The Hwang River has done most of this work. Find this river on the map on page 298 (*C3*) and trace its course across the plain to the sea. The Chinese word *hwang* means "yellow," and the river gets its name from the fact that it carries so much mud that it is yellowish in color. In building this plain on which so many millions of Chinese people live, the Hwang has shifted its course several times, and its mouth is now far to the north of the point where it entered the sea years ago.

"China's Sorrow." The Hwang is also known as "China's Sorrow" because it often overflows and floods vast areas of this lowland of its own making. Some of the plain is lower than the surface of the river, and the people have built high banks in an effort to keep the stream in its channel. In times of flood, however, the river breaks through the banks and spreads far and wide over the plain.

Each time the Hwang overflows, the mud which it carries settles on the land and forms a coating of new soil for the farmers to use, but the floods often destroy the crops and sweep away the people's houses. At times the flood comes so suddenly that thousands of

people are drowned. When great floods occur in China and crops are destroyed, periods of famine follow, and sometimes large numbers of people starve to death.

Canals and waterways. The Plain of China is covered with a network of waterways. Some of them are old courses of the Hwang and others are canals. The Grand Canal, which is nearly a thousand miles long, was completed more than six hundred years ago. These waterways are important highways of travel and transportation in the plain, and boats move slowly along them carrying farm products to market and passengers from one place to another. In the streams and canals here, and in all parts of China, many fish are caught, and fishing helps greatly to increase the food supply.

Peiping. One of the most interesting cities in the world is Peiping. It was formerly known as Peking, and for many centuries it was the capital of China. Find Peiping on the map on page 298 (*C3*) and notice its location near the northern margin of the Plain of China. Notice also that Peiping is better served by railroads than most of the Chinese cities, for it can be reached by train from Shanghai, from Mukden, in Manchuria, and from Hankow, in the Yangtze Valley. The railroad which runs southward from Peiping through Hankow goes to Canton, and is the only railroad line connecting north China with south China. *See Figure 333.*

Peiping is not a seaport and it is not on a navigable river, yet it is the second largest city of China. Its location was chosen by a Chinese emperor of long ago who did not care for advantages for manufacturing or trade, but who wanted a beautiful capital for his seat of government. As years passed, the Chinese emperors built magnificent palaces

James Sawders

Figure 334. Some of the shops in Peiping. Notice their beautifully carved fronts. The one at the left is a silk shop, the one in the middle a candle shop, and the one at the right a perfume shop.

Figure 335. An outdoor market in Peiping, where fresh vegetables from the surrounding countryside are sold.

and temples in the capital city and gathered together many of the most remarkable works of Chinese art.

In approaching Peiping you will see the thick walls which were built long ago to keep out enemies, and the great gates which were always closed and guarded at night. Within the city is an area surrounded by another wall and known as the "Forbidden City." In this area is the palace where the emperors lived with their families and their servants, and where they received representatives of other nations. Very few other people were ever allowed to enter it.

Street scenes in Peiping. Peiping, like the other large cities of China, has its old sections with narrow streets and little one-story houses and its new section with paved streets and modern buildings, some of which are built in Western style and some in Chinese style. Visitors enjoy especially the attractive shops where all kinds of Chinese goods are sold. *See Figures 334 and 335.*

Among the interesting sights in Peiping are the camel trains coming in from Inner Mongolia. They come from hundreds of miles away, loaded with wool, and they go back carrying food and other supplies. *See Figure 336.*

Some Chinese homes. In Peiping, as in the other cities of China, most of the people are very poor, but there are a few who live in great comfort. Their homes are made up of a number of buildings facing an inner court or garden. Different buildings serve different purposes. A Chinese gentleman's library and living room are often in a building on one side of his court, while the sleeping rooms are in another building on the other side. The

Figure 336. A camel train leaving Peiping for Inner Mongolia. Turn to the map on page 295 and see if you can discover why Peiping is the center for trade between Inner Mongolia and China.

James Sawders

Figure 337. A view of the Great Wall of China, showing how it climbs the mountain slopes. During the centuries when the wall was used for protection, it was patrolled by Chinese soldiers.

food is prepared in a third building and carried by servants to a fourth, which serves as a dining room. In homes of this kind there are beautiful works of art, books, and most of the comforts and luxuries found in wealthy homes in Europe and America.

A center of learning. Peiping is not a great commercial or industrial city, and it owes its importance today to the fact that so much wealth and culture came to center there in the centuries when it was the capital of China. It has an excellent medical school, and in and near the city there are many colleges and other institutions of learning.

The Great Wall. Many visitors to Peiping travel a little farther north to see the Great Wall which the Chinese built more than two thousand years ago to keep out invaders from the northwest. This wall is one of the wonders of the world, for it runs westward for more than 1500 miles, climbing steep mountain slopes and descending into deep river valleys and gorges. *See Figure 337.*

Tientsin. On the map on page 298 find Tientsin, the chief port of north China, and the third largest city of the republic (*C3*). This city is located about 40 miles from the coast on a river which has been made navigable by dredging and straightening. The map shows that it is the northern terminus of the Grand Canal and that it is connected with Peiping, Shanghai, and Mukden by railroads.

Because of its railroads and its shipping, Tientsin is a busy commercial center. Boats from other parts of China and from distant lands come to its wharves, bringing goods to be distributed to various parts of north China, and carry away products of that part of the country. Among the leading exports to distant lands are soy beans, bean cake, and raw cotton, which go chiefly to Japan. Can you explain why? Among the imports, various kinds of manufactured goods from Japan, the United States, Germany, and Great Britain held high rank before the war. What reason can you give for the fact that these countries supplied China with a great many of its imports?

Like Shanghai, Tientsin is a manufacturing city as well as a seaport, and has cotton mills and many other kinds of manufacturing plants. Long ago this city became a center for the weaving of Chinese rugs, using wool from Mongolia. Rug-making is still one of the leading industries of Tientsin, and large quantities of modern Chinese rugs are exported to our country.

Some things to explain. Explain why

1. Wheat is a more important crop than rice in the Plain of China.

2. The Hwang River is often called "China's Sorrow."

3. Peiping is a great center of Chinese culture and learning.

4. Tientsin is an important business and manufacturing center.

Figure 338. Two Mongolians with a camel cart. The cart consists simply of a pair of wheels with a wooden framework on which goods can be strapped. The Mongolians use these carts to transport their tents and other belongings as they move from place to place.

4. INNER MONGOLIA, SINKIANG, AND TIBET

West of China proper are the interior plateaus and mountains of the Chinese Republic. Review what you learned about these regions on page 308. What can you say about their climate? What reasons can you give for the fact that they contain only a small per cent of the people of the republic?

The interior plateaus and mountains are divided politically among the provinces of Inner Mongolia, Sinkiang, and Tibet. Find these provinces on the map on page 295. Which one borders the Soviet Union? Which two border India? From what you have already learned about the interior of the Chinese Republic, how do you think most of the people of these provinces make their living?

The gateway to the interior. On the map on page 298 find the town of Kalgan (*C 2*). Kalgan is located in a pass in the mountains, and is the eastern gateway to the interior plateaus of China. Camel caravans from the dry regions to the north and west have long used this pass to reach Peiping, and today a railroad from Peiping runs through Kalgan to the great northern bend of the Hwang River. Except for this one short stretch of railroad in the extreme east, travel and transportation in the interior regions of China are carried on either by camel caravan, or, where there are roads, by automobile.

Mongolian nomads. Mongolia is so dry that it has less than two people per square mile. Most of the Mongolians are nomads, who wander about with their sheep, cattle, ponies, and camels, always in search of fresh pasture lands. They travel in groups, and wherever they stop to allow the flocks and herds to graze for a time, they set up a village of tents. *See Figures 338 and 339.*

From their flocks and herds the Mongolians obtain most of their food, and large quantities of wool, hides, and skins to sell to the people of China proper. In exchange for these products they buy cotton and woolen cloth, sugar, tea, and other supplies which they need. The people who live on the Plain of China have always dreaded the Mongolian nomads, for in times of greater drought than usual Mongolian horsemen have often invaded the plain and robbed the farming people. It was to keep out these invaders from Mongolia that the Chinese long ago built the Great Wall.

Figure 339. Mongol tents. The tents are made of a framework of poles covered with matting of woven straw, and can be put up and taken down easily.

Figure 340. A Tibetan riding a yak. Yaks are the principal burden-carriers in Tibet, and they also furnish the people with meat, milk, and hides.

Sinkiang. Sinkiang is made up largely of the almost rainless regions known as the Zungarian Basin and the Plateau of East Turkestan. Turn to the map on page 70 and find the mountains which nearly surround these dry regions. Sufficient rain falls on the high mountains to give rise to streams which flow down the slopes bordering the deserts of Sinkiang. Because of this, western Sinkiang has a fringe of scattered farming villages along the mountainous margins of the deserts. Here the people keep sheep, and raise excellent crops of wheat, barley, cotton, fruits, and vegetables by means of irrigation. The rest of the people—about a tenth of the total population—are nomadic herdsmen.

Sinkiang has no railroads, and until quite recently camel caravans provided the only means of carrying on trade with outside areas. Now it is connected with China proper, the Soviet Union, and India by fairly good motor roads which follow the ancient caravan routes. Because Sinkiang is so far from the densely populated parts of China, much of the trade is with neighboring parts of the Soviet Union, and the rest is chiefly with India.

The Plateau of Tibet. On the map on page 70 find the Plateau of Tibet (*G5*). What is its elevation? What kind of land surrounds the plateau? What mountains separate it from the northern plain of India? Prove by the map that all the longer rivers of China, southeastern Asia, and India rise in or near the margins of the Plateau of Tibet.

The Plateau of Tibet is the highest plateau in the world, higher even than the Plateau of Bolivia. Like that South American plateau, it is surrounded by high, rugged mountains, and is therefore very dry. Because of its high altitude, Tibet is also a cold land. Even in summer the days are cool, and the nights are very cold.

Most of the people of Tibet live in the valleys on the southern and southeastern margins of the plateau, where they are somewhat protected from the cold winds. In these valleys they manage to raise a little barley and wheat, and small quantities of vegetables and fruit, but their most valuable possessions are their sheep and their yaks. The yaks are especially valuable, because, like the llamas of Bolivia and Peru, they can work well in the high altitude. *See Figures 340 and 341.*

The people of Tibet carry on a little trade with the people of the eastern lowlands of China. They pack wool and sheepskins on the backs of their yaks and take them eastward to the outer borders of the mountains. There they meet Chinese coolies carrying tea, sugar, cotton goods, and other supplies to be exchanged for the wool and skins from the plateau. There is also a little trade between Tibet and India, carried on by way of the high passes in the Himalaya Mountains.

The capital of Tibet is the old city of Lhasa. The people of Tibet have never wanted outsiders to enter their country, and it is often difficult for travelers and explorers to obtain permission to visit Lhasa.

Some things to explain. Explain why

1. Inner Mongolia, Sinkiang, and Tibet are thinly populated.
2. The Mongolians depend on camels for transporting goods, while the Tibetans depend on yaks.
3. Farming is of some importance in Sinkiang.

Figure 341. Yaks in the yard of a small inn in Tibet. They are on their way to the eastern border of Tibet, loaded with sheep's wool which their owner will exchange for supplies from China.

5. CHINA — PAST AND PRESENT

At the beginning of this chapter you learned that for thousands of years the Chinese lived by themselves and knew little of what was going on in the outside world. During all those years they were isolated, or kept apart, from other nations. Do you know what caused this isolation, and how it finally came to an end?

Land barriers and water barriers. As you know, the densely populated lowlands of China proper are bordered on the west by a vast stretch of high mountains and dry plateaus. Even today travel is difficult in these regions, and for thousands of years people feared to cross them. Thus the mountains and plateaus long formed a broad, uninhabited barrier between China and the countries farther west in Eurasia.

On the south and east, China is bordered by the ocean waters. These too were barriers for many centuries, for until a few hundred years ago there were no ships large enough and strong enough to withstand the ocean storms, and few sailors dared to venture out of sight of land.

Early Chinese civilization. Cut off from contact with the rest of the world by land barriers on the one hand and water barriers on the other, the Chinese developed a civilization all their own. From the earliest times most of the people were farmers. As population increased, there were more and more people to be fed, and since there was little or no trade with the outside world, the farmers had to find ways to make every acre of land produce all that it possibly could. Thus, little by little, China became an overcrowded country of small farms.

During the long period of isolation the Chinese learned how to make all the things they needed, and many of them became very skillful and artistic craftsmen. When Marco Polo, the Venetian traveler, reached China in the thirteenth century, he marveled at the beautiful silks, the fine porcelains, the furniture inlaid with pearl shell, and the carvings in ivory and jade which he found there.

During all these centuries China produced writers and scholars, some of whom were as great as any whom the Western world had produced, but their numbers were very few compared with the millions of people who had no education. Even today large numbers of the people of China have never had a chance to go to school, and cannot read or write.

The opening-up of China. It was several hundred years after Marco Polo's visit to China before the Chinese came to have much interest in the Western nations. In the meantime, the Western nations had been making wonderful progress in science and engineering. Large ships were built which could cross and recross the oceans safely. The steam engine was invented, and steam was put to work to help man in manufacturing and in transportation. The Western nations began to take a deep interest in all distant lands, for they needed to discover new sources of raw materials and new markets for manufactured goods.

These changes led the Western nations to attempt to carry on trade with China. The first efforts, however, were unsuccessful, for the Chinese were satisfied to continue living by themselves, and they did not welcome foreigners or foreign trade. At last, in 1842, the British were successful in getting the Chinese government to sign a treaty allowing foreign ships to trade at Canton, Shanghai, and three other Chinese ports. This was the end of Chinese isolation, and the beginning of the opening-up of China to trade and other contacts with the outside world.

Chinese trade. Today the ships of all nations are allowed to enter all the Chinese ports, and China carries on trade with many distant lands. The Chinese exports of highest value are tung oil, eggs, raw silk, and tea. What class of people in China produce three of these four leading exports?

Among the imports, manufactures hold the leading place, especially machinery and other products of iron and steel. Next come raw materials for China's manufacturing industries. Large quantities of kerosene and other mineral oils are also imported, chiefly from the United States and the Netherlands Indies.

Before the war the countries with which China carried on the most trade were the United States, Japan, Great Britain, and Germany. The reason for this is easy to understand. It is because these industrial countries provided markets for China's surplus raw materials and foodstuffs, and because they supplied the many different kinds of manufactured goods which are needed by the Chinese.

The new China. Ever since 1912, when the Chinese Empire became the Chinese Republic, China has had many troubles. Civil wars within the country were followed by the attack by Japan in July, 1937. For four and a half years the Chinese fought their powerful enemy alone and unaided, and it was not until August, 1945, that the full force of the Allied Nations brought defeat to Japan.

With the collapse of Japan as a great power China has risen to leadership among the nations of the Orient. The Chinese are now at work repairing the damage resulting from eight years of war, and their program for reconstruction calls for much fuller use of their resources so that China may become better balanced and more prosperous.

The plans center on greater industrialization. For this purpose China has abundant steam coal for power. It has coking coal and iron ore, and its mines produce a variety of other metal ores. Its farms and grazing lands produce textile fibers and other raw materials. Its enormous population supplies plenty of factory workers and large home markets for manufactures.

The Chinese know that all the plans for fuller use of the country's resources hinge on overcoming the present handicap of poor transportation. They are preparing to build more railroads and to improve and increase the present mileage of motor roads.

The Chinese have long been the world's greatest agricultural nation. If the manufacturing goals which they have set for themselves are reached, they will also be a great industrial nation.

Finding contrasts. You have learned that China is a land of great contrasts. Describe the contrasts listed below, using the pictures referred to as a help.

1. Contrasts in surface: Figures 324, 326, 332, and 337.

2. Contrasts in ways of doing work: Figures 326, 329, 332, 334, and 335.

3. Contrasts in means of transportation: Figures 323, 325, 328, 330, 331, 333, 336, and 341.

Giving reasons. Complete the following sentences by giving reasons:

1. More than nine tenths of the people of the Chinese Republic live in China proper because --------------------------------------.

2. China long ago became an overcrowded country of small farms because ------------- --------------------------------------.

3. Even today farming is far more important in China than manufacturing or commerce because ------------------------------.

4. In many parts of China travel and transportation are slow and difficult because ------ --------------------------------------.

5. The larger rivers of China are of great value to the people because --------------------.

Something to prove. You have learned that China has only just begun to carry on manufacturing in modern ways. By answering the questions below prove that it has great advantages for the development of manufacturing industries.

1. What mineral resource is sufficiently abundant in China to supply increasing numbers of mills and factories with power?

2. What three raw materials produced in various parts of the Chinese Republic can be used to increase the textile-manufacturing industries?

3. What advantages has China for increasing its manufactures of iron and steel products?

4. Why do manufacturers in China have no trouble in getting workers for their mills and factories?

5. Why does China itself provide large home markets for manufactured goods?

6. What advantages has China for marketing manufactured goods in foreign countries?

Naming cities. Name each Chinese city described below, and answer the questions about it.

1. The largest city and leading seaport of China. Why is it a great seaport? an important manufacturing city?

2. The second largest city of China, and for many centuries the capital of the country. In what part of China is it located? Why is it the chief center of wealth and culture in China?

3. The chief seaport of north China. For what densely populated lowland region is it the ocean gateway? Of what famous inland waterway of China is it the northern terminus?

4. The chief seaport of south China. For what densely populated lowland is it the ocean gateway? Why is it an important center for the making of silk goods? Why do large numbers of its people live in boats?

5. The three cities which form an industrial center in the Yangtze Valley. Why are they well located to manufacture cotton goods? silk goods? iron and steel?

6. The capital of the Chinese Republic. On what river is it located?

Some things to explain. 1. Give as many reasons as you can why the Chinese lived by themselves for so many hundreds of years, knowing almost nothing of the outside world.

2. Explain what happened in the outside world to make Great Britain and other Western nations anxious to open up China to foreign trade.

3. Give what you think may be the reasons why the Chinese preferred to go on living by themselves.

4. Describe some of the changes which have come about in China since the Chinese began to learn Western ways. Explain how the Chinese have benefited by these changes.

5. Give reasons for the following facts:

a. Many of the leading exports of China are agricultural products.

b. The leading imports are manufactures.

c. The Chinese import much rice in spite of the fact that China itself is a great rice-growing country.

d. A large part of China's trade was with the United States, Japan, Great Britain, and Germany before the war.

THE POLAR REGIONS

Foreword. As you know, the north pole and the south pole are the northernmost and southernmost points on the earth's surface. They are directly opposite each other, and the north pole is the same distance north of the equator as the south pole is south of the equator. Do you know how the polar regions, or the regions surrounding the two poles, differ from each other? The maps opposite this page will help you to answer this question.

The north polar region. The north pole is located in the midst of the Arctic Ocean, which is almost surrounded by the continents of the Northern Hemisphere. Prove by the map that the only broad opening to the Arctic Ocean is between Greenland and Europe.

For hundreds of miles outward in all directions from the north pole the Arctic Ocean is covered with ice the year round. The ice is very thick; but as it drifts with the winds and the currents, it cracks and breaks, and is often crumpled into long, high ridges. Because of the ice, it is impossible for any ship to make its way to the north pole.

Many explorers have tried to reach the north pole, but only a few have been successful. The first man to succeed was Rear Admiral Robert E. Peary, an American naval officer. Taking a Negro and four Eskimos with him as companions, and dog sledges to carry supplies of food, he crossed the frozen polar sea and reached the north pole on April 6, 1909. Trace his route on the map.

Seventeen years passed before anyone again reached the north pole. The man who made the second successful trip was another American naval officer, — Rear Admiral Richard E. Byrd. With one companion he flew in an airplane from Svalbard (Spitsbergen) to the north pole and back in about eighteen hours in May, 1926. In the same month Captain Roald Amundsen, a Norwegian explorer, and a group of companions flew in a dirigible from Svalbard to Point Barrow, in Alaska, passing over the north pole on their trip. Trace the routes of Byrd and Amundsen on the map.

North polar borderlands. You have already learned that the borderlands of the Arctic Ocean in Alaska, the mainland of Canada, and Eurasia (except the northwestern coast of Scandinavia) are cold treeless plains known as the tundra. Because the tundra is low land almost at sea level, the snow and ice which cover it most of the year melt away in the short Arctic summer, and grasses and flowering plants make their appearance for a few weeks.

Greenland and the northern islands belonging to Canada are higher, and because of this they are covered with ice and snow the year round. Only in a few scattered spots along their coasts is the land free from its covering of ice and snow during the summer.

You have also learned that the Arctic borderlands are very thinly populated, and that most of the people get their living by herding reindeer or by hunting the wild animals which live in the sea and on the land in these cold parts of the earth. Name the people of the polar borderlands of North America and of Europe. Why do these groups of people live nomadic lives?

On the upper map opposite this page find Etah, on the coast of Greenland, and Hammerfest, on the coast of Norway. Etah is an Eskimo village, and is the northernmost permanent settlement in the world. Hammerfest is the northernmost permanent settlement of white people in the world. What reason can you give for the fact that the extreme northwestern coast of Norway is not too cold for white people to make permanent homes there?

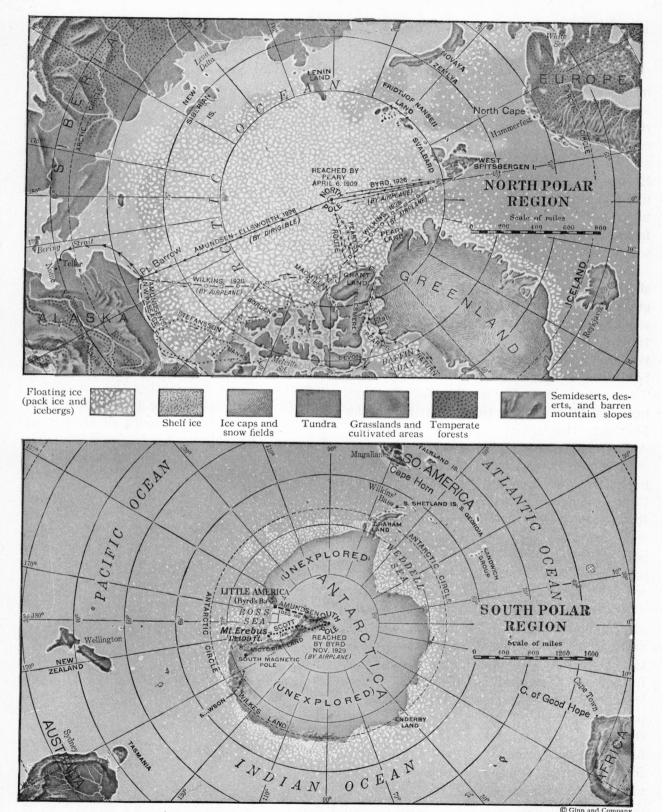

Floating ice (pack ice and icebergs) **Shelf ice** **Ice caps and snow fields** **Tundra** **Grasslands and cultivated areas** **Temperate forests** **Semideserts, deserts, and barren mountain slopes**

© Ginn and Company

The scale of the North Polar map is approximately twice that of the South Polar map

The south polar region. The map shows that the south polar region is quite different from the north polar region, for most of the area within the antarctic circle is occupied by the great mass of ice-covered land which we call Antarctica. The south pole is in this southern continent. Antarctica is larger than Europe or Australia, but there are no people living there. From the map on page 327 tell which one of the inhabited continents extends farthest south toward Antarctica. Name the southernmost settlement in that continent.

South polar explorations. It is only a short time since men began to explore this great southern continent, and even now vast stretches of it are unknown. The first men to catch glimpses of the land in this part of the world were those who went to the Far South on sealing trips and whaling trips. Their reports led to the sending out of exploring expeditions from the countries of the Northern Hemisphere, and the outlines of Antarctica are now fairly well mapped.

In 1911 two exploring parties set out to find the south pole. One was headed by Captain Amundsen, and the other by Captain Robert F. Scott, a British naval officer. Amundsen and his companions reached the pole in December, 1911, and Scott and his party reached it five weeks later. Trace their routes on the map on page 327.

No further attempt was made to reach the south pole until 1929. In that year Rear Admiral Byrd headed a large exploring expedition which made its base, or headquarters, at Little America on the margin of the Ross Sea ice barrier. In November Byrd and three companions flew in an airplane from their base to the pole and back in nineteen hours. This flight was very dangerous, for the plane had to fly over high mountain ranges and through narrow mountain passes that were almost hidden in fog. In 1933 Admiral Byrd led another expedition to Antarctica, again making his base

at Little America. On this trip Byrd and his men explored several new areas, and in places they found mineral ores. They kept careful records of the weather, thus adding to our knowledge of the climate.

A continent buried under ice. From the reports which explorers have brought back from the south polar region we believe that Antarctica is a huge plateau much of which is at least 6000 feet in elevation. Most of it is buried under a thick cap of ice and snow, and so it is impossible to tell just what the surface beneath may be. Here and there snow-capped mountain ranges from 10,000 to 15,000 feet in elevation tower above the surface of the ice cap, and moving slowly down their slopes are great glaciers.

In places along the coast there are stretches of bare, rocky land. Along much of the coast, however, the ice cap reaches the sea, and it is hard to tell where the land really ends. Since the ice is always moving slowly toward the sea, huge blocks break from its outer margin and float away, forming icebergs.

Whaling grounds in the Far South. Antarctica itself has no commercial value, but in the waters surrounding it there are large numbers of seals and whales. For more than a century the South Shetland Islands and South Georgia have been important centers of the sealing and whaling industries, and today seventy per cent of all the whales caught in the world come from the cold waters of the Far South. The Norwegians, as you know, lead in the whaling industry.

Sentences to complete. 1. No ships can reach the north pole because _____.

2. The northernmost permanent settlement in the world is ____ in _____. The people of this village are _____.

3. The northernmost permanent settlement of white people is _____ in _____.

4. Antarctica is uninhabited because _____.

5. The Norwegians send the most ships to the Far South because _____.

INTERNATIONAL RELATIONS

Our study of geography has shown us that the conditions which influence the lives and work of the people of the earth are constantly changing. For thousands of years the mountains, the deserts, and the oceans were barriers to travel. During that period of history progress was slow, and people went on doing about as their ancestors had done before them.

In those early times, when the various nations were more or less isolated, most of the people engaged in the simpler occupations such as hunting, fishing, or farming. When men began to use steam power and then electricity, a new civilization developed. This new civilization brought with it the development of manufacturing on a large scale, and this, in turn, led to the demand for raw materials from various parts of the world and the need for world markets for manufactured goods.

A period of wonderful progress in science and engineering followed, and men invented new means of transportation. They built railroads, automobiles, airplanes, and larger and stronger ships. Little by little, these new and better means of transportation overcame the barriers which had kept the people of the world apart.

Today mail is distributed by all the leading nations of the world. Cable messages, telegrams, telephone messages, and radio messages are sent back and forth across international boundaries, or boundaries between countries, and across the oceans. All the advanced people of the earth coöperate with one another in the development of rapid means of communication.

We have organizations such as the International Red Cross which assist people throughout the world in times of misfortune. When disasters such as floods, fires, earthquakes, or volcanic eruptions occur, people in many different countries contribute money and send workers to help those who have lost their homes and their property.

Many students of one country go to another to complete their studies. In the colleges, universities, and technical schools of the United States alone there are at least 10,000 foreign students every year. Professors and teachers from one country exchange positions with those of another, and thus, through education, a better understanding of the customs of the different countries is coming about.

We have learned that several of the leading nations are doing much to develop the resources and help the people in the backward countries of the world. They assist the native people by establishing good government, improving health conditions, opening schools, and introducing modern methods of farming, mining, and carrying on trade.

Friendly coöperation between all nations of the world is not only desirable but necessary, for backwardness, disasters, and misfortunes in any part of the world lessen the prosperity of the rest of the world. Wars, the worst disasters of all, result in nothing but loss to all the nations engaged in the fighting, and to the world as a whole. Nations can no longer live by themselves, for the days of isolation have passed.

In our international relations it is important that the people in each country shall have an intelligent sympathy for the people of all the other countries. Such sympathy depends on a knowledge of the living conditions in the various parts of the world, and on a kindly point of view. These, in the end, will do more than anything else to maintain peace and good will among the nations of the earth.

Turn over to page 332.

KEY TO NUMBERS

CENTRAL AMERICA

1. British Honduras
2. Costa Rica
3. Guatemala
4. Honduras
5. Nicaragua
6. Panama
7. El Salvador

SOUTH AMERICA

1. British Guiana
2. Surinam
3. Ecuador
4. French Guiana
5. Paraguay
6. Uruguay

EUROPE

1. Albania
2. Austria
3. Belgium
4. Bulgaria
5. Czechoslovakia
6. Denmark
7. Eire
8. England
9. Germany
10. Greece
11. Hungary
12. Netherlands
13. Northern Ireland
14. Poland
15. Portugal
16. Rumania
17. Scotland
18. Switzerland
19. Wales
20. Yugoslavia

AFRICA

1. Ashanti and Gold Coast
2. Bechuanaland
3. British Somaliland
4. Eritrea
5. French Somaliland
6. Italian Somaliland
7. Liberia
8. Nyasaland
9. Portuguese Guinea
10. Sierra Leone
11. Tunisia
12. Uganda

ASIA

1. Bhutan
2. British Malaya
3. Iraq
4. Nepal
5. Oman
6. Palestine
7. Syria and Lebanon
8. Trans-Jordan
9. Yemen

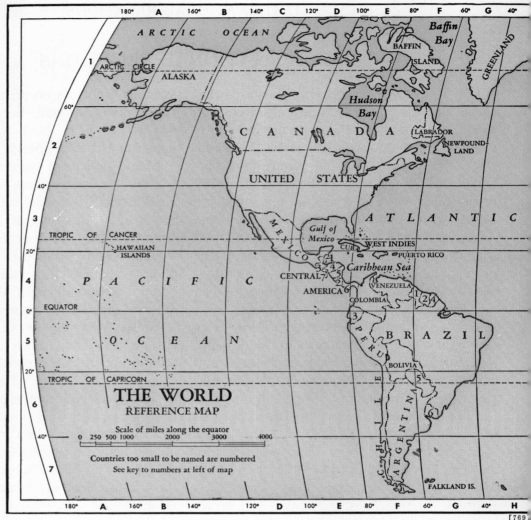

THE WORLD

REFERENCE MAP

Scale of miles along the equator

0   250 500 1000   2000   3000   4000

Countries too small to be named are numbered
See key to numbers at left of map

[769]

AREAS AND POPULATIONS OF THE

NORTH AMERICA

	AREA IN SQUARE MILES	POPULATION
Alaska	586,400	72,524
British Honduras	8,598	59,965
Canada	3,694,863	11,506,655
Costa Rica	23,000	639,197
Cuba	44,164	4,227,597
Dominican Republic	19,325	1,655,779
El Salvador	13,176	1,787,930
Greenland	736,518	16,630
Guatemala	45,452	3,284,269
Haiti	10,700	3,000,000
Honduras	44,275	1,105,504
Mexico	765,917	19,473,741
Newfoundland	42,734	300,000
Nicaragua	57,143	1,133,572
Panama	28,576	635,836
United States	3,022,387	131,669,275

SOUTH AMERICA

	AREA IN SQUARE MILES	POPULATION
Argentina	1,079,965	13,320,641
Bolivia	506,792	3,457,000
Brazil	3,275,510	45,002,176
British Guiana	89,480	346,982
Chile	296,717	4,677,089
Colombia	439,997	8,701,816
Ecuador	275,936	2,921,688
French Guiana	34,740	30,906
Paraguay	169,266	1,014,773
Peru	482,258	6,207,967
Surinam	54,291	181,044
Uruguay	72,153	2,122,628
Venezuela	352,143	3,491,159

EUROPE

	AREA IN SQUARE MILES	POPULATION
Albania	10,629	1,003,124
Austria	32,341	7,000,000
Belgium	11,775	8,386,553
Bulgaria	39,825	6,549,664
Czechoslovakia	54,244	14,729,536
Denmark	16,575	3,706,349
Eire	26,601	2,989,700
England	50,874	37,794,00
Finland	147,811	3,834,66
France	212,659	41,907,05
Germany	141,000	66,500,00
Greece	50,147	7,108,81
Hungary	35,875	9,106,25
Iceland	39,709	121,61
Italy	119,764	45,209,93
Netherlands	13,203	8,728,56
Northern Ireland	5,237	1,279,74
Norway	124,556	2,937,00
Poland	150,470	34,775,69
Portugal	34,254	7,539,48
Rumania	113,884	19,933,80
Scotland	30,405	4,842,98
Soviet Union	1,821,353	170,467,00
Spain	190,050	26,222,42
Sweden	173,341	6,370,53
Switzerland	15,944	4,260,71
Wales	7,466	2,158,37
Yugoslavia	95,576	15,703,00

330

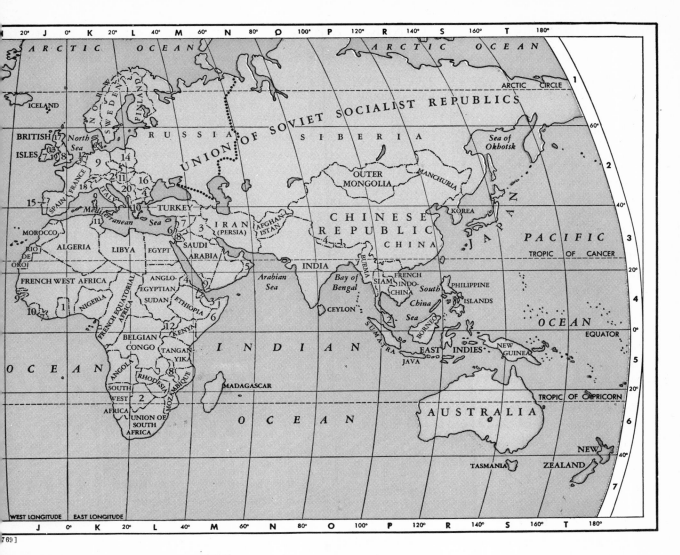

RINCIPAL COUNTRIES OF THE WORLD

ASIA	AREA IN SQUARE MILES	POPULA-TION
fghanistan	250,000	12,000,000
rabia	1,000,000	10,000,000
hutan	18,000	300,000
ritish Malaya	52,669	5,560,444
urma	261,610	14,667,146
eylon	25,332	5,981,000
hinese Re- public	3,750,106	470,000,000
rench Indo- China	286,000	23,853,500
dia	1,575,187	388,998,000
an	628,000	15,000,000
aq	116,600	3,560,456
pan	147,702	73,000,000
orea	85,246	22,800,647
ebanon	3,600	1,000,000
etherlands Indies	735,268	60,727,233
uter Mongolia	622,744	850,000
alestine	10,429	1,544,530
hilippine Is.	114,400	16,356,000

	AREA IN SQUARE MILES	POPULA-TION
Siam	200,148	15,718,000
Soviet Union	6,294,901	170,467,000[1]
Syria	54,300	3,000,000
Trans-Jordan	34,740	300,000
Turkey[1]	296,903	17,869,901
AFRICA		
Algeria	847,500	7,234,684
Anglo-Egyptian Sudan	967,500	6,288,852
Angola	481,226	3,225,015
Ashanti and Gold Coast	91,843	3,962,520
Bechuanaland	275,000	265,756
Belgian Congo	902,082	10,381,700
British Somali- land	68,000	344,700
Egypt	383,000	15,920,703
Eritrea	15,754	600,573
Ethiopia	350,000	12,100,000
French Equato- rial Africa	959,256	3,423,015

	AREA IN SQUARE MILES	POPULA-TION
French Somaliland	8,492	44,240
French West Africa	1,815,768	14,944,830
Italian Somali- land	194,000	1,021,572
Kenya	224,960	3,534,862
Liberia	43,000	1,500,000
Libya	679,358	888,401
Madagascar	241,094	3,797,936
Morocco	213,350	7,153,730
Mozambique	297,654	4,995,750
Nigeria	372,674	20,641,814
Northern Rho- desia	290,320	1,381,829
Nyasaland	37,374	1,686,045
Portuguese Guinea	13,944	426,009
Rio de Oro	100,200	386
Sierra Leone	27,669	1,672,000
Southern Rho- desia	150,333	1,448,393
Southwest Africa	317,725	314,194

	AREA IN SQUARE MILES	POPULA-TION
Tanganyika	360,000	5,283,893
Tunisia	48,300	2,608,310
Uganda	93,981	3,829,705
Union of South Africa	472,550	9,589,898
AUSTRALASIA		
Australia	2,974,581	6,997,326
Borneo	290,012	2,959,604
Java and Madura	51,032	41,718,364
New Guinea	344,232	1,209,191
New Zealand	103,723	1,573,810
Sumatra	164,148	7,677,826
CONTINENTS		
Africa	11,710,424	157,330,000
Antarctica	5,000,000	
Asia	17,000,000	1,160,000,000
Australia	2,974,581	6,997,326
Europe	3,750,000	550,000,000
No. America	8,664,864	184,260,000
So. America	6,937,551	88,680,000
[1]Europe and Asia		

331

A General Review

A map test. 1. On an outline map of Europe print these names in the correct places, doing the work from memory.

Atlantic Ocean	Apennine Mts.
Arctic Ocean	Ural Mts.
Mediterranean Sea	Caucasus Mts.
North Sea	Rhine River
Baltic Sea	Danube River
Black Sea	Seine River
Caspian Sea	Elbe River
Alps	Volga River
Carpathian Mts.	Vistula River
Pyrenees	Rhône River
Sierra Nevada	Po River

2. Print the name of each European country in the correct place.

3. When you have finished, check your map by the map on pages 144–145 to make sure you have made no mistakes.

Matching countries and capitals. Below is a list of the capitals of the countries which are wholly or partly in Europe. Name the countries in the order in which the capitals are listed.

Paris	Athens	Copenhagen
Oslo	Dublin	Amsterdam
Rome	Belgrade	Helsingfors
Sofia	Ankara	Bucharest
Bern	Brussels	Stockholm
London	Warsaw	Budapest
Berlin	Lisbon	Prague
Madrid	Moscow	

Some things to explain. Explain as fully as you can why

1. Great Britain, France, Germany, and Belgium are important manufacturing countries.

2. Norway, Sweden, Finland, and European Russia are able to supply other countries with lumber, wood pulp, and paper.

3. France, Germany, Denmark, and the Netherlands are important farming countries.

4. Italy and Switzerland, with no coal and little iron ore, are manufacturing countries.

5. Spain, with abundant coal and iron ore, is not a great manufacturing country.

6. Czechoslovakia is one of the important manufacturing countries of Europe.

7. Spain, Portugal, Italy, and Greece export fruits, nuts, wines, and olive oil.

8. Norway, Great Britain, Denmark, and the Netherlands are important fishing countries.

9. Yugoslavia and Rumania are the only two Balkan countries which export grain.

10. The southern part of European Russia is one of the great wheat-growing regions of the world.

11. Rumania and European Russia are able to supply some of the mineral oils needed in the other European countries.

12. The resources of the European part of the Soviet Union are much more fully developed than those of the Asiatic part.

13. The internationalized rivers of Europe are a great help to the landlocked countries and regions.

14. Great Britain has the largest fleet of merchant ships of any country in the world.

A map test. 1. On an outline map of Asia print the following names in the correct places, doing the work from memory.

Pacific Ocean	Indus River
Indian Ocean	Lena River
Arctic Ocean	Ob River
Lake Aral	Yenisei River
Caspian Sea	Tigris River
Red Sea	Euphrates River
Persian Gulf	Himalaya Mts.
Yangtze River	Ural Mts.
Hwang River	Caucasus Mts.
Brahmaputra River	Philippine Islands
Ganges River	East Indies

2. Print the name of each Asiatic country in the correct place.

3. When you have finished, check your map by the map on page 295 to make sure that you have made no mistakes.

Naming capitals. Name the capital of each of the Asiatic countries listed below:

Siam	Afghanistan
India	Chinese Republic
Iran	Japan
Iraq	Netherlands Indies
Ceylon	Philippine Islands

Topics for discussion. Following are some topics which you will find it interesting and worth while to discuss with your classmates.

1. Why so many millions of people are able to make a living in India, in China proper, and in Japan.

2. Why Siberia, southwestern Asia, and the interior of the Chinese Republic are so thinly populated.

3. Why the British regarded India as one of the most valuable of all their possessions.

4. Why so many of the Western nations are deeply interested in developing the resources of the Orient, and in carrying on trade with the Oriental nations.

5. Why Japan was the only Oriental country which ranked among the half-dozen most powerful countries of the world before the war.

6. What possibilities there are that China will become more prosperous and win for itself a more important place among the countries of the world.

A map test. 1. On an outline map of Africa print the following names in the correct places, doing the work from memory.

Mediterranean Sea	Sahara Desert
Suez Canal	Congo River
Red Sea	Nile River
Atlantic Ocean	Niger River
Gulf of Guinea	Zambezi River
Indian Ocean	Lake Victoria
Atlas Mts.	Lake Tanganyika

2. Print the names of the three independent countries of Africa in the correct places.

3. Print the names of the larger British possessions, French possessions, and former Italian possessions, and the name of the Belgian possession in the correct places.

4. When you have finished, check your map by the map on page 50 to make sure that you have made no mistakes.

Some questions about Africa. 1. What reasons can you give for the fact that the European nations have been so eager to obtain possessions in Africa?

2. Why have most of the native peoples of Africa been unable to remain independent of European control?

3. What problems do the Europeans face in developing the resources of the hot, rainy parts of Africa?

4. What parts of Africa are best developed today, and why?

Something to prove. In resources, occupations, and trade Australia and New Zealand are more like the countries of temperate South America than like any other parts of the world. Give as many facts as you can to prove that this is true.

A city test. 1. Write down the names of the cities described below. When you have finished, you will have a list of the fifteen largest cities of the Old World.

(1) The capital of the British Empire.
(2) The capital of Japan.
(3) The capital of Germany.
(4) The capital of the Union of Soviet Socialist Republics.
(5) The leading seaport of China.
(6) The leading industrial city of Japan.
(7) The capital of France.
(8) The chief Baltic seaport of Russia.
(9) The great city in Austria.
(10) The largest city of north China.
(11) The leading seaport of India.
(12) The leading seaport of north China.
(13) The largest city of Australia.
(14) The capital of Poland.
(15) The western seaport of India.

2. There are only nine cities in the New World with more than a million people. Five of them are in the United States. Try to make a list of these five cities from memory. Then check your list by the figures on page 337 and correct it if necessary.

3. The other four cities in the New World with over a million people are the capital of Argentina, the two largest cities of Brazil, and the capital of Mexico. Give their names.

4. Among these twenty-four largest cities of the world as a whole, how many are capitals of countries? How many are seaports? How many are lake ports? How many are river ports?

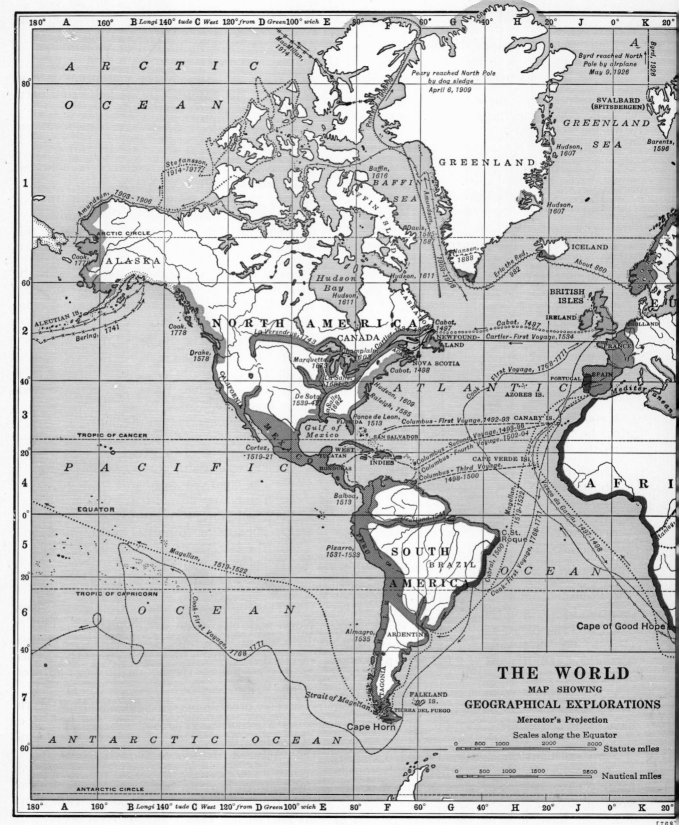

THE WORLD

MAP SHOWING

GEOGRAPHICAL EXPLORATIONS

Mercator's Projection

Scales along the Equator

334

[768]

ARCTIC OCEAN

80°

BARENTS SEA

NOVAYA

Barents, 1596-1597

TAIMIR PENINSULA

NEW SIBERIAN IS.

ZEMLYA

Amundsen, 1903-1906

North Cape

ARCTIC CIRCLE

1

Cook 1778

ALASKA

SIBERIA

BERING SEA

60°

KAMCHATKA PENINSULA

Bering, 1741

ALEUTIAN IS.

ASIA

Bering, 1741

EUROPE

SAKHALIN ISLAND

Bering, 1741

2

La Pérouse 1787

Bering, 1741

De Vries, 1643

Marco Polo

1271-1275

TIBET

JAPAN

PACIFIC

40°

PERSIA

CHINA

Sea

Albuquerque 1515

INDIA

TROPIC OF CANCER

3

EGYPT

ARABIA

PHILIPPINE IS.

Magellan, 1519-1522

20°

ARABIA

Red Sea

MALAY PENINSULA

SIAM

Death of Magellan 1521

4

CEYLON

Vasco da Gama, 1498

Albuquerque 1511

BORNEO

AFRICA

Stanley 1874

SUMATRA JAVA

CELEBES

NEW GUINEA

EQUATOR

0°

Stanley 1871

INDIAN

1616

1616

OCEAN

5

Livingstone 1840-73

Cook - First Voyage, 1768-1771

1622

OCEAN

20°

MADAGASCAR

Magellan's Voyage, completed by del Cano

1616 Dutch Explorers

AUSTRALIA

TROPIC OF CAPRICORN

6

1622

1628

Cook-First Voyage 1768-1771

40°

TASMANIA

Tasman, 1642

NEW ZEALAND

7

Tasman, 1642

Home countries and lands explored by

Norse

Portuguese

ANTARCTIC OCEAN

60°

English

French

Dutch

Spanish

Russians

Amundsen reached South Pole Dec. 14, 1911

Scott reached South Pole Jan. 18, 1912

Byrd reached South Pole by airplane Nov. 29, 1929

ANTARCTIC CIRCLE

POPULATION OF LARGEST CITIES IN COUNTRIES OF THE OLD WORLD

EUROPE

Austria
Vienna 1,874,130

Belgium
Antwerp 273,772
Brussels 900,228
Ghent 165,269
Liége 162,272

Bulgaria
Sofia 287,976

Czechoslovakia
Bratislava . . . 123,852
Brünn 264,925
Moravská Ostrava 125,347
Prague 848,823

Denmark
Copenhagen . . 843,168

Eire
Dublin 467,691

Finland
Helsingfors . . . 277,771

France
Bordeaux . . . 258,348
Le Havre . . . 164,083
Lille 200,575
Lyon 570,622
Marseille . . . 914,232
Nantes 195,185
Nice 241,916
Paris 2,829,746
St. Étienne . . . 190,236
Strasbourg . . . 193,119
Toulouse 213,220

Germany
Berlin 4,242,501
Cologne 756,605
Dortmund . . . 540,875
Dresden 642,143
Duisburg 440,419
Düsseldorf . . . 498,600
Essen 654,461
Frankfurt on
Main 555,857
Hamburg . . . 1,129,307
Hannover . . . 443,920
Leipzig 713,470
Munich 735,388
Nürnberg . . . 410,438
Stuttgart 415,028
Wuppertal . . . 408,602

Great Britain
Birmingham . . 1,013,700
Bradford 292,200
Bristol 413,100
Edinburgh . . . 464,600
Glasgow 1,124,300
Hull 322,200
Leeds 487,200
Liverpool . . . 854,500
London 8,474,900
Manchester . . 748,100
Newcastle on Tyne 292,700
Nottingham . . 280,200

Sheffield 520,500
Stoke on Trent . 274,100

Greece
Athens 452,919
Piræus 251,659

Hungary
Budapest . . . 1,051,804

Italy
Bologna 266,945
Catania 242,246
Florence 319,141
Genoa 625,355
Milan 1,103,960
Naples 860,176
Palermo 408,124
Rome 1,148,948
Trieste 242,681
Turin 623,454
Venice 260,991

Netherlands
Amsterdam . . . 781,645
Rotterdam . . . 595,448
The Hague . . . 482,397

Northern Ireland
Belfast 415,151

Norway
Bergen 98,303
Oslo 253,124

Poland
Breslau 625,198
Danzig 407,000
Krakow 237,532
Lodz 638,857
Posen 260,444
Warsaw 1,225,451

Portugal
Lisbon 594,390
Oporto 232,280

Rumania
Bucharest . . . 641,421

Spain
Barcelona . . . 1,148,129
Madrid 1,048,072
Seville 238,727
Valencia 352,802

Sweden
Göteborg 258,387
Malmö 141,485
Stockholm . . . 533,884

Switzerland
Basel 148,063
Bern 111,783
Geneva 124,121
Zürich 312,600

Turkey
Istanbul 740,805

Union of Soviet Socialist Republics
Gorki 451,500
Kharkov 654,300

Kiev 538,600
Kovno 105,370
Lemberg 316,461
Leningrad . . . 2,776,400
Moscow 3,663,300
Odessa 497,000
Revel 140,000
Riga 385,063
Rostov 520,700
Stalingrad . . . 388,000

Yugoslavia
Belgrade 238,775
Zagreb 185,581

ASIA

British Malaya
Penang 201,651
Singapore . . . 572,310

Burma
Mandalay . . . 147,932
Rangoon 400,415

Ceylon
Colombo 284,155

Chinese Republic
Amoy 234,159
Canton 861,024
Changsha . . . 606,972
Chungking . . . 635,000
Foochow 322,725
Hangchow . . . 506,930
Hankow 777,993
Harbin 458,379
Mukden 527,241
Nanking 1,019,148
Peiping 1,556,364
Shanghai . . . 3,489,998
Soochow 260,000
Taihoku 289,085
Tientsin 1,292,025
Tsingtao 514,769
Wenchow 631,276

French Indo-China
Cholon 134,000
Hanoi 124,000
Hue 123,000
Saigon 122,000

India
Ahmedabad . . 313,789
Amritsar 264,840
Bangalore . . . 306,470
Bombay 1,161,383
Calcutta 1,485,582
Delhi 447,442
Hyderabad . . . 466,894
Karachi 263,565
Lahore 429,747
Lucknow 274,659
Madras 647,230

Japan
Fukuoka 291,158
Hiroshima . . . 310,118
Kobe 912,179
Kyoto 1,080,593

Nagoya 1,082,816
Osaka 3,101,900
Tokyo 6,085,800
Yokohama . . . 704,290

Korea
Keijo 394,511

Netherlands Indies
Batavia 437,000
Surabaya . . . 313,000

Philippine Islands
Manila 353,418

Siam
Bangkok 931,170

Southwest Asia
Aleppo 177,313
Ankara 123,699
Baghdad 300,000
Beirut 134,655
Damascus . . . 193,912
Jerusalem . . . 125,000
Meshed 139,000
Smyrna 170,546
Tabriz 219,000
Tehran 360,000
Tel-Aviv 140,000

Union of Soviet Socialist Republics
Baku 709,500
Chelyabinsk . . 210,000
Novosibirsk . . 278,000
Omsk 227,000
Sverdlovsk . . . 400,800
Tashkent . . . 491,000
Tiflis 405,900
Vladivostok . . 190,000

AFRICA
Alexandria . . . 573,063
Algiers 257,122
Cairo 1,064,567
Cape Town . . . 322,221
Casablanca . . . 258,567
Durban 259,104
Fez 144,313
Johannesburg . . 378,593
Marrakech . . . 190,577
Oran 163,743
Tunis 202,405

AUSTRALIA AND NEW ZEALAND

Australia
Adelaide 315,130
Brisbane 309,772
Hobart 62,740
Melbourne . . . 1,008,300
Newcastle . . . 107,100
Perth 210,365
Sydney 1,254,780

New Zealand
Auckland . . . 212,159
Christchurch . . 132,559
Dunedin 81,961
Wellington . . . 149,971

AREA AND POPULATION OF STATES AND POSSESSIONS OF THE UNITED STATES

CENSUS OF 1940

	SQ. MILES	POPULATION		SQ. MILES	POPULATION		SQ. MILES	POPULATION
Alabama	51,609	2,832,961	Michigan	58,216	5,256,106	Tennessee	42,246	2,915,841
Arizona	113,909	499,261	Minnesota	84,068	2,792,300	Texas	267,339	6,414,824
Arkansas	53,102	1,949,387	Mississippi	47,716	2,183,796	Utah	84,916	550,310
California	158,693	6,907,387	Missouri	69,674	3,784,664	Vermont	9,609	359,231
Colorado	104,247	1,123,296	Montana	147,138	559,456	Virginia	40,815	2,677,773
Connecticut	5,009	1,709,242	Nebraska	77,237	1,315,834	Washington	68,192	1,736,191
Delaware	2,057	266,505	Nevada	110,540	110,247	West Virginia	24,181	1,901,974
District of Columbia	69	663,091	New Hampshire	9,304	491,524	Wisconsin	56,154	3,137,587
Florida	58,560	1,897,414	New Jersey	7,836	4,160,165	Wyoming	97,914	250,742
Georgia	58,876	3,123,723	New Mexico	121,666	531,818			
Idaho	83,557	524,873	New York	49,576	13,479,142			
Illinois	56,400	7,897,241	North Carolina	52,712	3,571,623	POSSESSIONS		
Indiana	36,291	3,427,796	North Dakota	70,665	641,935			
Iowa	56,280	2,538,268	Ohio	41,222	6,907,612	Alaska	586,400	72,524
Kansas	82,276	1,801,028	Oklahoma	69,919	2,336,434	Guam	206	22,290
Kentucky	40,395	2,845,627	Oregon	96,981	1,089,684	Hawaii	6,407	423,330
Louisiana	48,523	2,363,880	Pennsylvania	45,333	9,900,180	Panama Canal Zone	549	51,827
Maine	33,215	847,226	Rhode Island	1,214	713,346	Puerto Rico	3,435	1,869,255
Maryland	10,577	1,821,244	South Carolina	31,055	1,899,804	American Samoa	76	12,908
Massachusetts	8,257	4,316,721	South Dakota	77,047	642,961	Virgin Islands	133	24,889

CITIES IN THE UNITED STATES HAVING 100,000 OR MORE PEOPLE

CENSUS OF 1940

Akron, Ohio	244,791	Elizabeth, N.J.	109,912	Minneapolis, Minn.	492,370	Salt Lake City, Utah	149,934
Albany, N.Y.	130,577	Erie, Pa.	116,955	Nashville, Tenn.	167,402	San Antonio, Tex.	253,854
Atlanta, Ga.	302,288	Fall River, Mass.	115,428	Newark, N.J.	429,760	San Diego, Calif.	203,341
Baltimore, Md.	859,100	Flint, Mich.	151,543	New Bedford, Mass.	110,341	San Francisco, Calif.	634,536
Birmingham, Ala.	267,583	Fort Wayne, Ind.	118,410	New Haven, Conn.	160,605	Scranton, Pa.	140,404
Boston, Mass.	770,816	Fort Worth, Tex.	177,662	New Orleans, La.	494,537	Seattle, Wash.	368,302
Bridgeport, Conn.	147,121	Gary, Ind.	111,719	New York, N.Y.	7,454,995	Somerville, Mass.	102,177
Buffalo, N.Y.	575,901	Grand Rapids, Mich.	164,292	Norfolk, Va.	144,332	South Bend, Ind.	101,268
Cambridge, Mass.	110,879	Hartford, Conn.	166,267	Oakland, Calif.	302,163	Spokane, Wash.	122,001
Camden, N.J.	117,536	Houston, Tex.	384,514	Oklahoma City, Okla.	204,424	Springfield, Mass.	149,554
Canton, Ohio	108,401	Indianapolis, Ind.	386,972	Omaha, Nebr.	223,844	Syracuse, N.Y.	205,967
Charlotte, N.C.	100,899	Jacksonville, Fla.	173,065	Paterson, N.J.	139,656	Tacoma, Wash.	109,408
Chattanooga, Tenn.	128,163	Jersey City, N.J.	301,173	Peoria, Ill.	105,087	Tampa, Fla.	108,391
Chicago, Ill.	3,396,808	Kansas City, Kans.	121,458	Philadelphia, Pa.	1,931,334	Toledo, Ohio	282,349
Cincinnati, Ohio	455,610	Kansas City, Mo.	399,178	Pittsburgh, Pa.	671,659	Trenton, N.J.	124,697
Cleveland, Ohio	878,336	Knoxville, Tenn.	111,580	Portland, Oreg.	305,394	Tulsa, Okla.	142,157
Columbus, Ohio	306,087	Long Beach, Calif.	164,271	Providence, R.I.	253,504	Utica, N.Y.	100,518
Dallas, Tex.	294,734	Los Angeles, Calif.	1,504,277	Reading, Pa.	110,568	Washington, D.C.	663,091
Dayton, Ohio	210,718	Louisville, Ky.	319,077	Richmond, Va.	193,042	Wichita, Kans.	114,966
Denver, Colo.	322,412	Lowell, Mass.	101,389	Rochester, N.Y.	324,975	Wilmington, Del.	112,504
Des Moines, Ia.	159,819	Memphis, Tenn.	292,942	Sacramento, Calif.	105,958	Worcester, Mass.	193,694
Detroit, Mich.	1,623,452	Miami, Fla.	172,172	St. Louis, Mo.	816,048	Yonkers, N.Y.	142,598
Duluth, Minn.	101,065	Milwaukee, Wis.	587,472	St. Paul, Minn.	287,736	Youngstown, Ohio	167,720

POPULATION OF LARGEST CITIES IN OTHER COUNTRIES OF THE AMERICAS

Argentina
Avellaneda	386,372
Buenos Aires	2,505,332
Córdoba	310,070
La Plata	247,515
Rosario	516,668
Tucumán	157,480

Bolivia
La Paz	250,000

Brazil
Belém	294,944
Porto Alegre	321,628
Recife	472,764
Rio de Janeiro	1,896,998
São Paulo	1,120,405
São Salvador	363,726

Canada
Hamilton	166,337
Montreal	903,007
Ottawa	154,951
Quebec	150,757
Toronto	667,457
Vancouver	275,353
Winnipeg	221,960

Central America
Guatemala	176,780

Chile
Santiago	829,830
Valparaiso	263,228

Colombia
Bogotá	330,312

Ecuador
Quito	215,921

Mexico
Guadalajara	228,049
Mexico	1,464,556
Monterrey	180,942

Paraguay
Asunción	104,819

Peru
Lima	520,528

Uruguay
Montevideo	770,000

Venezuela
Caracas	203,342

West Indies
Habana	568,913
San Juan	169,247

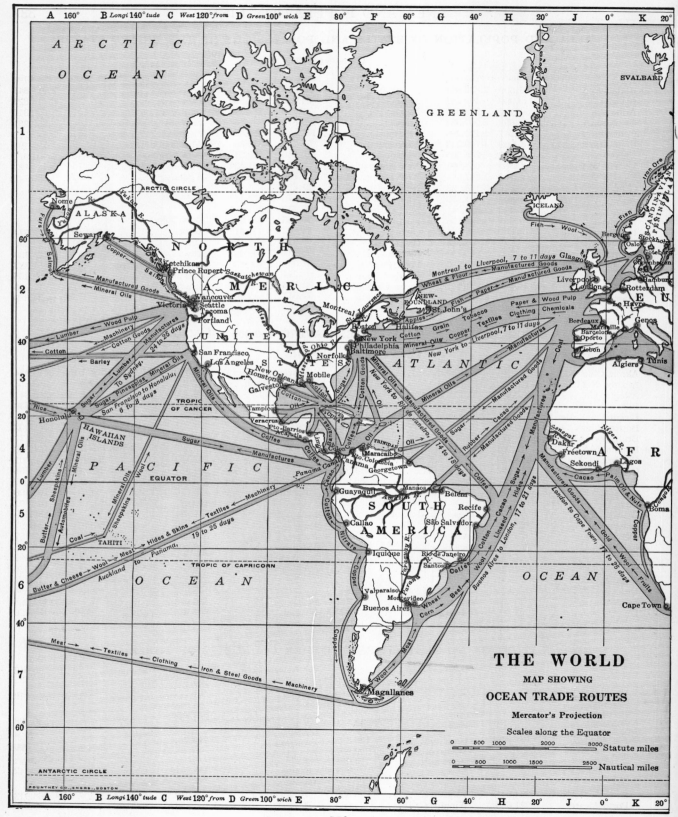

THE WORLD

MAP SHOWING

OCEAN TRADE ROUTES

Mercator's Projection

Scales along the Equator

[796]

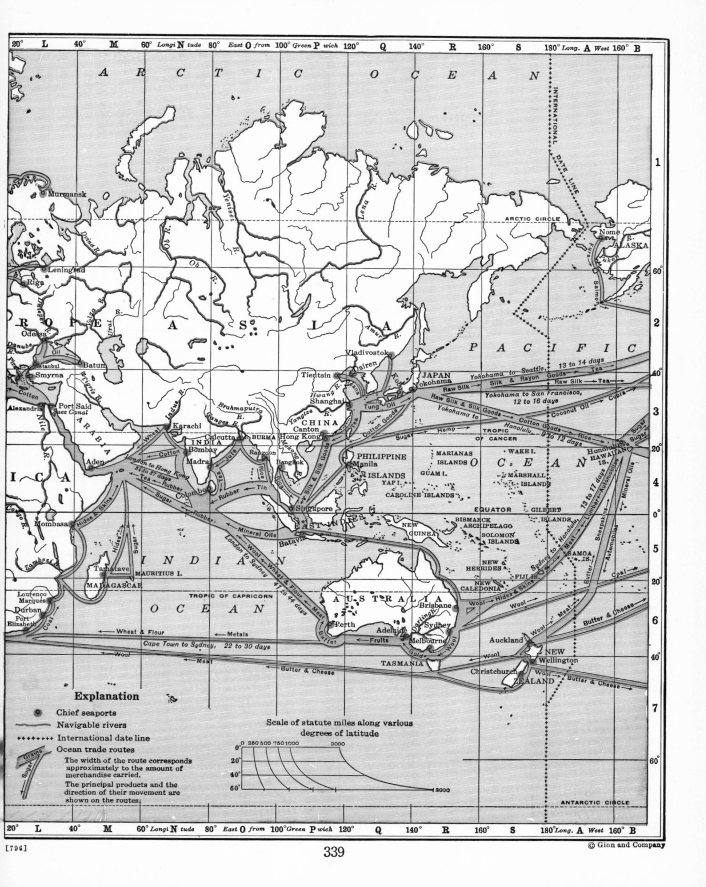

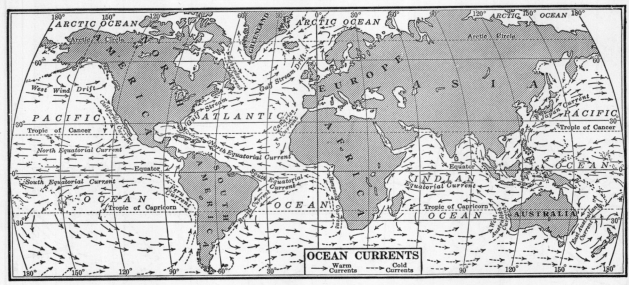

A map of the world showing ocean currents.

A LIST OF BOOKS FOR OUTSIDE READING

AKELEY, CARL E. and MARY LEE. Adventures in the African Jungle. Dodd, Mead & Company.

ALLEN, NELLIE B. Africa, Australia, and the Islands of the Pacific; Asia (Rev. Ed.); Europe. Ginn and Company.

ÁRNADÓTTIR, HÓLMFRÍDUR. When I was a Girl in Iceland. Lothrop, Lee & Shepard Company.

BUCK, ALAN M. When I was a Boy in Ireland. Lothrop, Lee & Shepard Company.

BUNKER, FRANK F. China and Japan. J. B. Lippincott Company.

BYRNE, BESS S. With Mikko through Finland. Robert M. McBride & Company.

CARPENTER, FRANK G. Africa; Asia; Australia, the Philippines, and Other Islands of the Sea; Europe. American Book Co.

CHAMBERLAIN, JAMES F. and ARTHUR H. Africa; Asia; Europe; Oceania. The Macmillan Company.

DAKIN, WILSON S. Great Rivers of the World. The Macmillan Company.

DU CHAILLU, PAUL B. In African Forest and Jungle. Charles Scribner's Sons.

FAIRGRIEVE, JAMES, and YOUNG, ERNEST. The British Empire; The British Isles (Secondary Series); Euro-Asia. George Philip & Son, Ltd., London.

FARIS, JOHN T. Real Stories of the Geography Makers. Ginn and Company.

FRANCK, HARRY A. China; The Japanese Empire. F. A. Owen Publishing Company.

FRANKE, S. The Last of the Zuider Zee. Stackpole Sons.

GREGORY, JOHN WALTER. Africa. Rand McNally & Company.

HALL, MAY EMERY. Dutch Days. Dodd, Mead & Company.

HAMSUN, MARIE. A Norwegian Family. J. B. Lippincott Company.

HODGDON, JEANNETTE R. The Enchanted Past. Ginn and Company.

HOLMES, BURTON. Travel Stories. China, by Eunice Tietjens; Egypt and the Suez Canal, by Susan Wilbur; Japan, Korea and Formosa, by Eunice Tietjens. The Wheeler Publishing Company.

IKBAL 'ALI SHAH, SIRDAR. Arabia. The Macmillan Company.

LEWIS, ELIZABETH F. Ho-Ming, Girl of New China; Young Fu of the Upper Yangtze. The John C. Winston Co.

MACVEAGH, LINCOLN and MARGARET. Greek Journey. Dodd, Mead & Company.

MIRZA, YOUEL B. Myself when Young — a Boy in Persia. Doubleday, Doran & Company.

MORRISON, LUCILE. The Lost Queen of Egypt. Frederick A. Stokes Company.

OWEN, RUTH B. Denmark Caravan. Dodd, Mead & Company.

ROY, SATYANANDA. When I was a Boy in India. Lothrop, Lee & Shepard Company.

RYAN, LORNA M. When I was a Girl in Australia. Lothrop, Lee & Shepard Company.

SCHOTT, HELENA C. Czechoslovakia. The Macmillan Company.

SCOTT, EVELYN and C. K. In the Endless Sands (Sahara Desert). Little, Brown & Company.

SEREDY, KATE. The Good Master (Hungary). Viking Press, Inc.

SIPLE, PAUL. A Boy Scout with Byrd; Scout to Explorer. G. P. Putnam's Sons.

SMITH, SUSAN. Made in Germany and Austria; Made in Sweden. Minton, Balch & Co.

SPAULL, HEBE. The Baltic States: Latvia, Lithuania and Estonia. The Macmillan Company.

TAYLOR, T. GRIFFITH. Australia. Rand McNally & Company.

THOMAS, LOWELL, and BARTON, REX. Wings over Asia. The John C. Winston Company.

WHITE, WILLIAM C. Made in Russia. Alfred A. Knopf, Inc.

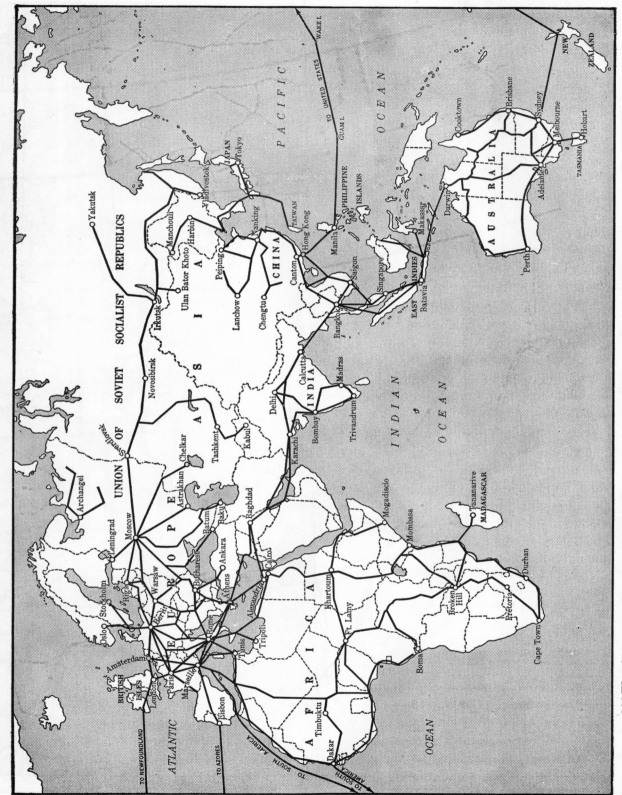

Old World airways. The black lines show the principal routes over which passenger airplanes are operated regularly.

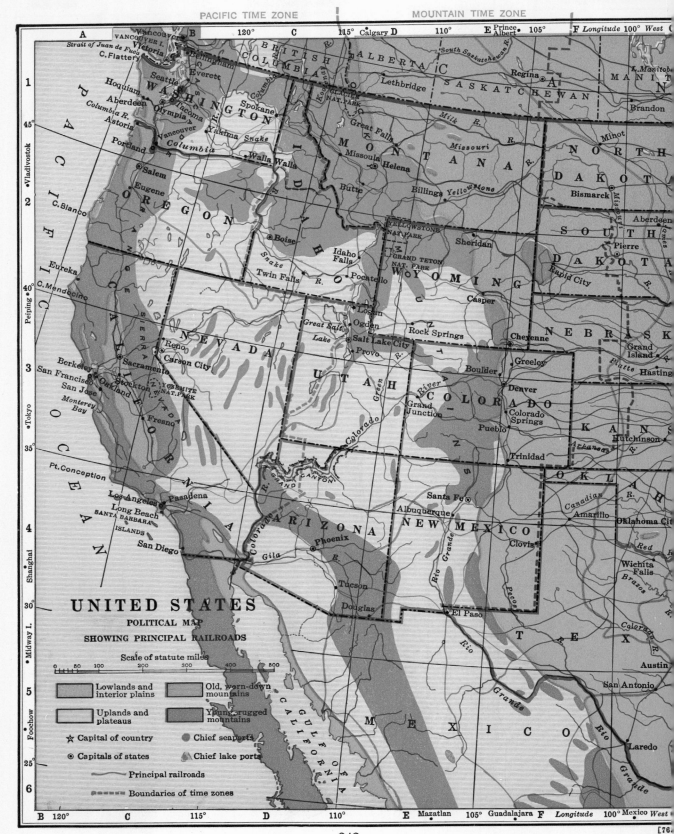

UNITED STATES

POLITICAL MAP

SHOWING PRINCIPAL RAILROADS

Scale of statute miles

| Lowlands and interior plains | Old, worn-down mountains |
| Uplands and plateaus | Young, rugged mountains |

☆ Capital of country   ● Chief seaports

◉ Capitals of states   ⛰ Chief lake ports

— Principal railroads

▬▬ Boundaries of time zones

from 95° Greenwich H 90° J 85° K 80° L 75° M 70° N

Lake Winnipeg
Winnipeg
Lake of the Woods
Grand Forks
Red L.
Fargo
L. Itasca
Duluth
Superior
St. Paul
Minneapolis
Sioux City
Council Bluffs
Lincoln
Topeka
Kansas City
Jefferson City
St. Joseph
St. Louis
MISSOURI
Joplin Springfield
Wichita
Tulsa
Muskogee
Fort Smith
ARKANSAS
Little Rock
Hot Springs
Pine Bluff
Texarkana
Dallas
Fort Worth
Waco
Shreveport
Alexandria
LOUISIANA
Beaumont
Houston
Port Arthur
Galveston Bay
Galveston
Brownsville

L. St. Joseph
Armstrong
Lake Nipigon
Port Arthur
Fort William
ISLE ROYALE
LAKE SUPERIOR
Marquette
Duluth
Superior
MICHIGAN
WISCONSIN
Green Bay
Oshkosh
La Crosse
Madison
Milwaukee
Rockford
Chicago
Joliet
Peoria
ILLINOIS
Decatur
Springfield
Terre Haute
Evansville
Cairo
TENNESSEE
Memphis
Nashville
MISSISSIPPI
Jackson
Vicksburg
Meridian
ALABAMA
Montgomery
Birmingham
Mobile
Pensacola
New Orleans
Mouths of the Mississippi R.

Hearst
Cochrane
Sault Ste. Marie
MANITOULIN I.
Escanaba
Mackinaw
Saginaw
Muskegon
Grand Rapids Flint
Bay City
Lansing
Kalamazoo
Detroit
South Bend
Gary Fort Wayne
Lima
INDIANA
Indianapolis
Covington
Frankfort
Lexington
Louisville
KENTUCKY
Chattanooga
Knoxville
Bristol
GEORGIA
Atlanta
Macon
Augusta
Columbus
Tallahassee
FLORIDA
Apalachee Bay
Tampa
St. Petersburg
Lake Okeechobee
Miami
C. Sable
Key West

North Bay
Cobalt
Sudbury
L. Nipissing
Ottawa
Toronto
L. Simcoe
Niagara Falls
LAKE ONTARIO
LAKE ERIE
Buffalo
Rochester
Cleveland
Youngstown
Akron
OHIO
Columbus
Dayton
Cincinnati
Huntington
WEST VIRGINIA
Charleston
Pittsburgh
Wheeling
PENNSYLVANIA
Harrisburg
Reading
Scranton
Winston Salem
NORTH CAROLINA
Raleigh
Charlotte
Asheville
SOUTH CAROLINA
Spartanburg
Columbia
Charleston
Savannah
Brunswick
St. Marys R.
Jacksonville
C. Canaveral

QUEBEC
L. St. John
Quebec
Sherbrooke
St. Lawrence R.
Montreal
Ottawa
Kingston
Utica
Syracuse
Schenectady
Albany
Binghamton
NEW YORK
Scranton
Newark
New York
Jersey City
LONG I.
Trenton
NEW JERSEY
Philadelphia
Wilmington
Atlantic City
Delaware Bay
Baltimore
Washington
Annapolis
Dover
DEL.
Richmond
Petersburg
Newport News
Norfolk
C. Charles
C. Henry
VIRGINIA
Lynchburg
Roanoke
Winston Salem
C. Hatteras
C. Lookout
Wilmington
C. Fear

N.B.
St. John
Fredericton
Bordeaux
Bangor
MAINE
Augusta
Lewiston
Portland
VT.
N.H.
Montpelier
Concord
Manchester
Lowell
Boston
C. Cod
MASS.
Springfield
Worcester
Fall River
Providence
CONN.
Hartford
New Haven
New York
Rome
Lisbon
Algiers
Baghdad
Jerusalem

ATLANTIC OCEAN

GULF OF MEXICO

West Palm Beach
GREAT ABACO I.
BAHAMA I.
BAHAMA ISLANDS (British)
NEW PROVIDENCE I.
ELEUTHERA I.
ANDROS IS.
Florida Strait

45°
40°
35°
30°
25°

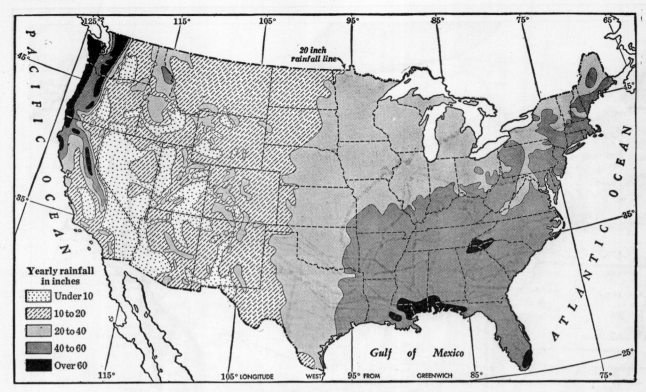

Distribution of rainfall in the United States.

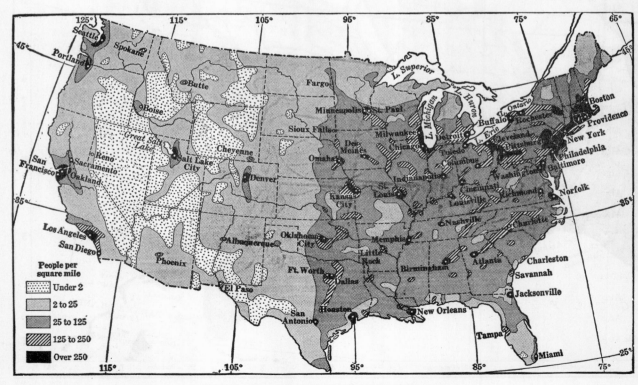

Distribution of people in the United States.

344

INDEX AND PRONOUNCING WORD LIST

NOTE. Map references are given thus: *161*, F 4. The number in italic type, *161*, = the map page; F 4 = the letter and number on the margins of the map. The F refers to the area between two meridians of longitude, and the 4 refers to the area between two parallels of latitude. The letter and the figure are to be used as guides in locating the place.

345

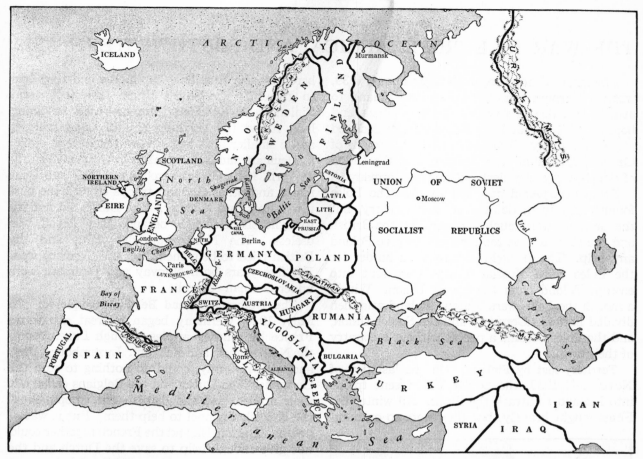

A map of Europe showing political boundaries before Germany commenced to change them in 1938.

WAR SUPPLEMENT

Foreword. The war which has just ended was called the Second World War because there was a First World War in 1914–1918. When that war was over, people hoped that there would never be another. But as years went by, men who wanted great power for themselves and their countries became leaders in Japan, Italy, and Germany. They began to build great armies, navies, and air forces, and to make plans for conquering other nations.

In 1937 Japan attacked China, and this started a war in eastern Asia. In 1939 Germany attacked Poland, and this started a war in Europe. These two wars spread far and wide until they grew into one giant war which drew in nations from all over the world.

The Second World War was between one group of nations who wished to conquer and rule the world and another group who believe, as we do, that all nations have the right to be free. The first group was led by Germany and Japan, and until September, 1943, Italy was on their side. They were called the Axis nations. Against them, on the side of freedom, were the United Nations, led by Great Britain, the United States, the Soviet Union, and China.

B

THE WAR IN EUROPE, AFRICA, AND SOUTHWESTERN ASIA

The war in Europe began on September 1, 1939, when a German army was sent into Poland to attack the Poles. Two days after this attack, and because of it, Great Britain and France declared war on Germany. Then the British dominions of Canada, Australia, New Zealand, and the Union of South Africa also declared war on Germany.

Poland conquered and divided up. The Poles fought bravely in defense of their country, but the Germans were much stronger, and the British and the French were too far away to give Poland any help. The struggle became even harder for the Poles when Russian troops were sent into eastern Poland from the Soviet Union. Within a month the Poles were beaten. Poland was then divided between Germany and the Soviet Union, and the Poles became a people without a country of their own.

Territory lost by Finland. On the last day of November, 1939, the Soviet Union sent troops into Finland to attack the Finns. All winter the Finns fought bravely, but they were so outnum-

bered by the Russians that in the end they had to give in. The Soviet Union then took from Finland the Karelian Isthmus, with adjoining land round the northern end of Lake Ladoga, and a smaller area just north of the arctic circle.

Denmark and Norway taken by Germany. Early in April, 1940, German troops marched into Denmark, and other German troops crossed the narrow waters into Norway. The Danes did not try to fight the Germans because they felt it was useless. The Norwegians did fight, and the British tried to help them, but the Germans won. For five years both Norway and Denmark were under German control.

The Netherlands and Belgium conquered. In May, 1940, Germany began a great attack on France by sending armies through Luxembourg, the Netherlands, and Belgium. Luxembourg, tiny, and with no army, could do nothing to stop the Germans. The Dutch and the Belgians called out their armies, and the British sent troops across the English Channel to help them. But it was of no use. The British and the French together could not give enough help to save the Dutch and the Belgians. Both Belgium and the Netherlands surrendered to the Germans, and the two countries were under German control until May, 1945. Little Luxembourg was annexed by Germany.

France defeated. Germany then went on with the attack against France. The German armies pushed the French armies back, and by the middle of June, 1940, the Germans were in the French capital of Paris. The French asked for an armistice; that is, for an agreement that the fighting should stop. The Germans granted the armistice and the fighting did stop, but the French had to pay for it by allowing Germany to take control of more than half of their country. Later Germany annexed outright two provinces of northeastern France: Alsace, bordering the Rhine, and Lorraine, with its rich iron mines.

After the armistice France was divided into two parts: the occupied area and the unoccupied area. Occupied France included the northern and western parts of the country and the entire

How Poland was divided after it lost its independence in 1939.

Atlantic coast. Like all the other territory conquered by Germany, it was guarded by German troops and governed by German officials. Unoccupied France was left under French control, and as its capital was at Vichy, it was called Vichy France. But even this part of France was not really free, for the French government officials had to take their orders from Germany. Some of them did so unwillingly, but there were others among them who were traitors to their country and sided with the Germans. In time the traitors gained the upper hand, and Vichy France became another enemy to the United Nations.

The battle of Britain. Many of the British soldiers who were sent across the English Channel to fight the Germans were killed. Of those who were left, many managed to get to the French port of Dunkerque. From there, in spite of terrible bombing by German planes, many thousands of the soldiers were taken back to England. All sorts of boats went over to get them, from warships to tiny launches and sailboats.

In the summer of 1940 the battle of Britain began. From bases on the coast of France the Germans sent over planes night after night to bomb the ports and the manufacturing centers of Britain. Hundreds of places were bombed again and again, and London the most of all.

The Germans hoped that the bombing would prevent the British from manufacturing enough war materials to keep on fighting, and that it would frighten the people so badly that they would be willing to make peace on any terms that Germany might offer. It did nothing of the sort. The British air force met every attack with fighter planes. The British people were not frightened; every raid made them work harder to get ready for the day when they would be able to carry the war to Germany. They repaired their damaged ports and shipyards and built more and more navy and merchant ships. They repaired their damaged factories, built new ones, and manufactured more and more guns, planes, and tanks.

The battle of Britain went on for months and months, and it was a losing battle for the Germans. It cost them so much in planes and lives and brought them so little that after the spring of 1941 they gave it up. From then on the air raids on Britain were much fewer.

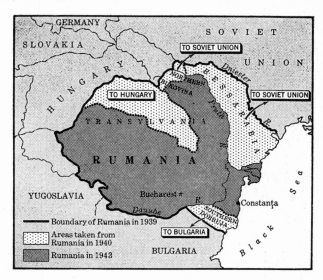

The territories lost by Rumania to the Soviet Union, Hungary, and Bulgaria in 1940.

Rumania's losses. At the end of June, 1940, the Russians took from Rumania two territories which the Rumanians had taken from them after the First World War: Bessarabia and Northern Bukovina. These territories became part of the Soviet Union in July.

The Germans wanted help from the Hungarians in the war, and so, as a bribe, they allowed Hungary to take about half of the part of Rumania known as Transylvania. This was late in August, 1940. At the same time, as another bribe for help, Germany allowed Bulgaria to take the section of southeastern Rumania known as Southern Dobruja. Thus Rumania lost land to three of its neighbors. Later both Rumania and Hungary were forced to join the Axis and to go to war on the side of Germany.

The Baltic countries taken by Russia. In July, 1940, the people of the three Baltic countries — Estonia, Latvia, and Lithuania — voted to ask to be taken into the Soviet Union. They did not do this of their own free will. They were told by the Russians that they must do it, and as they were small nations with no one to help them, they had no choice. Since then the Baltic countries have been states of the Soviet Union.

The Balkan Peninsula conquered. In April, 1939, before the European war began, Italy annexed Albania, the smallest of the Balkan countries. In June, 1940, the Italians declared war on France and Great Britain, but they had almost no part in the defeat of the French. In the last days of October, 1940, the Italians sent troops from Albania into Greece, expecting to conquer the Greeks in a very short time. The Greeks fought so bravely and so well all through the fall and winter that they pushed the Italians back into Albania, and it looked for a while as if they would be able to drive them back across the Adriatic Sea to Italy.

Things were going so badly for the Italians that the Germans had to take a hand in the Balkan Peninsula. At the beginning of March, 1941, the Bulgarians were forced to join the Axis and to allow German troops to enter their country from Rumania. Thus Bulgaria became another country at war on the side of Germany.

Late in March the Yugoslav government signed an agreement which would have made Yugoslavia an Axis partner, but the Yugoslav people rebelled and would not accept it. Early in April the Germans sent troops into Yugoslavia. The German armies quickly defeated the Yugoslavs and pushed on into Greece and Albania to help the Italians against the Greeks. The British sent forces to help the Greeks, but they could not send a big enough army to save them. By the end of April, 1941, the whole Balkan Peninsula was under Axis control. By the end of May the Germans had also captured the large Greek island of Crete, in the Mediterranean Sea.

Some of the soldiers of the Yugoslav army had escaped into the mountains, where they were joined by hundreds of strong, hardy Yugoslav mountaineers. Forming guerrilla bands, they attacked the German troops of occupation wherever they could get at them. The armies of brave Yugoslav patriots increased so fast and fought so well that the Germans had to keep sending in reinforcements to hold Yugoslavia as conquered territory.

The battle for the oil fields of Iraq. In May, 1941, after the defeat of Greece and Yugoslavia, the Germans set out to capture Iraq and the rich oil fields controlled by the British there, for they badly needed greater supplies of oil than they could get from the countries already under their control. The Germans had forced the French government in Vichy to let them use airfields in

Syria, and from there they sent bombing planes against British forces guarding the oil fields in Iraq. They got the Iraqi army to attack the British, but the Iraqi were soon beaten, and the German bombers were driven off. The Germans gave up trying to take Iraq, and the British kept control of the country and its oil fields.

The battle of Syria. Meanwhile, because Germany had the French government in Vichy in its power, the Germans were getting control of Syria. From the oil fields of Iraq a very important pipe line runs to a port on the Syrian coast. This pipe line was one of several reasons why the British had to take Syria away from the Vichy government and the Germans if they could. In June, 1941, they sent troops into Syria from Palestine and Iraq. Fighting French forces (French soldiers fighting on the side of the United Nations) helped the British, and together they got control of Syria by the middle of July.

Germany attacks the Soviet Union. On June 22, 1941, the Germans sent huge armies and air forces against the Soviet Union, attacking the Russians along a 2000-mile front from the Arctic Ocean in the north to the Black Sea in the south. In the south they had help from the Rumanians, and in the north from the Finns. Finland, by choosing to fight with the Germans against the Russians, became another Axis partner and an enemy of the United Nations.

One reason for the attack was that the Germans wanted to destroy the Russian army so as to be sure that the Russians could not attack Germany. Another reason was that the Germans wanted the rich resources of the Soviet Union: foodstuffs from its vast farm lands, iron and other metals from its mines, and, most of all, petroleum from its rich oil fields in the Caucasus region.

The Russians had large forces of soldiers and airmen, and they fought fiercely in defense of their country, but for months they had to retreat as the Germans pushed forward. In the north the Germans surrounded Leningrad, but they were not able to capture it. In central Russia they got within a few miles of Moscow, the Soviet capital. In the south they conquered the Ukraine, and they almost drove the Russians out of Crimea, the peninsula between the Sea of Azov and the Black Sea.

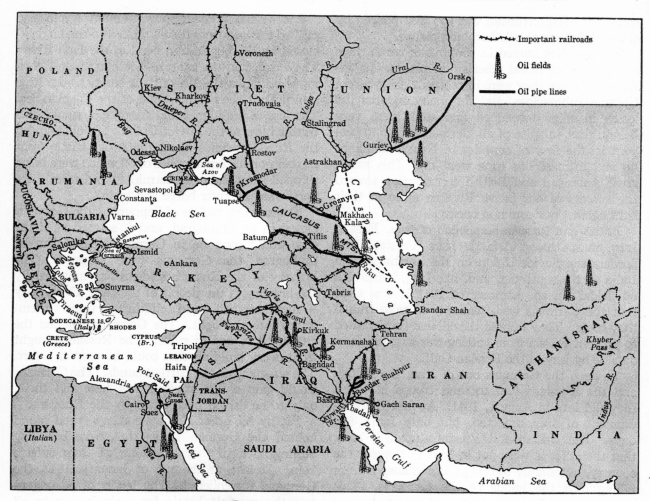

Political map of the Middle East.

Then, in December, 1941, the Russians began to drive the Germans back in a great counter-attack. All winter long, in bitter cold and deep snow, the Russians forced the Germans to retreat, a little here and a little there on the long fighting front, but the territory which they won back was only a small part of what they had lost earlier to the Germans.

By the time the first year of the Russo-German war had ended, in June of 1942, the Germans had begun another great offensive, or drive, against the Russians. Both sides were battling fiercely with fresh troops and new equipment. The Germans hoped to defeat the Russians before another winter. The Russians hoped to continue to drive the Germans back and to regain more Soviet territory.

British and American supplies for Russia. For the gigantic struggle against Germany the Soviet Union needed help from Britain and the United States in the form of war equipment and supplies. This help was not easy to give, because embattled Russia was cut off from the Atlantic Ocean and western Europe by the vast territory held by the Germans. For the first two years only two routes were open to the supply ships, and both were long and dangerous.

The northern route was round the northern end of the Scandinavian Peninsula to Arctic ports of the Soviet Union. The southern one was round the southern tip of Africa and then northward to ports of Iran on the Persian Gulf. The short cut through the Mediterranean Sea and the Suez Canal to the Persian Gulf could not be used because the Mediterranean was too well policed by enemy submarines and bombing planes.

The supplies moved in convoys of cargo ships and protecting naval vessels and planes. In the Atlantic Ocean they were in constant danger from German submarines, and for many months the losses in ships torpedoed and sunk were very heavy. But in spite of all German efforts to prevent it, the flow of supplies to Russia was kept up and increased as time went on. This was a great American and British contribution toward the success of our brave Russian allies in their fight against our common enemy.

British and Russian occupation of Iran. East of Iraq, in southwest Asia, is Iran (Persia). Iran borders the Soviet Union on the northwest and India on the southeast, and, like Iraq, it has rich oil fields. In the summer of 1941 it was clear that the Germans were planning to take Iran if they could. They wanted the oil, and they wanted to prevent Russia from getting war supplies from outside by way of the Persian Gulf.

To keep the Germans out of Iran, the British and the Russians had to send troops in. This they did late in August, 1941. At first the government of Iran objected, but only for a few days. The British and Russians made it clear that their troops were not in Iran to conquer the country, but simply to occupy it and keep it from falling into the hands of the Germans. This occupation of Iran saved the oil for the use of the United Nations and kept open the "back door" through which war supplies from Britain and the United States were reaching Russia.

The second year of the Russo-German war. The great battles of the summer of 1942 were in the south, where huge German armies with big tank divisions and thousands of planes made furious attacks on the Russians. The Russians put up such a strong defense, with so many counter-attacks, that the German advance was much slower than had been expected, but it did move eastward in spite of all that the brave Russians could do. By the middle of the summer the Germans had driven the Russians out of the peninsula of Crimea and had crossed the Don River just east of Rostov. From there they were pushing southward toward the Caucasus Mountains and the oil fields.

Meanwhile other strong German forces had pushed forward from the Ukraine into the land enclosed by the big eastern bend of the Don River. They expected to capture Stalingrad and then move on down the Volga to Astrakhan, the Russian port at the northern end of the Caspian Sea. The loss of Stalingrad and Astrakhan would be a terrific blow to the Soviet Union. It would cut off the Russian armies along the entire battle front farther north from supplies of oil which were being shipped from Baku to Astrakhan and from there northward by river barge and train.

Toward the middle of September the Germans closed in on Stalingrad, and it seemed as if the city would soon be in German hands. But at Stalingrad the Germans were stopped. The bravery of the Russian soldiers was matched by the bravery of the people of the city. Everybody — men, women, and children — threw themselves into the fight. The Germans bombed the city until it was in ruins. The Russians fought from every building that could be used as a fort. The streets were the battlegrounds. The Germans would gain a few hundred feet here and there, only to be driven back again by the Russians.

Bit by bit other Russian forces worked round behind the German forces that were besieging Stalingrad until they cut them off from outside help. At last, at the end of January, 1943, the Germans surrendered. The battle of Stalingrad was the greatest battle for a single city in all history, and it was a great Russian victory.

Meanwhile another Russian army was fighting against the German army that was moving southward through the belt of land between the Black Sea and the Caspian Sea. The Germans had captured the northernmost of the oil fields, and were pushing toward the next group round Grozny. But they never reached Grozny, and their great summer offensive ended in failure. They had taken only the least important of the Russian oil fields. They had not destroyed the Russian army. They had gained some ground in the south, but they had paid for it with millions of dead and wounded men. The Russians were still unconquered.

In December, 1942, the Russians began a big winter offensive all along the 2000-mile battle front. They recaptured much territory from the Germans, and in the north they drove back enemy troops which had been besieging Leningrad ever since the beginning of the war. In the south they pushed the Germans back to a small foothold round Novorossiisk, on the shore of the Black Sea. At the end of March, 1943, the winter campaign was over, and both sides began at once to prepare for the third summer of the war.

The retreat of the Germans in Russia. Early in July, 1943, the Germans started another offensive, but they were soon stopped. By the middle of the month the Russians began a great counter-offensive against the southern and central parts of the German lines. They drove forward with one smashing blow after another, forcing the Germans to retreat to the west, and again and again throughout the summer and autumn the victory guns in Moscow boomed as one key Russian city after another was recaptured from the enemy. The greatest Russian triumph came on November 5, when Kiev, the capital of the Ukraine, was retaken.

The tremendous Russian counter-offensive went on all through the winter and spring of 1943–1944, and it brought great victories. Fanning out from Kiev with furious attacks, the Russians sent the Germans reeling back into Poland and Rumania. In the north they drove the German forces westward to the boundary of Estonia. In the Crimean peninsula they crowded the enemy into a pocket around Sevastopol, and early in May they took that city and captured all the Germans who were not able to escape by sea.

It was now nearly three years since the Germans had first invaded the Soviet Union, expecting to destroy the Russian army and to enslave the Russian people. They had met with the failure they so richly deserved. They had been driven completely out of southern Russia, and their southern armies were being pushed deeper into

Map of the Russian-German front.

Poland and Rumania. The only Russian lands they now held were part of White Russia and narrow strips east of the boundaries of Latvia and Finland. They had lost millions of men and huge quantities of equipment. The whole Russian nation, soldiers and civilians alike, had fought so magnificently that the Germans had suffered one of the greatest defeats in all history.

On June 22, 1944, the Russians opened a great summer offensive in White Russia. Striking fast and furiously, they took one enemy stronghold after another, and the German retreat became a

Sovfoto

Buildings on a street in Stalingrad destroyed by enemy bombing.

disorderly rout. By the middle of August nearly all Soviet territory was back in Russian hands and the Russian armies had reached the border of East Prussia, and were pushing through Poland toward Germany itself.

Russia against Finland. Several times during the winter and spring of 1943-1944 the Russians gave Finland a chance to surrender before it was too late to save that country from again becoming a battleground, but the Finns refused. So, in June, 1944, the Russians began an attack to put Finland out of the war. Strong Russian armies advanced on both sides of Lake Ladoga, forcing the Finns to retreat so fast that German troops were sent to help them. By the end of the month it seemed clear that the Finns would be forced by the Germans to make a last-ditch fight, but most people believed that their surrender was only a matter of time. In September the Finnish government asked the German troops to withdraw, and made peace negotiations with Russia.

The Allied air offensive against Germany. In April, 1942, the British began a great air offensive against Germany. This was a series of terrific bombing attacks on manufacturing cities and seaports in Germany and in certain of the German-conquered countries. Canadian airmen played a major part in this offensive. Its purpose was to smash factories which were turning out German war equipment, and to force the Germans to keep

more of their fighting planes at home and in the conquered countries for defense. Thus the British helped the Russians by weakening the Germans.

In December, 1941, the United States entered the war against the Axis, and in January, 1942, began sending fighting forces to the British Isles. Big American camps and bases were built there, and since the summer of 1942 American fliers based in Britain played a big part in the bombing of Axis targets on the continent of Europe. Month after month British and American airmen kept pounding away day and night with heavier and heavier bombings of industrial cities in Germany itself and of others in France, Belgium, and the Netherlands, where the conquered peoples were forced to make war equipment for their German masters. The damage to industrial centers, railroads, ports, and bases was enormous, and seriously cut down the production of supplies needed by the Germans to continue their war against the United Nations on land, on sea, and in the air.

The war in East Africa. Since the British, the French, and the Italians had possessions in Africa, the war was bound to spread to that continent. The fighting began in the summer of 1940 between the Italians and the British in their colonies in East Africa. By the summer of 1941 the British had captured all three colonies of Italian East Africa: Ethiopia, Italian Somaliland, and

B

British Official Photo

A British cruiser tank in Libya passing a German tank hit and set on fire during an engagement with British units.

Eritrea. Ethiopia, which the Italians had conquered and annexed in 1936, was returned to its own people, under British protection.

The British against the Axis in North Africa. In the autumn of 1940 fighting between the British and the Italians began in the desert wastes of the Italian colony of Libya and the adjoining part of Egypt. Later, German forces joined the Italians and a German general took command of both. The Germans and Italians wanted to get across Egypt to gain control of the Suez Canal, and the British were determined that they should not do so.

For two years the fighting in North Africa seesawed back and forth, with first one side and then the other winning the victories. The battles were fought in terrible heat and dust, with tanks and planes playing a big part. Twice the British drove their enemies back halfway across Libya, but each time they, in turn, were driven back into Egypt.

Late in May, 1942, the Axis forces began their greatest drive to the east. By the first of July they were within seventy miles of Alexandria, the great British naval base in Egypt. Many people thought that this time the British would not be able to stop the Axis sweep to the Suez Canal, but the British did stop it. For months they held the

enemy forces along a line between the coast and a low, swampy area in the desert to the south.

Late in October, 1942, the British drove forward in a furious attack on the Axis line in the desert. This was the beginning of a great Axis retreat from Egypt all the way across Libya. The Germans and Italians fled westward, with the British forces always close on their heels. Now and then they stopped and tried to make a stand against the British, but it was of no use. By the end of November they had been driven 800 miles to the west. By early February, 1943, they had been pushed across the western border of Libya into the French colony of Tunisia. Egypt and the Suez Canal were safe at last, and the Italians had lost their entire empire in Africa.

The Americans in North Africa. On November 8, 1942, large forces of American troops landed at several places on the Atlantic and Mediterranean coasts of French North Africa. They came in hundreds of British and American ships, some directly from the United States, but more of them from the British Isles. They were fully equipped with tanks, planes, and all else needed for a big campaign.

French North Africa, made up of French Morocco, Algeria, and Tunisia, was under the

British Official Photo

An Atlantic convoy of troop and supply ships. Part of an escorting giant flying-boat is seen at the left.

control of Vichy France, but it was hoped that the French colonial troops would not put up a fight. Word was sent out to them, therefore, that the invasion was not a move against the French people, but rather a first step toward freeing them from German rule.

The landings were made at a number of different places in Morocco and Algeria. In some places the French troops did fight, but not for long. Within a few days the French colonial officials agreed to co-operate with the Americans, and this brought French Morocco and Algeria under United Nations control.

Meanwhile a British army reached Algeria, and by November 15 British and American forces had crossed the boundary from Algeria into Tunisia, where German and Italian troops held strongly fortified positions. The Allied plan was to capture Tunisia and keep the retreating Axis forces in Libya from escaping across the Mediterranean to Italy. Naturally the Germans and Italians moved swiftly to try to prevent this trapping of their forces in North Africa. From Italy and Sicily they sent additional troops and supplies across the narrow "bottleneck" of the Mediterranean to Tunisia and made ready to stop the Allied advance if they could.

The battle of Tunisia. The battle of Tunisia began at once, and all winter there was hard fighting in rain, sleet, and sticky mud. French colonial troops joined the British and Americans, and bit by bit the Allies gained ground and moved

eastward against fierce Axis defense and counter-attacks. Meanwhile the desert army of the Axis in Libya was nearing the Tunisian border, with the desert army of the British still close on its heels.

In February, 1943, when those two armies were inside Tunisia, the Allies began to close the trap, crowding the Axis forces closer and closer to the Tunisian coast. At last, on May 7, 1943, the British captured Tunis, and the Americans captured the Axis naval base of Bizerte. After that, the end came sooner than anyone had expected. Trapped in the northeastern corner of Tunisia, the Germans and Italians suddenly surrendered. By May 13 the battle of Tunisia had ended in a smashing victory for the United Nations, and the Axis had lost its last foothold on the continent of Africa.

All France occupied by the Germans. Because of the Allied invasion of French North Africa, the Germans broke a promise to the French not to send troops into Vichy France. Soon German troops were pouring down the Rhône Valley, and Vichy France lost what little independence it had had since the armistice of 1940. The entire area of France was now occupied and controlled by the Germans.

Sicily conquered. The victory in Tunisia gave the United Nations full control of the southern shores of the Mediterranean, with bases from which southern Europe could be invaded. The invasion began on July 10, 1943, when Allied

B

American and British troops landed on the southeast coast of the Italian island of Sicily. There were large German and Italian forces in Sicily, but the Italian soldiers were not very anxious to fight, and the Sicilian people were so happy over the prospect of being freed from their German-controlled government that they gave our troops a rousing welcome.

The Germans, with some help from the Italians, battled desperately to hold the island, but the Allied forces fought their way steadily northward. At the end of five weeks what were left of the enemy troops had been driven into the northeastern tip of the island and were beating a hasty retreat across the Strait of Messina into the toe of Italy. By August 17, 1943, the Allied conquest of Sicily was complete.

Italy changes sides. When Italy joined Germany against Britain and France in 1940, the Italian leaders thought they were choosing the winning side in the war. They promised the Italian people great victories and a greater empire when the war should be over. Three years later they had nothing but defeats to show for their choice. The Italians had been beaten by the Greeks, they had lost their African empire, and their country was being policed and controlled by the Germans. Their great industrial cities were being blasted by Allied bombings, and they knew that the Germans would use Italy as a battleground in order to keep the war away from Germany itself as long as possible.

Long before the invasion of Sicily, the Italian people were tired of the war and wanted to get out of it. Early in September, 1943, British and American forces landed on the toe and the heel of the Italian peninsula, and the battle for the mainland of Italy began. On September 8 Italy surrendered to the Allies, and the Italian troops which had been helping the Germans were withdrawn from the fighting. A few days later the Italian navy was turned over to the Allies. Then, on October 13, 1943, Italy declared war on Germany.

The Allies promised the Italians their freedom after the war under a democratic government of their own choice; but the decision to change sides came much too late to save Italy from becoming a battleground.

B

The Germans lose Sardinia and Corsica. One of the results of the surrender of Italy was the loss of Sardinia and Corsica by the Germans. These islands had long served as bases from which Axis planes bombed United Nations shipping in the western Mediterranean. Late in September, 1943, Italian forces, with the help of American forces, drove the Germans out of Sardinia.

As soon as the news of the Italian surrender reached Corsica, patriotic mountaineers of the island formed an army and attacked the German garrisons. They were soon joined by American Rangers and French colonial troops from North Africa, and by early October the whole island was in United Nations hands.

The battle for Italy. The Allied forces which had landed on the toe and the heel of Italy early in September, 1943, pushed northward, and by the middle of the month they had met and formed a line of offense across the peninsula north of the instep. Meanwhile other Allied forces had landed on the west coast a few miles south of Naples. After battling fiercely to hold their beachheads and to land equipment under heavy German fire, they began fighting their way toward the great Italian seaport. On October 1 they captured Naples. The next goal was Rome.

The battle for Italy now became a hard-fought struggle between the German line of defense across the peninsula and the Allied line of offense. The mountainous land made the offense harder than the defense, but the Allies kept on attacking, driving the Germans back a bit here and a bit there. Winter came, with rain, sleet, and snow that made the going terribly hard, and the Germans kept bringing reinforcements from northern Italy to strengthen their line. Month after month the Allies battled on, but they made slow headway. Spring came, and still they had not reached the Italian capital.

In May, 1944, the Allies began a much heavier offensive against the German line. This time the Germans reeled back, and on June 4 the Allies captured Rome. The Germans were now in full retreat with the Allies close on their heels. By April, 1945, the battle front in Italy had been pushed north of the Po, and more than three fourths of the peninsula was in Allied hands.

Political map of the Mediterranean region.

The war in the Mediterranean Sea. Ever since the Suez Canal was built, the Mediterranean Sea has been a very important short cut for shipping between the Atlantic and Pacific oceans. For many years before the war the British controlled this route because they held the key points to its use: Gibraltar at its western end, the island of Malta in its narrow "waistline," and the island of Cyprus and the Suez Canal at its eastern end. In times of peace they kept it open for the ships of all nations.

After Italy entered the war, in June, 1940, the Mediterranean Sea and the air above it became a battleground. With submarines, surface craft, and bombing planes the Germans and Italians tried to stop the British from using the Mediterranean route to deliver troops and supplies to Egypt, the main British base for all the fighting in northern and northeastern Africa. They succeeded in making the Mediterranean so dangerous that all the supply ships bound for Egypt had to take the long route to the south around Africa and up the Red Sea.

Most of all, the Axis wanted to knock out Malta, the great British naval and air base in the mid-Mediterranean. They bombed it many hundreds of times, but the people bore the raids heroically, and the British air forces based there met every attack with fighter planes and antiaircraft fire. The damage was often great, but no sooner was it done than all hands set to work to repair it. In spite of all the Axis could do at sea and in the air, British ships kept plowing the dangerous waters of the western Mediterranean to carry supplies to Malta, and it stood firm as a strong United Nations base.

By January, 1944, the Mediterranean had become much safer for United Nations shipping. There was no longer any danger from the Italian navy; and Sicily, Sardinia, Corsica, and all the smaller islands in the western Mediterranean which the Axis had used as naval and air bases

B

were in Allied hands. In the eastern Mediterranean the Germans still held Crete and the Dodecanese Islands, but German bombers from those bases were doing little damage, because the Germans needed most of their air force on the Russian and Italian fronts and in western Europe. Soon United Nations supply ships were going through to Egypt, and supplies for Russia were taking the Mediterranean short cut to the Persian Gulf. The battle for control of the Mediterranean Sea had been won by British-American teamwork.

The Allied invasion of France. In June, 1944, the Allies opened another fighting front in western Europe. The Germans had expected an invasion of their conquered lands from the west and had built strong defenses along the Dutch, Belgian, and French coasts. The Allies had prepared for it by training millions of American, Canadian, and British soldiers in England and gathering together enormous quantities of equipment.

On the night of June 5–6 four thousand ships carried the invasion forces across the English Channel to France. Mine sweepers cleared the way, and a huge "umbrella" of fighter planes gave protection against German air attack. The landings were made on open beaches on the coast of Normandy between Cherbourg and Le Havre. Fighting hard, the invasion forces won their beachheads and began battling their way inland against the German defenders. In three days they held a solid strip of coast and had captured several important inland towns.

The first big objective was to capture Cherbourg, so that the Allies would have a first-class port for landing more troops and supplies. This task was assigned to American troops. The German forces had been ordered to hold Cherbourg at all cost, and they put up a fierce fight; but our troops battered their way west, and on June 27 the great port was in our hands. Cherbourg was the first large French city to be liberated from German control.

Meanwhile British troops were fighting equally hard for Caen, the key point on the main railroad from Cherbourg to Paris. By the end of July Caen and the entire Cherbourg peninsula had been captured by Allied forces.

The invasion was the beginning of the liberation of the French people from four years of conquest and enslavement by the Germans. The Allied troops then drove westwood to Brest, south toward the Loire, and eastward in the direction of Paris. On August 15 further Allied landings took place on the Mediterranean coast of France. With the Russians rolling toward Germany from the east and the Allies pressing in from France and Italy in the south and from France in the west, the Germans were having to fight on four fronts, and everywhere they were being forced to withdraw.

The drive across France. The Allied armies drove ahead across France in the battle of Europe with amazing speed. While endeavoring to drive the enemy from the air, airmen pounded German military targets and attacked German cities. Ground forces, with their powerful, fast-moving tanks, drove the enemy back and broke holes in their defense lines. On August 25 Paris was freed from German occupation, and by the middle of September the greater part of France had been liberated. Canadian and British armies were moving across Belgium toward the Netherlands, and parachute troops were dropped in from transport planes to take possession of vital areas. The Germans used their best troops in an attempt to hold this coastal country. Southward three American armies were making a fierce drive to gain control of the gateways into southern Germany.

The march into Germany. When the march toward Germany began, the Eastern and Western Allies were 2300 miles apart. For the Russians the march began in November, 1942, in the foothills of the Caucasus, and for the Americans and British it began in June, 1944, on the beaches of Normandy. The Soviets had to fight their way across 1500 miles of plains and forests and across the Dnieper, Vistula, and Oder rivers. Between August, 1944, and April, 1945, they had signed armistices with Rumania, Bulgaria, and Hungary. They had brought about the fall of Vienna in Austria, and had battered their way into Berlin.

By April, 1945, American, Canadian, and British troops had broken the main defense line of the Germans in the West, had crossed the Rhine, and were advancing into central Germany. Belgium and part of the Netherlands had been cleared of Germans. Canadian units had cut off

A map of Europe showing territory held by Germany at its greatest extent.

A map of Europe on the eve of Germany's surrender.

all remaining troops in the Netherlands from land communication with Germany.

While the ground forces were fighting so valiantly, warplanes of five air forces had gained complete mastery of the air and had driven the German air force out of existence.

On April 26, 1945, after an 800-mile march across France and Germany, Americans joined the Russians at Torgau, on the Elbe River in the heart of Germany, cutting the country in two. By May 3, British and Russian troops had linked up on the Baltic coast, and the British had advanced to cut off the Danish peninsula at the north. Canadian forces had crossed into Germany from the Netherlands, and American and French forces were dealing out crushing blows to the enemy in the south. Berlin had been captured. Germany's collapse was near.

Victory for the Allies. Between May 5 and May 7 all German-held territory was surrendered unconditionally to the Allies. German troops in Italy, southern and western Austria, northwestern Germany, the Netherlands, and Denmark were the first to surrender. They were followed by troops in southern Germany, Norway, Czechoslovakia, and Yugoslavia.

Thus the first part of the Second World War came to an end after more than five years and eight months of fighting. Immediately after the surrender of Germany, Allied authorities moved to occupy the country. Plans were also put into effect to send troops from the European area to the Far Eastern area in an effort to defeat Japan. You will read about the war with Japan beginning on the following page.

THE WAR IN EASTERN ASIA, AUSTRALIA, AND THE PACIFIC

Japan against China. When the Japanese attacked the Chinese, in July, 1937, they were fully prepared for war. The Chinese were poorly prepared, and although they fought bravely, their armies were soon driven out of North China. Then the Japanese pushed southward, and before the year was ended, they had captured and almost destroyed Shanghai, and also Nanking, the capital of China.

The Chinese moved their capital up the Yangtze River to Hankow, but by the autumn of 1938 the Japanese had conquered the eastern part of Middle China and captured Hankow. They had also captured Canton and other ports on the coast of South China. Again the Chinese moved their capital, this time far inland to Chungking, in the Szechwan Basin. The country was thus divided into two parts: Occupied China, which was controlled by the Japanese army, and Free China, which was controlled by the Chinese.

After the capture of Hankow, millions of Chinese people traveled inland by any means they could find, mostly on foot, to the Szechwan Basin and other parts of the interior of Free China. There they built a new China. Cities and towns doubled and redoubled their population, and new ones sprang up. Factories for the manufacture of war supplies were built. Schools and colleges were established.

In order to keep on fighting from the interior of the country, the Chinese needed far more war supplies than they could produce. With all their ports so far away, and with most of them in the hands of the Japanese, they could not get supplies by sea. So, with picks and shovels, thousands of Chinese men and women went to work and built the Burma Road.

The Burma Road winds for hundreds of miles through rugged mountains. It connects the end of a road running south from Chungking with the end of a railroad running north from Rangoon, the largest port of Burma. As soon as it was finished, in 1939, it became China's "life line" for the transportation of supplies needed for carrying on the war.

To many people in the outside world the withdrawal into the interior seemed a sign of the defeat of China. It was just the opposite. It was the beginning of the magnificent fight which the brave Chinese people put up to drive the Japanese out of their country and to keep themselves a free nation.

Japan's push to the south. The Japanese had not expected that it would take very long to conquer China, but after the autumn of 1938 they made little headway. Their troops held the parts of the country which they had already taken, but whenever they tried to conquer more, sooner or later the Chinese armies thrust them back. For four and a half years the Chinese fought the Japanese alone, and when at last the British and Americans became their allies, they were worse off than before. This was because the Japanese soon took so much territory to the south and east of China that the whole country was blockaded and it was harder than ever for the Chinese to get supplies from outside. As late as the spring of 1944, an American air force fighting in China was the only armed help which the Chinese had received inside their own borders from their allies.

Early in 1941 the Japanese began to move southward from China. Within a few months they had French Indo-China and Thailand (Siam) under their control. It was thought that by these moves the Japanese were trying to get into a position to attack the interior of China from the south, but they were planning a much greater move, as was evident in the last month of 1941.

Japan against the United States and Britain. Early on the morning of December 7, 1941, without a word of warning, Japanese bombing planes made a savage attack on the American naval and air base at Pearl Harbor, in the Hawaiian Islands. The United States forces were taken by surprise, and before the Japanese planes were driven off, many American ships and planes were destroyed. As a result of this attack, the people of the United States immediately became fighting partners of the British and the other nations battling against the Axis in the Second World War.

B

At the same time, the Japanese attacked the tiny American Pacific islands of Midway, Wake, and Guam, and they landed troops in the Philippine Islands. They also attacked the British island of Hong Kong, just off the coast of South China, near Canton.

The Americans had very small forces of soldiers in Midway, Wake, and Guam, but they fought magnificently. Guam, the least well protected, was taken by the Japanese during the first week of the war. Wake held out longer. The Japanese did not capture it until the day before Christmas, and they paid a high price for it in lives, planes, and ships. At Midway the Americans beat off the Japanese, and this Pacific outpost was not captured.

The British forces in Hong Kong fought with equal bravery, but they too were forced to give in. They surrendered on Christmas Day, and the Japanese took over the island.

The battle for the Philippines. In the Philippine Islands an army of Americans and Filipinos put up another magnificent fight. The Japanese came with warships, swarms of planes, and an army much larger than the American army to capture the islands. They landed at several places on the coast of Luzon, the largest of the islands, and worked their way toward Manila, the capital city. American troops fought them every step of the way, but they captured Manila on January 2, 1942.

Meanwhile the Japanese had also landed troops in the southern part of the island of Mindanao, but the Philippines as a whole were by no means conquered. Even in Luzon, the Japanese had not yet succeeded in their purpose. Corregidor, the island fortress at the entrance to Manila Bay, was still in American hands, and the main American-Filipino army was in the Bataan Peninsula, between the bay and the South China Sea.

The Japanese wanted to use Manila Bay as a naval base, and they could not do so while American forces still held Bataan and Corregidor. For more than three months they poured fresh troops by thousands into Bataan, with hundreds of tanks and bombing planes. Their army outnumbered the Americans ten to one. They had control of the air with their planes; the Americans had hardly any planes. The Japanese had control of the South China Sea with their navy, and there

was no way for fresh American troops to reach Bataan. For every ship that managed to deliver equipment and supplies to the Americans, two were sunk by the Japanese.

Never in any war has an army fought more bravely with everything against it than did the men in the mountains and jungles of Bataan. By the middle of January they were short of food, but they never thought of giving in. They fought on until they were too weak from hunger and sickness to fight any longer. On April 9, 1942, they were forced to give up. The Japanese had at last captured Bataan, but they had been made to pay a high price for it in lives, equipment, and time.

But the capture of Bataan still did not give the Japanese control of Manila Bay, for the American flag still flew over Corregidor Fortress. The Japanese began a terrific attack on the fortress, battering it with shells from big guns at Manila and on Bataan, and bombing it day and night from the air. No help from outside could reach the little force of brave defenders; yet they held out for another four weeks. Finally, on May 6, 1942, the Japanese were able to land troops on the island, and there was nothing left for the defenders to do but surrender. This ended the five months' battle for the Philippines, but it did not end the firm determination of the American people and their leaders that the day should come, and as soon as possible, when the Filipinos should be freed.

Malaya and Singapore captured. Before the Japanese struck at the Philippines, they had troops in Thailand. Early in December, 1941, these troops began to push southward through the jungles of the Malay Peninsula. They were headed for British Malaya with its plantations and mines which supplied most of the rubber and tin used by the United States and Great Britain. The Japanese wanted the tin and rubber, and they knew that the loss of British Malaya would be a heavy blow to the British and Americans. They wanted also to capture the great British island fortress of Singapore, which guards the shortest shipping route between the Indian and Pacific oceans.

The British had too few troops in Malaya, and at the very beginning of the battle two of their great battleships were sunk off the coast by the Japanese. Their troops were forced to retreat

B

as the Japanese pushed southward, and by the first of February, 1942, they had lost the whole peninsula. Nothing was left now but Singapore, and this the British tried desperately to hold.

From across the narrow strait which separates the island from the mainland, the Japanese battered Singapore with shells from big guns and bombs from bombing planes. They destroyed its water supply, and finally they were able to land troops on the island. On February 15, 1942, the British were forced to surrender, and the Japanese took over the great fortress for their own uses.

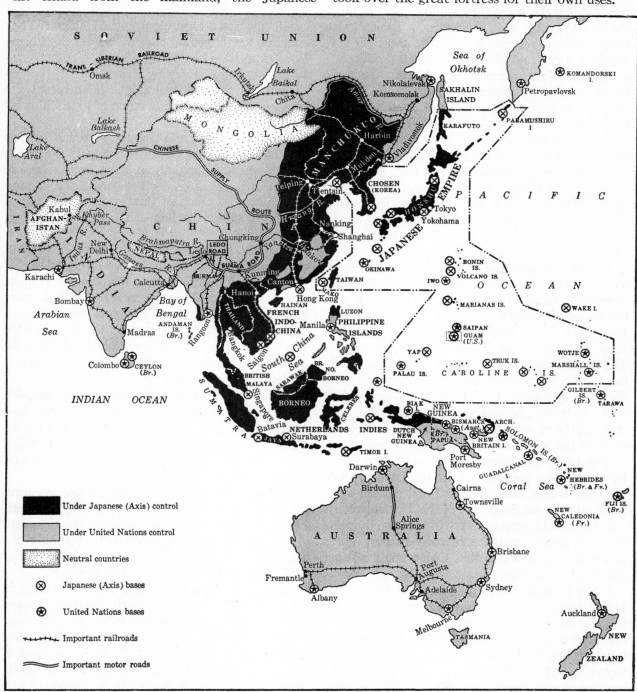

The Far East, June 1, 1945.

The battle for the East Indies. Long before the fall of Singapore, the Japanese made an attack on the large island of Borneo. By Christmas, 1941, they had captured most of the British part of the island, where there are valuable oil fields. It was clear that the Japanese were now beginning to strike for the prize they wanted most of all in southeast Asia: the Netherlands Indies, with their wealth of oil, rubber, and tin, and their vast supplies of rice and other agricultural products.

Soon the Japanese were bombing naval and air bases in the Netherlands Indies, and landing troops here and there in Celebes, Dutch Borneo, and Sumatra. The Dutch had an army in Java, and a small navy and air force, and they used them to the limit to fight off the Japanese. They had help from American, British, and Australian air and naval forces. There were great naval and air battles in which the Japanese lost many ships and planes, but the Allies also had heavy losses. Their combined strength was not so great as that of the Japanese.

Bit by bit the Japanese closed in on Java. They bombed the Dutch naval base at the port of Surabaya, and they finally managed to land troops on the island. The army of Dutch and Javanese soldiers fought bravely, but on March 7, 1942, the battle for the East Indies was over. The islands were in Japanese control, but not in the condition in which the Japanese would have liked to find them. The Dutch had done all they could to lessen the value of the conquest by destroying the oil wells and the buildings and equipment of the ports, airfields, and naval bases.

The battle for Burma. Meanwhile the battle for Burma was going on. Late in January, 1942, Japanese troops from Thailand had pushed westward into the southern part of this British colony. Their two main purposes were to take the Burmese oil fields and to cut the railroad running north to the Burma Road so that China could not get supplies by that route.

Little by little the British army in Burma was forced to retreat westward and northward. At the end of about seven weeks the Japanese had captured Rangoon and cut the railroad connecting that port with the Burma Road. Chinese forces joined the British in trying to stop the northward advance of the Japanese, but their com-

bined numbers were far too small and they had too little support from fighting and bombing planes. By the early summer of 1942 the battle for Burma was lost, and what was left of the small British army had retreated westward into India. Burma had been added to the list of Japanese conquests in southeast Asia.

All this was a hard blow to the Chinese. They could no longer get supplies by way of the Burma Road, and they had to fight hard to stop the invasion of their country by that route. If that invasion had succeeded, it might have meant the capture of Chungking and much of Free China by the Japanese.

In order to give the Chinese as much help as possible, the United Nations arranged for supplies to be flown to Chungking in planes from a base in Assam, a province of northeastern India. American pilots did much of this work, and it helped greatly to offset the loss of the Burma Road as a supply route.

Australia in danger. Toward the end of January, 1942, Japanese troops landed on the islands of the Bismarck Archipelago, in the Solomon Islands, and at points on the northern side of eastern New Guinea and began building bases there. From these bases they were expected to try to invade Australia. This fear increased when, later on, the Japanese began to bomb the Australian naval and air base at Port Darwin.

Meanwhile Port Moresby, on the southern side of eastern New Guinea, was made a strong Australian base. An east-west range of high mountains formed a barrier between the Australian forces at Port Moresby and the Japanese forces on the other side of the island.

In the spring of 1942 there were American army and air forces in Australia, and part of the American navy was in Australian waters. American and Australian fliers were continually bombing the Japanese in the islands to the north and northeast and their ships in the surrounding waters.

The battle of the Coral Sea. Beginning early in March, 1942, there was much fighting between Japanese and American-Australian naval and air forces in the Coral Sea. Then, early in May, came a big showdown in that sea. A large force of Japanese ships and planes, thought to be on its way to try to invade Australia, was defeated in a

From Ewing Galloway

A Japanese cruiser at Midway after having been bombed by United States naval aircraft.

five-day battle by the American and Australian forces. This was the first big victory of the United Nations over the Japanese in the southwest Pacific.

The battle of Midway. About a month later, in early June, 1942, another great Japanese naval and air force was discovered in the Pacific, headed for Midway, the American base northwest of the Hawaiian Islands. First the Army and Marine planes from Midway attacked the Japanese, and then Navy planes from aircraft carriers of the United States Pacific fleet joined in the fighting. The battle lasted three days. When it was over, about one fourth of the Japanese ships had been sunk or badly damaged, and the rest were steaming westward in a hasty retreat to the bases from which they had come. This was a second great victory at sea over the Japanese. They had hoped to capture Midway and then move on to attack the Hawaiian Islands. By stopping them and forcing them to turn back, the hard-fighting airmen prevented that disaster.

The Japanese in the Aleutian Islands. While the battle of Midway was going on, the Japanese managed to land troops on three small islands at the western end of the Aleutian chain. These landings were on American territory, and they were made under cover of the fog in which the Aleutian Islands are hidden much of the time. On

Kiska, the largest of the three islands, the Japanese began building an air and submarine base. Later they gave up one of the islands, but they held on to Kiska and to Attu, the westernmost island.

Month after month American forces from bases farther east in the Aleutians tried to blast the Japanese out of the islands by bombing raids. The raids did much damage, but they did not drive the Japanese out. Finally, on May 11, 1943, American troops made a surprise landing on Attu, and by the end of the month that island had been recaptured. On August 15 American and Canadian forces landed on Kiska. To their amazement they found the enemy gone. Expecting the landing and knowing that they could not hold the island against our attack, the Japanese had managed to sneak away a few nights earlier in the fog and darkness. All the Aleutians were now back in American hands, and from bases on the western ones our planes soon began bombing the northernmost of the islands of the Japanese Empire.

The battle of the Solomon Islands. During the spring and early summer of 1942 the Japanese were strengthening their bases on New Guinea and the Solomon Islands. It was clear that from the Solomons they intended to push southeastward, taking more of the islands in the southwest Pacific until they could cut the supply route from the United States to Australia.

B

On August 7, 1942, the United Nations took a step to try to stop this dangerous Japanese push to the southeast. American troops made hard-fought landings on two of the easternmost of the Solomon Islands. On Guadalcanal, the larger of the two islands, they captured a big airfield which the Japanese had just finished building. These landings were only "toe holds" in the Solomons, but they were held week after week against repeated Japanese attacks.

The battle of the Solomons soon became the big part of the war in the southwest Pacific. Land, sea, and air forces on each side were trying with all their might to destroy the forces of the other. One naval fight after another took place. American planes bombed Japanese positions, and their planes returned the bombing. In the middle of November, 1942, American forces won a really great victory. They went into battle against a strong Japanese fleet which was to land fresh troops and supplies on Guadalcanal, and they smashed it so badly that all the ships that were able to get away retreated as fast as they could.

The Australian-American drive in New Guinea. In the meantime combined Australian and American forces were fighting the enemy in New Guinea. Early in September, 1942, Japanese troops crossed the mountain range in eastern New Guinea from their bases on the northern side of the island and began moving down the southern slopes, headed for Port Moresby. As soon as it was known that they were on the march, Australian and American forces moved out of Port Moresby, bent on driving them back.

The Japanese got as far as the plains at the foot of the mountains, but there they were turned back. As they retreated over the mountain route, the Australians and Americans followed them. They were chased by ground troops and bombed by planes. In a few weeks Allied land, sea, and air forces were attacking the Japanese bases on the northern coast of New Guinea, and the fighting there became part of the great battle of the southwest Pacific.

The battles on land and sea in the southwest Pacific in the summer and fall of 1942 took so much of Japan's strength in troops, ships, and planes that the Japanese were unable to carry out their plan of taking more islands farther east in the South Pacific and cutting the American supply route to Australia. Keeping that route safely beyond Japanese reach was in itself a great United Nations victory.

The war in the southwest Pacific in 1943–1944. In 1943 the fighting in the southwest Pacific grew more furious. The Japanese fought fiercely to hold their bases in the Solomon Islands, in the Bismarck Archipelago, and on the northern coast of New Guinea. The Americans and Australians fought just as fiercely to drive the Japanese out of those bases. It was a year of great naval and air battles and of hard fighting by ground troops in the tropical jungles.

By the end of January the Japanese had been cleared out of the part of New Guinea known as Papua, and early in February our American forces wiped out the last of the enemy force on Guadalcanal. Early in March Allied planes won another smashing victory by destroying a whole fleet of Japanese troop and supply ships in the battle of the Bismarck Sea, off the coast of New Guinea.

In June our forces began what was called "island hopping." They landed on one after another of the Solomon Islands north of Guadalcanal, and by hard fighting they destroyed the Japanese garrisons. By the end of the year they had taken all of the Solomons and had made landings on the western end of New Britain Island in the Bismarck Archipelago. Meanwhile other Allied forces had pushed slowly but surely westward along the north coast of New Guinea, blasting the Japanese from bases there.

The first six months of 1944 brought the Japanese nearer to defeat in the southwest Pacific. American planes and ships bombed and shelled the enemy bases and made it harder and harder for Japanese ships to deliver much needed supplies. Allied troops captured more bases and airfields on New Guinea, New Britain, and smaller islands round about. In April Allied forces landed on the north coast of Dutch New Guinea and continued to push westward. Before the end of June, Biak Island, off the coast still farther west, had been taken, and this gave the Allies an air base only 880 miles from the Philippine Islands. At the beginning of July, 1944, the Japanese were still battling desperately to hold their remaining bases in the southwest Pacific. On July 21

American troops landed on Guam, thus opening another road to the Philippine Islands.

Taking Japan's inner defenses. In November, 1943, American forces captured the Gilbert Islands from the Japanese. This opened what soon came to be called the war in the central Pacific. Its purpose was to break through the islands that formed Japan's inner defenses, thus getting air and naval bases nearer Japan itself, and to clear the way for landing American troops in the Philippines and on the east coast of China later on.

Early in 1944 we took the main Japanese bases in the Marshall Islands. The enemy positions were first softened up by terrific bombing and shelling; then the troops landed and in hard fighting wiped out the enemy garrisons. In the following months the Caroline Islands and the Marianas were bombed and shelled again and again. Our fleet prevented Japanese reinforcements from reaching the Carolines, and the bases on those islands were so badly damaged that by late spring they were of little further use to the enemy.

On June 14, 1944, our troops landed on Saipan, in the Marianas, the key point in Japan's inner defenses. Saipan is only 1500 miles from Tokyo, and the Japanese could not afford to lose it. The troops on the island put up a fierce fight, and the Japanese sent several hundred carrier-based planes to help them. Our own airmen shot down nearly all the planes and then went after the fleet from which they had been launched. They found it midway between the Marianas and the Philippines, and they scored another great victory. Many of the enemy ships were sunk, and what was left of the battered fleet beat a hasty retreat. By the end of July Saipan was in American hands, and since November we had moved 2000 miles nearer to Japan proper.

Japan bombed. On June 15, 1944, the Japanese got another heavy blow. Huge American bombers from bases in China raided the great iron-and-steel center of Yawata on Kyushu, one of the four main islands of Japan. This raid did much damage, and it warned the Japanese that from now on their homeland was in danger.

The battle for the Peiping-Canton railroad. By the spring of 1944 Japan's supply route by sea to southeast Asia was almost blocked by American submarines and by American and Chinese bombers from newly built bases in the eastern part of Free China. The Japanese knew, as the June raid on Yawata soon proved, that these bases were dangerously near Japan proper. They also knew that with their inner island defenses in the Pacific crumbling, it was only a matter of time before it would be possible for American troops to land on the China coast to help the Chinese.

In face of these dangers they set out to capture the entire Peiping-Canton railroad. They already held the greater part of the northern section of the line, between Peiping and Hankow, and by the middle of May they had taken most of the remainder of that section. Then they began a big offensive against the Chinese who were holding the southern section. By the end of June they had taken about half of the railroad between Hankow and Canton, and had driven the Chinese and Americans out of one of the most important of the new air bases.

This was a setback for the American and Chinese allies, for if the Japanese had succeeded in their purpose, they would have had a supply route by land between their conquered territories in North China and southeast Asia. They would also have held a north-south strip of land in Free China where they could make a stand if Allied troops should advance inland from the coast to join forces with the Chinese. This would not have prevented the well-deserved defeat that was surely coming to the Japanese, but there was a chance that it might lengthen the war in Asia and make it more costly in Chinese and American lives.

Help for the Chinese in Burma. In 1943 British, Indian, Chinese, and American forces began co-operating in northern Burma to open a new supply route from Ledo, in the Indian province of Assam, to a point on the Burma Road just inside the Chinese border. The Ledo Road was being built as fast as the Allies could clear out the Japanese who were trying to prevent its completion. Month after month there was desperate fighting in the mountains and steaming jungles, but bit by bit the Japanese were forced to give way. In July, 1944, it looked as if the time were not far distant when supplies for China would be rolling in over the Ledo-Burma Road.

The Allies invade the Philippines. When American troops were forced to surrender the Philippine Islands to the Japanese in May, 1942, they promised that they would return to the islands, and return they did. On October 20, 1944, American troops, supported by American naval and air forces, made a successful landing on Leyte Island in the central Philippines. By the end of December the occupation of the island by the Americans was complete. Earlier in that month American troops had made a landing on Mindoro Island and in a short time had established air bases there and provided themselves with a springboard for the invasion of Luzon. Thus by the end of 1944 the Allied line in the Pacific had been extended from Mindoro in the Philippines west to Saipan in the Marianas, and northwest to the tip of the Aleutian Islands. In the meantime American naval and air forces had been pounding away at Japanese holdings from Paramushiru, one of the Kurile Islands, southward. They had destroyed hundreds of Japanese ships and aircraft.

Between the end of the year 1944 and May, 1945, Luzon and most of the other islands of the Philippine group had been conquered, and the Americans had also captured the island of Iwo and had invaded Okinawa, one of the Ryukyu group of islands. Australian troops had taken the island of Tarakan, off Borneo, and the British had cleared most of the Japanese out of Burma.

The last months of the war. The Allies knew how vital the conquest of Okinawa would be to them. The island is only about 330 miles from the Japanese mainland. The occupation of it would give the Allies bases from which operations in the invasion of Japan itself could be carried on. Knowing this, the Japanese defended the island for all they were worth. Thousands of them dug into Okinawa's many caves, from which they were difficult to dislodge. Furious fighting went on week after week until June 21, when the island fell to the Allies. The battle of this island was one of the fiercest and the most costly in number of killed and wounded of any battle in the Pacific. But when it was won, this sixty-two-mile-long island provided a springboard for the assault of Japan proper and the part of China occupied by the Japanese.

With the successful invasion of the inner defenses of Japan, especially the capture of Okinawa, the backbone of the Japanese fleet and air power was broken, but the main strength of the army was still intact. However, the Allies far surpassed the Japanese in the number of battleships and other naval vessels in the Pacific and in the number of planes. In strength of land troops the Japanese exceeded the strength of the combined American, British, and Australian troops by several divisions.

Up to the capture of Okinawa the Japanese still held most of the east coast of China, with its rivers and railroads, and the land route that they had developed from Manchukuo to Singapore; but American and Chinese air power was increasing in China, more and more equipment was reaching Chinese troops, and a pipeline had been built from Assam to carry oil into China.

The Allies fought on and on, determined to bring about Japan's defeat as they had brought about the defeat of Germany. In central China, in the jungles of Burma, in the forests of Borneo, New Guinea, and New Britain the fighting continued. British and American fleet forces pounded the Japanese islands with rockets, bombs, and shells. Planes dropped thousands of tons of explosives on Japan in a single day. On August 6 an atomic bomb, the most destructive weapon of war yet invented, was dropped on Hiroshima, in the southern part of Honshu, the largest island of Japan proper, with tragic results. Two days later Russia declared war on Japan and moved swiftly into Manchukuo. On August 9 a second atomic bomb was dropped on Nagasaki, on the island of Kyushu, destroying a large part of this important seaport.

By August 10 the Japanese announced that they were ready to surrender and asked for Allied terms. These were promptly given to them and were accepted by the Japanese August 14. On September 3, 1945, Japan time, the final surrender papers were signed, and this brought the Second World War to an end.

B

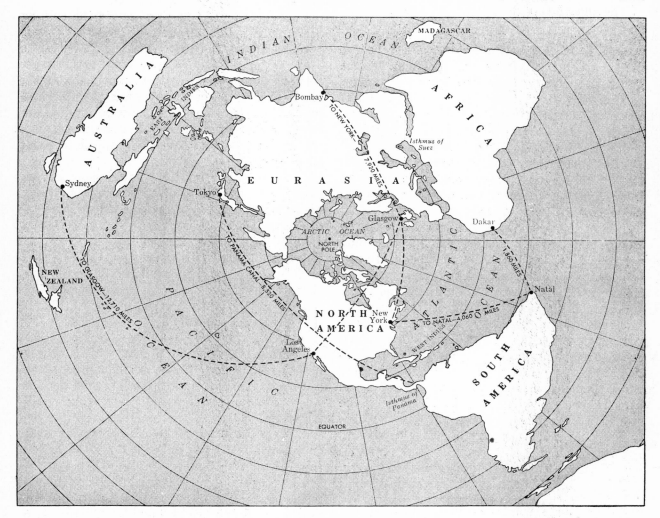

A polar projection map of the world.

A MAP FOR STUDYING THE GEOGRAPHY OF THE WAR

The war between the United Nations and the Axis nations was a new kind of war, different in many ways from all the wars that preceded it. One great difference was that this war was fought over a vastly larger area of the earth than any earlier one. Fighting took place in or near every continent except uninhabited Antarctica and on all the connecting seas and oceans. The war was fought in so many different parts of the world that it is called a "global war."

Another great difference was that this war was fought as much in the air as on the land or the sea. Armies and navies played a large part in it,

but most people believed that it would be won by the side whose army and naval forces had the greatest support from the fighting, bombing, and transport planes of its air forces.

In order to understand the geography of this global war you need a map such as the one given here; a map which shows how the inhabited lands of the earth are arranged in relation to one another and in relation to the oceans.

The map is drawn with its center at the north pole. It is not a full world map, but it shows all the inhabited lands of the earth. Notice that the meridians of longitude extend outward (southward) from the pole just as the spokes of a wheel extend outward from the hub. Notice also that the parallels of latitude form circles with the north pole as their center, and that they become larger with increasing distance from that point.

The map shows that the inhabited lands of the earth cluster round the Arctic Ocean. North America and Eurasia together almost encircle that ocean. South America, connected with North America by the Isthmus of Panama, extends southward far beyond the equator, somewhat like a pendant hanging from the main bracelet of the lands to the north.

Africa, connected with southwest Asia by the Isthmus of Suez, is another pendant extending southward beyond the equator. This continent, however, is so close to Europe and southwest Asia that it is almost part of the Eurasian land mass.

Australia is wholly south of the equator; but between this island continent and southeast Asia are the islands of the East Indies, which are like steppingstones between the one continent and the other. Thus Australia is like a third pendant, which is almost, but not quite, attached to the main bracelet of lands in the Northern Hemisphere.

The map shows also that the four oceans are not separate bodies of water; they form one vast world-ocean. This world-ocean, with its seas, gulfs, and bays, is the highway which all ships must use, in times of peace and war alike, to get from one part of the earth to another.

In studying the geography of the war you will want to remember that the shortest route between any two points on the earth is the one which, in connecting them, follows the curve of the earth's surface. All such routes are called "great circle" routes. They are very important in connection with transportation by sea and by air. A study of some of the sample routes drawn on the map will help you to understand why.

The line from Los Angeles to Sydney, Australia, is the great circle route by which the distance between those two ports is the shortest. Ships as well as planes can follow this route; ships because there is no land barrier in the way, and planes because their highway is the air. In

the air there are no barriers except the shifting ones of clouds and storms.

The line on the map from Los Angeles to Glasgow, in Scotland, is the great circle route between those two ports, and is about 5200 miles long. This is one of the many short cuts which only a plane can use. A ship bound for Glasgow from Los Angeles must take the roundabout route through the Panama Canal, a distance of about 8500 miles.

The great circle routes from Glasgow to New York and from Glasgow to Bombay, in India, are another example of the difference in the use of the sea and the use of the air in transportation. A ship sailing from Glasgow to New York can follow the shortest route between the two ports until it nears North America. There it must swing off the circle a little to get round Newfoundland and Nova Scotia. Planes can fly the direct route all the way.

Planes can likewise follow the great circle route from Glasgow to Bombay, a distance of about 4700 miles. Ships, on the other hand, must make a long roundabout voyage between the two ports, either round the southern tip of Africa, or by way of the Mediterranean Sea and the Suez Canal. By the Mediterranean route they sail about 6100 miles, and by the African route about 10,500 miles.

As you read about the war and about the part which ships and planes played in it, you will need to use maps on the polar projection again and again. You will find them a great help in understanding the use of the air and the sea in the fighting and in the transport of troops and supplies.

Perhaps you will like to look ahead and think what airplanes flying at speeds of several hundred miles an hour over the great circle routes of the earth will mean in the future. The airways will be used far more than ever before for pleasure travel and for the transportation of goods in international trade. Many inland airports will rival the seaports of today as exporting and importing centers. High-speed flying over the great circle routes will make distances seem so short that all the nations of the world will form one great neighborhood.